ANNIVERSARY ESSAYS ON TOLSTOY

A century after Leo Tolstoy's death, the author of *War and Peace* is widely admired but too often thought of only with reference to his realism and moral sense. The many sides of Tolstoy revealed in these new essays speak to today's readers with astonishing force, relevance, and complexity. In a lively, challenging style, leading scholars range over his long life, from his first work *Childhood* to the works of his old age like *Hadji Murat*, and the many genres in which he worked, from the major novels to aphorisms and short stories. The essays present new approaches to his central themes: love, death, religious faith and doubt, violence, the animal kingdom, and war. They also assess his reception both in his lifetime and subsequently. Setting new agendas for the study of this classic author, this volume provides a snapshot of current scholarship on Tolstoy.

DONNA TUSSING ORWIN is Professor of Slavic Languages and Literatures at the University of Toronto.

ANNIVERSARY ESSAYS ON TOLSTOY

EDITED BY
DONNA TUSSING ORWIN

CAMBRIDGE
UNIVERSITY PRESS

CAMBRIDGE UNIVERSITY PRESS
Cambridge, New York, Melbourne, Madrid, Cape Town, Singapore,
São Paulo, Delhi, Dubai, Tokyo

Cambridge University Press
The Edinburgh Building, Cambridge CB2 8RU, UK

Published in the United States of America by Cambridge University Press, New York

www.cambridge.org
Information on this title: www.cambridge.org/9780521514910

© Cambridge University Press 2010

First published 2010

Printed in the United Kingdom at the University Press, Cambridge

A catalogue record for this publication is available from the British Library

ISBN 978-0-521-51491-0 Hardback

To the memory of
Lidiia Dmitrievna Gromova-Opul' skaia
(1925–2003)

.

Contents

Acknowledgments

The Centre for European, Russian, and Eurasian Studies (CERES) at the University of Toronto and the Social Sciences and Humanities Research Council of Canada (SSHRC) contributed funds to realize this project. I would like to thank Dr. Edith Klein for editing the final manuscript for submission to Cambridge University Press, and Arkadi Klioutchanski for his preparation of the list of works cited and the index.

Many thanks to Linda Bree, Maartje Scheltens, and Frances Brown of Cambridge University Press for their help. As always, I thank my husband Clifford Orwin for his support and understanding during the process of assembling this volume. Academician L. D. Gromova-Opul'skaia, to whose memory this volume is dedicated, inspired Tolstoy scholars by her intelligence and dedication to her tasks as a textologist. She led by example; indeed, people naturally followed her because of her common sense and generosity of spirit. I admired her very much, and miss her and her good counsel.

Contributors

EDWINA CRUISE, Professor of Russian on the Alumnae Foundation, Mount Holyoke College

MICHAEL A. DENNER, Associate Professor of Russian Studies, Stetson University, and Editor of *Tolstoy Studies Journal*

CARYL EMERSON, A. WATSON ARMOUR III University Professor of Slavic Languages and Literatures, Princeton University

G. M. HAMBURG, Otho M. Behr Professor of History, Claremont McKenna College

ROBIN FEUER MILLER, Edytha Macy Gross Professor of Humanities, Professor of Russian and Comparative Literature, Brandeis University

GARY SAUL MORSON, Frances Hooper Professor of the Arts and Humanities, Northwestern University

DONNA TUSSING ORWIN, Professor of Slavic Languages and Literatures, University of Toronto

IRINA PAPERNO, Professor of Slavic Languages and Literatures, University of California, Berkeley

ANDREAS SCHÖNLE, Professor of Russian, Queen Mary University of London

ILYA VINITSKY, Associate Professor of Slavic Languages and Literatures, University of Pennsylvania

JUSTIN WEIR, Professor of Slavic Languages and Literatures, Harvard University

Introduction

Donna Tussing Orwin

One hundred years ago, on November 20, 1910 (or November 7, according to the Russian calendar at that time), Count Leo Tolstoy died of pneumonia in the home of the stationmaster at a railway stop called Astapovo. In the seven days during which he lingered, reporters gathered at the obscure station to wire capitals all over the world about his illness and death. It was the first great media circus, made possible by the existence of the telegraph, as well as by Tolstoy's own global reach. He was celebrated not only as a writer of fiction, but also as a moral thinker and reformer whose jeremiads and solutions influenced people everywhere, from Mahatma Gandhi in India, to the founders of the kibbutz movement in Palestine, to Jane Addams, the founder of the settlement movement in Chicago. When I lecture in the older buildings at the University of Toronto or at other universities in North America, I imagine Tolstoy's ideas echoing in these places from the days when my predecessors debated them in the later nineteenth and early twentieth centuries. After Tolstoy's death, there was a battle to assimilate his considerable authority to various causes often at odds with positions he had taken while he was alive and able to defend himself. The concluding chapter in this volume, by Michael A. Denner, documents the different and contradictory ways that Tolstoy was used during the Russian Revolution and its aftermath (1917–24) by all sides of the conflict, from dark red to lily white, about Russia and its future. Even the Bolsheviks embraced Tolstoy, especially in the early years after the Revolution. Once they began to consolidate their power, however, they regarded Tolstoyanism and Tolstoy as rivals, and they undertook an unprecedented propaganda campaign to separate the two. They persecuted the movement while assimilating the man, whose message they proceeded to tailor to their own specifications. Their unprecedented success in this propaganda effort created an official Soviet Tolstoy. (This Tolstoy and the "real" one are in fact distant cousins, though not kissing ones.) In the years since the fall of the USSR, scholars in Russia and abroad have been reading Tolstoy outside the Soviet lens. The present book continues that process with eleven original essays, each of which represents a new departure in Tolstoy studies. All of them engage Tolstoy's intentions, and therefore his thoughts. They have been arranged to encourage the reader to compare them, and this brief summary of their contents is intended to stimulate the comparison.

The book begins with Caryl Emerson's piece on Tolstoy and music. Tolstoy's abiding love of music, and, more importantly, his reliance on it in his aesthetics, reveals the romantic in the realist. If music expresses feeling (as Tolstoy declared in a diary entry in 1852), then psychological prose must depend in various ways on music, as Emerson indeed shows. Tolstoy's theory of art as infection, according to which an artist pours his feelings into the recipient of his art, is deeply musical. He wanted to believe that in and of itself infection as a form of pure communication was good, though it could be used to bad ends. He thus distinguished between means and ends in the folk story "The Empty Drum" (1891). The hero Emelyan uses the drum employed by the Tsar to summon soldiers to war to lead them to a river, where he smashes the drum, and releases the soldiers from the Tsar's power. In a reverse direction, Emerson explores how in *The Kreutzer Sonata* (1889) an initially pure infection by art can over time, and in relation to the character and situation of the recipient, mutate into something ugly, even murderous. In a "coda," Emerson discusses musical adaptations of Tolstoy that might have pleased or infuriated him.

The second chapter, by Andreas Schönle, treats something even more fundamental to Tolstoy (and life) than music: death. All great art either depicts or responds to it, of course, but I would observe that Tolstoy's anarchic individualism makes it central to his aesthetics. Schönle starts with the death of Maman in *Childhood* (1852) and the boy's reaction to it. The sublimity of this dread and incomprehensible event generates both fear and pleasure as the bereaved child distances himself from it by absorbing it in imagination. This form of the sublime is Kantian, though Tolstoy need not have learnt it directly from the master. (Schönle digresses to bring in the astonishingly relevant reaction of the poet Zhukovsky to the death of his friend, and Russia's greatest poet, Alexander Pushkin.) The chapter goes on to reveal Tolstoy's fascination with corpses, and "their ability to generate aesthetic pleasure": the dead Chechen in *The Cossacks* is but one instance of this. An obsession with the dead continues throughout Tolstoy's long creative life, but Schönle does detect a change in his attitude which he attributes to the writings of Schopenhauer, whose notion of the sublime "enables the self to rise above the will to live, which had produced an illusory notion of individuality." But what Schönle calls the "seduction" of the

Schopenhauerian sublime is counterbalanced in Tolstoy's later years by an absorption in life, and a Kantian emphasis on moral action in the everyday.

Nature and the material world are also formative themes in Tolstoy's art, which in this respect as in so many is influenced by philosopher Jean-Jacques Rousseau. Fundamentally for Tolstoy, human beings are animals with big brains. This means that we have a special relation to other animals, and also obligations to them as our kin. Robin Feuer Miller's chapter compares Tolstoy's view of animals to those of present-day thinkers like Peter Singer, Martha Nussbaum, and especially Nobel Prize winner J. M. Coetzee, author of *The Lives of Animals.* Tolstoy's attention to the animal in man helps account for the earthiness of his fiction. Overall, however, its effect is not to denigrate humans, but to raise animals to the level of "non-human autonomous beings" which we cannot simply regard as objects to serve our needs and pleasure. In Tolstoy's aesthetics, "[a] successful artistic rendering of the hare or the wolf would embody both the feelings of the artist and the essential quiddity of the animal itself." Although human beings are usually held to a higher moral standard than other animals in Tolstoy's art, at times they act simply in accord with their animal natures. This happens most brutally but under-standably in war, and here Miller's study intersects with mine on war in Tolstoy and the untranslatable Russian concept of *molodechestvo.*

My chapter ponders why an author so opposed to war might write so much about it, and even describe it sympathetically. The answer resides partly in Tolstoy's cultural heritage, but also in a wartime experience that taught him the joys of anger, which he had to depict and somehow explain. Combat can also educate. War is hell in Tolstoy's art, but some good things can result for those who must engage in it.

On the hunt and at war, man is an animal, and experiences animal fears and pleasures, but that is not the whole story in Tolstoy's art. Irina Paperno investigates precisely the side of Tolstoy that develops out of his "big brain," and is *not* simply natural. She argues that in the late 1870s Tolstoy was fed up with art, which tended to slip out of the moral control of the artist, and was looking to philosophy to express more clearly and precisely what the moral "I" wanted to say. He therefore proposed to his close friend Nikolai Strakhov that they explore and elucidate their religious worldview together in a dialogue on "personal faith in the age of reason and science." Strakhov turned out not to be the ideal partner in this endeavor, but through it Tolstoy got to the point, in 1879, where he wanted to write his own confession, which he finished in 1882. In it the general reader took the place of Strakhov as his interlocutor, and, after 1879, Tolstoy's letters to

Strakhov lost their confessional tone and content. Strakhov continued to treat Tolstoy as his guru, although it was the man and his art, and not his philosophizing, that most impressed him. Meanwhile, Tolstoy had found a way to communicate more directly with others than through art.

Tolstoy's preoccupation with spirituality did not come out of the blue, and it was mediated by a respect for science typical for his age. Ilya Vinitsky explores the way science and forms of transcendentalism intermix in Tolstoy and his contemporaries in the 1860s. The key elements in this counterintuitive marriage are ethical; all Russian thinkers of the time, whatever their political stripe or bent toward science, had moral goals. Focusing on the death of Andrei in *War and Peace* (1865–69), Vinitsky argues that Tolstoy imagines life after death as a merging into all that is living in nature. He discards the notion of a hierarchical Herderian chain of being that Pierre celebrates in his conversation with Andrei at the ford. But at the same time, the individual soul seems still to exist "as one of the countless phenomena of life in nature."

Gary Hamburg discusses the content of Tolstoy's later spirituality. In his old age, Tolstoy rejected the distinction between reason and revelation. Nonetheless, the teachings of reason require faith, because human beings are still more sentient animals than reasoning beings. According to Hamburg, *On Life* (1887) translates into philosophical terms the Christian ethical code discussed in *What Do I Believe?* (1884), and it also refashions Christian notions of personal immortality into a philosophical conception connecting altruism, memory of the good, and "soul force."

The remaining contributors to this volume concentrate on Tolstoy's art. Edwina Cruise may have finally put to rest (by rendering it irrelevant) the dispute about which English novel Anna Karenina might be reading on her return by train to St. Petersburg. Having read dozens of such novels herself, many of them forgotten today, Cruise concludes that Anna's novel is a palimpsest, or perfect parody of them. She provides crucial new insight into the role of the English novel in Tolstoy's own version of the perfect one; although Anna never reads another English novel after that train ride, she and other female characters are formed by their reading habits. Cruise focuses on four novelists – Anthony Trollope, George Eliot, Mary Elizabeth Braddon, and Mrs. Henry Wood – who each meant different things to Tolstoy, and each influenced his art. This chapter also broadens into a larger discussion of the English novel in the Russia of the 1860s and 1870s.

Justin Weir explains why Tolstoy's aesthetics generally made drama unattractive to him as a mode of art; without the assistance of a narrator, play-goers (or readers) can know little about the inner life of a character. On the other hand, Tolstoy's greatest play, *The Realm of Darkness* (1887), is an appropriate vehicle for the story he tells. The very limitations of drama as Tolstoy conceived it make it suitable for this play about infanticide and its consequences. Evil destroys conscience, and drama, according to Tolstoy, cannot depict either it, or memory, through which conscience operates. *The Realm of Darkness* dramatizes inexplicable evil without having to explain it, and ends with the repentance of the main protagonist and his return to humanity. Weir places *The Realm of Darkness* in the larger context of Tolstoyan drama, and the theme of violence in his art.

Finally, Gary Saul Morson discovers a new genre in Tolstoy's oeuvre hidden in plain view: the short form. Morson ranges over vast territory in aesthetics gathering the fundamentals of this form and proving its historical existence. Having documented Tolstoy's lifelong interest in short forms of many types, he provides some wonderful interpretations of a subgroup of stories that are elaborations of the "wise saying." I would suggest that the short form may have engaged Tolstoy because it provided a bridge between universal truths, and truths that the individual can grasp and use for moral guidance. In other words, Tolstoy's interest in the form attests to his moral anarchism, or the extreme moral individualism manifest from his earliest writings.

Tolstoyanism and related phenomena like Tolstoyan communes did not survive the chastening horrors of the last hundred years. As it turned out, human beings were too imperfect, too capable of evil, to live in the peaceful and rational way that the movement promoted. But Tolstoy does survive, both as a man and as a writer of fiction. For a long time, many scholars in Russia and abroad rescued him from his association with Tolstoyanism or Marxist-Leninism by, implicitly or explicitly, driving a wedge between the thinker and the writer. In recent times that distinction, most famously drawn in the West by Isaiah Berlin in his landmark *The Hedgehog and the Fox* (1953), has been questioned if not denied outright. All the contributions to this anniversary volume engage Tolstoy as both a writer and a thinker; and all unearth nourishing capillaries running between the two roles. This is not to say that Tolstoy's thought or ideology explains his fiction or vice versa. A mixture of hope and stark realism about the human condition informs both, but while Tolstoy's hopefulness can be a defect in his thought, which can expect too much of human beings and sweep too much of human history under the carpet, in his fiction it is yet another element of his unsurpassed realism, which would be less true and less complete without it.

Even Tolstoy's thought remains relevant, especially but not exclusively as expressed in his fiction. One may well ask why, given his preoccupation with feelings and their association in his own mind with music, Tolstoy became an artist of the word rather than a musician. The answer is complex. First of all, as Caryl Emerson so ably demonstrates in her discussion of musical adaptations of Tolstoy, words sing in his fiction, and the great Russian realist is a poet in this regard. Second, much of Tolstoy's prose is dedicated to *proving* the primacy of feeling in human nature. Tolstoy uses words in order to stake poetry's claim to superiority over philosophy. Beyond this essential romantic paradox, however, lurks a dedication, not always acknowledged by Tolstoy but omnipresent in his writing, to the word as the instrument of reason and its all-important manifestation in human nature: the conscience. (Reason also functions as the voice of mere self-serving calculation, of course.) If the voice of conscience usually speaks later and more softly than other, stronger impulses in the human soul, it acts to correct these, thereby enforcing natural moral discipline in what would otherwise be a tyranny of feeling. According to Tolstoyan psychology, human reason both exacerbates the bad consequences of the natural self-absorption such as obtains in other animals, and provides us with a dignity potential if not always active in our souls. We have moral choice, and we reason our way to right or wrong action with words. Over and over again Tolstoy's fiction demonstrates this paradigmatic action for good or ill in the soul. The educated need self-analysis to reform themselves, while the uncorrupted and uneducated unselfconsciously access the folk wisdom that embodies what Tolstoy calls "common sense." Either way, morality speaks in paradoxes that reflect the existence of moral choice in human nature. This ethical component of Tolstoy's prose differentiates it, at least theoretically, from the Nietzschean-influenced Symbolist prose that follows it in Russian literature, and connects it to the Russian eighteenth-century Enlightenment that precedes it. The essays in this book all demonstrate in different ways the unique admixture of narrative and ethical thought that makes Tolstoy such a fascinating figure and a great writer.

A NOTE ON TRANSLITERATION AND DATES

Throughout the book, except in quotations and titles, we have used spellings of well-known Russian names that are conventional in English. Where the name is not familiar, and in Russian quotations, we have followed a modified form of Library of Congress transliteration to render Cyrillic into the Latin alphabet.

Readers should keep in mind that, until after the Revolution, Russia used the Julian Calendar (often called Old Style), which in the nineteenth century was twelve days behind the Gregorian one used in most other countries. When two dates are given for the same event, the first is in Old Style and the second as the Gregorian equivalent.

Ellipses in square brackets are not in the original quotation.

CHAPTER I

Tolstoy and music

Caryl Emerson

Tolstoy's relations with music – the least mediated of the temporal arts, and thus for him the most potent – were reverent, wary, and on occasion punitive. He was fascinated by the *force* of music, just as he was by the force of sexuality, beauty, and war. By "force" Tolstoy did not mean violence or disruption, but the power to organize, suddenly and irresistibly, all our scattered actions and feelings into a coherent meaningful whole. Thus focused in its energies, the human organism would fear nothing, not even its own mortality. But since this heightened condition lent itself equally well to sublime insight and to irrational acts, it had to be carefully watched. Furthermore, music, being neither an instinct nor a force of nature but the product of creative human striving, obligated its practitioners to positive deeds as our more animal sides did not. The intensely receptive and aesthetically arousable Tolstoy worked hard at the piano as a young man, and he continued to revere music long after he had abjured war, sex, and beauty. Everything he wanted to accomplish through words happened faster and more purely through music.

These fundamentally Romantic priorities manifested themselves early. In a diary entry from November 1851, the 23-year-old Tolstoy charted the fine arts according to their ability to act on the imagination.[1] The realm of visual art or painting is space, where we realize an image of nature. The realm of music is harmony and time, where we realize feelings. Poetry, by expressing our feelings toward nature, partakes of both. The transition from visual art to music passes through dance; from music to poetry, through song. Although poetry might be "clearer" in its referents, music is "fuller in its imitation of a feeling" than any verbal (and spatial) art could ever be. As Tolstoy would subsequently argue through his treatises and the experience of his fictional heroes, emotional fullness in music is an autonomous quality. It cannot be prompted or sustained by any image, concept, or narrative "program," which inevitably confuses and blurs the purity of musical effect.[2] Purity in this instance is not a moral category but more a thermodynamic one. The key parameters are accuracy and efficiency: how to communicate a feeling and unite people through it without loss of precision and heat. In his mature theory of art, Tolstoy would call this energy transfer "infection" – perhaps to emphasize its involuntary, irresistible dissemination among all live organisms exposed to it. Emotions, Tolstoy believed, were our single wholly reliable human common denominator. But the experiences that produce these emotions are inevitably individualized, locked up in the personal: they are impenetrable and can be reconstructed only after the fact, partially, and at great risk. The Tolstoyan word laboriously recreated this uniquely experiencing individual. The musical utterance was more fortunate; being universal, it could be conveyed without intermediaries. Its effect was of unsegmented, unreflective, spontaneous flow. This competition between words, the professional medium that Tolstoy came to control absolutely, and music, the passionate avocation that (if successful) controlled him, lasted until the end of his life. Melody and rhythm affected him with disastrous directness.

Tolstoy judged the legitimacy of a piece of music intuitively, subjectively, on the evidence of his own motor reflexes and psychic reactions. If a performance caused him to weep or tap his feet, it was authentic – so much so that later in life he would beg his young friend, the pianist Alexander Gol'denveizer, *not* to play Chopin for fear he would "burst into tears."[3] If a musical experience failed to move him or required of him sustained, calculated intellectual attention, it was summarily dismissed as counterfeit. By our later, more scientific standards of physiology, Tolstoy was probably naïve as regards the body's immediacy[4] – and in any event, Tolstoy's custom was to assume that the needs and sensitivities of his own organism were the norm for all humanity. Nevertheless, music's ability to transform our psychological state, even against our will or logical judgment, remained for him a touchstone for all art, the aesthetic equivalent to a love relation and thus a source of the most severe anxiety as well as bliss.

In a letter to his son Lev and daughter Tatiana in March 1894, Tolstoy described a tirade he had been delivering on the dismal state of contemporary music to a student at the Moscow Conservatory. Suddenly, from somewhere, two students began to sing *Là ci darem la mano*, the seduction duet between Don Giovanni and Zerlina from Mozart's opera. "I stopped talking and began to listen, to feel joyful and to smile at something," Tolstoy confessed. "What a terrible force this is" (*PSS* 67: 79).[5] Tolstoy refers often to the "terror" (*strakh*) of music. From the "terrifying and joyful" (*strashno i radostno*) reaction of young Petya Rostov dreaming a choral symphony the night before his death in *War and Peace* to the half-mad Pozdnyshev's ruminations in *The Kreutzer Sonata* – "It's a terrible thing, that sonata [...] and in general music is a terrible thing" (*PSS* 27: 61) – we are coaxed into accepting music as the great harmonizer and human reconciler as well as a stimulus for murder on par with jealous rage and possessive love. In April 1910, after Gol'denveizer had performed one of his host's favourite Chopin études, Tolstoy confirmed that he "loved music more than all the other arts."[6]

This chapter samples three aspects of Tolstoy's relationship to music: as part of his own life (both as pianist-performer and audience); as episodes in his verbal texts (fiction, semi-autobiographical writings, and philosophy of art); and, in a coda, Tolstoy's works set to music. A special constraint applies to this last category, since the mature Tolstoy did not approve of mixed-media art. He believed that each art form, in order to retain its focus and the infectious force peculiar to it, should cultivate its own field and not combine with neighboring media.[7] In principle, then, Tolstoy would condemn musical-dramatic settings of his verbal texts. But since nay-saying is so routine and easy to predict with this writer, we will take the more challenging path – briefly noting several twentieth-century musicalizations that Tolstoy, under certain conditions, might have welcomed.

MUSIC IN TOLSTOY'S LIFE

At Iasnaia Poliana as on most well-to-do Russian gentry estates, music-making was as integrated into daily life as the making of honey, boots, or jam. As a child Tolstoy received basic instruction in piano and at 17 began seriously improving his keyboard skills. Two years later, in 1849, he invited a German pianist from St. Petersburg to visit, whose companionship inspired him to sketch out a treatise on the "Foundations of Music and Rules for its Study"; in his unfinished novella, "Holy Night" (*Sviatochnaia noch'*, 1853), sessions with this pianist-theorist reappear as a first-person digression on the merits of Russian gypsy music versus German common practice.[8] Given his later celebration of the ethical tasks of art, it must be emphasized that Tolstoy never confused the authenticity of music as art with its social or moral setting. Although "visiting the gypsies" might be shameful according to his Rules of Life, Tolstoy always admired gypsy singing – with its rich chest tones, rhythmic variability, and pliable interweaving of solo and chorus. He paid it rapturous tribute throughout his life, from his 1856 "Two Hussars" (*Dva gusara*) to his drama *The Living Corpse* (*Zhivoi trup*) (1900), which features a gypsy chorus singing on stage at the end of the first act.

An early convert to Rousseau, Tolstoy shared his mentor's belief that the simpler forms of vocal music, especially folk music, were potentially redemptive for alienated, over-civilized European society. Laconic diary entries made over half a century, rating the music he had heard that day, suggest that for Tolstoy the more massive, complex, pretentiously serious and "staged" the musical spectacle, the less he liked it.[9] But Tolstoy did not oppose all musical instruction for the common people. Throughout the winter of 1861–62 he had notable success in his experimental Iasnaia Poliana schools teaching peasant children the fundamentals of music through singing (intervals, chords, scales). He did believe, however, that it was essential to begin right away with art, not exercises; systematic drill might be suitable for young ladies, but "it's better not to teach village children at all than to teach them mechanically" (*PSS* 8: 120–25).[10] Nor did Tolstoy habitually denigrate all upper-class music, even for the stage. Eighteenth-century works usually delighted him, as did staged comic genres (comedy, he believed, was more honest than tragedy because less premeditated). He played a huge variety of music in four-hand piano arrangements with family members as well as with visiting musicians, and at home he was a much-valued accompanist for art songs. Relaxation at the keyboard could overlap with literary creativity. Tolstoy often worked out human and plot relations "harmonically." His brother-in-law Stepan Bers and son Lev L'vovich recall that during the 1860s–70s Tolstoy would sit at the piano for hours and improvise chord sequences, inspiring and focusing his mind before he got down to verbal work.[11]

As a member of the upper nobility, Tolstoy was acquainted with all the prominent Russian composers. He shared a box with Dargomyzhsky at the premiere of the latter's opera *Rusalka* at the Mariinsky Theater in St. Petersburg in May 1856; in 1858, before the founding of the first Russian conservatory, Tolstoy helped set up a musical society in Moscow. Closest to him were the more cosmopolitan wing of Russian musicians: the Rubinstein brothers, Tchaikovsky, Rimsky-Korsakov in his later conservatory period, Taneyev, Skriabin. Tolstoy's meeting with Tchaikovsky in 1876, and its aftermath in letters and musical evenings until 1886, has left rich (if disputed) traces.[12] According to Tchaikovsky's account, Tolstoy's first comment upon being introduced was that "'Beethoven has no talent' – and everything began from there." Tolstoy and Tchaikovsky charmed each other utterly. In December 1876, Nicholas Rubinstein arranged a private concert of Tchaikovsky's chamber music for Tolstoy in Moscow, taking care to select folk-based works that would please the master. The composer wrote endearingly in his diary that he was "enchanted and touched in his authorial vanity" when Tolstoy broke down and wept during the Andante of his First Quartet.

It must be said, however, that such filtering of Tchaikovsky's chamber music to highlight its folk melodies was quite unnecessary. Tolstoy's first loves in music were not Russian, but mainstream European: Mozart, Haydn, Weber, selected Beethoven, Mendelssohn, and above all Chopin (whom Tolstoy called the musical equal to Pushkin in poetry).[13] This list might seem arbitrary to us, but Tolstoy, it appears, had his criteria. To Gol'denveizer in 1896 he remarked:

In every art – I know this from experience – there are two extremes difficult to avoid: vulgar triviality and over-refinement or virtuosity. For example, Mozart, whom I love so much, sometimes falls into vulgarity, but then soars up to an extraordinary height. Schumann's defect is excessive refinement. Of these two defects, over-refinement is worse than vulgarity, if only because it's harder to get rid of it. The greatness of Chopin is that however simple he might be he never falls into vulgarity, and his most complex compositions are never over-refined.[14]

The high priority Tolstoy placed on the delicate (and highly subjective) boundary between "vulgar" and "virtuosic" helps explain why this great epic Realist in literary representation displayed so little interest in the realistic musical experiments of Russia's most radical nationalist composer, Modest Musorgsky. According to Sergei Bertenson, son of the doctor who tended both Musorgsky and Tolstoy, when his father queried the writer on this point Tolstoy remarked that he "liked neither talented drunks nor drunken talents."[15] It took one persuasive performance to change that verdict. In 1901, the Russian-French singer Maria Olenina-d'Alheim visited Iasnaia Poliana and sang "The Fieldmarshal" (in French) from the cycle *Songs and Dances of Death*. "How is it people keep telling me Musorgsky is a poor composer?" Tolstoy exclaimed. "What we heard just now was more than splendid."[16] Still, too much attention to words – to the narrative program in texted music – always raised Tolstoy's suspicions. "Words first" (and especially the Russian word) was a strong bias in Russian Realist songwriting. Gol'denveizer recalls that one year earlier, in January 1900, the great bass Fyodor Chaliapin sang for the Tolstoy household; his German lieder were better received than either the over-refined Rakhmaninov or the vulgar, hyper-prosy Musorgsky.[17] In his memoirs, Doctor Bertenson noted that Tolstoy did not care for Chaliapin's concert repertoire or character pieces such as "The Flea," calling them "melo-declamation and not music."[18]

We mention one final musical landmark in Tolstoy's life, at age 75: the advent of the gramophone. The household was anxious. Would the old man be curious about this new instrument, or would he consider it one more dehumanizing technological gadget? Aleksei Sergeenko, Chertkov's secretary, recalls a demonstration session at Iasnaia Poliana in December 1903.[19] The machine was wound up and the recordings brought out: Beethoven, Chopin, Tchaikovsky, opera arias. Tolstoy listened. Amazed, he began to mutter. When a folk dance tune began, he grinned, shook his head, and began to tap out the beat with his feet. This was not done for show, Sergeenko wrote: "even alone in the hall, without us, he could not have kept his feet still."

These reflexes are telling. For among the paradoxes of Tolstoy's over-documented life is the gap between eye-witness accounts of the master listening to chamber music – passionately, lovingly, with tears in his eyes, tapping his feet – and the many punitive assaults he made on upper-class musical art in his theoretical writings. Part of the problem, surely, is Tolstoy's insistence that virtue and honesty are simple, whereas formal musical structure or "musical development" (as in sonata form) prides itself on complication and refined variation. Also problematic is Tolstoy's keen solicitude for the receiving, reacting body. Feelings aroused must be provided an outlet. Thus work songs, funeral laments, and military bands priming soldiers for violence were far more honest as musical experiences than an orchestral concert – scheduled in advance, tied to no special purpose, and always trapping people immobile in their seats. There was a more suspicious side to Tolstoy's later assaults on music, however, unrelated to listener response. It arose out of keen disappointment about origins rather than affects. "Art, poetry […], painting, and especially music give us the impression that they are emanating from an extraordinarily good and kind place," he wrote in his diary for March 13, 1900. "But there's nothing there" (*PSS* 54: 13).[20] Terror was his response to a sublime feeling that could not be traced back to a morally reliable source.

MUSIC IN TOLSTOY'S FICTION AND PHILOSOPHY

The hundreds of musical episodes or exemplars in Tolstoy's writing can be grouped under various rubrics: chronological placement in his life, social class (folk or aristocratic), musical genre, moral or immoral effect, the presence or absence of a stage, the trustworthiness of the composer, the aural material, the sonic source. That source might be a human construct (string quartet), a natural backdrop (nightingales), or some soundscape in between (say, the musical *pooff! boom-boom-boom! trakh-ta-ta-takh!* of cannonballs before the Battle of Borodino in volume 3, part 2, chapter 30 of *War and Peace*).

My discussion here is limited to human constructs and takes its organizing principle from Richard Gustafson: "When Tolstoy the writer writes of art, he always thinks of a musical event … Tolstoy's art of infection is the art of a good performance."[21] This "performative" criterion is appropriate, because it highlights the similarities between a successful musical experience – which for the nineteenth century was always live – and Tolstoy's participatory ideal for all art. It also distributes responsibility for the transfiguring force of music equally among three agents: the composer, the "realizer" (singer or instrumentalist), and the receiver (audience). A false note by any of these three components could misdirect the musical force to unclean ends. We now sample various types of music performance (solo voice, vocal chorus, instrumental solo, instrumental ensemble, orchestral fantasy), concluding with a curious "psychological" subset of musical production in Tolstoy: music dreamed.

The solo singing voice, unaccompanied or supported by a single instrument, is always a piercing communicator in Tolstoy. It both focuses our ethical sense and, crucially, is capable of transcending that sense. One early example is the itinerant street singer in "Lucerne" (1857), an episode lifted from Tolstoy's travel diaries in Switzerland and permeated, appropriately, with Rousseau. The autobiographical Prince Nekhliudov befriends a beggared little man peddling his music to a wealthy hotel crowd; the singer's graceful melodies have lifted the Prince from a mood of weary indifference to "a need for love, a fullness of hope, a spontaneous joy of life" (*potrebnost' liubvi, polnotu nadezhdy i besprichinnuiu radost' zhizni*) (*PSS* 5: 8). After this initial grateful transformation, however, the Prince becomes increasingly bitter. None of the laughing hotel guests donates a centime. Feeling "indescribable anger," Nekhliudov invites the singer for a drink and rages at a negligent waiter, thereby embarrassing the poor musician. Then the diary entry trails off into a treatise against evil, greed, high-society idleness, and the lament that everyone loves and seeks art but "no one acknowledges its force, nor values or thanks those who give it to people" (*PSS* 5: 21). By the end of the tale, however, the sweet distant sounds of the singer prompt Nekhliudov to transcend even his indignation. He withdraws his right to judge and submits to a higher, unknown universal law.

A far more famous instance of the same double-tiered dynamic occurs in *War and Peace*, volume 2, part 1, chapter 16. Nikolai Rostov has just lost 43,000 rubles to Dolokhov. In despair, he returns home to find his sister Natasha and Sonia at the clavichord. At 15, Natasha is singing seriously but her voice is not yet trained. As she warms to the climax of *Oh mio crudele affetto*, Nikolai is transfixed; will she take the high B? When she does, her brother involuntarily sings the second voice a third below. And then his astonishing conclusion, emerging from "what was best in Rostov's soul": "What are gambling losses, and Dolokhovs, and words of honor! Nonsense! One can kill, and steal, and still be happy!" (*PSS* 10: 59).[22] In *War and Peace*, the supremely musical Rostov family is the locus for the irresponsible fullness of the present. No one can resist a dance rhythm. They whirl spontaneously, take risks, give generously, fail to keep financial accounts, act on impulse, rarely plan – and the survivors are rewarded with wealth and fertility. The Rostov spirit, written down, fares as poorly as live music trapped and transferred to a score. This dynamic was explained by Fedya Protasov, protagonist of *The Living Corpse*, to the musician who is fretting that he cannot transcribe a gypsy song because "each time it's new, and the scale is different." "He won't write it down," Fedya says. "And if he writes it down and sticks it into some opera, everything will be ruined" (act 1, sc. 2; *PSS* 34: 22).

In the Epilogue to *War and Peace*, the two Rostov siblings mature into thrifty (even stingy) household managers. Music, it appears, has been superannuated. Nikolai counts every ruble and orders his lazy peasants flogged. Natasha Rostova-Bezukhova has become a jealous, penny-pinching matron, and (here Tolstoy registers profound approval) has quit singing for good, having found full emotional outlet in her husband and children. But a detail near the end of chapter 13 reassures us that the family economy is still in place. Three-year-old Natasha Rostova, Nikolai and Marya's daughter, is shrieking with joy in the children's room. Hearing this happy sound, her father exclaims: "Now there's marvelous music!" (*Vot muzyka-to chudnaia!*).

Group singing in Tolstoy, especially folk music, is overwhelmingly affirmative. Its closeness to the speaking voice and the evidence it provides of coordinated, harmonious communal activity make it a safe repository for musical energy. The most positive chorus of all is the work song, which infects its weary participants joyously after a day of agricultural labor (Tolstoy's standard for all honest work). In part 3, chapter 12 of *Anna Karenina*, Konstantin Levin, still recovering from Kitty's rejection, lying in a haystack on his estate, hears several dozen peasant women break into a rollicking song: "it seemed to him that a thundercloud of merriment was coming upon him" (*PSS* 18: 290). He envies their high spirits, their physical exhaustion in common labor, and despairs at his own loneliness. As did Nekhliudov in "Lucerne," he first turns this keen musical experience against himself and his social class, resolving to change his "burdensome, idle, artificial and individual life" (*PSS* 18: 290–91).[23] But like the raging

Prince Nekhliudov in Lucerne and Nikolai Rostov after his gambling fiasco, Levin is reconciled with himself by the end of the scene. He catches a glimpse of Kitty in her carriage at dawn and confirms his love for her. Singing has this layered effect in Tolstoy. It stuns the organism that hears it, hints at access to a sublime realm, triggers severe self-criticism, then finally allows the listener's error and pride to be reabsorbed in a larger, more tolerant harmony.

Tolstoy excelled at a second sort of "chorus," superficially at odds with peasants singing after a day of productive labor but in fact closely aligned with it. These are the soldiers' songs that break out on the march to the front. A great master of war, Tolstoy is in no way naïve about the slaughter and horror of the battlefield. But for half a century, from "The Raid" (*Nabeg* [1853]) to *Hadji Murat* (1896–1905, published 1912), Tolstoy persists in affirming the exhilaration, communal purpose, and heightened sense of life and rhythm that precedes contact with the enemy. One especially infectious scene is described in *War and Peace*, volume 1, part 2, chapter 2, before the disaster at Austerlitz. Dolokhov, reduced to the ranks, is conversing reluctantly with the hussar cornet Zherkov against the constantly interrupting backdrop of the marchers' song. As the insolent Dolokhov strides along, remarking curtly on his own disgrace and rehabilitation while keeping time to the music, its refrain mingles with the dialogue and frames the replies. "Their conversation would probably have been different," Tolstoy notes, "if they had not been talking to the sounds of the song" (*PSS* 9: 146).[24] In what way different he does not say, but the reader senses a larger vortex, set in musical motion by the marching, joyously singing men, which now governs the army. Even Zherkov's horse gallops off and catches up with a carriage "in time with the song" (*PSS* 9: 147).

Such harmony, affirmation of life, and rhythmic ecstasy are not denied to instrumental chamber music. But as the complexity and "stagedness" of the performance increase, pitfalls and contaminations multiply. Solo piano, the purest instrumental mode and the one Tolstoy knew most intimately, is almost danger-free. It is paid beautiful tribute in *Childhood* (*Detstvo*, 1852), where Nikolenka recalls his mother playing Beethoven's Eighth Piano Sonata, the *Pathétique*. In this first fictional hint of his later physiological aesthetics, Tolstoy as narrator insists: "Music acts neither on the mind nor on the imagination […] I think about nothing, imagine nothing, but some strange sweet feeling so fills my soul that I lose consciousness of my existence" (*PSS* 1: 182).[25] Strangeness, sweetness, and loss of conscious ego: this is Tolstoy's initial recipe for "infection," the communicative dynamic that he will later posit for all successful art. Authentic art breaks down boundaries between composer, performer, and listener so that an unconscious unity is realized – a condition not easy to paraphrase in words but piercingly specific, transparent, and sincere. This instantaneous, inchoate sharing of an emotion, with its intonations of divine grace, can be traced to a young child's longing for union with a loving, but irrevocably lost, parent. It has properly been called Eucharistic.[26]

Music restores the sense of being loved. Unsurprisingly, Tolstoy as musician was moved deeply by the "expectedness" of chord progressions, which he considered indispensable to the science of music. The security of "knowing everything in advance" was one of the reasons he so enjoyed the *Sonate Pathétique*.[27] Nikolenka's critical faculties – indeed, his very desire to think or speak as a sovereign self – melt away under his mother's playing. The scene is foundational. To infect others by a work of art is not to invite from them a differentiated, open-ended, unexpected response. Quite the opposite: sincerity (*iskrennost'*) of artistic expression dissolves all outside points of view in a one-way, unbroken transmission of feeling. "Sincerity is that state in which there is a natural, unselfconscious coincidence between the public and private, between stem and root," writes one recent student of Tolstoyan aesthetics. Although we are *with* others, marvelously, we are not nervous about their reception of us. (For Tolstoy, who considered himself unattractively awkward and self-conscious in social situations, this was relief indeed.) "In a moment of true sincerity, a person has no more regard for how others will perceive him and his actions than a root sending up a stem and leaves has for its observers."[28] Such exiling of constructive interlocutors, onlookers, and differentiated dialogue from the realm of authentic art is among the more curious aspects of Tolstoy's aesthetics – especially because music is a temporal art and its infectious processes must flourish complexly over time. But differentiation is already a falling-away, a decay; and reconstruction or analysis is treacherous. No piece of fiction by Tolstoy better illustrates these paradoxical moments than the late, scandalous novella *The Kreutzer Sonata* (*Kreitserova sonata*, 1889), our exemplar of the instrumental ensemble in Tolstoy. It is testimony to music's lethal force when performed, received, and remembered under flawed conditions. But this remarkable story not only testifies to music "gone wrong"; it also tests, perhaps against Tolstoy's wishes, the sincerity–infection theory of art. That theory had worked splendidly with Natasha Rostova's high B, with peasant work songs, with soldiers singing their way to the front, and in the blissful unconscious unity brought about between mother and child by the *Pathétique*. In this novella it confounds and misleads.

Tolstoy's *Kreutzer Sonata* is musical on several levels. Its eponymous plot event is a chamber music recital, by the protagonist's piano-playing wife together with a visiting violinist, of Beethoven's Sonata in A major, op. 47. It would have been a routine social event except for the murderer's self-obsessed (self-accusatory, self-absolving) recontextualization of it in morbid retrospect. The fictional narrative, structured by Tolstoy in verbal imitation of sonata-allegro form, is itself a flashback "performed" by Pozdnyshev to an unknown (but sympathetic, which is to say, "infected") traveling companion in a train carriage.[29] Leaving aside the question of the murderer-husband's sanity, it must be stressed that the performance of Beethoven's sonata that evening was neither a failure nor a scandal. Pozdnyshev himself admits that the pair "played splendidly," that the violinist Trukhachevsky had "to the highest degree what was called tone" and even "refined and elevated taste"; Pozdnyshev also admits that his wife was "simple and natural" in the violinist's presence (*PSS* 27: 54). The husband's jealousy and subsequent decision to murder his wife develop much later, after the sublime moment of infection has worn off and he has begun to ponder the matter in his mind. Although he does not perform on an instrument himself, Pozdnyshev is very musical. He has been despising his wife (and himself) for several years, largely because he refuses to seek any justification for their cohabitation except animal pleasure. As with Prince Nekhliudov in "Lucerne," music for Pozdnyshev functions as that almost random trigger which, once pressed, releases a flood of disgust at the vices of his social class. The addition of the failed-marriage theme to *The Kreutzer Sonata* complicates the musical matter irreparably. For we have here not mere social critique, nor mere sexual jealousy on the husband's side toward some apparent competitor, but a complex Mozart-and-Salieri scenario for envy, where the envier is aware of the superiority of his rival – a category that expands to include his wife at the keyboard alongside the violinist. The envier admits the value of the higher purpose that his rival serves, and fears like fire the reciprocal infection that will inevitably spread out around his rival's successful performance.

In that infectious zone, all creativity and desire are dangerously enhanced. But here the non-musician Pozdnyshev is clearly disadvantaged: he performs as a creator solely in words and images, that is, in imagination. To be sure, these verbal and visual props come into play only later, stealthily, silently, after the musical event is over. During the performance, the musically vulnerable Pozdnyshev succumbs to the magical art of Beethoven's sonata, to its ability to fuse performers and listeners into a single pulsing whole. But he soon reverts to the more divisive effects of temporal, aurally transmitted art natural to his possessive and suspicious temperament. For musical narrative, similar to its inefficient cousin the narrative utterance, does not always unite. It can also divide, differentiate, leave unresolved, mysteriously darken rather than elevate or clarify. Heard fully, musical narrative can complicate and enrich the world over time with multiple voices and incompatible vocabularies. Even when such divisive or unresolved musical energies do not become pathological, as they do in this murder story, one still senses Tolstoy's reluctance to confirm them as authentic. An incorrigibly idealistic musicophile, he would like to believe that only words laid out in a row, which so ponderously mediate experience and prompt us not to joy or reconciliation but to barren logical thought, can fail as instruments of human communion.

Thinking back on that chamber music evening, Pozdnyshev pointedly blames the environment for failing to provide appropriate release. If idle, overfed high society, exposed to this powerful music, is permitted to respond with no more than polite applause followed by small talk and sherbet, illicit sex is certain to break out somewhere. But one suspects a more damning dynamic at work. Remembering how his wife had realized Beethoven's music with the violinist, more than mere spousal possessiveness began to drive Pozdnyshev crazy. It was also the irresistibly dialogic nature of the sonata's opening passages, the fact that violin and piano are equal partners, each answering the other and adjusting to the other in sequential or overlapping themes, tempos, rhythms, and intentions. "Listened to" for the first time in her married life, Pozdnyshev's wife was growing ever more articulate, self-confident, and creative at the keyboard while rehearsing this difficult and rewarding music with the stranger-violinist. It would appear that Pozdnyshev could not abide witnessing this growth in his wife's participatory autonomy (she does not even have a name in the story her husband tells) – and so he activates words and images to create the worst possible "program" for their music, a piece of narrative text that he can again control and condemn. The murdered wife's technical fidelity or infidelity is immaterial; the story does not rule on that point. But the failure of this successful musical performance to bind minds and bodies together in trust or brotherhood is devastating.

In Pozdnyshev's anxious reaction to Beethoven's music, then, Tolstoy has the courage to confront the most vulnerable aspects of his art-as-infection theory. These aspects include an indifference to real duration, a rejection of dramatic or tonal antagonism, an insistence on the cloning of identical feelings in all participants (when contrast and confusion might have been more honest to the purpose of the artwork), a reluctance to address the bitter fallout of musical euphoria when reconstructed as verbal or pictorial memory. It seems that Tolstoy himself was not wholly at rest on this issue. His initial inspiration for the story had been an amateur performance of the Kreutzer Sonata in July 1887, with his son Sergei at the piano and the family music teacher, one Monsieur Liasotta, as violinist. In 1895 Tolstoy heard the Sonata again, this time performed by the accomplished Czech violist Oskar Nedbal, a guest at Iasnaia Poliana. Nedbal reproached Tolstoy for his disrespectful treatment of Beethoven in his (now world-famous) novella. Tolstoy allegedly replied: "Perhaps you are right, but I would have never written 'The Kreutzer Sonata' if I had heard it performed by noble-minded musicians. In the rendition of two students, each of whom played poorly, it impressed me as an erotic work."[30] But the comment is itself curious. Why should Eros – even if we grant Tolstoy the right to shame it out of court – be equated with technical awkwardness, lack of mastery, and incomplete or immoral infection?

The answer lies in the huge number of negative human traits that Tolstoy would like the wrong sort of music to illustrate and the proper ("noble-minded") sort of music to make right. Like any beloved object, music is applied by Tolstoy with fastidious care. In the celebrated episode from *War and Peace* (vol. 2, pt. 5, chs. 8–10), where a humiliated Natasha Rostova attends the opera and is intoxicated into an almost-fatal flirtation with Anatole Kuragin, Tolstoy gives us almost no sound; the narrator's wrath is directed against the naked legs of ballet dancers, the fat torsos of singers, the flimsy fakery of the stage set, the stupidity of the plot. In the operas he despises – which include the grander, more clogged, supernatural nineteenth-century variants – Tolstoy concentrates on the visuals and plays down any possible infection through music. Mozart was another matter. *Don Giovanni*, for all its undisguised and amoral Eros, delighted Tolstoy whenever he heard a snatch of it (as in that instance at the Moscow Conservatory in 1894). Mozart is so tuneful and life-affirming that even a decadent storyline cannot contaminate him. But in principle Tolstoy opposed all plotted or program music, since it literally "pre-programs" the audience with the crudest of markers – people and events. This can only hinder the individual trajectory of emotional infection appropriate to each listener.

Our final example of instrumental music, from part 7, chapter 5 of *Anna Karenina*, is censured for precisely this flaw. Konstantin Levin is in Moscow for his wife's confinement. One afternoon he attends a matinée concert of a recently composed fantasia, in extra-novelistic life a composite of Milii Balakirev's "King Lear on the Heath" (*Korol' Lir v stepi*, 1860) and

Tchaikovsky's fantasy on "The Tempest" (*Buria*, 1873), the first based on a Shakespeare tragedy that Tolstoy especially detested. Levin avoids reading any music critics on the work (just as Tolstoy would have done); he wants to make up his own aural mind. But Tolstoy assures us that the longer Levin listened to the "King Lear" fantasia, the further he felt from "any possibility of forming some definite opinion for himself" (*PSS* 19: 261). "The musical expression of feeling was ceaselessly beginning, as if gathering itself up, but it fell apart at once into fragments of new beginnings of musical expressions and sometimes into extremely complex sounds, connected by nothing other than the mere whim of the composer [...] He was in utter complexity when the piece ended and felt great fatigue from such strained but in no way rewarded attention" (*PSS* 19: 261–62).[31] When an acquaintance enthusiastically begins matching musical episodes to events in Shakespeare's tragedy, "Levin timidly asks: 'But what does Cordelia have to do with it?'" (*PSS* 19: 262). The irrelevance of Cordelia is at the heart of Tolstoy's rebuke: here Levin was trying to lose himself, but instead of being guided by autonomous musical movement into a sublime realm, the music had been guided (that is, distorted) by a sequence of imported images, personalities, and plots. Measured by the four criteria Tolstoy will posit in *What Is Art?* (*Chto takoe isskustvo?*), Balakirev's "King Lear" fantasy qualifies as thoroughly counterfeit art: it borrows (its story), imitates (images), peddles striking effects (insanity and suicide), and requires of the receiver cleverness, bookish preparation, and a huge amount of mental effort if the work is to be grasped at all.

An orchestral fantasy is fatiguing enough. But for Tolstoy, full-scale grand opera was quite simply insulting: intellectually, musically, dramatically, socio-economically, humanely. In the first chapter of *What Is Art?* he recalls attending a rehearsal of "one of the most ordinary new operas" (*PSS* 30: 28).[32] It becomes immediately clear that he did not attend to enjoy, however, but sleuthed around backstage, in the underground of musical art, spying on the musicians' dark stalls, on the stage crew's sweaty work, and on a six-hour rehearsal during which the irritable conductor, "in a suffering and spiteful voice," abused orchestra and singers with such epithets as "asses, fools, idiots, swine," compelling a "crippled person" to repeat the same musical phrase "twenty times over [...] It is hard to imagine a more repulsive sight" (6; *PSS* 30: 30). Never is there the suggestion that the participants in this project might welcome rehearsals to improve the quality of the musical performance. In chapter 13, Tolstoy savagely caricatures a staging of Wagner's *Ring of the Nibelung*, libretto as well as music. He dismisses the idea that a performance in Bayreuth could better justify this nonsense; sit for four days with other half-mad people, he writes, and the physical inactivity, darkness of the theatre, fantastical illusions of stage art, nymphs, gnomes, and incest will work their dire effect. The audience he observed in Moscow, also in an "abnormal state," was simply hypnotized; spiritualists and opium-dealers could have manipulated the same phenomena (III; *PSS* 30: 139). In his penultimate chapter 19, Tolstoy reveals the true *Zukunftkunstwerk* (artwork of the future), which will emerge on different principles: it will be the work of amateurs, spontaneous and unstaged. Everybody will agree that to invent on the spot a "little fairy-tale or song" that provides consolation or joy will be "incomparably more important and fruitful than to write a novel or a symphony" (155; *PSS* 30: 183).

It remains to consider one final category of musical expression in Tolstoy's writings: music dreamed. In chapter 23 of his *Musicophilia* (2007), Oliver Sacks describes the quasi-pathological, quasi-creative phenomenon of musical dreams.[33] He mentions several composers – Wagner, Ravel, Stravinsky, Berlioz – who created (or channeled) substantial musical ideas, often fully orchestrated, in hallucinatory "hypnagogic" (pre-sleep) and "hypnopomnic" (post-awakening) states. Sacks also notes two acute musical dreams of his own, one of them a guilt dream "full of melancholy and a sort of horror" (280). The latter hallucination would have surprised Tolstoy. His fictional use of dreamed music is overwhelmingly affirmative, integrative, and blissful. It matches the emotional profile of the character and is well motivated in the dreamer's life; often, coterminous real-world sounds are woven in, prompting or supplementing the music. But no matter how somber the real-life events surrounding the dream, joyful anticipation is its dominant musical mood.

Anna Karenina opens on one such hypnopomnic moment. Stiva Oblonsky, recently discovered in adultery by his wife, has been exiled to the sofa in his study. He wakes up, rolls over, hugs the pillow, and recalls his dream: a dinner given on glass tables, and the tables were singing *Il mio tesoro*, "only it wasn't *Il mio tesoro* but something better, and there were some little carafes, which were also women" (*PSS* 18: 4).[34] This difficult tenor aria from act II of Mozart's *Don Giovanni*, sung by Donna Anna's fiancé Don Ottavio, should have given pause to the philandering Oblonsky – but in fact, as the unfolding novel will show, the most potent trait of Oblonsky's personality is his ability to forget or simplify any unpleasantness in the larger context and intuitively pursue the immediate bodily satisfaction. This instinct justifies the sensible advice he gives his sister Anna when she begins to go off the tragic-operatic deep end (get a divorce, marry the man you love), but it also testifies to his own hopeless shallowness as a moral being. There is much of music's infectiousness in Oblonsky, which is why it is so hard to dislike or blame him. His far less flexible friend Levin, who broods, remembers, embarrasses himself, tests himself, and everywhere resists the spontaneous way, is not a naturally musical man.

Our second dream is experienced by Petya Rostov, 16-year-old officer attached to a partisan brigade, in volume 4, part 3, chapter 10 of *War and Peace*. While his sabre is being sharpened by a Cossack nearby, Petya drowses off. The rhythmic sound of the whetstone – *ozhik, zhik, zhik* – triggers a hypnagogic auditory hallucination of gorgeous complexity, a choral symphony that Petya himself eventually conducts. First he hears a majestic hymn, then a fugue, then male and female voices make their entry; Petya closes his eyes, and "on all sides, as if from far away, sounds trembled, began to harmonize, scattered, merged, and again all joined in the same sweet and solemn hymn" (*PSS* 12: 147).[35] The music Petya summons forth is a fair description of Beethoven's Ninth Symphony, which premiered in 1824. It could not have been dreamed in 1812 – a fact that adds to its eerie timelessness. Petya will be killed the next morning, in the raid that frees Pierre Bezukhov from French captivity. Through some mysterious harmony, the sacrificial death of this young, musically primed Peter (Petya) works to save the life of another Peter (Pierre), who by the end of the novel has just fathered a new Petya, Natasha's first son. This refrain, or recycling, is part of the "marvelous music" that is starting up in the Rostov–Bezukhov nursery.

In Tolstoy's fiction, music is frequently present at transitions between life and death. For all its dependence on the resonating body, it has a strong metaphysical dimension. Petya's triumphant symphony occurs at such a threshold, as does the translucent "whispering music" of the *piti-piti* chorus heard by the fatally wounded Prince Andrei in his delirium at Mytishchi (*War and Peace*, vol. 3, pt. 3, ch. 32). With this Janus-faced function in mind, part chaotic mystery and part an ordered progression toward the Light, we might now try to place Tolstoy and music in larger perspective. European aesthetics generated at least four distinct, quite incompatible concepts about music's essence. Most ancient is the classical idea of the "music of the spheres": a mathematically expressed spirit of harmony and proportionality in which the internal music of the human body is linked with the inaudible "universal music" created by the orbits of celestial bodies. Romantic theories of music offered the opposite definition, that music was not a matter of whole-number ratios or cosmic calibrations but of structureless flow, ineffable and inexpressible. Still more recent "listener-response" theories hold that music is best understood as a sonic stimulus designed to elicit certain emotions and actions. In a dark fourth option that Tolstoy wrestled with and eventually repudiated, music is related to conscious will, intentionality, and desire (Schopenhauer's concept of the "world will"). Through what it embraces and what it rejects, Tolstoy's synthesis partakes of all four.

The judgments on music in *What Is Art?* did not originate in the post-conversion years. In a notebook jotting from 1852, Tolstoy, at the age of 24, divided the knowledge of music into two parts. To the objective realm belonged music theory; to the subjective realm, rules and musical production. "The basis of music is the ability to express some musical thought," Tolstoy wrote. This process entails "the linking-up and unifying of sounds that compose a single whole [...] we call *musical feeling* the ability to reproduce a musical thought so that its unity is not disturbed in our soul" (*PSS* 1: 242).[36] The unity Tolstoy would bring about through music need not imply complete homogenization, nor must it dissolve all interpersonal boundaries. But it is cleansed of impatience and violent disharmonies; it seeks a cadence. By unification Tolstoy intends above all the emotional state Nekhliudov experienced under the starry sky at the end of "Lucerne": a moment of reconciliation with oneself, which then enables tolerance of others, a transcendence of angry judgment, and clarity. Clarity could almost do the work of love.

Let us return to the terms invoked at the beginning of this chapter. Tolstoy understood art in general as a kind of optimal energy transfer, with musical art as the ideal. Music succeeds to the extent that it generates both heat and light. Heat in this case is thermodynamic efficiency; it is achieved most quickly through purity of medium, spontaneity, intensity of utterance, and simplicity of idiom. As Tolstoy noted in his diary for December 18, 1899: "People have the habit of saying: that's very profound and thus not fully understandable. That isn't true. Everything deep is transparently clear" (*PSS* 53: 234).[37] In Tolstoy's musical utopia, clear depths are made murky by rehearsing, remembering, "staging," mastering a new form intellectually, negotiating or accommodating the mind's prior associations. Only clarity and immediacy can guarantee light.

CODA: TOLSTOY SET TO MUSIC
(RISKING THE MASTER'S PLEASURE)

The Soviet-era compendium *Tolstoi i muzyka* (1977) lists over two dozen attempts to set Tolstoy's work as opera, ballet, or instrumental composition.[38] Considering the vast scope of Tolstoy's collected works and compared with several thousand musicalizations of Pushkin and hundreds for Gogol and Dostoevsky, the number is soberingly small. Is this because there is no poetry from Tolstoy's pen, and art-songs – poetry set to music – always inflate the count? Or because Tolstoyan prose is too luxurious, complex, and meandering to fit musical form or the conventions of a libretto? Or perhaps the master's stern, disapproving eye has warded off potential musical adaptors of his prose? As this chapter has tried to suggest, even Tolstoy's disapproval was shot through with passionate attraction. In closing we note two operas that Tolstoy, perhaps against his better theoretical judgment, might have liked, and then the stub of a third.

The first is also the greatest and most famous, Sergei Prokofiev's monumental opera *War and Peace*. It was begun in April 1941, subjected to massive and capricious censorship, revised under pressure for a decade, and still unpremiered in its entirety at the time of the composer's death in 1953.[39] Prokofiev was passionate about opera; he was also committed to serving the state. Tolstoy condemned both. But Prokofiev and his librettist Mira Mendelson brought to the task other skills that might well have caused Tolstoy to tap his feet and attend closely, with mounting astonishment and respect, to its prose libretto. He would have heard long stretches of himself sung but otherwise unaltered, the rhythms and emotional curve of the lengthy Tolstoyan sentence even intensified. Like Tolstoy's beloved Mozart, Prokofiev had a spectacular lyrical gift. But unlike Mozart and eighteenth-century operatic practice generally, Prokofiev could sustain a prose utterance in a mesmerizing musical line. Radically for opera, he could develop this prosaic line toward serious rather than comic purpose. What is more, Prokofiev in music (like Tolstoy in literary prose) was a master at blending lyrical intimacy with patriotic military spectacle.

Mira Mendelson extracted all episodes for part 1 of the opera, "Peace," from volume 2, parts 3 and 4. The unifying theme is Natasha Rostova's fall from innocence and its repercussions on the three men who desire her: her fiancé, her seducer, and the confessor who will become her husband. At the epicentre of these events is a scene that Prokofiev did *not* set, "Natasha at the Opera." Quite possibly the original scene in the novel is the meanest parody of the genre in all nineteenth-century literature. Mean, because opera is represented with no respect for its conventions (the spectacle Natasha sees, anachronistically, is modeled on Meyerbeer's 1831 *Robert le Diable*, an immensely popular French grand opera that played in Moscow between 1861 and 1864 and which Tolstoy intensely disliked).[40] Mean also, because of what this opera sets Natasha up to do – to those who love her, and to herself. And mean, finally, because there is almost no music described in it (just fat ladies and fake sets), and stage decorations can never infect, only music can. The opera-loving Prokofiev had nothing to gain by reproducing Tolstoy's disgust at operatic convention. He had everything to gain, however, by showcasing the seductiveness of music. Thus in act 1, scene iv, he replaces the absent centerpiece of Natasha at the Opera with an equally intoxicating device of his own: an E-flat major waltz in compelling 3/4 time, which none of the musical Rostovs is able to resist. Modulating in and out of more sinister minor keys, Hélène and Anatole keep this waltz going throughout the scene. Natasha and her father try feebly to counter its rhythmic field with a 4/4 beat of their own, and they fail; their words might resist, but they sing in time with the waltz. Even the impeccably moral Sonia, horrified at Natasha's profligacy, cannot assert a successful 4/4 beat against the swirl. The waltz was Europe's dance of illicit passion, and Tolstoy knew what it meant when one's foot began to tap to it.

This same theme of seduction followed by betrayal is repeated in part 2 of the opera, "War." But now Natasha has become all of Russia; the Frenchified salon of the Kuragins has become the French Grande Armée. Russia is seduced, betrayed, falls. Fieldmarshal Kutuzov preserves her, as Pierre preserves Natasha, but at a terrible cost. If the seductive rhythms of the waltz dominate "Peace," then the mass choral hymn, military march, and patriotic aria infect in "War." Although Prokofiev was compelled repeatedly to inflate Kutuzov's arias, in fact the chauvinistic pageantry of this opera is immensely stirring, even frightening, true to the novel and even to a portion of Tolstoy's later musical aesthetic. In the black year 1943, with the nation again under siege, Russia needed to see, hear, and be mobilized by the triumph of 1812. Prokofiev's opera could have satisfied that need. Music is depraved only when performed in inappropriate contexts. But the opera never passed ideological muster, and the inspired, necessary moment passed.

Curiously, in the early 1940s Prokofiev also considered setting a second Tolstoyan novel, *Resurrection*, which would have emphasized a later, lonelier Tolstoyan approach to salvation. A prose libretto, "Katiusha Maslova," was produced by the playwright Anatoly Mariengof in 1941 for Dmitry Shostakovich, from whom the Kirov Theater had commissioned the opera. But Shostakovich lost interest and offered the project to Prokofiev. Prokofiev remained with *War and Peace* – sensibly, it turned out, for the Mariengof libretto was banned in May 1941. The surviving typescript of "Katiusha Maslova" suggests an operatic condensation for the Stalinist stage with sufficient tunefulness and subversiveness to appeal to Tolstoy himself.[41] Gypsies sing in the brothel in act II, scene ii (the heroine, we recall, was fathered by a "passing gypsy"), against a backdrop of uninter-rupted, unrepentant state violence. The ending is abrupt and non-novelistic. After Simonson stammers out his confession of love, romance as a motif is abruptly curtailed; only a hurried shout "Farewell" passes between Katiusha and Nekhliudov as she is led away in a throng deeper into Siberia, to a plaintive folk lament. The Prince disappears from the text.

Such a mass "Siberian" finale is congenial to Russian time-space under all regimes. But other Tolstoyan emphases are also possible with this novel. An American operatic version of *Resurrection*, by Tod Machover, premiered in Houston in 1999 with a more sentimental – and at the same time more lonely and self-reliant – denouement.[42] Its theme was individuality, one area in which the eighteenth-century Tolstoy, enamored of the Franklin diaries, overlaps with the pragmatic and resilient North American States. At the end, Nekhliudov and Katiusha sing of a world changed one person at a time, where a prince can do what a former prostitute cannot. After a non-love duet confirming their separation, Katiusha, now pardoned, remains behind to tend Simonson, whose back has been flayed by a whipping. The final stage direction reads: "(Nekhlyudov is left alone on stage as Siberia fades away behind him. He turns and walks away into the dawn, back to the world. The resurrection is complete.)"[43] Is this later Prince Nekhliudov finally making good on his conciliatory visions by Lake Lucerne?

Both these operas, built off two great Tolstoy novels, contain much that would have moved the novelist to tears in terms of moral content. Musically too they might have appealed: Prokofiev's lyrical mastery, combined with a mass of infectious dances, would surely have pleased Tolstoy's ear. Likewise, Machover's devotion to tonal consonance, his expertise with medieval chants and American folk hymns, and his conservative use of "hyperinstru-mentation" to embellish select moments of live music electronically, might have intrigued Tolstoy much as did the gramophone in 1903.[44] But these two works are nevertheless operas: big expensive affairs produced on big professional stages, requiring well-trained if not virtuosic voices, rehearsals, costumes, and capital layout. Our final example of Tolstoy set to music is still opera, but moves to overcome these final objections.

In the mid-1990s, the House of Hope Presbyterian Church commis-sioned the American composer Stephen Paulus and his librettist Michael Dennis Browne to compose a one-act opera on Tolstoy's 1886 variant of a Volga District legend, "Three Hermits" (*Tri startsa*).[45] This tiny parable relates the conversion of a Russian Orthodox bishop by three hermits of Solovetskii Monastery, whose garbled homespun prayer – "Three are Ye, Three are we, Have mercy on us!" – the bishop had tried to "correct" by teaching them the authorized Lord's Prayer. The bishop leaves their island after administering the lesson. But the three hermits cannot remember the new words and so they hasten over the water to the high cleric's ship to be taught afresh. The bishop is chastised by the humble faith of the three hermits and is reminded of the falseness of mere words.

Tolstoy heard the legend from a wandering storyteller in 1879 and "transcribed" it in 1885 for his *Twenty-Three Tales*. Within his own faith system, of course, Tolstoy must discount any miracle. He tenderly and lovingly parodies the apocryphal "walking on water" motif of the legend, all the while seriously endorsing the bishop's epiphany.[46] When Stephen Paulus set Tolstoy's text, however, he did so for an audience of Christian believers who did not necessarily discredit the miraculous episodes of the Gospel. In scene iii, the dramatic peak of the piece, the passengers on the bishop's vessel (his mother, several nuns, a chorus of pilgrims) witness, to shimmering music and dazzling moonlight, "the hermits running over the water / as though it were dry land." It is to this physically present, eye-witnessed miracle that the bishop bows and admits his own need for humility: "It is not for me to teach you," he sings. "In my pride, I tried to change you. / Pray for us, you holy ones." The music to *Three Hermits* is luminous, vocally non-virtuosic throughout, with intermittent modality marking the religiously most fervent moments. Several reviews of the opera note its appropriateness for church and amateur groups. Tolstoy would say that the psychological effect of the work – what the art *does* rather than what it *is* – argues for its authenticity. Verifying the fact-content of an experience (whether the hermits were paddling in a skiff or walking the surface of the waves) is far less important than fostering humility and brotherhood. With that purpose achieved, does it make any difference, in the end, who sees what under the moon? All the tasks of true art are accomplished through the return of the hermits. The high are brought low, although gently and at their own volition. The bishop, who thought he commanded all the right verbal formulas, is converted by the homespun, simple, and humble. Of course the legend is a fantasy, but it is not the pernicious fantasy of Natasha at the Opera, which intoxicated her body so disastrously. *Three Hermits* is transformational and affirmative. It is also (in Tolstoy's special sense) pragmatic, that is, useful for keeping faith alive – an aid in "forcing people to love life" and to forgive life its trespasses. For this to happen, the "infectious impulse" must be simple, intensely emotional, unmediated, and ideally resolved in unison. The technical difficulty of balancing this prescript with the vagaries of human expression and communication, not to mention our natural curiosity to experience new forms, is hinted at in that diary entry from December 18, 1899. The entry is prefaced with the word "nonsense" (*pustiaki*) – but one suspects that Tolstoy, smiling at himself, is also serious. "About polyphonic music," he writes. "A voice ought to say something, but in this case there are many voices, and each one says nothing" (*PSS* 53: 232).[47]

NOTES

1. "Dnevnik. 1851. 29 noiabria. Tiflis." L. N. Tolstoi, *Polnoe sobranie sochineniia*, 90 vols. (Moscow: Gosudarstvennoe izdatel'stvo "Khudozhestvennaia literatura," 1928–58), 46: 239–40. Hereafter cited as *PSS* followed by volume and page numbers.
2. For Tolstoy's argument against *programnost'* or storytelling in music, see Iosif Eiges, "Vozzrenie Tolstogo na muzyku," in P. N. Sakulin, ed., *Estetika L'va Tolstogo: sbornik statei* (Moscow: Gosudarstvennaia Akademiia Khudozhestvennykh Nauk, 1929), 241–308, esp. 253–54 and 277–80.
3. Recorded for December 7, 1899. A. B. Gol'denveizer, *Vblizi Tolstogo* (Moscow: Goslitizdat, 1959), 58.
4. See Leonard B. Meyer, *Emotion and Meaning in Music* (Chicago: University of Chicago Press, 1956), 81: "[I]t seems clear that almost all motor behavior is basically a product of mental activity rather than a kind of direct response made to the stimulus as such."
5. From Tolstoy to his children L. L. and T. L. Tolstoi, March 12, 1894. "What wizardry," Tolstoy continues. "It's no joke, but a horrifying power. And it seems that people want only the bad influence" (Kak za koldovstvo … Eto ne shutka, a uzhasnaia vlast'. A okazyvaetsia, chto liudi khotiat tol'ko durnogo vozdeistviia). PSS: 67: 79.
6. V. Bulgakov, *L. N. Tolstoi v poslednii god ego zhizni* (Moscow: Pravda, 1989), 147.
7. See diary entry for July 12, 1900: "People who are not capable of penetrating to the depth [of their own art] raid the neighboring arts for the benefit of their own field and think that they create something new: poetry into music and vice versa, painting into music, etc." (Liudi zhe ne mogushchie uglubit' prikhvatyvaiut v svoe pole iz sosednikh iskusstv i dumaiut, chto tvoriat novoe: poeziia – muzyku, i naoborot, zhivopis' – poeziiu i t.d.). PSS 54: 29.
8. Cf. the autobiographical patch from "Sviatochnaia noch'," VIII [IX] "Mechty," where Tolstoy laments the fall in status of this popular form: "There was a time in Russia when no music was more loved than gypsy music […] even to prefer it to the Italians did not seem strange […] Gypsy music in Russia was the only transition from folk music to learned music" (Byvalo vremia, kogda na Rusi ni odnoi muzyki ne liubili bol'she Tsyganskoi […] i predpochitat' ikh Ital'iantsam ne kazalos' strannym. Tsyganskaia muzyka byla u nas v Rossii edinstvennym perekhodom ot muzyki narodnoi k muzyke uchenoi). PSS 3: 262.
9. Indispensable to this task is Z. G. Paliukh and A. V. Prokhorova, eds., *Lev Tolstoi i muzyka: khronika, notografiia, bibliografiia* (Moscow: Sovetskii kompozitor,

1977), 41–258 ("Muzykal'naia khronika zhizni L. N. Tolstogo," a digest of comments on music from diaries, letters, memoirs, and Tolstoy's fiction). All citations checked against the Jubilee edition and occasionally filled out or corrected.

10. From his 1861 article "Iasnopolianskaia shkola za noiabr' i dekabr' mesiatsy," *PSS* 8: 120–25, cited in *Lev Tolstoi i muzyka*, 83.

11. Cited in Eiges, "Vozzrenie Tolstogo na muzyku," 242–43.

12. For a good overview of the relationship, see N. N. Gusev, *Lev Nikolaevich Tolstoi: materialy k biografii s 1870 po 1881 god* (Moscow: Izd. AN SSSR, 1963), ch. 37, 245–48. Quoted phrases are on 245 and 247.

13. "L. N. Tolstoi i muzyka (iz arkhiva N. N. Guseva)," in *Iasnopolianskii sbornik* (Tula: Prioskoe knizhnoe izdatel'stvo, 1986), 171.

14. Gol'denveizer, *Vblizi Tolstogo*, 38. The English translation differs somewhat from later Soviet-era Russian versions; translation amended here from A. B. Gol'denveizer, *Talks with Tolstoy*, trans. S. S. Koteliansky and Virginia Woolf (London: The Hogarth Press, 1923), 10–11.

15. *The Musorgsky Reader: A Life of Modeste Petrovich Musorgsky in Letters and Documents*, ed. and trans. Jay Leyda and Sergei Bertensson (New York: Norton, 1947), xix.

16. This visit is described in Alexander Tumanov, *The Life and Artistry of Maria Olenina-d'Alheim*, trans. Christopher Barnes (Edmonton: University of Alberta Press, 2000), 99–105. Quote on 103. (Original Russian text: A. Tumanov, *"Ona i muzyka i slovo": zhizn' i tvorchestvo M. A. Oleninoi-d'Algeim* [Moscow: Muzyka, 1995, 119]).

17. Gol'denveizer, *Vblizi Tolstogo*, 58. The pianist attributes this indifference to Chaliapin on that day to Tolstoy's bad mood.

18. L. B. Bertenson, "Stranichka vospominaniiam o L. N. Tolstom" (1911), cited in *Lev Tolstoi i muzyka*, 182.

19. A. P. Sergeenko, "Tantseval'naia muzyka," in *L. N. Tolstoi v vospominaniiakh sovremennikov*, vol. 2 (Moscow: GosIzdKhudLit, 1960), 219–21.

20. "Dnevnik. 13 marta 1900." *PSS* 54: 13.

21. Richard F. Gustafson, *Leo Tolstoy. Resident and Stranger: A Study in Fiction and Theology* (Princeton, NJ: Princeton University Press, 1986), 374.

22. Leo Tolstoy, *War and Peace*, vol. 2, pt. 1, ch. 16, trans. Richard Pevear and Larissa Volokhovsky (New York: Knopf, 2007), 343.

23. Leo Tolstoy, *Anna Karenina*, trans. Richard Pevear and Larissa Volokhovsky (New York: Penguin, 2000), pt. 3, ch. 12, 275.

24. Tolstoy, *War and Peace*, vol. 1, pt. 2, ch. 2, 121–22.

25. *Detstvo*, third redaction, ch. 10 "Maman igraet." – Muzyka. *PSS* 1: 181–83, esp. 181.

26. See Amy Mandelker, "Tolstoy's Eucharistic Aesthetics," in Andrew Donskov and John Woodsworth, eds., *Lev Tolstoy and the Concept of Brotherhood* (New York and Ottawa: Legas, 1996), 116–27, esp. 117.

27. A. E. Babaev, "Lev Tolstoi i muzyka" [introductory essay] in *Lev Tolstoi i muzyka* (1977), 17–18.

28. Michael A. Denner, "Accidental Art: Tolstoy's Poetics of Unintentionality," *Philosophy and Literature* 27 (2003): 284–303, esp. 291.
29. For a detailed analysis of musical and narrative parallels, see Janneke van de Stadt, "Narrative, Music, and Performance: Tolstoy's *Kreutzer Sonata* and the Example of Beethoven," in *Tolstoy Studies Journal* 12 (2000): 57–70, esp. 58–64.
30. V. Sukhinenko, "Tolstoi i muzyka," in *Novaia Sibir'* (Irkutsk), 1935, 131, as cited in *Lev Tolstoi i muzyka*, 134.
31. Tolstoy continues: "These fragments of musical expressions, good ones on occasion, were unpleasant because they were totally unexpected and in no way prepared for […], like a madman's feelings. And, just as with a madman, these feelings passed unexpectedly" (No i samye otryvki etikh muzikal'nykh vyrazhenii, inogda khoroshikh, byli nepriiatny, potomu chto byli sovershenno neozhidanny i nichem ne prigotovleny […] tochno chuvstva sumasshedshego. I, tak zhe kak u sumasshedshego, chuvstva eti prikhodili neozhidanno) (*PSS* 19: 261–62). Tolstoy, *Anna Karenina*, pt. 7, ch. 5, 685.
32. Leo Tolstoy, *What Is Art?*, trans. Richard Pevear and Larissa Volokhonsky (London: Penguin Books, 1995), 4. Henceforth cited in text by page number, followed by *PSS*.
33. Oliver Sacks, *Musicophilia: Tales of Music and the Brain* (New York: Knopf, 2007), 279–84.
34. Tolstoy, *Anna Karenina*, pt. 1, ch. 1, 2.
35. Tolstoy, *War and Peace*, vol. 4, pt. 3, ch. 10, 1055.
36. "Tri otryvka o muzyke" [*Otryvok II] [1848–50], in *PSS* 1: 242.
37. Entry for December 18, 1899, Moscow. In *Tolstoy's Diaries*, ed. and trans. R. F. Christian (New York: Charles Scribner's Sons, 1985), vol. 2, 473.
38. *Lev Tolstoi i muzyka*, 259–66. A 2008 Russian on-line search reveals a scarcely updated list.
39. For a detailed and complete history of the *War and Peace* project, both libretto and music, see Simon Morrison, *The People's Artist: Prokofiev's Soviet Years* (Oxford: Oxford University Press, 2008), chs. 4, 6, 7. I thank Morrison for sharing his materials on this and a second potential Tolstoy–Prokofiev project based on *Resurrection*.
40. See Margo Rosen, "Natasha Rostova at Meyerbeer's *Robert le Diable*," *Tolstoy Studies Journal* 17 (2005): 71–90.
41. "Katiusha Maslova (*Voskresenie*)," TsGALI (Sankt-Peterburg) f. 337, op. 1, d. 206, 54 ll.
42. *Resurrection*, music by Tod Machover, libretto by Laura Harrington (with additional material by Braham Murray), premiered April 1999 by Houston Grand Opera. CD Albany Records 2001, Houston Grand Opera conducted by Patrick Summers.
43. Libretto for the Houston premiere of *Resurrection*, printed April 1, 1999, 44. My thanks to Gary Gibbs, Director of Education and Outreach for Houston Grand Opera, for the packet of promotional materials.

44. See Charles Ward, "How to Sing Tolstoy / Tolstoy Transformed," *Houston Chronicle* (Sunday, April 18, 1999), 1, 9.

45. *The Three Hermits*, an Opera in One Act after a story by Leo Tolstoy, music by Stephen Paulus, libretto by Michael Dennis Browne. CD by d'Note Entertainment Classics, recorded April 29, 1997, at House of Hope Presbyterian Church, choir conducted by Thomas Lancaster.

46. For a discussion of Tolstoy's procedures for these transformations, including this legend, see Inessa Medzhibovskaya, *Tolstoy and the Religious Culture of his Time: A Biography of a Long Conversion, 1845–1887* (Lanham, MD and Boulder, CO: Lexington Books, 2008), "Rhetoric of Holiness, Moral Action, and Synthesis of a Religious Art-Form," 276–77.

47. Entry for December 18, 1899, Moscow. In *Tolstoy's Diaries*, trans. Christian, vol. 2, 472.

CHAPTER 2

Sublime vision and self-derision: the aesthetics of death in Tolstoy

Andreas Schönle

Death features prominently in Tolstoy's artistic and intellectual universe. Tolstoy's very first work, *Childhood*, a semi-fictional account of scenes inspired by his childhood, relates the 10-year-old protagonist's first confrontation with death when his mother unexpectedly succumbs to an illness. Tolstoy was about 2 years old when his mother died, and 9 when his father followed her. This initial painful realization of human mortality clearly exerted a profound impact, prompting him to recreate the image of his mother in *Childhood* and to return again and again to the theme of death in his subsequent works. Both *War and Peace* and *Anna Karenina* contain celebrated death scenes unparalleled in world literature, but shorter works have been just as powerful, in particular "Three Deaths," *The Death of Ivan Ilych*, and *The Kreutzer Sonata*. Notable death scenes are also scattered in many, if not most, of his other pieces, including the Sevastopol sketches, *The Cossacks*, and *Hadji Murat*. The prominence of death in Tolstoy's oeuvre can hardly be overstated, and so it is no surprise that Philippe Ariès discusses Tolstoy's treatment of death at length in his seminal *The Hour of Death*, a survey of the history of dying in Western civilization.[1]

Little Nikolenka, the protagonist and first-person narrator of *Childhood*, does not witness the final moments of his mother's life; he and his brother are led away from her deathbed, more out of concern for the dying mother than to spare the boys. Yet on the next day, he feels the urge to see her again and in the late hours, having overcome "an involuntary feeling of fear," he sneaks into the room where she is lying in a coffin.[2] His initial gaze is blurred: his eyes are so clouded by tears that objects seem "strangely to merge," yet among other things he distinguishes "something transparent, the color of wax." He gets up on a chair to glance at her face, but again sees only a palish yellow, translucent object. When he realizes that this is in fact his mother's face, he is seized with "horror." Progressively he gains a measure of the changes her face endured. He is surprised at the "stern and cold" expression on her face and at the shape of her lips, which is "so beautiful, so sublime" and expresses such "unearthly calm," that it sends cold shivers through his body.

This short description presents themes characteristic of Tolstoy's aesthetics. The child's first unpreconceived glance at the spectacle of death rests on the divorce between visual impression and cognitive understanding. In Kantian terms, this is the hallmark of aesthetic contemplation, as the imagination requires no concept of the object to appreciate its beauty. This ability to behold objects in their intrinsic form, rather than with an automatic leap to their presumed, and often socially sanctioned, signification, underpins Tolstoy's experiments in what Viktor Shklovsky has called defamiliarization. In this case, however, the gap between intuition and comprehension, between visual perception and habitual understanding, is unfathomable, as it is caused by the occurrence of death. The object is the mother, but not quite, for the ontological status of her corpse is painfully unclear. Can her body still be called her if her spirit has departed? The experience of defamiliarization is often described as an attempt to see an object *anew*, as if for the first time, in a manner unencumbered by any preconceived notion of it. But in this instance, defamiliarization is seeing the object for the *last* time.[3] In any case, horror overwhelms Nikolenka only when he makes the link between the corpse in front of him and his mother, as their seeming identity conceals an insuperable incongruity, of which the visible changes in her face serve as subtle indicators. Between the inert matter in the coffin and all he remembers about his mother, a faint relation of resemblance obtains, but one that he finds incomprehensible and shocking. His experience of death reveals the mystifying nature of metaphor: for him the yellowish translucent object lying in the coffin can in no way stand for his mother. The little boy "kept forgetting that the dead body, at which he looked senselessly as if at an object that has nothing in common with his memories, was *her*" (ch. 27; *PSS* 1: 85). Obfuscating the resemblance between the two wards off the necessity of coming to terms with the reality of death.

Yet at the same time, the narrator does not deny that the corpse of his mother exerts an uncanny power over him. Not only is he surprised by the expression on her face – a coldness and severity that seem vaguely to reproach him for something – but he also discovers something attractive in the features of her face, a folding of her lips called at once beautiful and sublime. Altogether his mother seems imbued with "unearthly calm," contrasting resolutely with the state of agitation he experiences. His mother has seen something that eludes him, which lends her a definite superiority over him, and it is as if she were now both physically distant and psychologically uninterested in him. He is irresistibly drawn to her face, as if through it he could catch a glimpse of what she has beheld beyond the pale of life. Indeed, his imagination then produces compensatory visions of his mother not only alive and lively, but also joyful and smiling, the opposite of her present condition. And after shifting a few times between the sobering vision of his dead mother and the imaginary recreation of her post-mortem reincarnation, he loses his sense of reality altogether and succumbs to "a lofty, inexpressibly pleasant and sad bliss" (ch. 27; *PSS* 1: 85).

In aesthetic terms, the experience described here closely resembles what has been called the sublime. In the most basic sense, the sublime involves a confrontation with something unexpected, which exceeds human faculties and therefore seems threatening. Yet dreadful as it is, the sight of this overpowering object affords pleasure, as it enables the beholder to become cognizant of his or her ability to withstand the threat, mitigate it, or else compensate for it. The menacing element is normally tied to some infinitude, whether one of magnitude or power, and in the latter case it conveys a foreboding of death. The sublime thus leads to some kind of self-discovery resulting in enhanced self-awareness and self-confidence.

The sublime emerged as a critical aesthetic category in the late seventeenth century, as a result of the Copernican revolution that usurped God's position and put the human self at the center of the world.[4] It provided a context for experimenting, theoretically as well as practically, with consciousness, for testing its powers and limits. Predictably, the issue involved the relationship among human faculties such as perception or intuition, imagination, and reason. Chaos made its entry into aesthetics, at least in the guise of the "beau désordre" evoked by Boileau and echoed by Edmund Burke as the "magnificent" disorder, which produces "an appearance of infinity."[5]

Thus, the self became aware of itself, actualized its potential, and, as it were, took shape in part through this experience of the sublime. Knowledge of the self was no longer to be attained by means of a religious epiphany or philosophical deduction, but only through the aesthetic experience, the last opportunity to assemble the bits and pieces of the world into a vision of totality.[6] At the same time as nature became a kind of objective analogue for the self, a figurative representation of the totality of the soul, it was in its turn preserved from disintegration by being unified in the prism of aesthetic consciousness. Yet because it rests on a solitary experience and, unlike the beautiful, fails to invoke values shared by a community, the sublime underpins a form of self-consciousness staunchly individual and autonomous.

Boileau sparked off the fascination for the sublime with his translation of Longinus' treatise *On the Sublime* in 1674. From then on, the development of ideas about the sublime ran through the eighteenth century in both literature and philosophy. Major contributions to this debate included Burke's empiricist *Inquiry into the Origins of Our Ideas of the Sublime and Beautiful* and Immanuel Kant's idealist *Critique of Judgment*.[7] The sublime continued to be influential in the nineteenth century, exerting notably an important impact on Schopenhauer's aesthetics, itself an inspiration for Tolstoy (as will be discussed below), and inspiring renewed interest in the late twentieth century in the context of post-structuralist cultural theory.[8]

This is not the place to attempt even a summary of Kant's aesthetic philosophy, which is both complex and problematic, but in anticipation of the discussion of death in Tolstoy a few points should be emphasized. Kant distinguishes between two types of sublime. The mathematical sublime, which pertains to cases in which the subject experiences the inadequacy of the senses to grasp a formless and unlimited object, need not concern us here. The dynamical sublime, in contrast, describes situations in which an external phenomenon threatens to destroy the self through its physical power. The threat to the self, however, is more imaginary than real, for in an actual situation we would run for our lives rather than experience the refined pleasure of the sublime. This form of sublime "reveals in us at the same time an ability to judge ourselves independent of nature [...] Hence nature is here called sublime (*erhaben*) merely because it elevates (*erhebt*) our imagination, [making] it exhibit those cases where the mind can come to feel its own sublimity, which lies in its vocation and elevates it even above nature."[9] What we learn in this process, then, is an ability to distance ourselves from our immediate needs. Our pleasure at a sublime sight stems from our ability to resist the claims of nature, both external and internal, over us and thus to affirm our moral autonomy.

Of course we have no evidence that Tolstoy will have read Kant's *Critique of Judgment* by 1852, when he writes *Childhood*. The first incontrovertible evidence of Tolstoy's interest in Kant does not come until the summer of 1869, when he writes to Afanasii Fet that he reads Schopenhauer and Kant (*PSS* 61: 219).[10] Nevertheless the very combination of "beautiful" and "sublime" in the description of the dead mother suggests that Tolstoy is at least vaguely aware of the existence in aesthetics of this conceptual pair. He may have been apprised of it indirectly, for example through the works of Nikolai Gogol or Vasily Zhukovsky, or through his readings of Western philosophy and literature, for example Friedrich Schiller. Yet conflating the two terms, as Tolstoy seems to do in this case, implies that his grasp of the difference between the beautiful and the sublime is anything but rigorous. Nevertheless, his subsequent description of Nikolenka's response to the sight of his mother's corpse neatly features the ambivalence of the experience of the sublime, the combination of repulsion and attraction, of fear and pleasure, which Kant conceived at times as a two-stage process and at times as a continuous alternation, as it is in this case.[11] And the whole experience ultimately leads to a feeling of elation, an "elevation" of the imagination, very much as Kant would have described it.

Most intriguing, however, is the lexical thread Tolstoy spins around the sublime, which he repeats in *The Cossacks*, his piece most sustainedly concerned with this aesthetic category. Indeed, the stern expression the boy discovers on the face of his dead mother returns in Tolstoy's epic novella in the vision of Caucasian peaks as stern sublimity. As Olenin travels to the Caucasus and sees the mountains for the first time, he slowly penetrates the character of the topography, until he "felt the mountains." "And from this moment," the narrator continues, "everything he saw, everything he thought, everything he felt, acquired for him the new, sternly sublime (*strogo velichavyi*) character of the mountains" (ch. 3; *PSS* 6: 14).[12] Under the spell of the towering peaks, his entire moral constitution becomes loftier, so that all his previous concerns now seem trivial. Everything he sees and feels is imbued with the might of the mountains: "A look at the sky – and he recalls the mountains. A look at himself, at Vaniushka – the mountains again. Two Cossacks are riding their horses [...] and the mountains [...] The Arbeks are roaming on the steppe, and I travel, without fear, I have a gun, and strength, and youth; and the mountains" (*ibid.*). The narrator clearly experiences an ingress of power under the influence of the lofty scenery, which exerts such a profound impact upon him that this encounter of the sublime becomes a turning point in his life. The lexical combination of *stern sublimity* recurs several times in the story in relation both to the mountains ("he gazed again at the mountains and the sky, and the stern sense of sublime [*velichavoi*] nature permeated all his memories and dreams" [ch. 11; *PSS* 6: 43]) and to its inhabitants ("Olenin was struck by the sublimity [*velichestvennost'*] and sternness of expression on the face of the *dzhigit*" [ch. 21; *PSS* 6: 80]; Mariana "frowned and sternly drew him away with her hand. Again she seemed sublimely beautiful [*velichestvenno khorosha*] to Olenin" [ch. 25; *PSS* 6: 99] etc.). Later on in *The Cossacks*, Tolstoy links mountainous and female beauty together in an evocation of primordial beauty (ch. 33; *PSS* 6: 120). Finally the same cluster of loftiness and sternness resurfaces in *War and Peace*, in the description of Andrei's frame of mind as he lies wounded on the battlefield at Austerlitz, although here sublimity inheres more clearly in his frame of mind than in the physical properties of nature (or women!): "Everything seemed so futile and trivial in comparison with the stern and sublime train of thought (*s tem strogim i velichestvennym stroem mysli*) that weakness from loss of blood, suffering, and the nearness of death, aroused in him" (vol. 1, pt. 3, ch. 19; *PSS* 9: 355).

This recurrent nexus between sternness and sublimity acquires a strongly gendered character in the associative link between mountain and woman. Combined with the devaluation of daily life and its commonplace concerns, it seems designed to ward off the emergence of sexual desire. In *The Cossacks* the impregnability of the mountains serves as a direct analogue for the unapproachability of Caucasian women. Mariana's proud, composed, and seemingly indifferent demeanor leaves Olenin in a position where he can admire her, but must fear and hesitate to enter into more immediate contact with her. He is confined to a purely aesthetic stance, which manifests itself in the reification of mountain and woman alike. Similarly, Andrei's experience of the sublime at Austerlitz, reinforced by the subsequent death of his wife, initiates a wholly de-eroticized, self-punishing way of life for him. The elevation of the self inspired by sublime scenery comes then at a cost, namely the suppression of erotic impulses.[13]

It is now possible, after this brief digression into the psychology of the sublime, to return to *Childhood* and to the depiction of a cold and stern mother. The description of her face at once bespeaks and represses desire. The narrator's prolonged attention to the beautiful fold of her lips, which sends "cold shivers" through his back and hair, reveals the subliminal pulsation of desire. To prevent its actualization, the sublime intervenes as a sort of barrier, removing the mother from face-to-face interaction, suggesting in the evocation of her "unearthly calm" that she has withdrawn from human contact, and implying ever so slightly a sense of rebuke in the cold and stern expression of her face. In other words, the awareness of guilt promptly suppresses the emergent necrophiliac velleities of the narrator. We are left with a disjunctive vision of the mother as a cold, distant corpse and a "beautiful soul that looked back with sadness at [this world] and saw my sorrow, took pity at it and on the wings of love descended to earth with a heavenly smile of mercy to console and bless me" (ch. 27; *PSS* 1: 85). Stripped of a body and acting more like the Virgin Mary, the mother can now safely enter into contact with the boy, undoing all the hieratic distance and coldness the corpse has exuded and prompting the child's unmitigated delight at reviving the fantasies of intimacy with the mother expressed earlier in the story (ch. 15; *PSS* 1: 43–45). The sublime, in other words, distills sexual energy into spiritual communion, offering respite from the barrenness of real life in the form of short-lived dreams of spiritual intimacy with the departed mother. Death has become a spectacle, but one that keeps the senses in check in order to foster a moral vision of metaphysical plenitude. The boy's shocking experience of time is momentarily overcome through the invention of an imaginary totality, in which life and love triumph over death. Only this moment of "self-forgetfulness," the narrator adds, represents authentic sorrow, suggesting that the child's response is to be distinguished from the strategies of denial and the display of self-righteousness in which people normally engage on occasions of bereavement, as the narrator shrewdly proceeds to analyze (ch. 27; *PSS* 1: 85–86). The only other genuine response to the cadaver is that exhibited by a 5-year-old girl brought to the funeral, who shrieks with unmitigated horror at the sight of the corpse. For Nikolenka, her visceral repulsion finally brings home the "bitter reality" (as opposed to the sublime ideality) of his mother's passing (ch. 27; *PSS* 1: 88).

Although Tolstoy's portrayal of death will hardly ever be as reassuring again as this sublime vision of love beyond the grave, his description in *Childhood* sets the terms of his treatment of death in many subsequent pieces. In many of his works Tolstoy uses pronouns in the neuter to convey the inability of the beholder to recognize the reality of death and the identity of the corpse.[14] The formula "something transparent" (*chto-to prozrachnoe*) in *Childhood* is echoed by the phrase "Something in a greatcoat was lying prone where Volodia stood" (*Chto-to v shineli*) in the story "Sevastopol in August, 1855" (ch. 26; *PSS* 4: 116) or by the clause "Something large" (*Chto-to bol'shoe*) in reference to the Chechen killed by Lukashka in *The Cossacks* (ch. 8; *PSS* 6: 33), not to speak of the "something alien and hostile" (*chto-chuzhdoe i vrazhdebnoe*) in Princess Marya's impression of her dead father in *War and Peace* (vol. 3, pt. 2, ch. 8; *PSS* 11: 142). The delay between perception and understanding signals the immensity of what is to be construed and the revolting incongruity between the visible and the metaphysical. Phrases such as "This dead body was his live brother" with regard to the death of Konstantin Levin's brother Nikolai in *Anna Karenina* capture in compressed form the unfathomable transition between life and death (pt. 5, ch. 17; *PSS* 19: 60). Likewise the sentence "The same evening the ill woman was already a corpse" (*V tot zhe vecher bol'naia byla uzhe telo*) from "Three Deaths" indicates through its strange syntax the ineluctability and finality of death (ch. 3; *PSS* 6: 63). In keeping with narrative requirements, we might have expected a verb such as "to become" or simply "to die" to signal the process whereby life turned into death, or we might have anticipated a formula that confers on death agency and describes the eventful moment of its intervention. Instead, the syntax here telescopes two conditions, the state of being ill and that of being dead, without any indication of their relations and temporal boundaries, conveying only a sense that death was either quick or premature ("already"). Furthermore the state of "deathness" is conveyed through a brutal materialization – rather than being dead, she is a corpse – which hammers down the point that the woman by that moment is nothing more than a corpse. And yet the syntax insists on continuity and identity (the ill woman *was* a corpse), as if the intervening changes were inconsequential and as if the property of being could be seen to inhere in corpses. The breakdown of narrative, much like the breakdown of metaphor in *Childhood*, reveals the inability of language and, more broadly, of human understanding to come to terms with the brutal reality of death.[15]

Anna Karenina, too, hints at the paradoxical nature of the condition of being dead. After Anna commits suicide at the train station, her blood-stained body in Vronsky's recollection is described as "still full of recent life" as if life and death were not mutually exclusive conditions or as if there was a carry-over of vitality or energy between the two states, so that death can appear as a form of plenitude (pt. 8, ch. 5; *PSS* 19: 362). This overlapping between life and death recurs in many forms in Tolstoy's works. Andrei Kodjak has interpreted it as an ingredient of Tolstoy's "personal myth of immortality."[16] In this reading, the inability of conventional symptoms of life and death to enable the identification of a person's genuine condition shores up the writer's intuitive notion of immortality. The problem with this thesis is not so much its conclusion – Tolstoy undoubtedly harbored a diffuse sense of life beyond the grave – as the fact that it sweeps under the carpet the very real tensions, paradoxes, doubts, and anxieties in Tolstoy's thinking about death.

The attractiveness of corpses and their ability to generate aesthetic pleasure play a role in several of Tolstoy's works. In *The Cossacks* the fighters stand around the corpse of the Chechen shot by Lukashka, admiring his handsome features in awed silence (his brown body is depicted as "beautiful and shapely"). This is a rare moment when the Cossacks are shown engrossed in contemplation. There is no sense of eroticism here, of course. With his glassy open eyes, the corpse seems to look beyond anything in life and his lips seem frozen in "good-natured, subtle derision," as if he was no longer concerned with earthly matters. Just like Nikolenka's mother, the dead Chechen here shuns interaction with the living. And yet paradoxically this is the moment when the Cossacks take measure of the humanity of their enemy: "He, too, was a person!," one of the Cossacks exclaims, "with visible admiration for the dead" (*mertvets*) (ch. 9; *PSS* 6: 38). The use of *mertvets* here (dead man), rather than *trup* (corpse), is significant, as it implies the survival of identity. Indeed, the Cossacks then evoke what it would mean to battle against him, assuming, as it were, his fighting powers to be intact. What they discover in this scene then is grudging respect for the Chechen, whose death has only elevated him in their eyes. Thus, in the Chechen's case death results in an enhancement of manliness. Something similar happens to Ivan Ilych in *The Death of Ivan Ilych*, who clearly gains in stature from being dead: "as with all the dead (*mertvetsov*), his face was more handsome and, crucially, more imposing (*znachitel'noe*), than that of the living" (ch. 1; *PSS* 26: 64). Note the narrator's generalization about the ennobling effect of death.

Women, in contrast, often preserve their charm and attractiveness in their deceased condition and seem to remain just as keen on expressing themselves. In *War and Peace*, for example, Liza, who had seemed withdrawn when she was alive, is resolutely engaged in communication now that she is dead. Indeed, "her charming, pitiful, dead face" finally dares to voice the reproaches she was too shy to utter previously: "I love you all and did no harm to anyone and look at what you did to me," her face seems to "speak" (vol. 2, pt. 1, ch. 9; *PSS* 10: 40). Liza's face is further endowed with enviable tenacity, as three days later, during the funeral ceremony, it still speaks the same words, which elicit guilt in Andrei and anger in his father. Anna, too, keeps her "charming face" intact, with her heavy hair and curls and a half-opened rosy mouth, telltale signs of vitality, although her eyes seem to express, "as if in words, the terrifying warning that he [Vronsky] will repent" (pt. 8, ch. 5; *PSS* 19: 362). Death becomes a unique opportunity to settle scores, and Anna's corpse seems not to have lost any of her intensity. Indeed, earlier in the novel she had imagined her death as a way to punish Vronsky and had anticipated his reaction.

These examples also illustrate the uncanny expressiveness of corpses, which all seem keen to flaunt facial markers of their owners' experiences at the threshold of death. In "Three Deaths," the aristocratic lady exhibits a "stern, calm and lofty" face, much reminiscent of the mother in *Childhood*, despite the profound moral differences between the two women (ch. 3; *PSS* 6: 63). As Andrei slowly succumbs to death in *War and Peace*, he, too, casts a "cold, stern" gaze at his sister, making her feel guilty for being alive (vol. 4, pt. 1, ch. 15; *PSS* 12: 57). He becomes increasingly detached from life and resentful of being called back to the living. When his sister enjoins him to look at his son, he responds with a "derisive" smile. Much like the Chechen warrior in *The Cossacks*, he has put all need for human commerce behind him. Finally, Ivan Ilych is not to be outdone. Firmly assured that he died a proper death, he confronts the living "with reproach or exhortation," which his former colleague finds positively unseemly (ch. 1; *PSS* 26: 64). In short, all these corpses confront the living from a position of moral privilege, which expresses itself in their calm and sovereign posture. Enhanced by the experience of death they have just sustained or are about to experience, they look back at the living with a bemused impatience at the triviality of their existence. To survivors, however, corpses seem almost consistently to instill a feeling of guilt, guilt not from any specific failing, but from a diffuse sense of being mired in a trivial, inauthentic existence.

Tolstoy's depiction of corpses can be profitably compared to Zhukovsky's 1837 account of Pushkin's death. Here, too, death leaves the imprint of "deep, sublime (*velichestvennoi*), solemn thought" on the face of the deceased. And Zhukovsky resorts to a similar clinical precision in describing the events. The final farewell with the poet evokes a Tolstoy-like brutal matter-of-factness: "and everything that was the earthly Pushkin forever disappeared from my eyes."[17] Yet Zhukovsky's account is devoid of any sense of defamiliarizing horror, let alone of the moral censure at the living, which many Tolstoyan corpses inspire or display. Instead, it is couched in the pacifying rhetoric of reconciliation with the Tsar, national unity, and faith in the other world, of which the dying poet has acquired "a full, deep, gratified knowledge," a vision also evoked in Zhukovsky's poem "On lezhal bez dvizhen'ia ..." (He lay without moving).[18]

Yet what is most striking in Tolstoy's treatment of death is that it steadfastly remains a visual spectacle, and self-consciously so. The scopic nature of dying becomes explicit in *The Death of Ivan Ilych*: "*she* [death; italics are in the original, suggesting that the female pronoun is of the essence] diverted his attention to herself [...] so that he would look at her, straight into the eyes, and, without doing anything, suffered inexpressibly" (ch. 6; *PSS* 26: 94). The experience of death is thus resolutely aesthetic, both in the original sense of the word as "reception" and in the sense of becoming sensitive to a certain kind of beauty, which can only be called sublime, given that it invokes ideas of threat, loss, unfathomability, and unspeakability.

These examples also reveal the basic consistency of Tolstoy's treatment of death, as if the original description of death in *Childhood*, which was very much visual, had determined Tolstoy's treatment of death throughout his life. Indeed, the absence of recognition or defamiliarization of the loved one, the beauty and expressiveness of corpses, the survival of some form of identity, the overlapping between life and death, the sublime dignity of the corpse, if not its menace to the survivors, all these notions pervade Tolstoy's representation of death throughout his works. The foundational impact of the death of the mother in *Childhood* can hardly be denied. And yet this sense of continuity should not be overstated. As Tolstoy became engrossed in philosophy and subsequently religion, his presentation of death acquired new dimensions and especially new imagery, and it is to changes in his treatment of the sublimity of death that the remainder of this chapter will be devoted.

Andrei's experience of the sublime on the battlefield at Austerlitz undercuts his pursuit of Romantic heroism and punctures his inflated view of Napoleon as the quintessential hero. Confronted with a vision of the sublimity of the sky, Andrei comes to the realization that "everything is empty, everything is delusion, except this infinite sky. Apart from it, there is nothing, nothing" (vol. 1, pt. 3, ch. 16; *PSS* 9: 341). This experience of the sublime is less Kantian than it seems at first glance, for rather than bringing about a strengthening of reason or ingress of power, it creates a blissful feeling of peace and quietness gained from an intuition of the triviality of individual pursuits: "how quiet, how calm and solemn, not at all as when I was running," it occurs to Andrei as he lies wounded on the battlefield. He comes out personally diminished from this experience, abandoning his overriding goal of achieving fame. Contrary to the scenarios we have discussed so far, his encounter with the sublime seems paradoxically to undermine individual self-consciousness.

This version of the sublime resonates with Schopenhauer's rewriting of the Kantian sublime, which envisions a process through which the subject, threatened by an external object that clashes with his will, can "forcibly tear himself from his will and its relations, and, giving himself entirely to knowledge, may quietly contemplate, as pure, will-less subject of knowing, those very objects so terrible to the will."[19] The Schopenhauerian sublime enables the self to rise above the will to live, which had produced an illusory notion of individuality. Viewing a sublime object, the self gains the ability to see through the vacuity of individuation and to distance itself from blind will. From an unwitting victim of the will, the person becomes, however briefly, a pure subject of knowledge. This ability to transcend quotidian needs instills in the subject a feeling of happiness and peace. In tune with such denigration of everyday life, Andrei becomes fleetingly aware of the triviality of life and the "greatness of something incomprehensible, but most essential." The apparent imminence of death inspires in him a "stern and sublime train of thought," which throws into relief the urgency of overcoming habitual knowledge, which seems now inauthentic (vol. 1, pt. 3, ch. 19; *PSS* 9: 355–56). At this stage of *War and Peace*, these similarities with Schopenhauer's philosophy may be serendipitous, as we have no proof of Tolstoy's interest in Schopenhauer before the autumn of 1868. Rather than demonstrating direct influence, these echoes suggest why Tolstoy was so enthusiastic when he finally took to reading the German philosopher. As often with him, he found in Schopenhauer's philosophy a mirror of his own views.[20]

Echoes of the Schopenhauerian sublime are, however, even more explicit in Andrei's death scene in vol. 4 of *War and Peace*, written when Tolstoy was engrossed in Schopenhauer.[21] The German philosopher drew an analogy between the short-lived pleasure of aesthetic contemplation, as we rise above our desires and are briefly "rid of ourselves," and the more prolonged blissful self-abnegation of a person on the brink of death:

Such a man who, after many bitter struggles with his own nature, has at last completely conquered, is then left only as pure knowing being, as the undimmed mirror of the world. Nothing can distress or alarm him any more; nothing can any longer move him; for he has cut all the thousand threads of willing which hold us bound to the world, and which as craving, fear, envy, and anger drag us here and there in constant pain. He now looks back calmly and with a smile on the phantasmagoria of this world which was once able to move and agonize even his mind [...] Life and its forms merely float before him as a fleeting phenomenon, as a light morning dream to one half-awake, through which reality already shines, and which can no longer deceive.[22]

Andrei's "alienation from all worldly things," the sense that he is engrossed in the contemplation of "something else, more important," the faint smile of "calm, meek derision" he directs at his sister when she evokes his son to call him back to life, all these moments are congruent with Schopenhauer's description of dying (vol. 4, pt. 1, ch. 15; *PSS* 12: 57–59). Andrei's revelation "I died – I awoke. Yes, death is waking up" could have come straight out of Schopenhauer. Even the notion of universal (if abstract) love that Andrei discovers once he is fatally wounded, which has enabled him to forgive his nemesis Anatole Kuragin – an idea which is often seen through a Christian prism – harks back to the German philosopher. Schopenhauer had described the ways in which suffering fosters in people the denial of the will, "first producing perfect goodness of disposition and universal love of mankind, and finally enabling them to recognize as their own all the sufferings of the world."[23] At this point, people "forgive their enemies, even those through whom they innocently suffered."[24] These feelings, which in a different context would sound Christological and messianic, are here presented as symptoms of the eradication of the will.

The circumstances of Andrei's dying clearly invoke the sublime. The advent of death brings home an unspecified "threatening, eternal, unknown and faraway element," of which he has been conscious throughout his life.

In a dream, he envisions death as a force, expressed as "it" (*ono*), which threatens to crash through a door he tries his utmost to keep shut. In the end, "it" breaks in, but death turns into an exhilarating deliverance accompanied with a strange feeling of lightness (vol. 4, pt. 1, ch. 16; *PSS* 12: 63–64). The main reward from this oneiric experience of death, aside from the sensation of lightness, is cognitive: a veil covering the unknown lifts before Andrei's "spiritual gaze," evoking Schopenhauer's notion of pure contemplation, which obtains when the will is overcome by suffering or aesthetic experience. Similarly, Pierre's contemplation of the nightly stars above ruined Moscow, as he identifies himself with the immensity of the universe ("and all of this is mine, and all of this is in me, and all of this is me!" [vol. 4, pt. 2, ch. 14; *PSS* 12: 106]) – a response to Andrei's discovery of the sky at Austerlitz – unmistakably evokes Schopenhauer, who had averred that

if the heavens at night actually bring innumerable worlds before our eyes, and so impress on our consciousness the immensity of the universe, we feel ourselves reduced to nothing [...] But against such a ghost of our own nothingness [...] there arises the immediate consciousness that all these worlds exist only in our representation [...] The vastness of the world, which previously disturbed our peace of mind, now rests within us; our dependence on it is now annulled by its dependence on us.[25]

Yet here we also sense a difference between the two writers. The external sublime, in Schopenhauer's interpretation, is nothing but an illusion of perspective, which imputes to the world an objectness that we merely project into it, the only reality being our will to live. As Donna Orwin has argued, Tolstoy does not share Schopenhauer's radical subjectivism.[26] The world to him possesses independent reality, with which we are, however, at one. Pierre's vision is of a totality that includes the objective world, rather than of a solipsistic universe, as in Schopenhauer.

Schopenhauer's idea of life as a continuous striving to expand, knowing full well that one ultimately faces defeat, may have influenced Tolstoy's imagery. The writer's famous image of a sphere of drops, which seek to stretch and are held in check only by other continuous drops, reprises the philosopher's image of life as a soap bubble we blow "as large as possible, although with the perfect certainty that it will burst."[27] Yet here, too, an important difference between Schopenhauer and Tolstoy comes to light. For if for the German philosopher life serves merely the survival of the species, in light of which individual existence becomes nearly pointless, in Tolstoy's spheric imagery each individual drop seeks to reflect the light of God and is thus endowed with a vocation that makes its existence both indispensable and meaningful.[28] Tolstoy did not fully share Schopenhauer's denigration of instinctual life, at least at this stage in his philosophical development. At the time of his encounter with Schopenhauer, he still harbored a fascination for unconscious existence, which he embodied in the figure of Platon Karataev, who identifies with the totality of life and is thus free of any notion of his separate individuality: "But his life [Karataev's], as he saw it himself, had no meaning as a separate existence. It made sense only as a small part of the whole, which he continuously felt" (vol. 4, pt. 1, ch. 13; *PSS* 12: 51).[29] Karataev, who has the knack of forgetting what he has just said and is entirely deprived of self-analysis, exhibits Schopenhauer's notion that to espouse the will to live is to exist in an eternal present. Despite his intuition of the totality to which he belongs, he is not devoid of self-love and is engaged in the pursuit of happiness.[30] He exemplifies the legitimacy of instinctual life and illustrates the notion that a natural sense of individuality does not preclude harmonious integration within the totality of life.

Yet, instinctual life – unreflected adherence to the will to live – is not the final word of the novel.[31] In captivity, Pierre also discovers the power of his mind. He learns to ignore both his own pain and that of his fellow prisoners. He discovers the resilience of his mind, "the salutary force of attention displacement," and finds pleasure in gaining distance from his ordeal, feeding his mind with "joyful and calming thoughts" (vol. 4, pt. 3, ch. 12; *PSS* 12: 153). This attempt to rise above the claims of the body and the logic of instinctual life extends to his relationship with others, and so Pierre ends up denying the ailing Karataev compassion, as "he feared his pity toward this man" (vol. 4, pt. 3, ch. 13; *PSS* 12: 154). Ultimately Pierre turns a blind eye to Karataev's execution, preferring to complete some calculations in his mind, despite the peasant's pressing call for attention (vol. 4, pt. 3, ch. 14; *PSS* 12: 157).[32] This cold-minded denial of sympathy suggests Pierre's unwillingness to succumb to his instincts and signals the beginning of a process through which he will overcome Karataev's philosophy and reaffirm an aristocratic identity.[33] Both Andrei and Pierre end up espousing a stoic rejection of the needs of the body and a distancing from everyday life, including the claims of their close ones.

In its association with death, the version of the sublime Tolstoy articulates after his encounter with Schopenhauer then serves the project of overcoming not only the will to be distinct, but also the logic of immersion into the claims of everyday life. It brings about a re-dedication to what is at once personal and universal in our nature and empowers us to transcend the body. It strengthens the virtues of self-control, indeed instills a salutary diffidence of our very selves, and thus enables us to overcome the fear of death. Only such self-transcendence can explain why Andrei's deathbed commitment to universal love fails to translate into personal and preeminent love for Natasha, his sister, and his son, and why, despite his love for his family, Pierre, in the first epilogue, insists on disregarding its needs for the sake of his political activities on behalf of Russia as a whole. Yet this version of the sublime hardly represents a resolution of the antinomies Tolstoy articulated throughout *War and Peace*. Indeed, this stoicism stands in a tense relationship with the embrace of instinctual life embodied by Karataev, and, in the first epilogue, by Natasha.[34] The difficulties in Pierre's and Natasha's marital relationship stem precisely from this unresolved disagreement about the importance of immersion into the everyday and the reliance on the ideals of the mind.

Tolstoy's subsequent works, which there is unfortunately no space to analyze in detail, undertake to divorce the sublime from the experience of death. For Anna and Vronsky in *Anna Karenina*, as well as for the protagonist of *The Death of Ivan Ilych*, death appears no longer as dreaded and longed-for immensity, but as a dark sack into which one is unwillingly pushed. The feeling of constriction, rather than liberation, associated with the experience of death betokens, of course, the fear of annihilation. There is nothing redeeming about Anna's relentless drive toward self-willed death, suggesting that Tolstoy has become more pessimistic about the prospects of a grand Schopenhauerian self-transcendence and more critical of the resulting alienation from life and, in particular, from others. Indeed, Levin's experience of the sublime at the end of the novel – another sky scene – explicitly renounces the attempt to comprehend infinitude: "Lying on his back, he now looked at the lofty cloudless sky. 'Do I not know that this is unlimited space and not a rounded arch? Yet however strongly I narrowed and strained my eyes, I cannot help seeing it rounded and limited, and despite my knowledge of infinite space, I am undoubtedly correct, when I see a firm blue vault, indeed I am more correct than when I strain to see beyond'" (pt. 8, ch. 13; *PSS* 19: 381–82). Faith, handed down through tradition, takes the place of reason, consigning the stoic denial of the will to the dustbin. Levin discovers in himself an injunction to live "for God, rather than for oneself" and thus to engage in the daily practice of goodness toward others. This revision of the sublime acquires Kantian overtones and results in a position reminiscent of the philosopher's categorical imperative.[35] Similarly, in *The Death of Ivan Ilych*, a resolution to the suffocating experience of death in a sack is found only with the discovery of human compassion, which transforms death into a joyful experience of dissolution into light (ch. 12; *PSS* 26: 113). Tolstoy's increasing pessimism about human nature led him, perhaps paradoxically and less than compellingly, to affirm the importance of compassion and hence of moral investment in the sphere of the everyday, thereby renouncing the seductions of the sublime.

The gruesome violent death of Hadji Murat confirms Tolstoy's dyspeptic views. Framed by the story of a burdock, which holds on to life in defiance of systematic and repeated human attempts to cut down the field, the death of Hadji Murat bespeaks not the passage into a transcendent realm, but his extraordinary resilience, as he battles to the very end despite finding himself in a desperate situation. His severely disfigured dead face displays "a childish, kind expression," as if he had found deep satisfaction in his fighting death (ch. 24; *PSS* 35: 109). At best, the manner of his demise illustrates some sort of primordial vitality that underpins human life, one we share with nature and one that is therefore resolutely immanent. The unseemly, albeit strangely respectful way Russians and Cossacks then parade his cut-off head implies a bitter acceptance that the meaning of life lies purely in fighting, as well as parodying the scopic import of death. At this stage, there is nothing meta-physical to be learned anymore from looking at a corpse.

NOTES

1. P. Ariès, *The Hour of Death*, trans. H. Weaver (New York: Oxford University Press, 1991).
2. Ch. 27. L. N. Tolstoi. *Polnoe sobranie sochineniia*, 90 vols. (Moscow: Gosudarstvennoe izdatel'stvo "Khudozhestvennaia literatura," 1928–58), 1: 84–85. This Academy edition is hereafter cited as *PSS*. All translations from Tolstoy in this chapter are my own.
3. One is tempted to speculate whether this imagined experience of mortality serves a paradigmatic role for Tolstoy's notion of defamiliarization. For a discussion of the paradoxical relationship between the death or destruction of the object and attempts to bring it alive through defamiliarization in the work of the Russian Formalists, see I. Kalinin, "Vernut': veshchi, plat'e, mebel', zhenu i strakh voiny. Viktor Shklovskii mezhdu revoliutsionnym bytom i teoriei ostra-neniia," *Wiener Slawistischer Almanach* 62 (2005): 351–86, and I. A. Kalinin, "Istoriia kak iskusstvo chlenorazdel'nosti (istoricheskii opyt i meta/literaturnaia praktika russkikh formalistov)," *Novoe literaturnoe obozrenie* 71 (2005): 103–31.
4. A traditional survey of the sublime is to be found in S. Monk, *The Sublime: A Study of Critical Theories in Eighteenth-Century England*, reprint (Ann Arbor: University of Michigan Press, 1960).
5. N. Boileau, *L'art poétique*, II, verses 71–72; E. Burke, *A Philosophical Enquiry into the Origin of Our Ideas of the Sublime and Beautiful* (Oxford: Oxford University Press, 1990), 71 (pt. II, sec. XIII).

6. See J. Ritter, "Landschaft: Zur Funktion des Ästhetischen in der modernen Gesellschaft," in Ritter, *Subjektivität* (Frankfurt a.M.: Suhrkamp, 1974), 141–63 (153), and H. R. Jauss, *Ästhetische Erfahrung und literarische Hermeneutik* (Munich: Fink, 1977), 121–23.

7. For a discussion of the opposition between these two approaches and its implication for contemporary cultural theory, see F. Ferguson, *Solitude and the Sublime: Romanticism and the Aesthetics of Individuation* (New York and London: Routledge, 1992).

8. H. Bloom, "Introduction," in H. Bloom, ed., *Poets of Sensibility and the Sublime* (New York: Chelsea House Publishers, 1986), 1–9; N. Hertz, *The End of The Line* (New York: Columbia University Press, 1985); J.-F. Lyotard, "Answering the Question: What Is Postmodernism?" in Thomas Docherty, ed., *Postmodernism: A Reader* (New York: Columbia University Press, 1993), 38–46; J.-F. Lyotard, *Lessons on the Analytic of the Sublime* (Palo Alto, CA: Stanford University Press, 1994); T. Weiskel, *The Romantic Sublime: Studies in the Structure and Psychology of Transcendence* (Baltimore, MD: Johns Hopkins University Press, 1976).

9. I. Kant, *Critique of Judgment*, trans. W. S. Pluhar (Indianapolis, IN: Hackett Publishing Company, 1987), 120–21.

10. On Tolstoy's reception of Kant, see G. R. Jahn, "Tolstoi and Kant," in G. J. Gutsche and L. G. Leighton, eds., *New Perspectives on Nineteenth-Century Prose* (Columbus, OH: Slavica, 1982), 60–70.

11. P. Crowther, *The Kantian Sublime: From Morality to Art* (Oxford: Clarendon Press, 1989), 81.

12. At this stage of his artistic development, Tolstoy uses the terms *velichavyi* and *velichestvennyi* interchangeably. In his later period, he settles for the latter.

13. For a sustained psychoanalytical interpretation of the sublime, see Weiskel, *The Romantic Sublime*.

14. For a discussion of Tolstoy's use of pronouns in his representation of death, see K. Parthé, "Death Masks in Tolstoi," *Slavic Review* 41, no. 2 (1982): 297–305.

15. On the nexus between mistrust of language and the representation of death, see L. Knapp, "'Tue-la, Tue-la!': Death Sentences, Words, and Inner Monologues in Tolstoy's *Anna Karenina* and Three More Deaths," *Tolstoy Studies Journal* 11 (1999): 1–19.

16. A. Kodjak, "Tolstoy's Personal Myth of Immortality," in A. Kodjak *et al.*, eds., *Myth in Literature* (Columbus, OH: Slavica, 1985), 188–207.

17. V. A. Zhukovsky, "S. L. Pushkinu" (February 15, 1837), in *PSS* 4: 602–16 (615, 616). My thanks to several participants at *Tynianovskie chteniia* in the summer of 2008 who pointed out this likely subtext to me.

18. Owing to the prominence of the deceased, it is not inconceivable that Tolstoy would have been aware of Zhukovsky's account, given that it was published in *Sovremennik* in 1837, albeit in a truncated, censored form. In any case, Zhukovsky stands here for a widespread quietist, metaphysically assured, and patriotic relationship to death, which Tolstoy rejected.

19. A. Schopenhauer, *The World as Will and Representation*, trans. E. F. J. Payne, 2 vols. (New York: Dover Publications, 1969), vol. 1, 210. Lev Shestov was the first to draw attention to the Schopenhauerian dimension of Andrei's death scene. See L. Shestov, *Dostoevskii i Nitsshe, Sochineniia v dvukh tomakh*, vol. 1 (Tomsk: Vodolei, 1996), 361–62.

20. The letter Tolstoy writes to A. A. Fet on the occasion of his brother's death in October 1860 sounds uncannily pre-Schopenhauerian, and also confirms Tolstoy's scopic treatment of death: "A few minutes before his death he dozed off and awoke suddenly, whispering in horror: 'what the hell was this?' – He saw it – this absorption of himself into nothing" (*PSS* 60: 357).

21. See S. McLaughlin, "Some Aspects of Tolstoy's Intellectual Development: Tolstoy and Schopenhauer," *California Slavic Studies* 5 (1970): 187–245 (188, 189n8). McLaughlin drew attention to the Schopenhauerian dimension of Andrei's death scene (199), in particular to the notion of awakening and the annihilation of individuality.

22. Schopenhauer, *The World*, vol. 1, 390–91.

23. *Ibid.* 392.

24. *Ibid.* 393.

25. *Ibid.* 205.

26. D. T. Orwin, *Tolstoy's Art and Thought, 1847–1880* (Princeton, NJ: Princeton University Press, 1993), 162.

27. Schopenhauer, *The World*, vol. 1, 311; Tolstoi, vol. 4, pt. 3, ch. 15; *PSS* 12: 158. Schopenhauer also writes of our selves as drops dissolving in the ocean (vol. 1, 205).

28. McLaughlin presents evidence suggesting that by 1870 Tolstoy explicitly identified the will with God. McLaughlin, "Some Aspects," 204.

29. McLaughlin also finds Schopenhauerian elements in Karataev, but tempered by the continuing influence of Rousseau, notably in the "romantization of the peasant." McLaughlin, "Some Aspects," 197.

30. Orwin, *Tolstoy's Art*, 105.

31. Irina Reyfman has revealed Tolstoy's ambivalence about his notion of instinctual acceptance of death as early as in the 1858 story "Three Deaths." See Reyfman, "Turgenev's 'Death' and Tolstoy's 'Three Deaths'," in Lazar Fleishman *et al.*, eds., *Word, Music, History: A Festschrift for Caryl Emerson, Stanford Slavic Studies* 29/30 (2005): 312–26.

32. For a different reading of this passage, see R. L. Jackson, "The Ethics of Vision II: The Tolstoyan Synthesis," in *Dialogues with Dostoevsky: The Overwhelming Questions* (Stanford, CA: Stanford University Press, 1993), 55–74, in particular 73–74.

33. For a discussion of this evolution, see A. Schönle, "Modernity as a 'Destroyed Anthill': Tolstoi on History and the Aesthetics of Ruins," in J. Hell and A. Schönle, eds., *Ruins of Modernity* (Durham, NC: Duke University Press, in press).

34. This tension is sometimes seen as an antinomy between Andrei's wisdom and Karataev's. See Orwin, *Tolstoy's Art*, 107–9.

35. In a letter on October 16, 1887, Tolstoy claims to read for the first time Kant's *Critique of Practical Reason*, blaming Schopenhauer for giving him a biased understanding of his moral philosophy. However, this letter is seemingly contradicted by his earlier acknowledgment in his letter to A. A. Fet on August 30, 1869, that he reads Schopenhauer and "I read Kant, too," using the perfective verb *prochel*, which implies completion (*PSS* 61: 19).

CHAPTER 3

Tolstoy's peaceable kingdom

Robin Feuer Miller

Tolstoy stands before us as a monumental chronicler of the human experience throughout every stage of life as individual, as member of a complex society, as seeker after truth through philosophy, religion, and art. But the other animals of the biosphere are also essential to Tolstoy's vision; man is, as characters like Pierre or Levin realize full well, merely one link in the great chain of being. The animal kingdom permeates Tolstoy's written world – as it did his actual existence – in myriad and often contradictory ways. Animals helped shape his views of art, death, happiness, life, history, causality, order and chaos, friendship, relations between men and women, morality, and philosophy – indeed all the preoccupations that alternately perplexed Tolstoy, drove him to despair, and gave his life meaning. Animals figure in countless permutations but are always close to the center of his ruminations.

This chapter begins by tentatively exploring ways in which Tolstoy's ideological views on animals mesh with those of some philosophers and writers who are interested in these questions today. The question of animal rights and the degree to which animals resemble human beings has reengaged philosophers and scientists in the past several decades, perhaps as a result of what has been learned about animal behaviors and the animal brain.

My primary interest, however, is in Tolstoy's representations of animals in his fiction. Animals are essential to Tolstoy's framing of aesthetic, moral, social, personal, and philosophic questions. They contribute to his framing of these questions and to his attempts to answer them. With this in mind, I shall touch upon several disparate examples of the ways in which animals give voice to Tolstoy's primary ideas as an artist and a thinker.

Tolstoy's famous embrace of vegetarianism was triggered in large part by his intensifying philosophy of non-violence, his horror of doing harm to animals and witnessing them suffer. One wonders if he ever read Jeremy Bentham's *Introduction to the Principles of Morals and Legislation*:

The day *may* come when the rest of the animal creation may acquire those rights which never could have been withheld from them but by the hand of tyranny. The French have already discovered that the blackness of the skin is no reason why a human being should be abandoned without redress to the caprice of a tormentor. It may one day come to be recognized that the number of the legs, the villosity of the skin, or the termination of the *os sacrum* are reasons equally insufficient for abandoning a sensitive being to the same fate. What else is it that should trace the insuperable line? Is it the faculty of reason, or perhaps the faculty of discourse? But a full-grown horse or dog is beyond comparison a more rational, as well as a more conversable animal, than an infant of a day or a week or even a month, old. But suppose they were otherwise, what would it avail? The question is not, Can they *reason*? Nor Can they *talk*?, but, Can they *suffer*?[1]

The philosopher Peter Singer makes much of this passage in his own utilitarian arguments and uses it as primary ballast for his ongoing philosophical endeavor to promulgate the rights of animals. He accuses humans of "speciesism" and suggests that the "basic signals we use to convey pain, fear, anger, love, joy, surprise, sexual arousal, and many other emotional states are not specific to our own species."[2]

Tolstoy would have read with relish the numerous modern-day philosophers such as Singer, Mark Bekoff, Peter Carruthers, Julian Franklin, Martha Nussbaum, and the many others who are writing about animals today. These philosophers bring to bear the whole gamut of traditional philosophical approaches to seek the most powerful and persuasive arguments on behalf of animal rights. Yet they disagree with each other, not so much in their ends, as in their means of reaching it. These current debates pit the utilitarians (like Singer) against those who frame the case for animal rights in terms of moral theory. There are also those who "attempt to develop a theory of respect for animals from human feelings of compassion."[3] This approach also dovetails with that of Nussbaum, who extends her ideas about civic justice to include non-human animals by virtue of what she calls a "capabilities approach" which she argues is "an approach to issues of basic justice and entitlement and to the making of fundamental political principles – that provides better theoretical guidance […] than that supplied by contractarian and utilitarian approaches to the question of animal entitlements, because it is capable of recognizing a wide range of types of animal dignity, and of corresponding needs for flourishing."[4] In the end, however, her capabilities approach, despite its grounding in compassion, remains pragmatic.

It is likely that Tolstoy would have participated vigorously in these current inquiries into the nature of animal rights occurring within the realms of moral philosophy, anthropology, imaginative literature, and neuroscience. Peter Singer, however – perhaps the most outspoken of the philosophical animal liberationists – eschews the kind of deep, personal affection for animals Tolstoy experienced. (In the preface to the 1975 edition of *Animal Liberation*, Singer wrote of himself and his wife: "we were not especially 'interested in' animals. Neither of us had ever been inordinately fond of dogs, cats, or horses in the way that many people are. We didn't 'love' animals. We simply wanted them treated as the independent, sentient beings that they are, and not as a means to human ends."[5]) Tolstoy, on the contrary, was deeply interested in animals and did know the experience of profound personal affection for them. At the same time, he avoided sentimentalizing that affection, as the following anecdote illustrates:

Testimony is abundant that Gorky had many stories about Tolstoy which, as Victor Shklovsky put it, "he either failed to write down or didn't want to." As an example ("of course not verbatim") Shklovsky offers this: Tolstoy's daughters brought a rabbit with a broken leg up to the balcony. "Oh, the poor little rabbit!" Lev Nikolayevich came down the stairs. Almost without stopping, he took the rabbit's head in his big hand and, with the practiced movement of a professional hunter, throttled it with two fingers. "It's a shame," Shklovsky comments, "that this was never written down." One has to agree.[6]

Like Singer, however, he increasingly treated animals as "independent, sentient beings," and, to the extent possible, "not as a means to human ends."

Tolstoy's multi-faceted relationship to the animal world in both fiction and non-fiction writing seems closest in its complexity, imaginativeness, and variety to that of J. M. Coetzee. As with the fictional writings of Tolstoy, the autobiographical and philosophical overlap between Coetzee and some of his characters is dense. If at times the boundary between the voice of Tolstoy in *Confession* and Levin in *Anna Karenina* or the narrator of *Memoirs of a Madman* is difficult to discern, that between Coetzee and a character like the eponymous Elizabeth Costello can be even more so. Two lectures she gives about animals ("The Philosophers and the Animals" and "The Poets and the Animals") also constituted Coetzee's own lectures at Princeton University in 1997–98 (along with the ensuing critiques and commentary of the other characters upon hearing these two talks). Despite the complex overlap between author and character, however, Tolstoy is decidedly not Levin or the "madman" (or *Strider*, or Pozdnyshev, etc.), nor is Coetzee Elizabeth Costello or any of his other characters. Both writers also separate themselves from the arguments of those philosophers who explore the question of whether animals possess reason or immortal souls. Moreover, although Tolstoy and Coetzee each have strong opinions about the proper treatment of non-human animals, they write instead, with all their imaginative and rational power, about animals as animals per se, and about the varieties of suffering that humans impose on them. They present their ideas most powerfully in the fictional context of characters (human and non-human), conversations and plots.[7] For both writers the capacity to place oneself into the being of another and to awaken "the sympathetic imagination" of the reader is ultimately more effective in producing change than is the application of reason.

Coetzee and his character Elizabeth Costello thus offer a paradigm here for focusing on Tolstoy's "sympathetic imagination" of animals, as the reader encounters it repeatedly in his work. These acts of sympathetic imagination give voice even more eloquently to Tolstoy's views about animals than do his more philosophical non-fiction writings on vegetarianism and non-violence. By relentlessly exploiting his own capacity for sympathetic imagination, he alters ours. He uses the sympathetic imagination to explore not just the boundaries between animals and humans but the extent of human creativity and perhaps the essence of humanity itself.

Violence toward animals dehumanizes the perpetrator, and thus Tolstoy's descriptions of it evoke more than simply our pity. Tolstoy's 1890 account of watching a pig slaughtered offers a hair-raising description of man's violence toward animals which rivals any of the battle scenes in his fiction:

On entering the village we saw a well-fed, naked, pink pig being dragged out of the [...] yard to be slaughtered. It squealed in a dreadful voice, resembling the shriek of a man [...] A man gashed its throat with a knife. The pig squalled still more loudly and piercingly, broke away from the men, and ran off covered with blood. Being near-sighted I did not see all the details. I saw only the human-looking pink body of the pig and heard its desperate squeal.[8]

This individual killing, awful as it is, cannot compare to the slaughter that he witnesses in his two visits to the Tula slaughterhouse.

A few days ago I visited the slaughterhouse [...] It is built on the new and improved system [...] with a view to causing the animals as little suffering as possible [...] Long before this [...] I had wished to visit a slaughterhouse, in order to see with my own eyes the reality of the question raised when vegetarianism is discussed. But at first I felt ashamed to do so, as one is always ashamed at going to look at suffering which one knows is about to take place. (*PSS* 29: 78; "The First Step," 1)

Tolstoy then reports his conversation with a butcher, who described the killing of cattle, who "are quiet, tame cattle. They come poor things! Trusting you. It is very pitiful." He goes on to invoke the terrible smell in the slaughterhouse of "warm blood," "congealed black blood" (*PSS* 29: 79–80). Tolstoy first invokes our pity in simple, factual prose with such sentences as:

From beneath the head [of the ox] there flowed a stream of blackish-red blood, which a besmeared boy caught in a tin basin. All the time this was going on the ox kept incessantly twitching its head as if trying to get up, and waved its four legs in the air. The basin was quickly filling, but the ox still lived. (*PSS* 29: 81; "The First Step," 3)

Tolstoy continues to describe in minute detail the prolonged, horrifying death of the ox and of several others.

It is significant, however, that Tolstoy's argument does not cease at the point where he has awakened human pity for the suffering animals. The horror he invokes outweighs the carnage of the battlefield precisely because human sympathy seems absent, and the business at hand, while gruesome, is mundane. Most startling, however, is that he frames his argument in terms, not so much of the pitiful violence done to the animals, but rather in terms of the incalculable violation and cost to men of suppressing their own capacity for sympathy and pity. This suppression, coupled with the acute feeling of shame which he had already described at the outset, is profoundly harmful. Man violates himself as much as the animal. In essence, Tolstoy's argument is not to make the animals seem more human, but to show how people can become less so. The shadow of these essays of the late Tolstoy inevitably casts its measure of somber darkness on his art.

Even before this 1890 account, animals had long been primary characters in Tolstoy's simple, didactic fables and stories for peasants and children. Aside from these overtly prescriptive animal-centered texts, however, such works as *Childhood*, *Family Happiness*, *The Cossacks*, *War and Peace*, *Anna Karenina*, "Two Hussars," *Master and Man*, *Confession*, *Strider*, *The Kreutzer Sonata*, and *Hadji Murat* exhibit the multitude of ways in which the presence of animals has always been essential to Leo Tolstoy's fictive kingdom, even if he is frequently its undisputed leonine ruler and absolute narrator. Like his character Eroshka in *The Cossacks*, Tolstoy knew his animals and observed them closely. Eroshka, the hunter with a resonant, unconscious reverence for animals, describes the boar, the eaglet, the cock, the goose, the wild sow and her piglets, the tiny moth circling the candle. The characters in Tolstoy's animal world are even more diverse and range from large animals to insects, bees, and ants. All have a detectable voice or instinct of some kind; all have lives that exist independently from man, even if man seeks analogies and answers through them. As Eroshka says, "You have your laws, and the pig has its own. And although it's a pig, it's just as good as you; it's one of God's creatures just like you are."[9] Tolstoy, however, was to question intermittently whether or not man and the other animals in fact lived by the same set of laws or whether those laws differed strongly.[10] He understood each kind of animal in its own right and did not seek easy or sentimental analogies between man and beast. Thus Anna and Frou-Frou may undergo related experiences, or the French army may be "like a wounded animal," but the differences are always as important as the similarities.

Animals appear throughout Tolstoy's canon as subject and object, as a source of extended complex analogies, in fables as parsed, sometimes transparent stand-ins for particular human strengths and weaknesses, as nuanced philosophic terms of reference, as definitive of the boundaries of artistic representation, and even as profoundly serious first-person narrators. Animals can offer Tolstoy substantive answers to his perennial questions, "How then shall I live?" and "How shall I die?" But they remain animals.

Tolstoy's early and late attempts to describe animals as autonomous, non-human beings also double as important articulations of his aesthetics. In *Childhood*, the semi-fictional semi-autobiographical hero Nikolenka Irtenev is, at 24, looking back to his childhood at the age of 10. Through a focus on several particular extended moments in his childhood, the narrator encapsulates both its general contour and flavor and its momentous changes. In each of these episodes – that simultaneously epitomize childhood itself, its looming end, its moral and spiritual conflicts – the reader witnesses facets of the birth of the narrator (and by implication of Tolstoy) as artist.

As a little boy, Nikolenka is preoccupied with the boundary between truth and falsehood and the ways in which, when he practices deception – whether in describing a prophetic nightmare about his mother's death that he never actually had, playing games, writing a disingenuous poem to please his grandmother, or displaying a picturesque grief at the news of the death of his mother that he did not yet feel – his words and gestures are effective and move others. The quick success of these lies is both pleasurable and morally disturbing. Nikolenka's first important attempt to create a work of art comes at the end of a day that has been both a typical and a final day of an epoch of his childhood.

This day has earlier included a hunt – Tolstoy's first extended depiction of an activity that, in whatever work it appears, usually presages an important realization for some character. Here, and at other such moments depicting the hunt, the narrator or central character becomes simultaneously an observer and a member of the animal kingdom. Nikolenka and the dog Zhiran have found themselves settled in at the foot of an oak tree: while awaiting the appearance of the hunted hare, the boy has observed swarms of ants carrying their burdens, and a butterfly with yellow wings who finally has become still. Nikolenka has gazed at the butterfly and it presumably has gazed at him.[11] Suddenly the hare appears. The child narrator resembles Tolstoy's other heroes at the hunt in his solitude, his immersion in the activities of several kinds of animals at once, in the rapid switch of perspective from what is inches before his eyes to what is farther away. His attention darts from the ant to the butterfly to the hare, from a metaphor for utopian society, to one of arrested beauty, to the dynamic embodiment of desire itself.

The story of Tolstoy and the "Ant-Brotherhood" he and his brothers formed as children is well known.[12] Even if, as is generally thought, the name of this brotherhood was a misunderstanding of *Muravsksie brat'ia* ("Moravian Brothers") which the Tolstoy brothers probably "mistakenly transformed" into *Muraveinye brat'ia* ("Ant Brothers"), it also highlights the lifelong importance to Tolstoy of those small inhabitants of the animal kingdom who seem most able to achieve a highly organized social structure: the ants and the bees. These creatures exist enmeshed in a brotherhood that transcends the life of the individual, yet where individual choices and desires exist. These acts and desires mesh perfectly, however, with those of the whole group – so that an individual decision seemingly reflective of one private choice among many remains an activity ultimately in harmony with the purpose of the whole colony. For example, Nikolenka watches the ants:

They hurried one after another along the smooth tracks they had made for themselves, some carrying burdens, others un-laden. I picked up a twig and barred their way. It was a sight to see how some of them, despising the danger, crawled underneath and others climbed over it; while some, especially those who had loads to carry, quite lost their heads: they stopped, not knowing what to do, looked for a way round, or turned back, or came up the twig to my hand with the idea, I think, of crawling up the sleeve of my jacket.[13]

The 10-year-old child in the glen observes the spectacle of individual choice among the various ants within the framework of a larger necessity (the preservation of the anthill). His minute observations of the ants are quickly displaced, however, by the beauty of the butterfly and the appearance of the hare. In this first hunt on the Tolstoyan canvas, the hare escapes, and the child feels shame, as though the author were punishing himself for his lingering interest in the extremes of idealized social theory (the ants) and disengaged beauty (the butterfly). His passionate desire to capture the hare (and perhaps also to expiate his guilt) provokes a remarkable early statement of Tolstoy's aesthetics, which runs counter to politicized theories of art as well as art for art's sake.

Most important, however, is that later that same day he transmits the experience of the hunt for the hare and the other experiences of his day into art. Chapter 11 opens with two paragraphs full of material that Tolstoy was to mine for the rest of his life and that herald the late Tolstoy in the voice of the fledgling writer.[14] To summarize these first two paragraphs: as his mother plays Field's second concerto and Beethoven's *Sonate Pathétique*, the 24-year-old narrator, Nikolenka, writes of his 10-year-old self hearing the music of these two pieces: "I well remember the feelings they aroused in me. They resembled memories – but memories of what? It almost seemed as if I were remembering something that had never been" (*PSS* 1: 31; *Childhood*, 40). In *Family Happiness*, Masha's playing of the piano (Mozart and Beethoven) evokes similarly complex emotions in which desire and reality intertwine in an ultimately dissatisfying way. Nikolenka's words herald those of *The Kreutzer Sonata*'s Pozdnyshev decades later. Pozdnyshev cries out, "Music makes me forget myself, my real position; it transports me to some other position not my own. Under the influence of music it seems to me that I feel what I do not feel."[15]

It is while this music is playing that the young narrator Nikolenka ventures into the realm of an artistic representation of the hunt.

I only had blue paint; but for all that I took it into my head to draw a picture of the hunt. After representing in very lively style a blue boy on a blue horse, and some blue dogs, I stopped, uncertain whether one could paint a blue hare, and ran into papa's study to consult him. Papa was reading something and in answer to my question, "Are there blue hares?" replied without lifting his head, "Yes, my dear, there are." Returning to the round table, I painted a blue hare but then found it necessary to turn it into a bush. I did not like the bush either and made it into a tree, then the tree into a hayrick, and the hayrick into a cloud, until finally I had so smeared my whole sheet of paper with blue paint that I tore it up in vexation and went off to meditate in the high-backed arm-chair. (*PSS* 1: 30–31; *Childhood*, 40)

Like any artist, his tools for representing an experienced reality (the hunt) are limited. The chosen medium cannot absorb the full complexity of the event he wishes to portray. He only has blue paint. Nevertheless it is possible to convey in a "very lively," albeit blue style, a boy, a horse, and some dogs. But this process of artistic creation has its own laws and boundaries. "I stopped, uncertain whether one could paint a blue hare."

Why is the depiction of a blue hare a stumbling block in this world of blue boys, horses, and dogs? Even though the artist is guided most accurately by his own inner logic, he asks for a response, an authentic one, from someone he trusts and admires. "Are there blue hares?" Without lifting his head, his father replies, "Yes, there are." The narrator senses unconsciously that this absent-minded answer is a lie – a lie in a different mode from the necessary lie that exists at the centre of all artistic or fictive representations of reality, or even from the false memories that music can engender. Nikolenka's father lies from inattention, habit, and an impulse to stifle conversation and inquiry. Nikolenka nevertheless returns to his painting and continues to work. The blue hare becomes a bush, then a tree, a hayrick, and finally a cloud. The painting becomes unintelligible. Unlike the artist Mikhaylov in *Anna Karenina* over twenty years later, in this case a smudge becomes a source not of inspiration but rather of vexation. The blue hare is emblematic of the individual artist's private, inviolable sense of the boundaries of his art, its inner laws and limits. It may not seem logically to be a problem that the hare was blue, since the horse was also blue. But for the artist the blueness of the hare perhaps represented the point where his authentic expression collapsed into the artificial. He had sought to represent the feeling of the entirety of the hunt – a process – but the blueness of the hare somehow disfigured the whole and dissipated the feeling the artist had been trying to recapture. Tolstoy – through his 10-year-old character Nikolenka – was perhaps learning that his art would attempt to represent the process of life (not a particular single particle of it) articulated within a moment in time.

Near the end of his life, when Tolstoy wrote *What Is Art?*, he endeavored to return to the well-springs of the artistic impulse. In attempting to describe the essence of art, he returns to the world of nature and, in particular, to a boy's emotions in an encounter with an animal. In this case the object of representation is not a hare, but a wolf.

Art begins when one person, with the object of joining another or others to himself in one and the same feeling, expresses that feeling by certain external indications. To take the simplest example: a boy, having experienced, let us say, fear on encountering a wolf, relates that encounter: and, in order to evoke in others the feeling he has experienced, describes himself, his condition before the encounter, the surroundings, the wood, his own lightheartedness, and the wolf's appearance, its movements, the distance between himself and the wolf, etc. All this, if only the boy, when telling the story, again experiences the feelings he had lived through and infects the hearers and compels them to feel what the narrator had experienced, is art. If even the boy had not seen a wolf but had frequently been afraid of one, and if, wishing to evoke in others the fear he had felt, he invented an encounter with a wolf and recounted it so as to make his hearers share the feelings he experienced when he feared the wolf, that also would be art.[16]

This discussion of the boy and the wolf, which nearly immediately precedes a frequently cited passage of *What Is Art?* defining art as the transmission of feeling, offers a clue to the young Nikolenka's artistic dilemmas and frustrations of so long ago.

Nikolenka had begun his painting, despite the limiting fact that he possessed only blue paint, because he wished to represent his feeling about the hunt. With the blue paint, the boy was able to express some of his experience (the boy, the dog, the clouds) in "lively style" until it became time to represent the most important part, the hare – the desired object of the hunt – whose escape was the source of his subsequent shame. At this point his representation of the experience faltered. The hare had been both the object of his desire and the source of his shame. The medium of blue paint ceased to suffice. His audience – his father – was not in the least infected or engaged by the child's artistic endeavor. The child immediately sensed the inauthentic response of the father. There was no sharing of feelings, no stirring of the sympathetic imagination. The painting suddenly became an object of vexation rather than of communication, and the artist destroyed it.

The hare is the object of desire and of subsequent shame for Nikolenka, and the wolf the object of desire and fear for the hypothetical boy in *What Is Art?* The hare and the wolf also each exist as living, moving, animal beings, who are ultimately independent of the feelings about them that the two would-be artists seek to represent. A successful artistic rendering of the hare or the wolf would embody both the feelings of the artist and the essential quiddity of the animal itself.

It is as if the boy Nikolenka realized fully what the old man Tolstoy asserted (in italics):

To evoke in oneself a feeling one has once experienced, and having evoked it in oneself, then, by means of movements, lines, colors, sounds, or forms expressed in words, so to transmit that feeling that others may experience the same feeling – that is the activity of art.

Art is a human activity consisting in this, that one man consciously, by means of certain external signs, hands on to others feelings he has lived through, and that other people are infected by these feelings and also experience them. (*PSS* 20: 65; *What Is Art?*, 51)

In Nikolenka's case, however, he was unable to evoke the feeling of the hare through his medium of blue paint, whether to himself or his father. In a larger and darker sense, he could not transmit to his father the feelings of desire, excitement, and shame he had lived through on that momentous day of childhood; his father remained unmoved, absently uninterested – as signified by his automatic, absent-minded reply – both to his son's inquiry and, by extension, to his son's experience. He remained uninfected by what his son tried to impart to him.[17]

Animals inform Tolstoy's ideas about the nature of happiness, the possibilities for societal organization, and the acquisition of knowledge. Tolstoy articulates some of these notions through the many animals in *War and Peace*. Its animals abound – whether as metaphors, characters, or philosophical tools. Of the numerous non-human animals of the novel – its birds, bees, ants, tortoises, rams, carp, animals of the hunt, dogs, cats, hens, farm animals – I will touch briefly upon three, the wolf, the bee, and the ant, and upon Tolstoy's general use of the term "animal."

The wolves in this novel differ from the wolf of *What Is Art?* That wolf embodied the emotion to which the would-be artist consciously desires to give form in order to communicate feelings and infect others with what he has experienced. Wolves appear several times in *War and Peace*, and their presence offers insights into primary human experience rather than into aesthetic questions. Consider the scene in which the young Nikolai Rostov participates in a hunt. The sudden but fervently desired appearance of this first wolf constitutes, the narrator tells us, the happiest moment of Rostov's life. The narrator also makes clear that Rostov undoubtedly will never realize that this was the happiest moment of his life. Gary Saul Morson has identified here a moment that epitomizes both Tolstoy's use of detail and the hallmark of his narrative stance.

> We recognize as Tolstoyan an absolute assurance about details whose significance is unfathomable and whose existence might not even have been noticed [...] Tolstoy is absolutely certain: it is not just a happy moment, not even "one of the finest moments," but, without qualification, it is the happiest moment of Rostov's life. [Moreover,] [i]f at some future time, Rostov was asked to name the happiest moment of his life, he would probably not even think of this one [...] The happiest moment of his life lies outside of all imagined narratives or patterns. It is perceptible only to God and the author, who knows that plots and plotting exclude the unnoticed, unplottable events, hidden in plain view, that are truly important in all their exceptional richness.[18]

The hunter's perspective and all its accompanying metaphors are comfortable ones for both Tolstoy and his character.

These same "unnoticed, unplottable events, hidden in plain view" can also, however, expose the ways in which the unhappiest moments similarly lie outside of "imagined narratives or patterns." For example, much later in the novel when Rostov is on the battlefield he unconsciously slips back into his easy hunter's role.

> Rostov, with his keen sportsman's eye, was one of the first to catch sight of these blue French dragoons pursuing our Uhlands [...] Rostov gazed at what was happening before him as at a hunt [...] He acted as he did when hunting, without reflecting or considering [...] With the same feeling with which he had galloped across the path of a wolf, Rostov gave rein to his Donets horse.[19]

But his target now is a human one, and once he strikes the Frenchman with his saber, "The instant he had done this, all Rostov's animation vanished" (*PSS* 11: 64; *War and Peace*, 724). As the two soldiers gaze into each other's eyes, the easy hunt metaphor collapses in the face of a more complex human reality. Rostov is passionate, but no killer. His suspension of consciousness in the wolf hunt had allowed him (and the reader) to glimpse the other side of rational reflection – to experience the height of animation and happiness. Yet on the battlefield his return from that other side – that boundary of human existence when one acts "without reflecting or considering" – exposes him to an unhappiness as sudden and profound as his happiness had been at the hunt, and as he realizes he is harming another human being, makes him more human still.

Yet the violent moment when Rostov had seen the wolf struggling in the gully, the moment when he had seen "her outstretched hind leg and her frightened choking head" had been "the happiest moment of his life" (*PSS* 10: 253; *War and Peace*, 552). The contours of these two moments are strikingly similar; in each case Rostov watches the suffering of a living creature. Yet Rostov in hunting down his human prey experiences moral revulsion and a sudden loss of animation, whereas in hunting down the wolf he feels utter, complete, albeit unconscious happiness.

Tolstoy deliberately links these two passages through his narrative, but he does not illuminate for his readers why the moment on the battlefield is one of moral degradation and the moment at the wolf hunt is one of pure joy. In the hunting passage Tolstoy observes that "the height of happiness was reached – and so simply, without warning, or noise, or display" (*PSS* 10: 251; *War and Peace*, 550). Could it be that this kind of happiness, reached simply, without warning, noise, or display and then just as quickly forgotten, is, in fact, the closest that a human can ever come to experiencing what could be described as pure animal happiness? Could this moment at the hunt be one where Rostov, despite his gun and dog, is in fact the equal of the wolf – an animal himself – and able to transcend, however briefly, the usual boundaries of his species?

Is this what Prince Andrei is thinking of when, in a fit of depression, he says to Pierre, "'You talk of schools [...] education and so forth; that is, you want to raise him' (pointing to a peasant who passed by them taking off his cap) 'from his animal condition and awaken in him spiritual needs, while it seems to me that animal happiness is the only happiness possible, and that is just what you want to deprive him of'" (*PSS* 10: 112; *War and Peace*, 417). Andrei's praise of "animal happiness," however, is rationally inspired and born of despairing thoughts rather than of surprising, unheeded joy. It is an idea about animal happiness and not the experience or process of animal happiness itself.

Yet even as Andrei flirts glumly with the ideal of "animal happiness," that is, of living for oneself, in the present, and presumably with a minimum of the corrosive consciousness of ideas and their ramifications, it is Pierre – his ideological opponent in this Dostoevsky-like exchange – who actually possesses a capacity for that kind of happiness as well as a firmly rooted sense of his own position in the great chain of being:

I have felt myself, a part of that vast invisible chain the beginning of which is hidden in heaven [...] Don't I feel in my soul that I am part of this vast harmonious whole? Don't I feel in my soul that I form one link, one step, between the lower and higher beings [...] If I see, clearly see, that ladder leading from plant to man, why should I suppose it breaks off at me and does not go farther and farther? I feel that I cannot vanish, since nothing vanishes in this world, but that I shall always exist and always have existed. (*PSS* 10: 115–16; *War and Peace*, 420–21).[20]

This exchange between Andrei and Pierre exemplifies Tolstoy's employment of a narrative mode quite different from the prevailing didactic, absolute tone that reigns throughout much of *War and Peace*; here he is at his subtle best, for Pierre's eloquent, heartfelt affirmation about his place in the world of plants, animals, and the heavens – so close in some respects to Levin's more sustained epiphanies in *Anna Karenina* – is, ironically, in fact part and parcel of his attempt to recruit Andrei to dogmatic free-masonry, an object of ridicule in the novel. And Andrei, despite his observation that "animal happiness" is the only possible kind, actually embraces this doctrine less than perhaps any other character in the novel. Nevertheless, the notions that human animals have something to learn about happiness from non-human ones and that each plant and animal has its place in the world were to become increasingly important for Tolstoy.

Eventually Tolstoy extends his metaphor of the hunt to an even broader canvas. Rostov's moment of supreme happiness when hunting the wolf had offered a point of analogy for the very different moment when he found himself hunting one of his own species. In the hundreds of pages devoted to the Russian army's defeat of the French, the narrator intersperses another sequential, but now purely metaphoric, description of a hunt, much like that first hunt, the occasion of Rostov's happiness. Extracting its contours scattered over many pages, we read that the French invaders are "like an infuriated animal that has in its onslaught received a mortal wound" (*PSS*: 11: 263; *War and Peace*, 914). It "licks its wounds" (*PSS* 11: 268; *War and Peace*, 920); "the hunter did not know" whether the beast was dead or alive. "Suddenly the beast was heard to moan" (*PSS* 12: 70; *War and Peace*, 1,099). "The plight of the whole army resembled that of a wounded animal which feels it is perishing and does not know what it is doing"; it rushed forward "onto the hunter's gun, reached him, turned back, and finally – like any wild beast – ran back along the most disadvantageous and dangerous path, where the old scent was familiar" (*PSS* 12: 91–92; *War and Peace*, 1,118). General Kutuzov, "like an experienced sportsman […] knew that the beast was wounded […] but whether it was mortally wounded or not was still an undecided question" (*PSS* 12: 111; *War and Peace*, 1,136). Hence the Russian army, in its role of hunter, "had to act like a whip to a running animal. And the experienced driver knew it was better to hold the whip raised as a menace than to strike the running animal on the head" (*PSS* 12: 170; *War and Peace*, 1,191). The French army fled "liked a wounded animal, and it was impossible to block its path" (*PSS* 12: 197; *War and Peace*, 1,219).[21] This hunt is no metaphor for joy, unhappiness, or moral degradation, but rather one that evokes a frantic struggle against inevitability.

The collective, organized life of animals in groups at times offered Tolstoy a way to think about human society. For example, Tolstoy's narrator declares that Napoleon, "while thinking he was acting on his own volition" in fact "perform[ed] for the hive life – that is to say, for history – whatever had to be performed" (*PSS* 11: 6; *War and Peace*, 670). The chaotic aftermath of the collision of the two armies near Smolensk is rendered starkly through the image of a disrupted swarm: "Through the streets, soldiers in various uniforms walked or ran confusedly in different directions like ants from a ruined anthill" (*PSS* 11: 117; *War and Peace*, 779). In a sustained metaphor of epic proportion, Tolstoy's narrator compares Moscow to an abandoned hive. The precise description of the dying hive; the beekeeper whose tap on the hive's walls does not produce the "former instant unanimous humming"; the bees flying out of the hive laden with honey; the robber-bees who appear; the beekeeper's closing of the hive and burning it clean – this elaborate, yet dry, textbook-like description of the dying hive and its beekeeper dwarfs the subsequent descriptions of Napoleon's entrance into Moscow, relegating a massive, complex military operation to a natural process rather than a willful, heroic invasion (*PSS* 11: 327–28; *War and Peace*, 974–75).

Throughout the novel, however, the groupings of bees in their beehives, ants in their hills, and animals in their herds do more than offer metaphors for the ways in which men, thinking they are acting individually, are in fact acting in some unknowable way for the interests of the whole. For Tolstoy, in trying to understand swarm intelligence, seemed to suggest a way in which the chaos of individual choices and acts could rationally be subsumed in the more ordered intentions of animals in a swarm. The study of swarm instinct is currently a focus of scientific inquiry that seems uncannily to back up some of Tolstoy's assumptions. Through computer models scientists are deciphering how the separate actions of millions of individuals can form "a collective brain able to make decisions and move like a single organism."[22] Ian D. Couzin and his colleagues have built a computer model to describe how information flows through swarms: "There is a swarm intelligence [...] What makes this collective decision-making all the more puzzling is that each individual can behave only based on its own experience [...] Each individual has to balance two instincts: to stay with the group and move in a desired direction."[23] This attempt to analyze how the desire of an individual in a swarm (free choice) and the movement of the group as a whole (the larger laws of history or necessity) seems to continue, from a scientific vantage point, the historiographic perspective that Tolstoy developed in *War and Peace*, where contemplation of bees, ants, and herds helped him to frame his own philosophical discourse about freedom and necessity.[24]

Humans are but one among the species of animals. Within the group, each individual's capacity for knowledge of the whole is always and necessarily partial, whether it is a human being seeking to understand the bees, or a herd of rams observing that one of its number is growing much fatter.

A bee settling on a flower has stung a child. And the child is afraid of bees and declares that bees exist to sting people. A poet admires the bee sucking from the chalice of a flower and says it exists to suck the fragrance of flowers. A beekeeper, seeing the bee collect pollen from flowers and carry it to the hive, says that it exists to gather honey. Another beekeeper [...] says that the bee gathers pollen dust to feed the young bees and rear a queen, and that it exists to perpetuate its race. A botanist notices that the bee flying with the pollen of a male flower to a pistil fertilizes the latter, and sees in this the purpose of the bee's existence. Another, observing the migration of plants, notices that the bee helps in this work, and may say that in this lies the purpose of the bee. But the ultimate purpose of the bee is not exhausted by the first, the second, or any of the processes the human mind can discern. The higher the human intellect rises in the discovery of these purposes, the more obvious it becomes that the ultimate purpose is beyond our comprehension.

All that is accessible to man is the relation of the life of the bee to other manifestations of life. And so it is with the purpose of historic characters and nations. (*PSS* 12: 246, *War and Peace*, 1,264)

In addition to demonstrating, through the example of observation of the bee, that knowledge is always partial, this passage also offers a kind of shorthand list of the various narrative voices that Tolstoy assumes through-out his novel – whether it is the "innocent" perspective of the child (through the technique of *ostranenie*), the poet (in the beauty of the metaphors and similes), or the beekeeper, or botanist (as the narrator takes on the role of sifting through practical, historical, philosophic, and scientific evidence). Tolstoy's narrator modulates at will from one perspective to the next.

There is a perspective hitherto unexplored. Tolstoy gives a completely different gloss to the meaning of "animal life" in his story *Strider*. Tolstoy worked on this story in the early 1860s, in the period just before he gave himself completely over to the writing of *War and Peace*, and again in the mid-1880s, during the period when he wrote *Confession*. As a result the story exhibits an idiosyncratic commingling of the early and the late Tolstoy – all told primarily through the narrative of a piebald gelding, *Strider*. As early as 1856 Tolstoy had written in his journal, "I would like to write the story of a horse." And presumably Turgenev had jokingly remarked to him that he must once have been a horse.

We were walking through [a] pasture [...] when we looked up and saw standing there [...] an old horse of the most pitiful and wretched appearance [...] old age and toil had somehow utterly bent him out of shape ... he just stood there [...] We went up to this unfortunate gelding, and Tolstoi began petting him while saying what he thought the horse was feeling and thinking. I was positively spellbound [...] "Listen, Lev Nikolaevich, you must have been a horse once yourself." You couldn't find a better rendering of the inner condition of a horse.[25]

Throughout the eleven chapters of *Strider*, the narrative centers on the famous piebald gelding *Strider*, initially through a third-person narrator. But early in the fifth chapter, the narrative actually emanates from *Strider* himself. He tells his life story to the other horses over a period of five nights during the course of which he narrates his autobiography from birth until the present moment: "And here I am," at which point his narrative ceases.[26] He dies several days later.

Tolstoy's wife, who had gained publication rights to the story, had wanted to give it the subtitle "An Experience of the Fantastic Kind. 1861."[27] Sonya's subtitle, although it was rejected by Tolstoy, seems apt, for, like Dostoevsky's two experiments with first-person narrative "fantastic stories" in the 1870s ("A Gentle Creature" and "Dream of a Ridiculous Man"), this tale, in asking its audience to enter the realm of the fantastic by reading the narrative of a horse, also seeks to illuminate and comment upon contemporary society.

As such, the story draws upon the form of the *rêve* or *voyage imaginaire* so popular in the eighteenth century and earlier, as much as it does from the popular tradition of the physiological sketch. Moreover, Tolstoy's story seems strongly reminiscent of that most famous fantastic, first-person narrative journey, Jonathan Swift's *Gulliver's Travels*. In the fourth voyage Gulliver encounters a rational breed of horses, the Houyhnhnms, and finds himself in deep and abiding admiration of them. Both the Houyhnhnms and *Strider* offer an occasion to point up didactically what ails the contemporary society of Swift and Tolstoy. Tolstoy's narrator describes *Strider* in terms that could be a poignant description of the aging Tolstoy himself, the Tolstoy of 1886.

There was really something majestic in [his] figure and in the terrible union in him of repulsive indications of decrepitude, emphasized by the motley colour of his hair, and his manner which expressed the self-confidence and calm assurance that go with beauty and strength. Like a living ruin he stood alone in the mist of the dewy meadow. (*PSS* 26: 8; *Portable Tolstoy*, 440)

Like Tolstoy, *Strider* loses his mother and grieves mightily. "Such passionate anger overcame me that I began to beat my head and knees against the walls of the stall" (*PSS* 26: 16; *Portable Tolstoy*, 449). *Strider*'s mother in fact returns, but no longer loves him. *Strider*, as a transparent echo of Tolstoy himself, ponders the "injustice of men," "the inconstancy of mother-love and feminine love in general," and "above all I pondered on the characteristics of that strange race of animals with whom we are so closely connected, and whom we call men" (*PSS* 26: 18; *Portable Tolstoy*, 452). These men are almost as repulsive as Swift's human Yahoos, and the rational un-animal-like horses find them to be a lower order of being. *Strider* then, in Swiftian fashion, considers private property, violence, religion, and especially ownership of one living being by another. "The words '*my* horse' applied to me, a live horse, seemed to me as strange as to say 'my land,' 'my air,' or 'my water'" (*PSS* 26: 19; *Portable Tolstoy*, 453). Likewise Gulliver admires how the Houyhnhnms do not discolor reason by "passion and interest." When they die, "their friends and relations [express] neither joy nor grief." And, most important, their language has no words for "lie, doubt, opinion, or evil." The verb *to die* meant simply "to retire to one's first mother."[28] Tolstoy and Swift before him delete our common understanding of the "animal nature" of these horses and replace it with extreme rationalism.

A few days after completing his narration to the other horses, *Strider* dies the most ideal death anywhere in Tolstoy's oeuvre, except perhaps that of another horse, Mukhorty, in *Master and Man*. As the knacker slaughtered him with his knife, after the pain, *Strider* heaved a sigh and "felt much better. The whole burden of his life was eased [...] Everything was so new to him" (*PSS* 26: 36; *Portable Tolstoy*, 472–73). After his death, the herd experiences a horsey *ostranenie*; they see something red surrounded by dogs, hawks, and crows. At dawn, five wolf cubs and their lean old mother arrive and devour his body. The violent passage is nearly as cosmically beautiful as the end of Chekhov's story *Gusev*, when the sharks devour Gusev's dead body. In each case there is a solemnity, a sense of fittingness, a lofty calm amidst the consumption of the hero's corpse. The wolf cubs come and stand around their mother.

She went up to the smallest, and bending her knee and holding her muzzle down, made some convulsive movements, and opening her large sharp-toothed jaws disgorged a large piece of horseflesh. The bigger cubs rushed toward her, but she moved threateningly at them and let the little one have it all. The little one, growling as if in anger, pulled the horseflesh under him and began to gorge. In the same way the mother wolf coughed up a piece for the second, the third, and all five of them, and then lay down in front of them to rest. (*PSS* 26: 36–37; *Portable Tolstoy*, 473)

In this magnificent scene, the experience of death coalesces seamlessly with the continuance of life, as so often with Tolstoy's human characters. But here the depiction of the contiguity of death with life attains a soundless sublimity that passages like those describing the concurrency of Lise's death and the birth of Andrei's son, or Nikolai Levin's death and the pregnancy of Kitty, cannot achieve.

Resemblances to *Gulliver's Travels* continue into a subsequent work of Tolstoy's in which animals also figure importantly, *The Kreutzer Sonata* (1889). Pozdnyshev shares much of the general sense of disillusionment with human beings of the third-person human narrator of *Strider*. They both evince a Gulliverian disgust for humankind, although Pozdnyshev, unlike Gulliver, never actually converses with an animal, nor does the third-person narrator of *Strider*, although he does report the equine narrative. Moreover,

Pozdnyshev shares Gulliver's moral nausea. When Gulliver returns, unwillingly, to human civilization, he experiences such an extreme disgust at the life and behavior of human beings that he cannot bear to be around them. Pozdnyshev, upon his release from prison, experiences a similar metaphysical and philosophical horror of his fellow man. He seems to find a deeper rationalism and philosophic peace existing in the non-human animal kingdom than in his own. Remembering the coarse sensuality of his courtship, he declares:

There was nothing to talk about. All that could be said about the life that awaited us, our arrangements and plans, had been said, and what was there more? Now if we had been animals we should have known that speech was unnecessary, but here on the contrary it was necessary to speak, and there was nothing to say, because we were not occupied with what finds vent in speech. (*PSS* 27: 27; *Kreutzer Sonata*, 375)

If men and women were as rational as animals, they would realize that in this situation they need make no effort to speak. The nightingale does not sing nor the lion roar while mating.

Pozdnyshev ultimately finds his answer to the problem of human sexuality by contemplating the bees. "The highest race of animals, the human race, in order to maintain itself in the struggle with other animals ought to unite into one whole like a swarm of bees, and not breed continually; it should bring up sexless members as the bees do; that is, again, it should strive towards continence and not towards inflaming desire – to which the whole system of our life is now directed" (*PSS* 27: 30–31; *Kreutzer Sonata*, 379). The bees and the other animals thus offer him a clue to how both human society and human desire should be organized. "Animals, you see, only come together at times when they are capable of producing progeny, but the filthy lord of nature is at it any time if only it pleases him!" (*PSS* 27: 36; *Kreutzer Sonata*, 384).

Like Gulliver upon his return home, Pozdnyshev, returned from prison, now tries to live in an isolation which is punctuated only by the obsessive desire to tell his story that other men may learn by it. Both are like Coleridge's ancient mariner, telling his story yet "alone, alone, all, all alone." Pozdnyshev even tries to explain away the necessity for maternal grief over the death or illness of a child by seeking an analogy (as Gulliver had done) in the rational world of animals:

A hen is not afraid of what may happen to her chick, does not know all the diseases that may befall it, and does not know all those remedies with which people imagine that they can save from illness and death. And for a hen her young are not a source of torment. She does for them what it is natural and pleasurable for her to do; her young ones are a pleasure to her. When a chick falls ill her duties are quite definite: she warms it and feeds it. And doing this she knows that she is doing all that is necessary. If her chick dies she does not ask herself why it died, or where it has gone to; she cackles for a while, and then leaves off and goes on living as before. (*PSS* 27: 42; *Kreutzer Sonata*, 390)

Both Gulliver and Pozdnyshev are mad, use the tools of reason to fuel their madness, and create a world in which animals are of a higher moral and rational order than men.

Both find the highest capacity for moderation and reason in the animal kingdom, rather than among humans. They do not seek poetic analogies to human beings in the life of animals; instead animal life, as they each imagine it, offers a model for an ideal existence profoundly different from human existence, contaminated as it is by uncontrollable desire. The animals are to be emulated. Indeed, in the variant notes for *The Kreutzer Sonata*, Tolstoy has Pozdnyshev take his argument even further:

Just notice: a hen, a goose, a she-wolf are always unattainable models of animal love for our women. Few women would at the risk of their lives rush at an elephant to take their baby from him, but no hen, and no she-cow even, would fail to fly at a dog; and each of them would sacrifice itself for its children, while few women would do so. Notice that a human mother can refrain from physical love of her children while an animal cannot do so. (*PSS* 27: 318; *Kreutzer Sonata*, 441)

Pozdnyshev's madness, like Gulliver's, reverberates with a haunting tragic grandeur, and their moral nausea is contagious. Readers have speculated that both Swift and Tolstoy have been infected by their characters, or vice versa.

One of the most negative contemporary assessments of *Anna Karenina* unconsciously forecasts, in an unkind but humorous way, what will become of the reverence for animals Tolstoy displays in both *Strider* and, indirectly, *The Kreutzer Sonata*. In 1875, before the publication of either of those stories, the Russian radical P. N. Tkachov, under the pseudonym of P. Nikitin, wrote of his imagined sequel to *Anna Karenina*:

[The author] discovers tragedy in Vronsky's relations not only with Anna but with his mare Frou-Frou too and makes these relations the object of as much detailed artistic analysis as he does those with Anna […] If he wishes to be even more consistent, if he wants his work to move further along this new and original path, then I permit myself to suggest […] a wonderful subject for his next novel […] Here briefly is my outline for the story. Levin married Kitty and lives with her in seclusion in the country, scorning all political and civic activity as fruitless and tedious concerns which lead to progress and civilization which themselves put a break upon the growth of happiness. In a short period of time there appears in Levin's heart a more spontaneous and consequently more powerful and legitimate feeling than that of love for his wife: Levin experiences an agricultural love for his cow, Pava. Kitty notices her husband's new passion and seeing in it, because of her feminine frivolity, a certain danger to family happiness feels jealous and no longer wishes to look after Pava's calves as if they were her own children. There follows a series of peripeteia, both romantic and tragic, the sufferings of Kitty, the torments of Pava, the explanations of Levin to Pava [...] the most subtle psychological analysis of the feelings of humans and cows [...] would stretch over scores of pages.[29]

After Kitty's inevitable suicide, Levin grasps the idea that this "agricultural love" is a higher "natural happiness" than "family happiness with a woman." In this cunning, humorous, mean-spirited review, one can almost discern the shapes of the unwritten *Strider* and *The Kreutzer Sonata* low on the horizon.

Other major writers of the nineteenth century in Russia – for example, Gogol, Dostoevsky, Turgenev, and Chekhov – also depict animals as significant players in the human drama. The unparalleled canine epistolary exchange in Gogol's "Diary of a Madman" or the thoughts of Chichikov's horse spring instantly to mind. With Dostoevsky one thinks immediately of Raskolnikov's dream of the horse in *Crime and Punishment*, of the birds, the dog, and the goose in *The Brothers Karamazov*, or of the underground man's mice, bulls, and anthills, or Myshkin's gnats, or Stavrogin's spiders. But Dostoevsky's animals do not really exist independently as animals or exhibit the varieties of awareness with which Tolstoy endows his animals. Turgenev perhaps comes closer to Tolstoy's approach: think, for example, of the dog in "Yermolai and the Miller's Wife." The horse in Chekhov's "Misery" or the sharks of *Gusev* likewise evince the qualities of Tolstoy's animals. The animals of Turgenev and Chekhov could perhaps inhabit Tolstoy's peaceable kingdom, but they do not present themselves with such complete fullness or independence as do Tolstoy's animals.

Finally, following Isaiah Berlin's paradigm, it is productive to contemplate whether Tolstoy is a hedgehog, or a fox, or a fox desiring to be a hedgehog. But the wolf, the hare, the horse, the dog, the ant, and the bee may also loom large in our attempt to understand Tolstoy. He lived his life as an artist and a thinker amidst the other animals among whom he firmly places his characters, his readers, and himself. Tolstoy's peaceable kingdom admits violence and death: the wolves devour *Strider*'s body; the hen is not afraid for what will happen to her chick, and though she warms it when it is ill, she does not ask herself why it died. Tolstoy's animal kingdom retains its solemnity and peaceful grandeur because its inhabitants balance reason, instinct, and even passion in an ideal way. Tolstoy's animals are not burdened by their creator's perennial questions, "How then shall I live?" "How shall I die?"

NOTES

1. See Peter Singer, *Animal Liberation* (New York: HarperCollins, 2002), 7. Singer is quoting Jeremy Bentham, *Introduction to the Principles of Morals and Legislation*, ch. 17.
2. Singer, *Animal Liberation*, 14.
3. Julian H. Franklin, *Animal Rights and Moral Philosophy* (New York: Columbia University Press, 2005), xiii. Franklin provides a thoughtful and readable summary of the various philosophical approaches to animal rights and develops his own theory by a revision of Kant's categorical imperative.
4. Martha Nussbaum, "Beyond 'Compassion and Humanity': Justice for Nonhuman Animals," in Cass R. Sunstein and Martha Nussbaum, eds., *Animal Rights: Current Debates and New Directions* (Oxford and New York: Oxford University Press, 2004), 300.
5. Singer, *Animal Liberation*, xxi.
6. Donald Fanger, ed., trans., intro., *Gorky's Tolstoy and Other Reminiscences: Key Writings by and about Maxim Gorky* (New Haven, CT: Yale University Press, 2008), 78.
7. J. M. Coetzee, in *The Lives of Animals: J. M. Coetzee* (with essays also by Marjorie Garber, Peter Singer, Wendy Doniger, and Barbara Smuts), ed. and intro. Amy Gutman (Princeton, NJ: Princeton University Press, 1999), 35.
8. L. N. Tolstoi, *Polnoe sobranie sochinenii*, 90 vols. (Moscow: Gosudarstvennoe izdatel'stvo "Khudozhestvennaia literatura," 1928–58), 29: 79. Hereafter cited in the text as *PSS* plus volume and page number. See also Leo Tolstoy, "The First Step," in *Essays and Letters*, trans. Aylmer Maude (New York: H. Frowde, 1909), 82–91. PDF version (5 pages), 2.
9. *PSS* 6: 58; Leo Tolstoy, *The Cossacks and The Raid*, trans. Andrew MacAndrew (New York: Signet, 1961), 73.
10. See Donna Tussing Orwin's excellent reading of the implications of Olenin's experience of nature, in particular within the stag's lair. Donna Orwin, "Nature and Civilization in *The Cossacks*," in *Tolstoy's Art and Thought, 1847–1880* (Princeton, NJ: Princeton University Press, 1993), 85–98.
11. Nikolenka and other characters of Tolstoy who are depicted amidst the wildlife of nature during a hunt share a kind of intimacy with the beings around them. At such moments man and animal are somehow on a more ancient footing and have a different kind of interaction than that of humans with animals in a zoo.
12. The most readable English-language account of this episode in Tolstoy's childhood is found in Ernest J. Simmons, *Leo Tolstoy* (2 vols.), vol. 1 (New York: Vintage Books, 1960), 23–24. Tolstoy's brother Nikolai solemnly announced to them one day that he possessed a wonderful secret that could

make all men happy. If it became generally known, a kind of Golden Age would exist on earth: there would be no more disease, no human misery, and no anger. All would love one another and become "Ant Brothers" (23). The children then organized a game of Ant Brothers where they huddled in the dark under chairs or boxes covered with shawls. Nikolai also devised conditions for his younger brothers under which he would show them a secret place. "The first was to stand in a corner and not think of a white bear. The second was to walk along a crack in the floor without wavering; and the third was to keep from seeing a hare, alive or dead or cooked, for a whole year" (23). Nikolai also invited his younger brothers to each confide one wish that would come true. Interestingly, all of these childish wishes involved animals and/or the making of art: "Seryozha wished to be able to model a horse and a hen out of wax: Mitenka wished to be able to draw everything in life size, like a real artist; and the five-year-old Lyovochka, clearly puzzled, lamely wished to be able to draw things in miniature" (24).

13. *PSS* 1: 25; Leo Tolstoy, *Childhood, Boyhood and Youth*, trans. and intro. Rosemary Edmonds (Harmondsworth: Penguin, 1961), 34.

14. Ironically Dostoevsky wrote from exile to Maikov, upon reading *Childhood*, "I like L. T. very much, but in my opinion he won't write much (perhaps I'm mistaken, however)." See F. M. Dostoevskii, *Polnoe sobranie sochinenii v tridtsati tomakh*, 28 (1), 210.

15. *PSS* 27: 61; *The Kreutzer Sonata*, trans. Louise and Aylmer Maude, in *Great Short Works of Leo Tolstoy*, intro. John Bayley (New York: Harper and Row, 1967), 410. What is fascinating about Pozdnyshev's diatribe against music is that it casts in negative terms much of the kind of positive infection of which art is capable that Tolstoy describes in *What Is Art?*

16. *PSS* 30: 64–65; *What Is Art?*, trans. Aylmer Maude, intro. Vincent Thomas (New York: Bobbs-Merrill, 1960), 50–51. Note that in the previous paragraph, Tolstoy returns to the yawning image that he used in *The Kreutzer Sonata* and which is cited in the previous note. He suggests that such direct infection "does not amount to art."

17. Nikolenka's acute awareness that his foray into painting has been unsuccessful presages Vronsky's abandonment of painting after his failed portrait of Anna. The would-be artist, whether child or man, should instinctively know when his artistic endeavor has failed. (See pt. 5, ch. 13 of *Anna Karenina*.)

18. Gary Saul Morson, *Hidden in Plain View: Narrative and Creative Potentials in "War and Peace"* (Stanford, CA: Stanford University Press, 1987), 156–57.

19. *PSS* 11: 62–63; Leo Tolstoy, *War and Peace*, ed. George Gibian, trans. Aylmer Maude (New York: Norton: 1966), 723–24.

20. As Andrei points out, Pierre is citing Herder here. For a full discussion of the idea of the great chain of being, see Arthur L. Lovejoy, *The Great Chain of Being: A Study of the History of an Idea* (Cambridge, MA: Harvard University Press, 1936).

21. Even as Tolstoy portrays the French army as a wounded animal in such a sustained metaphor he is also scientifically aware that the French army "melted

away at the uniform rate of a mathematical progression," which was confirmed by one of the first and most famous graphs of the nineteenth century. See *PSS* 12: 196; *War and Peace*, 1,218.

22. Carl Zimmer, "From Ants to People, An Instinct to Swarm," *New York Times*, November 13, 2007: D1.

23. *Ibid.* D4.

24. See also Tolstoy's analogy to a herd of rams and a herdsman to explain the reasons why effects beyond the scope of ordinary human agency are frequently described in terms of genius (*PSS* 12: 239; *War and Peace*, 1,257).

25. See I. S. Turgenev, *I. S. Turgenev v vospominaniiakh revoliutsionervo-semidesiatnikov*, ed. M. K. Kleman (Moscow: Academia, 1930), 237, quoted by Eikhenbaum, 101. The best accounts of Tolstoy's writing of this work are in Boris Eikhenbaum's, *Tolstoy in the Sixties*, trans. Duffield White (Ann Arbor, MI: Ardis, 1982), 91–103; and Viktor Shklovsky's *Lev Tolstoy*, trans. Olga Shartze (Moscow: Progress Publishers, 1978), 350–54. Eikhenbaum labels it a "didactic epic (*poema*)," a "fable," and eventually an "animal epic." He writes at length about the story, perhaps because it evolved over three epochs in Tolstoy's life – the mid-1850s, the early 1860s, and the mid-1880s – and, as such, seems to combine the younger Tolstoy's social concerns with his subsequent complex emotions about aging.

26. *PSS* 26: 27; *Strider*, in *The Portable Tolstoy*, ed. John Bayley, trans. Louise and Aylmer Maude (New York: Viking Penguin, 1978), 462.

27. See Shklovsky, *Lev Tolstoy*, 350. Shklovsky's analysis focuses on the differences between the 1861 version of the story and the one completed in 1885. He describes the strong link between *Strider* and his author. "Tolstoy was a thoroughbred, he was a genius, but he was a piebald both in life and in literature: his coat colour, his special position in the world, and his apartness were denied recognition. That is why the story is so dear to Tolstoy's heart" (351).

28. Jonathan Swift, *Gulliver's Travels* (1726: New York: New American Library, 1960), 288, 296.

29. "Tkachov Attacks Tolstoy's Aristocratism: 1875," in A. V. Knowles, ed. and trans., *Tolstoy: The Critical Heritage* (London: Routledge and Kegan Paul, 1978), 259–60.

CHAPTER 4

Leo Tolstoy: *pacifist, patriot, and* molodets

Donna Tussing Orwin

What if there were a war and nobody came? Bumper stickers in college towns all over the United States in the 1960s broadcast this slogan, but today, fifty years later, no end to war is in sight. Count Lev (Leo) Nikolaevich Tolstoy, advocate of conscientious war resistance and author of the greatest war fiction in modern times, hated war but understood its role in human life. He fought in two conflicts, the long-running battle against mountain tribes in the Caucasus, and the Crimean War. Born into a family of warrior aristocrats, with his oldest brother Nikolai already in the army, his decision to take up arms came naturally, and so, presumably, did his celebration of Russian martial spirit at the siege of Sevastopol. Yet the seeds of his later pacifism are evident in his earliest war stories. A draft of his first one, "The Raid" (1853), defines war as "murder,"[1] while the patriotic "Sevastopol in December" (1855) calls it "blood, suffering, and death." War seemed evil to him for religious reasons,[2] and in the final chapter of "Sevastopol in May" (1855) he asks how "all those [Christians] who profess the same great law of love and self-sacrifice" could fight one other. In his old age, by then a world-famous pacifist, Tolstoy returned in *Hadji Murat* (published posthumously, 1911) to the Caucasian wars of his youth to depict them as an imperialist adventure by Russia. Yet this anti-war masterpiece contains his most sympathetic portrait of a warrior.

This chapter explores the psychological and cultural reasons why Tolstoy's soldiers go to war. Having read and heard a great deal about war, having observed it as an eye-witness and participated in various forms of it over five years, Tolstoy collected a mass of impressions that did not boil down to any one easily digestible teaching. Different aspects of his understanding, in isolation, lead to different (potentially conflicting) conclusions, and this is why he seems like a patriot in some readings and a pacifist in others.[3] We will use the particulars of Tolstoy's life so far as we can reconstruct them from his own writings and other sources to follow him to his general conclusions.[4]

MOLODECHESTVO

When Tolstoy first joined the army, he worried mostly about his own performance. Two entries in his diary, the first as he leaves with his detachment for the winter campaign, and the second as he is returning from it after his first serious combat, document a loss of confidence in himself as a warrior.

February 5, 1852 (Nikolaevka – riding in the detachment.) I'm indifferent to a life in which I've experienced too little happiness to love it; therefore, I don't fear death. I am not afraid of torments either, but I am afraid that I won't be able to bear torments and death well. I'm not completely calm; and I'm aware of this because I shift from one spiritual state and view about many things to another. It's strange that my childish view of war – *molodechestvo* – is the most comfortable for me. In many ways I am returning to my childish view of things. (*PSS* 46: 90–91)

February 28, 1852 (In the detachment, near Teplichek.) The expectations of my imagination have never been justified in reality. I wanted fate to put me in difficult situations for which spiritual strength and virtue were necessary. My imagination loved to present these situations to me, and inner feeling told me that I would have sufficient strength and virtue for them. My vanity and confidence in my strength of soul, encountering no obstacles, grew. Circumstances in which I might have put my confidence to the test, but in which I did not do so, I excused because they presented too few difficulties, and I would not be using all the strengths of my soul.

I was proud, but my pride did not found itself on deeds, but on the firm hope that I was capable of everything. Because of that, my outward pride lacked certainty, firmness, and constancy, [and] I would swing from extreme haughtiness to excessive modesty.

My state during danger opened my eyes. I had loved to imagine myself completely cold-blooded and calm in danger. But in the operations of the 17th and 18th, I wasn't. I didn't have the excuse that I usually use, that the danger was not as great as I imagined it to be. This was my one chance to show all my strength of soul. And I was weak and therefore I'm not satisfied with myself.

I have only now understood that confidence based on future deeds is deceptive, and I can count on myself only in those matters where I already have experience. That this confidence actually destroys strength, and that I must not consider a single circumstance too negligible to apply all my strength to it. (*PSS* 46: 91–92)

On February 5, the novice artillery NCO expected to prove himself in battle. On February 18, during a second day of engagement with enemy forces, he almost died when a cannonball struck the gun carriage he was operating. The fact that this happened on his name day heightened its significance for him, and it became the basis of his fictional accounts of the experience of the untested soldier.[5] In the second diary entry, written the day before the end of the campaign, Tolstoy was not satisfied with his performance. Henceforth he would miss no opportunity to try his resolve, because only experience steels the soul for battle.

It is tempting to slide with Tolstoy in these two war diary entries from fantasies of glory to experience. That said, however, some fantasies have deeper roots than others in Tolstoyan reality. The Russian imitating a Caucasian *dzhigit* (warrior) always looks silly, while the young officer, with his youthful enthusiasm for war, is always positive.[6] His youthful high spirits may kill him – as they do Alanin ("The Raid"), Volodya Kozel'tsov ("Sevastopol in August"), and Petya Rostov (*War and Peace*) – but careerists like Berg and Boris Drubetskoi in *War and Peace*, wholly lacking these spirits, are always despicable. On the one hand, Tolstoy wanted to put an end to dangerous, false romantic illusions about war;[7] on the other, he treasured the spontaneity and confidence inherent in what he called, in the entry of February 5, *molodechestvo*.

To understand Tolstoy's soldier, one must explore the meaning of this word. A *molodets* is a youth fine in body and spirit. The word *molodechestvo* with its abstract suffix 'stvo' indicates the essence of such a youth, so it should be, and fundamentally is, positive.[8] Although the concept is applied quite frequently in a broader context, in folk poetry it is associated with war: the heroes of Russian epic folk poetry are called *molodtsy*, usually with the epithet "fine" (*dobrye*) attached.[9] A frequent synonym for the word is *udalets*, another difficult word to translate that refers to courage and skill, often, though not always, in battle. The closest English equivalents to *molodechestvo* might be "pluck" or "boldness," but, as we shall see, these concepts resonate differently in the Russian context.

In a late diary entry Tolstoy disparages the *molodechestvo* of his youth as a kind of corrupting convention.

> January 24, 1909. While I was out walking I was thinking about two things: childish wisdom, and my upbringing, how, as in my childhood I was taught to direct all my energy to *molodechestvo* in hunting and war, so it is possible to inspire children to direct all their energy to a battle with themselves, to an enlargement of love. (*PSS* 57: 18)

The story *Father Sergius* (published posthumously, 1911) dramatizes this desirable transformation from soldier to saint.[10] After discovering that his fiancée has been the mistress of his beloved Tsar, the officer hero resigns his commission, joins the church, and concludes his quest to vanquish pride as an anonymous vagabond working for a rich peasant in Siberia. In the diary passage of February 28, 1852, however, Tolstoy says nothing about rejecting *molodechestvo* as not moral. On the contrary, it seems that he judges himself not strong and virtuous enough to be a *molodets* in combat. The word *sila*, "strength," as a synonym for courage, appears six times in the passage from February 28; in the first two it is paired with *dobrodetel'*, "virtue," and the other four appearances imply the pairing as well. The suggestion is that an uncorrupted youth goes to war for moral reasons.[11] In Tolstoy's war fiction, real martial courage in both officers and men is usually portrayed as positive; the problem is that most of what passes for courage is false, and Tolstoy provides copious evidence of this.

The youthful Tolstoy considered the military an honorable profession, and even later in his life he occasionally alluded to the virtuous motives of officers in earlier times. In 1896, in an unfinished anti-war document, Tolstoy contrasted them to the debased corps of the present day.

In the past, a military man of the 1830s, 40s, 50s, and even the 60s, constituting an inseparable and indispensable part of society then, not only was not something disagreeable, but as it was then among us and most probably everywhere, he was, especially among the guards, the flower of the educated class of the time. Our Decembrists in the 1820s were such men. Military men at that time not only did not doubt the justice of their calling, but were proud of it, often choosing it out of a feeling of selflessness. (*PSS* 39: 219)[12]

The young Tolstoy came out of the tradition described in this passage and made it his own. As a Rousseauian, he believed in a natural goodness that was constantly being undermined by passions artificially inflated by civilization. Joining the war effort in the Caucasus, he was hoping to exchange bad habits for a career of public service, but he soon became acquainted with army vices and practiced them with gusto himself.[13] In Bucharest, however, where he was stationed for a few months before being transferred to the Crimea, he met a group of idealistic young officers with whom he tried, unsuccessfully, to found a newspaper for soldiers.[14] Like Tolstoy and his friends, the young officers in his fiction recklessly rushing into battle combine the personal desire to test themselves with the virtuous intentions that he insisted were necessary for true courage.

Yet even if it seems as though Tolstoy embraces *molodechestvo* as an ideal in the diary entries for 1852, it cannot simply be equated with virtue in his fiction, which would be much less profound if this were so. It is not the Russian equivalent of knightliness (*rytsarstvo*). As we shall see, he understood and illustrated all the implications, good and bad, of *molodechestvo* in his war fiction, though he emphasized some more than others. In *The Cossacks* (1863), Lukashka is called "Snatcher" (*urvan*) for the *molodechestvo* that he displayed as a boy in rescuing a drowning child (*PSS* 6: 21). Vaska Denisov in *War and*

Peace shows himself to be a true *"molodets"* when he is dancing the mazurka or on horseback (*PSS* 10: 50), and Russian soldiers are admiringly called *"molodtsy"* (the plural form) many times there. Hadji Murat remembers "the expression of pride and *molodechestvo*" with which his son Iosif has promised his father to care for his mother and grandmother (*PSS* 35: 106). But *molodechestvo* can be foolhardy, as with Alanin or Petya Rostov. It can be mere convention: in *Anna Karenina*, Vronsky is disgusted at having to entertain a foreign prince with a bear hunt as a "display of Russian *molodechestvo*" (*PSS* 18: 374). The cult of *molodechestvo* can lead to depravity, so that in *The Kreutzer Sonata* the protagonist's friends urge him to have casual sex both for his health, and also as a form of *"molodechestvo"* (*PSS* 27: 18).

As a mask for mere vanity or narcissism, *molodechestvo* is negative in the language and most definitely in Tolstoy's fiction, but even when authentic it can be problematic. The *dzhigit* and the Cossack are true *molodtsy* in it, yet, as Olenin discovers in *The Cossacks*, *molodets* Lukashka is not sufficiently moral; in particular, he is not ashamed of killing men in war. Tolstoy had learned from earlier writers that Caucasian braves allow themselves the freedom to pursue all their passions, including hatred and vengeance, which they satisfy in war. The *molodechestvo* ascribed to the eponymous hero of A. Bestuzhev-Marlinsky's *Ammalat Bek* (a childhood favorite of Tolstoy) is presented by the author as attractive but tragically flawed, while M. Lermontov "unequivocally identified" with the eponymous hero of his poem *Ismail-Bei*.[15] Tolstoy loved this poem. In July 1854, just after he had left the Caucasus, its opening lines helped him "understand and love" the place "in which so strangely and poetically two completely opposing things – war and freedom – are joined."[16]

> And the tribes of those gorges are savage;
> Their god is freedom, their law – war.
> They grow up amidst clandestine raids,
> Cruel deeds, and extraordinary ones;
> In the cradle there the songs of mothers
> Frighten children with Russian names;
> There to destroy an enemy is no crime;
> Friendship is certain there, but more certain is revenge;
> There good is returned for good, and blood for blood,
> And hatred is as boundless as love.

In Lermontov's writings, Tolstoy found an anarchic individualism, or freedom, implicit in *molodechestvo* that makes it seductive and also, in its extreme forms, taboo within Russian culture except in particular situations which we will enumerate below.[17]

Tolstoy had other sources in Russian culture, direct and indirect, for the concept of *molodechestvo*. In the 1830s, A. Pushkin used folk poetry collected in the eighteenth century by M. Chulkov to conjure Emelyan Pugachev and his men into existence in *The Captain's Daughter* (1836) as courageous, reckless, and lawless *molodtsy*. (I refer to the use of related words in epigraphs to chapters and in folk songs interpolated into the text.) The Cossacks in N. Gogol's *Taras Bulba* (1842), though rarely called *molodtsy* in the text, are models of *molodechestvo*, and so, in real life, and frequently named as such, were the Russian soldiers of Tolstoy's time. F. Bulgarin's memoirs, published in the late 1840s, applied the term specifically to officers in the 1820s.

The character, spirit, and tone of the military youth and even the older cavalry officers epitomized *molodechestvo* or daring (*udal'stvo*). *Spend as though there's no tomorrow* and *Life's not worth a damn, don't bother your head about it*: these sayings of ancient Russian daring were our motto and our guide. In both war and peace we sought dangers so as to distinguish ourselves by our fearlessness and daring. Feasting, duelling with swords, raising hell where we shouldn't, that's what our military life consisted of in peacetime.[18]

Bulgarin's *molodtsy* are loyal to one another, but think nothing of humiliating civilians and seducing their wives. In constant trouble with the police, they may also overstep military authority and are demoted or even imprisoned for this. Later in the memoirs Bulgarin discusses Tolstoy's relative, Fyodor Ivanovich Tolstoy, "The American" (1782–1846), who "took [*molodechestvo*] to its farthest extreme."[19] Tolstoy did not read Bulgarin's memoirs so far as we know, but he remembered Fyodor Tolstoy from his childhood, and in his own unfinished memoirs (1903–6), in language encapsulating Bulgarin's definition of *molodechestvo*, referred to him as "an extraordinary, transgressive, and attractive person."[20] As is well known, Fyodor Tolstoy was a prototype for Dolokhov in *War and Peace*. *Molodechestvo* appears in the novel for the first time at Dolokhov's wild party, where the host earns the title *molodets* for a daring stunt. In war, Dolokhov is a cold-blooded killer, though a useful one.

Bulgarin's discussion of *molodechestvo* begins with an epigraph from a poem by hussar poet Denis Vasilievich Davydov (1784–1839), and contains a quotation from another one of Davydov's poems:

I do love a bloody battle;
I'm born to serve the Tsar!
Sabre, vodka, Hussar steed,
You're partners in my golden life!
I do love a bloody battle;
I'm born to serve the Tsar!

As Bulgarin explains in a note to this epigraph, Davydov "copied the cavalry life of his time from life"; that is, what Davydov called "gusarshchina" is Bulgarin's *molodechestvo*.[21] Tolstoy knew Davydov's writing very well. His "Two Hussars" (1856), comparing the youths of a father and son, has an epigraph from a poem by the hussar poet. Count Turbin, the older hussar from the early nineteenth century, resembles both Fyodor "The American" Tolstoy and the hussar as immortalized in Davydov's poetry. Whereas Davydov himself rarely uses the word *molodechestvo* or related forms, Tolstoy applies them to the count. A braggart in the story who wants to link his name with Turbin calls him a *molodets* and a "real hussar": in sum, the older Turbin is as charming and "transgressive" as his prototype, and Bulgarin's *molodets*.[22] In *War and Peace*, Tolstoy invoked the entire hussar world out of Davydov's poems, memoirs, and essays, and placed Denisov at its head to acknowledge his debt.[23]

"Sevastopol in August" is an "idyll" of *molodechestvo* in which the Kozeltsov brothers together represent the front-line Russian officer as Tolstoy encountered him in the Crimean War.[24] Volodya, the younger brother, sets out for Sevastopol with ideals nurtured in his military academy, and in chapter 9, just like Tolstoy on February 5, 1852, he imagines himself as a *molodets* in battle. His journey down into the heart of the embattled city coincides with a catastrophic fall in spirits, but prayer revives him. His older brother Mikhail, who chooses to return to the front even before a wound has healed, raises hell with his mates in the bunker in the spirit of *molodechestvo*. Both brothers die idyllicly, that is, bravely. To satisfy his sense of pride and love of competition, Mikhail must either "excel or … expire."[25] The best place to do this is at war, which, if Mikhail represents a natural type, would seem to be an inevitable part of human life.

WAR

A seasoned *molodets* understands the reality of war. Just as he brought a concept of *molodechestvo* with him to the Caucasus, in later reminiscences Tolstoy claimed that he already knew what war was when he arrived there. His teachers were his brother Nikolai and Stendhal in *The Charterhouse of Parma*.

"Stendhal," Tolstoy told Paul Boyer, "taught me to understand war. In *The Charterhouse of Parma*, you should reread the story about the Battle of Waterloo. Who before him had described war that way, that is, the way it really is? Remember Fabrizio, riding over the battlefield and understanding "nothing." And how the hussars lightly tossed him over the back end of his horse, his magnificent general's horse? Then my brother, who served in the Caucasus earlier than me, confirmed the truthfulness of Stendhal's descriptions. Nikolai loved war very much, but he was not one of those who believed in the bridge at Arcole. These are all embellishments, he told me, and in war there are no embellishments. Soon after that it was easy for me in the Crimea to see all this with my own eyes. But, I repeat, everything that I know about war I learned first from Stendhal.[26]

In 1900, recalling his first combat in 1852, Tolstoy mentions the morning fog, the noise of battle, his near death, and then unexpected enemy fire during the retreat at which "I felt fright such as I had never before experienced."[27] His emphasis on chaos as the most frightening element in war owes something to Stendhal.[28] Fabrizio's comical loss of his horse (to a general on his own side), which so tickled Tolstoy, stands for the lesson learned by all his untried soldiers about the loss of control in battle. Tolstoy also borrowed Stendhal's technique of making battle strange by representing it from the perspective of single individuals. It may illustrate either the impossibility of one individual's grasping the whole picture in battle (as when an officer tries to explain the Russian position to Pierre at Borodino), or the bewilderment of an individual under fire (Pierre's loss of his "home" with the artillery battery). The warnings of Nikolai Tolstoy against the "embellishments" of war are related to Stendhal's lessons. Showy feats of glory such as Napoleon's supposed taking of the bridge at Arcole presuppose a degree of control impossible in war. Experienced soldiers like Nikolai Tolstoy know what war is, and courage for them, as in the case of Captain Khlopov in "The Raid," consists in keeping their cool.[29] Hence in 1900, Tolstoy praised his brother for his "astonishing presence of mind" during the engagement of February 18, 1852.

War blows away the imagined defenses of the young. On the other hand, for *molodtsy*, war as "blood, suffering, and death" poses the ultimate challenge to their manhood. This is one reason why Nikolai Tolstoy "loved" it, as his then pacifist brother reported in 1900 without comment, and also the reason that Denis Davydov gives for his exhilaration as a young soldier under fire.

Those were the first bullets to whistle past my ears. I am no Charles XII, but at that age, in that moment, in the intoxicating fumes of first dangers, I understood the vow of that crowned seeker of adventures. I looked proudly at myself, blackened by gunpowder, and the whole civilian world and everything outside of military service, all of this in my opinion sank beneath me, down to the antipodes![30]

The *molodets* loves war *because* of its deadly chaos. In his memoirs, Colonel P. N. Glebov, under whom Tolstoy served in the Crimean War, disparaged him as just such a thrill-seeker.[31] When Tolstoy was reading histories and memoirs while writing *War and Peace*, it was Davydov whose account "was the first to ring true" about the wars between Russia and Napoleon (*PSS* 15: 240). Tolstoy agreed with him that chance governs war. Davydov argued that the effective soldier must train for the unexpected, the "chance happenings in battle," and he blames the Prussian loss at Jena (1806) for a lack of preparedness in precisely this regard.[32]

Davydov preferred partisan war, which allows maximum flexibility in the field and therefore maximum response to chance, and so did Tolstoy. It is no accident that career army officer Colonel Glebov disapprovingly dubbed Tolstoy a "partisan."[33] Of course partisan warfare, as opposed to individual risk-taking, is possible only under certain conditions. Lacking the usual defenses built into a hierarchical army structure, it requires initiative, willingness to gamble, and daring. Soldiers will only engage in it for plunder or when fighting on their home territory. Davydov explains that the idea of partisan warfare first came to him at Borodino because it happened to take place near his ancestral estate; therefore he knew the terrain, and he was especially motivated to defend it.[34] (Similarly, in *War and Peace*, the defiling of his Smolensk estates infuriates Prince Andrei.) In the Caucasus, Tolstoy had found himself on the wrong side of a partisan effort. As he ponders in a draft to "The Raid," the mountain warrior defending his village has a personal interest in fighting that is absent in the Russian (*PSS* 3: 234–35). A career soldier like Captain Khlopov fights from duty in the one story written in the Caucasus ("The Raid"), but there is no talk of patriotism here or in Tolstoy's letters or diaries from the period. Indeed, within a few months of having joined the army, Tolstoy was thinking of leaving it, and this theme recurs from time to time in his Caucasian diary. His attitude changed markedly during the Crimean War once he and his comrades were fighting invaders. Under those conditions Russian soldiers and front-line officers like Tolstoy, undersupplied, with inferior weaponry, and poorly led at the top, fought ferociously and willingly engaged in partisan-like night raids on enemy trenches.

It is significant that the first outburst of patriotic rhetoric in Tolstoy's diary comes in response to the disastrous Battle of Inkerman, which the Russians had expected to win.[35] Railing against leaders he considered responsible for the defeat, Tolstoy defiantly celebrates "the moral strength of the Russian people" as demonstrated in the fighting spirit of the doomed warriors, conscripts and officers alike. He is determined to fight in Sevastopol, especially after the "useless" death at Inkerman of his friend Staff Captain Komstadius, writing that "It's as if I feel ashamed before him" (*PSS* 47: 28). At the end of

"Sevastopol in August," anger (*zloba*) and shame along with "repentance" are what the Russian soldiers evacuating Sevastopol are said to feel as they vow revenge for their humiliation. These are the circumstances under which Tolstoy himself embraced the cult of *molodechestvo*.

The most alien element for Tolstoy in *molodechestvo* was the role in it of anger and revenge, and yet his war experience allowed him to understand even this, if he did not condone it. In a draft to "The Raid," he had asserted that the feeling of "fury" (*zlost'*) could not be sustained though a whole conflict and therefore could not explain war (*PSS* 3: 228). In the Crimean War, he discovered its power to provoke and feed it. On December 7, 1854, he reported without criticism many raids against French positions that were "not so much bloody as cruel." In one such raid, a Lieutenant Titov sprayed enemy trenches with gunfire, and "they say that in the trench there was such a groan that it could be heard in the third and the fifth bastions" (*PSS* 47: 33–34). This horrific story and no doubt others like it did not restrain Tolstoy himself from joining a raiding party on March 10 (*PSS* 47: 37); he never divulged what he did or saw during it, nor did he choose to describe this common tactic in his Sevastopol stories. A front-line officer in "Sevastopol in December" does report the death of a "*molodets*" who had participated in six raids. And in that same story, speaking from the notorious fourth bastion, the narrator reveals to a surprised viewer "the feeling of anger (*zloba*) and "vengeance" (*mshchenie*) that motivates the soldiers there (*PSS* 4: 14).

If war is "murder," then all the bloodletting during it cannot be accidental or in justifiable self-defense. Tolstoy knew this, of course, but he underemphasizes it in his war fiction. The Sevastopol sketches do not dramatize a single killing committed with intentional malice. In *War and Peace*, the most terrible such death is the mob killing of Vereshchagin incited by Count Rostopchin. We know that Dolokhov and the peasant Shcherbatyi kill defenseless French prisoners offstage. (As if to make up for this earlier squeamishness, *Hadji Murat* ends with the beheading of the hero in detail, and from the point of view of the victim; here the motivation is revenge and intimidation.) There are a number of killings in *War and Peace*, like those of the arsonists in Moscow or of Platon Karataev, that are ascribed to an anonymous murderous force (*sila*) that deprives the direct perpetrators of free will. But how does this ferocious *sila* possess its agents? Fear is usually a catalyst. In the execution of the arsonists, it grips everyone, from the victims to the firing squad of French soldiers who know that they will be punished if they do not shoot (*PSS* 12: 41). On the battlefield, too, fear motivates fighters. In the encounter at Borodino between Pierre and a

French officer, Pierre, "beside himself with fear" – in Russian, literally, "not remembering himself" (*ne pomnia sebia*) – loses his moral center of gravity and starts to throttle his adversary from sheer impulse of self-defense (vol. 3, pt. 2, ch. 32; *PSS* 11: 236–37). Fear can provoke first anger and then courageous action. In "Sevastopol in August," as the storming of the fifth bastion begins, *molodets* Mikhail Kozeltsov, overcoming an initial chill of fear with anger, goes on to a heroic death. But anger is also responsible for atrocities in war, and therefore it is a primary cause for the murderous *sila* that stalks the battlefield.

The spokesman in *War and Peace* for righteous anger as the motivator of the warrior is Prince Andrei. His speech to Pierre on the eve of Borodino makes a positive case for war in its most brutal form (*PSS* 11: 205–12). According to Andrei, it should be waged only as an unconditional fight to the death. Laws that limit it make it less deadly, more like gaming for glory, and therefore more frequent. Andrei specifically recommends that no prisoners be taken; this is the policy of Dolokhov that so horrifies Denisov during the partisan war. Andrei speaks with the tone of *zloba* (anger; *PSS* 11: 207) that Tolstoy noted in the soldiers retreating from Sevastopol, and Andrei's men, represented by Timokhin, who care nothing for glory, share his feeling. It is precisely in Andrei's call for no mercy and a fight to the death that Pierre finally discovers the meaning of the expression that he has been seeing on every Russian face before Borodino. Just as the defeat does in "Sevastopol in August," patriotism here expresses itself in a tone of justifiable *zloba*.

He understood the hidden (latent, as they say in physics) warmth of patriotism, which was in all of the people whom he saw, and which explained to him why all these people calmly and as it were, light-heartedly, were preparing themselves for death. (*PSS* 11: 210)

The reference to physics is significant. As Andrei defines war, it violates human nature by engaging *only* the determined, the animal, in man; it is in this sense that we are not ourselves when we slaughter others in battle. We may do this from simple motives of self-preservation, or from more complicated but still related ones. Patriotism as Tolstoy presents it may be understood as the extension of the animal goal of self-preservation to include the preservation of home and family. Hence Andrei's diatribe climaxes in rage against enemies who "*worst of all*, kill my children, my father, and then they talk about the laws of war and magnanimity to enemies" (*PSS* 11: 210; my emphasis). Patriotism is therefore an expression of the brutal *sila* that prevails in war and generates atrocities otherwise not humanly comprehensible. Faced with a life or death situation, men lash out as animals in defense of themselves and their own. Such feelings are not confined to Russians, of course; in chapter 17 of *Hadji Murat*, after Russian troops have destroyed their *aoul* (village), the Chechens set about rebuilding and resisting under the influence of a feeling "stronger than hatred."

What all the Chechens, from youngest to oldest, felt, was stronger than hatred. It was not hatred, but a refusal to acknowledge these Russian dogs as human beings and such repulsion, disgust, and incomprehension in the face of the absurd cruelty of these beings that the desire to destroy them, like the desire to destroy rats, poisonous spiders, and wolves, was as natural a feeling as the feeling of self-preservation.

A hostile contemporary reader, N. Flerovskii, picked up on the larger context and importance of Andrei's speech for the novel.

All the war scenes in the novel are full of sympathetic stories about Denisov's obtuse lack of control, about the savage, destructive instincts of the army, which mows unripe grain, about the bloodthirstiness of Bolkonsky, who recommends not taking prisoners. The novel consistently takes the same attitude toward the business of war as drunken marauders.[36]

Though Tolstoy and Davydov abhor cruelty for its own sake, understandable rage and desire for vengeance, the "savage, destructive instincts" of *zloba* deplored by Flerovskii, keep the Russians upright and fighting at Borodino against repeated French attacks. Partisan warfare too feeds off *zloba*, as Davydov illustrates in his memoirs.[37]

   Andrei finds his insight into the true nature of war almost unbearable, but Tolstoy's text contains a more shocking truth that Flerovskii detects in the "disgusting" hunting scenes.

With a kind of disgust you read the rapturous description of hunting with hounds, where people melt with delight watching as whole packs of dogs tear a single hare to pieces; and the author strives to describe these people as strong and energetic.[38]

Merriment is a leitmotif in vol. 3, pt. 2 of the novel in which the Battle of Borodino takes place: words with the root *vesel-*, "merry," occur twenty-eight times in this part, most of these related to the war. On the battlefield, soldiers fight "merrily" (*veselo*). On and off it, they crack jokes. Most difficult for Tolstoy and many of his readers to acknowledge, the practice of war itself can bring pleasure. Tolstoy does not dwell on what his "merry" soldiers do in battle, but Davydov does. The first quotation records his own joy in battle, the second – that of his men.

The pursuit continued until noon. We cut, slashed, shot, and dragged into captivity officers, soldiers, and horses – in a word, the victory was complete. I was overflowing with joy!

[Davydov tells his Cossacks not to take prisoners because there isn't the time or manpower to do so.] My Scythians needed no further urging, while you should have seen the terror that suddenly gripped the whole enormous crowd of travelers! You had to have witnessed yourself the mix of screams of desperation with encouraging voices, the shots of the defenders, the crackle of artillery shots flying through the air, and the thunderous *Hurrahs* of my Cossacks![39]

It is pleasant to indulge our anger; this is why Lermontov's mountaineers love revenge so much. This explains the "joyful exclamations" of the men fighting in the fourth bastion when they see that enemies have been killed in "Sevastopol in December" (*PSS* 14: 14). Tolstoy does not emphasize this fact, but he records it. The soldiers feel "the attraction and charm of rage" that comes over Pierre in *War and Peace* when he threatens his adulterous wife Helene (vol. 1, pt. 4, ch. 6), or the "joy of rage" that Pierre feels as he attacks a French soldier molesting a young woman in occupied Moscow (vol. 3, pt. 3, ch. 34).

Fury has its own rewards. The pleasure described by Davydov may occur when the very desperation of their situation carries fighting men beyond fear. This happens to Kozeltsov senior ("Sevastopol in August"), who fights more bravely because he is certain he will die (*PSS* 4: 113). Freed from preoccupation with themselves, soldiers in this state throw themselves into communal activity in a way that mimics and indeed produces self-sacrifice. The only other such pleasurable self-forgetting is sexual. Boris Eikhenbaum characterized war in Davydov's poetry as "eroticized" because it is depicted through the "rampage of feelings" of the soldier narrator.[40] As Eikhenbaum's formulation suggests, the escape in war from all restraints imposed by others and by the self is pleasurable. Young soldiers like Nikolai Rostov are looking for this experience as they go to war. Nikolai's moral sensitivity overweighs his merry energy when he looks into the eyes of the French youth whom he captures; after this he will do his duty as an officer, but restrict the expression of unrestrained *molodechestvo* to the hunt. The "Scythians" who fight for Davydov feel no such scruples, and Davydov himself is not ashamed to call himself a descendant of "Genghis Khan," who "powerfully cleaved with his Tatar's hand / All that opposed the mighty hero."[41] For Russian officers like Davydov, *molodechestvo* was lawless free-dom permissible up to a certain point within loyal service to the Tsar.[42] Under conditions of all-out and justifiable war, it allowed them to behave like Genghis Khan and his followers rather than according to rules of chivalry. Tolstoy references this element of the Russian warrior code in

War and Peace when, responding to invasion, Russians lay down their swords and take up clubs to drive out the invaders (vol. 4, pt. 3, ch. 1).[43] It is Denis Davydov, with his "Russian instinct," who first understands and formalizes this response (vol. 4, pt. 3, ch. 3). Denisov, Davydov's fictional double in the novel, leads the partisan effort, and Tolstoy, later the world-famous pacifist, calls this effort "blessed" (*ibid.*).

In Tolstoy's conscripted soldiers, *molodechestvo* can also be pleasurable, and can have ugly consequences. Tolstoy knew that soldiers could be brutes, writing in his 1857 diary that "you have only to dress a man in uniform, distance him from his family, and beat a drum, to make a beast out of him."[44] He usually blamed this state of mind on the arbitrary discipline of military life to which the soldier adjusts by regarding himself as not morally culpable for deeds he must commit.[45] Elaborating this argument in the second epilogue to *War and Peace*, Tolstoy imagines an army in the shape of a cone, in which those who do the killing form the base, and the one who orders it the tip. But in the first epilogue he makes a significant exception to this rule for a "national war," in which the soldiers willfully commit brutal deeds, and do not need a leader to justify these. This is illustrated in the novel during the partisan war. Denisov's own right-hand man, the Cossack NCO Lovaiskii, approves of Dolokhov's take no prisoners ethos.[46] Mounted, Lovaiskii, with a "calm, self-satisfied expression both on his face and in his ride … is not a man sitting on a horse, but man and horse together, a being doubled in strength (*sila*)" (vol. 4, pt. 3, ch. 4). Centaurs like this, terrorizing the enemy, are the epitome of Cossack *molodechestvo*. Though Tolstoy is uncomfortable with such a model, he presents it here as a necessary and therefore legitimate part of Russian resistance.

Napoleon's animal will to power for its own sake is criminal, while Alexander I acts in justifiable defense of his country; this makes it easier for Tolstoy to depict Russians enjoying themselves in battle in *War and Peace*. Nonetheless, he observed the merry animal spirits of Russian soldiers even in the Caucasus, and records its existence as a kind of puzzle in a prominent place at the very end of "The Raid." Whatever its cause, it is a crucial part of the "incommunicable experience of war" that American Civil War veteran Oliver Wendell Holmes called "the passion of life to its top."[47] Holmes' war – fought to save his nation and end slavery – was a just one, and this allowed him to celebrate it. But the experience to which Holmes alludes is not in itself virtuous, and the desire for it may be one underlying cause of the persistence of war.

No other Russian wars besides the Siege of Sevastopol during Tolstoy's lifetime were "national" (*narodnyi*), and therefore, in Tolstoy's opinion, none gained the consent of the people. During unnecessary wars, decent soldiers fight from fear or from a sense of duty that is not the same as informed consent. Thus, in *Anna Karenina*, the old peasant beekeeper, when asked his opinion of the Russo-Turkish War, defers to the judgment of his sovereign just as Tolstoy says that soldiers do when they find themselves forced to fight wars not of their choosing. Necessary wars are part of what Tolstoy in *War and Peace* calls the swarm life of mankind; the beekeeper in *Anna Karenina* is busy controlling swarms. In that novel military *molodechestvo* is mostly negative, while *molodtsy* like the peasant Ivan Parmenev and the successful suitor Konstantin Levin occupy themselves with peaceful elements of swarm life such as harvests, weddings, and births. If the *molodets* could satisfy himself with such pursuits, there would be no war, or at least no willing warriors. As Levin's triumphant wooing of Kitty after his bear hunt (a deliberate counter-pose to the one staged for the foreign prince) suggests, however, exposure to danger scores victories even in the peaceful shire (*PSS* 18: 404–5).

The tide of war in Tolstoy's fiction crests in *War and Peace* and then retreats. The novel is his most expansive and complete treatment of the subject, and therefore of *molodechestvo*. The *molodets* of Tolstoy's old age is *dzhigit* Hadji Murat, whose life unfolds within a war of Russian imperialism. Raised in a warrior culture, he fights for honor and revenge, but in the end chooses his family over potential glory. Although he therefore dies for the one cause that Prince Andrei deemed sufficient for war, its inherent tragedy and injustice is illustrated by the fact that Murat kills someone else's son while attempting to rescue his own.[48] As in earlier works, in *Hadji Murat* warriors – soldiers, officers, and Caucasian warriors alike – are "merry," and war itself makes a merry impression on Butler, last of the stand-ins for Tolstoy as a young officer. In this work, however, the narrator intervenes directly in chapter 16 to inform us that Butler "unconsciously" avoids thinking about "the other side of war: death, the wounds of soldiers, officers, and mountaineers," because that would undercut his merriment (*PSS* 35: 79). The "merry" engagement in which Butler tests his manhood results in the destruction of a mountain village and the decision of its enraged inhabitants to take up arms to defend themselves. Readers may justly conclude that war is to be avoided whenever possible, and should never be fought for pleasure, no matter how keen and natural.

Yet a reader of Tolstoy's epic would also have to conclude that without war there could be no Hadji Murat, and that poses a dilemma for the reader who vicariously lives "the passion of life to its top" through him. Tolstoy himself models this role by placing himself in the frame narrative, from which he both comments as a pacifist on the action, and creates a timeless fantasy of a warrior. Murat is more hero than villain or victim. As he does in *War and Peace*, Tolstoy assigns the most frightening aspects of *molodechestvo* to minor characters (the inhabitants of the *aoul*, the killers of Murat, and Murat's menacing side-kick Gamzalo, for instance), and does not show Murat enraged except momentarily when (in chapter 20) he must defend himself against an unexpected attack. Unlike Achilles, Murat commits no egregious crime from excessive rage, nor does he display the excessive craftiness of an Odysseus or, in the novel, of Shamil and Vorontsov. Like Denis Davydov, he does not agonize over the need to kill in what he regards as a just cause, but, unlike Davydov, he is not shown to fight "merrily" (although such a man as he would surely have done so). We cannot imagine Murat walking away from a fight, and we would not respect him for it. In the chaos of war, he acts decisively in one crisis after another. Prince Andrei thinks his way out of the desire for glory, but still dies fighting in a just war, so that his son Nikolenka dreams of emulating him as a warrior. Murat does not reject glory on principle, but he easily turns his back on it when something more important intervenes. He too dies in battle, and he too will be a model for his son. His thinking can be moral as well as strategic, but it is not self-castigating; he does not reject his warrior ethos. Most seductive for us as for Tolstoy, Murat can look death in the eye and not blink; in the final episode of the work he both accepts the probability of his death, and fights to live. Like Petya Rostov, we mostly do not dwell on the ferocity of the *molodets* in battle; indeed, at times we wonder whether, if it were necessary, we could be as ferocious. We want to be *molodtsy*, as whole, strong, and self-confident as Hadji Murat, and so does Tolstoy's narrator. As long as people want to test themselves against death and chaos, as long as injustice or the perception of it exists, it seems that when wars call, *molodtsy* will come.

NOTES

1. L. N. Tolstoi, *Polnoe sobranie sochineniia*, 90 vols. (Moscow: Gosudarstvennoe izdatel'stvo "Khudozhestvennaia literatura," 1928–58), 3: 228. Hereafter cited as *PSS*. Unless otherwise stated, all translations in this chapter are my own.
2. See the diary entry for January 4, 1853, *PSS* 46: 155. See John L. N. Keep, *Soldiers of the Tsar: Army and Society in Russia, 1462–1874* (Oxford: Clarendon Press, 1985), 210, for this as a problem in the Russian ranks.
3. The literature on war in Tolstoy is vast, especially in Russia, and reflects the confusing situation that I have sketched. I. Ianovskii reconciles the two sides of Tolstoy by blaming his pacifism on the injustice of the Old Regime in Russia and

the wars it waged (*Chelovek i voina v tvorchestve L. N. Tolstogo* [Kiev: Vishcha shkola, 1978]). More often, because Tolstoy's treatment of war is complex, critics tend to focus on what is essential to themselves and their own times. Compare, for instance, Leonid Grossman's 1916 antiwar article, which emphasizes the horror of war ("Stendal' i Tolstoi. Batalizm i psikhologiia ras v literature XIX veka," *Russkaia mysl'* [June, 1916]: 32–51), and anticipates Boris Eikhenbaum's *The Young Tolstoi* (1921; trans. Gary Kern, Ann Arbor, MI: Ardis, 1972); with M. Tsiavlovskii's approving summary of Tolstoy as patriot and warrior, published in 1940 in *Literaturnaia gazeta*, November 17. In general the war theme in Tolstoy became very important in Soviet criticism with the outbreak of World War II. (Russians call the invasion of Russia by Germany the Great Patriotic War, thereby linking it to the Patriotic War of 1812, and thence to *War and Peace*.) Compare Shklovsky's attack in 1936 ("O staroi russkoi voennoi i o sovetskoi oboronnoi proze," *Znamia* 1 [1936]: 218–27) on Tolstoy as a "barin" who, in publications like "Sevastopol in December" and "The Wood-Felling," soft-pedaled the truth about the tsarist army as he depicted it in unpublished works like "A Note on the negative sides of the Russian soldier and officer" (*PSS* 4: 285–94; 1855), to Lidiia Ginzburg's "O romane Tolstogo 'Voina i mir'" (*Zvezda* 1 [1944]: 125–38), which, like many other positive Soviet discussions of Tolstoy, emphasizes his skill at portraying the triumph of "communal life" during war. Ginzburg's article appeared just as the siege of Leningrad, which she endured, was lifted.

4. S. Chubakov (*Lev Tolstoi o voine i militarizme* [Minsk: Izdatel'stvo BFU, 1973]) and especially S. Doroshenko (*Lev Tolstoi – voin i patriot: voennaia sud'ba i voennaia deiatel'nost'* [Moscow: Sovetskii pisatel', 1966]) provide the most information about Tolstoy's military service.

5. Tolstoy recalled the battle several times, often on its anniversary. See his diary entry for February 18, 1897 (*PSS* 53: 138) and a letter to G. Rusanov, February 18, 1906 (*PSS* 76: 103). Nikolai Tolstoy wrote his brother on February 18, 1855 reminding him of the dual significance of the date (*Perepiska L. N. Tolstogo s sestrami i brat'iami* [Moscow: Khudozhestvennaia literatura, 1990], 180).

6. For the positive semantics surrounding the young officer, see A. T. Gulak, "'Raspuskaiushchiisia': stilistiko-rechevye kraski obraza iunogo voina v rasskazakh L. Tolstogo 50-kh gg.," *Russkii iazyk v shkole* 5 (September 2000): 70–74.

7. See Eikhenbaum's *The Young Tolstoi*, ch. 3, for the first exposition of this theory.

8. On the formation of such abstract nouns, see Charles E. Townsend, *Russian Word-Formation* (New York: McGraw-Hill, 1968), 167.

9. *Tolkovyi slovar' russkogo iazyka*, ed. D. Ushakov (Moscow: Gosudarstvennoe izdatel'stvo inostrannykh i natsional'nykh slovarei, 1938). The word exists in two forms with different stresses. The Common Slavic *mólodets*, associated with folk poetry, is first attested in Old Russian in 1186; *molodéts* is a specifically Russian variation that is neutral in tone. See *Etimologicheskii slovar' russkogo iazyka*, ed. A. F. Zhuravlev and N. M. Shanskii, vol. 10 (Moscow: Izdatel'stvo Moskovskogo universiteta, 2007). The first attestation of *molodechestvo* according to the authoritative *Slovar' sovremennogo russkogo literaturnogo iazyka*, ed. V. Chernyshev, vol. 6 (Moscow and Leningrad, 1957) is in a dictionary in the year 1731.

10. *Molodechestvo* is negative in anti-war and anti-military works like A. Kuprin's *The Duel* (1905), in which it never appears in a positive light.

11. For Tolstoy's unquestioning love of country and military valor in childhood, see "A ma chère Tante. Amour de la Patrie," *PSS* 1: 215.

12. *PSS* 39: 219. The last sentence is crossed out. See also his discussion in 1886 with French author and politician Paul Déroulède (1846–1914) (as transcribed by Tolstoy's distant cousin E. F. Iunge, who was present; *Literaturnoe nasledstvo* 75, no. 1 [1965]: 536–40).

13. He was especially dismayed by the behavior of his beloved and admired brother Nikolai. See diary entries for March 30 and 31, 1852, *PSS* 46: 103–6.

14. On the circle in Bucharest, see Chubakov, *Lev Tolstoi o voine i militarizme*, 43.

15. Susan Layton, *Russian Literature and Empire: The Conquest of the Caucasus from Pushkin to Tolstoy* (Cambridge: Cambridge University Press, 1994), 134. Layton has chapters on both works, which were written at the same time, in the early 1830s, although Lermontov's poem was only published in 1843.

16. *PSS* 47: 10. Tolstoy read Lermontov intensively and more than once during his army service; see *PSS* 46: 154; 47: 7, 9–10. Note the Lermontovian lament that begins the diary entry of February 5, 1852, quoted above.

17. The best exposition of anarchic individualism in Lermontov is David Powelstock, *Becoming Mikhail Lermontov: The Ironies of Romantic Individualism in Nicholas I's Russia* (Evanston, IL: Northwestern University Press, 2005).

18. See Faddei Bulgarin, *Vospominaniia* (Moscow: Zakharov, 2001), 173 (pt. 2, ch. 3). The cautious Bulgarin assures his readers (and the censors) that soldiers today do not behave this way (*ibid.*).

19. *Ibid.* 606 (pt. 5, ch. 3). An exact translation would be that he took it to the point of "desperation" (*otchaianie*). For the meaning of this word in both Tolstoy and Dostoevsky, see Orwin, *Consequences of Consciousness: Turgenev, Dostoevsky, and Tolstoy* (Palo Alto, CA: Stanford University Press, 2007), 161–66.

20. *PSS* 34: 393. P. Biriukov, *L. N. Tolstoi, Biografiia*, 3 vols. (Berlin, Izd. I. P. Ladyzhnikova, 1921), vol. 1, 89. "Transgressive" is an exact etymological equivalent in English of the word *prestupnyi*, usually rendered as "criminal."

21. Bulgarin, *Vospominaniia*, 172.

22. On the indebtedness of "Dva gusara" to Davydov, see E. M. Zhiliakova, "Denis Davydov i povest' L. N. Tolstogo *Dva gusara*," in A. S. Ianushkevich, ed., *Russkaia povest' kak forma vremeni* (Tomsk: Izd. Tomskogo un-ta, 2002), 216–26.

23. Besides the well-known references to partisan warfare, there are many other implicit ones to Davydov's memoirs in *War and Peace*.

24. Tolstoy himself called the work an idyll when he first conceived it. See *PSS* 47: 40.

25. The excellent translation of these lines in ch. 1 is by David McDuff.

26. N. Apostolov, *Lev Tolstoi nad strannitsami istorii: istoriko-literaturnye nabliu-deniia* (Moscow: Komissiia po oznamenovaniiu stoletiia so dnia rozhdeniia L. N. Tolstogo, 1928), 24. Apostolov took this quote from Boyer's memoirs, published in 1901, of his visit to Tolstoy.

27. See P. A. Sergeenko, *Kak zhivet i rabotaet L. N. Tolstoi* (Moscow, 1908), 106–7.

28. Doroshenko, *Lev Tolstoi – voin i patriot* (76–79), provides a more thorough depiction of the operation on February 18 from other sources.
29. For Tolstoy's debt to Plato in this regard, see Orwin, "Tolstoy and Courage" in Donna Tussing Orwin, ed., *The Cambridge Companion to Tolstoy* (Cambridge: Cambridge University Press, 2002), 222–36.
30. *Voennye zapiski partizana Denisa Davydova* (Moscow: Gosudarstvennoe izda-tel'stvo "Khudozhestvennaia literatura," 1940), 78. Charles XII (reigned 1697–1718) was a daring Swedish king who fought Peter I in the Great Northern War that led to the downfall of the Swedish empire.
31. "Zapiski Porfiriia Nikolaevicha Glebova," *Russkaia starina* 3 (1905): 528–29.
32. *Voennye zapiski*, 118, 153.
33. "Zapiski Porfiriia Nikolaevicha Glebova," 528.
34. *Voennye zapiski*, 197.
35. *PSS* 47: 27–28. On the Battle of Inkerman, see John Shelton Curtiss, *Russia's Crimean War* (Durham, NC: Duke University Press, 1979), 332–41.
36. "Iziashchnyi romanist i ego iziashchnye kritiki," *Delo* 6 (1868): Sovremennoe obozrenie, 1–28 (27). Flerovskii (1829–1918), a well-known leftist economist and sociologist, is also known by the pseudonym V. V. Bervi, and signed this particular article as S. Navalin.
37. See, for instance, his advice to peasants in occupied territory about how to kill French marauders without alerting the authorities (*Voennye zapiski*, 209); his order to set fire to huts full of French soldiers in revenge for an earlier battle in which he lost thirty-five men (221); and the execution of a turncoat (242–43). For a similar Soviet defense of cruelty in war, see A. A. Saburov, "Obraz russkogo voina v 'Voine i mire'," in D. D. Blagoi, ed., *L. N. Tolstoi: Sbornik stat'ei i materialov* (Moscow: Izd-stvo Akademii nauk SSSR, 1951), 390–424 (402–5).
38. Flerovskii, "Iziashchnyi romanist i ego iziashchnye kritiki," 23.
39. Davydov, *Voennye zapiski*, 234–35, 252.
40. "Ot voennoi ody k 'gusarskoi pesne'," in B. M. Eikhenbaum, *O poezii* (Leningrad: Sovetskii pisatel', 1969), 148–68 (166–67).
41. *Grafu P. A. Stroganovu*. See also *Voennye zapiski*, 262, where, having ordered huts full of enemy soldiers set alight, he calls himself "a true son of Genghis Khan."
42. See Laurence Leighton ("Denis Davydov's Hussar Style," *Slavic and East European Journal* 7 [1963]: 349–60 [349–50]) on Davydov's participation in a loyal opposition of officers who opposed Alexander's Prussianization of the army.
43. On the Russian perception of dueling as alien, see Irina Reyfman, *Ritualized Violence Russian Style: The Duel in Russian Culture and Literature* (Stanford, CA: Stanford University Press, 1999).
44. April 1/13, Geneva; *PSS* 47: 204.
45. See also his "Diaden'ka Zhdanov i kavaler Chernov" (*PSS* 3: 271–73; 1854) and "Zapiska ob otritsatel'nykh storonakh russkogo soldata i ofitsera"(*PSS* 4: 285–94; 1855).

46. Lovaiskii smiles approvingly when Dolokhov articulates this. See vol. 4, pt. 3, ch. 8.
47. The first phrase is from a speech delivered on Memorial Day, 1895, to the Harvard graduating class; and the second one from another Memorial Day speech, this one delivered in 1884, in Keene, New Hampshire.
48. See Donald Fanger, "Nazarov's Mother: Notes toward an Interpretation of *Hadji Murat*," *Iberomania* (1974): 99–104.

CHAPTER 5

Leo Tolstoy's correspondence with Nikolai Strakhov: the dialogue on faith

Irina Paperno

ABOUT THE CORRESPONDENCE

Among Leo Tolstoy's voluminous letters, his correspondence with Nikolai Strakhov stands out for its intensity, intimacy, reciprocity, and confessional nature.[1] As a literary critic and philosophical writer, Nikolai Nikolaevich Strakhov (1828–96) participated in the major intellectual debates and publishing ventures of the 1860s–80s. In his prodigious role as editor, private correspondent, and confidant, he served as a conveyor of diverse ideas and a mediator between disparate people. (In many ways, he served as a "link" between Tolstoy and Dostoevsky.)[2] What Strakhov self-consciously offered to Tolstoy was his special ability, and need, to "enter other people's interests and thoughts" (1: 207; April 22, 1875). Tolstoy insisted on reciprocating. At his urging, in spring 1875 (after four years of friendship), Strakhov confessed that he had been desperately searching for a "cause" in life (1: 207). Tolstoy wanted to probe the matter further: "Your spiritual condition has been revealed to me a little, and I want all the more to penetrate it further" (1: 211; May 5, 1875). He suspected that they were both yearning for faith. Thus, Strakhov admitted to the same desire that Tolstoy himself had experienced as of late: to visit Optina Pustyn' – a monastery and hermitage celebrated for its elders (*startsy*), charismatic Orthodox spiritual advisers eager to advise laymen and even hear their informal (non-sacramental) confessions (1: 211).[3] (For the next two years they would plan and discuss a visit to Optina, which took place only in July 1877.) But for Tolstoy, an unfinished project stood in the way of his new aspirations: "I'm at work at the moment on that dreary, vulgar A[nna] Karen[ina] and all I ask God is that he give me the strength to be rid of it as soon as possible, to free some space […] for other, more pressing matters" (1: 215; August 25, 1875). For some time now, Tolstoy had felt an urge to abandon belles-lettres for a higher cause. In May 1874, he told Strakhov that he had neglected the novel to work on an article "in the form of my pedagogical *profession de foi*" (1: 164; May 10, 1874). Come the fall of 1875, it was religious-philosophical thoughts on the "meaning of life and death."

When the two met in Iasnaia Poliana in late September 1875, Tolstoy felt a "remarkable spiritual affinity" between them. In letters that followed, he urged Strakhov to join him in the urgent task to "elucidate and define" their "religious worldview" (1: 222; October 26 [?], 1875). Tolstoy felt that they both were at a crossroads: suspended, like many of their contemporaries, between "Christian belief" and "nihilistic materialism" and, in their individual life journeys, between life and death, they had a common duty to speak out, so as to "help those who are in the same miserable lonely condition." Strakhov responded that he would follow Tolstoy's advice and do what he could (1: 224; November 4, 1875). Tolstoy sealed their pact: "I rejoice at your plan and challenge you to a correspondence." He immediately added: "My God, if only somebody would finish A. Karenina for me!" (1: 226; November 8–9, 1875).

And so the two men began a philosophical dialogue; its subject was personal faith in the age of reason and science. Scholars have long used this correspondence to trace Tolstoy's dramatic evolution in the late 1870s, between *Anna Karenina* and *A Confession*, into a religious-philosophical writer. In the words of Andrew Donskov, under whose editorship this correspondence has been recently published in full, "the germ of almost all the moral/religious principles [Tolstoy] expounded in the last three decades of his life can be found in his pre-1880 letters to Strakhov."[4] In this chapter, I will focus on the correspondence itself: an act of intimate communication between two friends established for the purpose of elucidating and defining their respective religious outlooks.

The act itself was a matter of irresistible need and a social duty, but its success was not guaranteed. Tolstoy was tormented by the problem of self-expression: *how* to speak about one's faith, that is, about that which lies apart from reason and language. In these years, Tolstoy's writing on faith, much of which he discarded, was experimental in nature. Then, after more than four years of intense epistolary exchange, Tolstoy described the development of his religious views in the work we know under the title *A Confession* (*Ispoved'*, written between 1879 and 1882).

The correspondence between Tolstoy and Strakhov in the years 1875–79 may be the most important strand in the story of Tolstoy's religious conversion and his evolution from belles-lettres to religious-philosophical writings.[5] Side-by-side with everyday matters, their letters contained a self-conscious philosophical dialogue. Such dialogue, of course, has a long and venerable tradition as philosophical genre, from Plato to Hume to

Rousseau, and beyond, which endowed this intimate conversation with an aura of larger significance.

THE PHILOSOPHICAL DIALOGUE

When, at Tolstoy's instigation, Strakhov opened their dialogue, he used Kant's three fundamental questions to set the agenda: 1. What can I know? 2. What ought I to do? 3. What may I hope? (*Critique of Pure Reason*, A 805/ B 833). The second question was the most important for him: indifferent (he wrote) to the question of the immortality of the soul, Strakhov wanted to know "what is to be done," or, "translated into Christian language, how to save one's soul" (1: 228; November 16, 1875). Like many a Russian intellectual, Strakhov sought specific instructions for "active involvement in life" (his words), but, unlike others, he approached the matter in a religious key.

In his response, Tolstoy focused on a different question, which had preoccupied him since childhood: "What may we hope for?" – by which he meant the future, eternal life of the soul. But he believed that all three questions were inextricably linked into one: "What am I?" (1: 230; November 30, 1875). A question about his own character – and simultaneously about the nature of man – "What am I?" was a theological issue for Tolstoy.

Commenting that it might seem irresponsible to address such questions "on two sheets of note-paper," he added that this was something he would have done even if he were not writing a letter to an intimate friend, but rather a "*profession de foi*, to which the whole of humankind attended" (1: 230). So, writing to an intimate friend, he was as if making a solemn declaration of a religious creed.

Then Tolstoy made "a digression on method" (his words) – pages of tedious repetitions and paraphrases (1: 230–35). In brief, he tried to say that "scientific method," which relied on logical reasoning, was inapplicable to philosophy – the "true" philosophy, concerned with the meaning of human life and death. True philosophy relied on "harmony" rather than logic, on "linking disparate notions into a single whole," which convinced "instantly," without deductions and proofs (1: 234). He offered an emblematic image: "a philosophical outlook spawned directly from life is a circle or a sphere with no end, middle or beginning" (1: 235). (In *War and Peace*, Tolstoy associated his perfectly harmonious character, the peasant Platon Karataev, with a sphere or ball.) He also offered examples of philosophers who had pursued the ideal of such "true philosophy," and named the one who had come closest: Plato (1: 232). (Tolstoy did not comment on the role of the dialogue form in promoting this accomplishment, but it would be hard to imagine that he did not have in mind that Plato had set the standard for the genre of philosophical dialogue.)

Appended to the November 30 letter, was "an introduction of sorts" (transcribed by a copyist) to an "as yet unwritten philosophical work" (the introduction was entitled "Why do I write?" [*Dlia chego ia pishu*]).[6] Tolstoy started in the first person and in the autobiographical mode:

I'm forty-seven years old [...] I feel that old age has set in.

Old age is what I call that inner, spiritual condition in which all the world's external phenomena have lost interest for me [...] If a sorceress were to appear before me and ask me what I desired, I would not be able to express one single wish.

(As scholars have noticed, years later, in *Confession*, Tolstoy would appeal to this same image.) He had lived (wrote Tolstoy) through "childhood, adolescence, youth," reached "maturity," that is, had gone "up the mountain," reached the "summit" – and started the descent. What next? This much seemed clear: death (1: 236). Having considered, and rejected, the idea that life might be inherently meaningless, Tolstoy started searching for a view on life that would relieve this sense of meaninglessness. The purpose of his writing was "To tell how it was that I passed from a state of hopelessness and despair to an explanation for myself of the meaning of life" (1: 237). At this point, the copied manuscript comes to an end. Resuming his letter (in his own hand), Tolstoy commented that he could not give the rest to the copyist. That which followed argued that these questions were fully answered by religion, admitting that, "with the knowledge we possess, it is impossible for us to believe in the principles of religion." Exposure to such material "could have led the copyist into temptation" (1: 237).

As Tolstoy made clear, he started writing at the very moment of transition (from the state of hopelessness to uncertain groping for meaning) and in the presence of others (the addressee and the copyist). The writing itself was an act of religious self-definition. Accordingly, he focused on the *how*: on the process and method.

Tolstoy concluded his first philosophical letter by inviting his correspondent to respond. The philosophical method, he reiterated, rests on harmonious linking of disparate notions into a single whole. He awaited Strakhov's response and objections in order to demonstrate the "harmony" in the assembly of his "religious (philosophical) views" (1: 239). Thus, Tolstoy wanted an interlocutor – a philosophical writer whom he urged to embark on a parallel quest – in order to validate that his credo was properly harmonized or, at most, to fine tune it.

In response, Strakhov suggested that in his "digression on method" Tolstoy seemed to be saying that science employed "analysis" (division of the whole into parts), while philosophy strove for "synthesis" (1: 240–41; December 25, 1875). Tolstoy responded firmly that he did not agree with this simple "substitution of terms," but he urged Strakhov to respond to his next philosophical letter, which would go out in a few days (1: 243; January 1–2, 1876).

Tolstoy's long-delayed second philosophical letter, mailed only on February 14–15, 1876, contained an unfinished essay, "The soul and its life outside of the life that is known and understood by us" (*O dushe i zhizni ee vne izvestnoi i poniatnoi nam zhizni*).[7] Turning to a different mode – not spiritual autobiography, but abstract philosophy – Tolstoy, again, started with the word "I": "I exist" (*PSS* 17: 340). Having crossed out this statement, he made an attempt to approach the problem from the view point of his antagonists, the materialists: I live and, as I know from experience (*opyt*), I will die. Nothing remains, then, but dead matter (*PSS* 17: 351–52). And what about the soul: how would one "define" the soul – that which lies, and lasts, beyond reason? How would one speak of that something which is larger than both the living and the dead, the "I" and the "non-I"? After many pages of repetitive and barely penetrable philosophizing, Tolstoy returned to his initial point: What am I? He mused: "I don't know to what extent Descartes' formulation is accurate: I think, therefore I live; but I know that if I say – *I know myself above all, that I live*, – this cannot be inaccurate" (*PSS* 17: 351).

It was not easy for Strakhov to engage in a philosophical dialogue with the man he venerated: "I cannot write to you, my inestimable Lev Nikolaevich, about philosophy" (1: 255; March 20, 1876). When he finally forced himself to respond, he rephrased and contextualized Tolstoy's main arguments in the language of a well-informed student of Western philosophy: "Your letter is an attempt to tread the same path as Descartes, Fichte, Schelling, Hegel, Schopenhauer. They began in precisely the same way, from themselves, from Cogito ergo sum, from the I, from the consciousness of the will, – and from there derived their understanding of all else that exists" (1: 256; April 8, 1876). He praised Tolstoy for the "power" of his thoughts. Yet, his compliment notwithstanding, Strakhov felt that retracing the steps of post-Cartesian philosophy from its starting point in the subject would not bring what both men desired: something that lay beyond human reason and the human subject (1: 256–67). Moreover, Strakhov told Tolstoy that the form he chose for the expression of his view on life did not show him at his best:

You are trying […] to contain your views in the formulas of general knowledge. I am certain that the results you receive will be one hundred times more impoverished than the content of your poetic meditations. Consider, for instance, whether I can place the view on life diffused in your works above what Schopenhauer or Hegel or anyone else has to say about life? (1: 257)

He then turned the conversation to readers' reactions to the published installments of Tolstoy's novel (chs. 7–19 of pt. 5 appeared in the April issues of *Russkii vestnik*): "*Anna Karenina* is arousing admiration and rancour such as I never before remember in literature" (1: 258). But Tolstoy wanted to hear not the praise, but only the critical comments about *Anna Karenina* (1: 259; April 8–9, 1876). As for Strakhov's response to his philosophical letter, he, again, rejected his interlocutor's interpretation of his ideas. Admitting that he was unable to express himself, he put his trust in Strakhov's special ability to understand: "I am afraid that I cannot say what I want to […] I hope that you will understand even that which is ill-expressed" (1: 261; April 14 [?],1876). Responding to his interlocutor's objections, Tolstoy extended his initial ideas further, naming that one principle which embraced everything, the living and the dead; the "I" and the "non-I": "the living God and the God of love" (1: 261).

Strakhov began his response immediately, but he mailed his unfinished "*philosophical letter*" (1: 27; his italics) much later, as an addendum to the regular letter of May 8, 1876:

You see in the world the living God and feel his love. Now your meaning is clear to me, and I can, I feel, tell you frankly that it can be developed logically in the same strict form as other philosophical systems possess. It will be a pantheism, the fundamental principle of which will be love, just as the will is for Schopenhauer, as thought is for Hegel. (1: 263; written after April 14; mailed on May 8, 1876)

Strakhov then asked Tolstoy to define his understanding of evil, but Tolstoy returned to their philosophical correspondence only more than six months later (1: 291; November 12–13, 1876). In summer 1876, Strakhov twice visited Iasnaia Poliana, where the two men continued their philosophical conversations in person.

As for their correspondence, I would argue that as an attempt to elucidate their respective professions of faith, the exchange of philosophical formulas that took place between May 1875 and May 1876 led to a dead end. Philosophizing did not seem to bring Tolstoy closer to answering questions about the meaning of life and death. Moreover, he did not seem encouraged by Strakhov's responses – he was not a man to accept being associated with existing philosophical conceptions. (The name of Hegel alone would have been extremely annoying: Tolstoy did not share Strakhov's devotion to Hegel.)

While the regular exchange of the "philosophical letters" proper came to a halt after one year, another topic came to the fore in their continuing correspondence: *Anna Karenina*. Over the course of the year, Strakhov again and again tried to turn the conversation to Tolstoy's unfinished novel. As Tolstoy commented on April 23, 1876, in more than one way, their correspondence "doubled" (*razdvoilas'*) (1: 267).

"I WISH THAT YOU, INSTEAD OF READING *ANNA KAR[ENINA]*, WOULD FINISH IT ..."

Tolstoy was increasingly irritated by Strakhov's exhortations to return to *Anna Karenina*. Literature – an institution replete with professional authors, journals, criticism – disgusted him (1: 259; April 8–9[?], 1876). He even coined a new spelling for the word itself, expressing his disdain by transcribing from the French: "In spite of your great, independent mind, you pay tribute to Petersburg and to *littérature*" (1: 244; January 1–2, 1876.) He found the writing profession morally dangerous: "The rank of writer is loathsome; it's depraving" (1: 259; April 8–9 [?], 1876). Tolstoy was now fearful of both criticism and praise of *Anna Karenina* and he felt disgusted by the novel itself. Strakhov responded with intense emotion:

You are losing your usual calm and, it seems, you want me to advise you to cease printing *Anna Karenina* and leave the thousands of readers who are all asking and waiting for how it will end cruelly in the dark? [...] You've worked me up into such a state of agitation as if I had to write the end of the novel myself. (1: 264–65; late April [?], 1876)

Strakhov also reproached Tolstoy for failing to respond to his reflections in his letters on the novel. He now asked Tolstoy: did he correctly understand the "idea" of the novel? (1: 264). Tolstoy finally rose to Strakhov's challenge: "your opinion of my novel holds true, but this is not everything – that is, it's all true, but what you've said is not everything that I wanted to say" (1: 266; April 26, 1876). What he said next has been since cited by numerous scholars. In order to express all that is in his novel, he would have to write the same work over again. Expression is only realized through the "linkage" (*stseplenie*) of parts, and evades plain verbal summary:

every idea, expressed by itself in words, loses its meaning, is terribly debased, when taken alone out of that linkage in which it is found. The linkage itself is not constituted by an idea [...] but by something else, and to express the basis of this linkage directly in words is quite impossible; but it is possible only indirectly – in words describing images, actions, situations.

He gave an example: the scene of Vronsky's attempted suicide, highly praised by Strakhov. When Tolstoy was revising this chapter, Vronsky, "completely unexpectedly" for him, the author, "but quite decidedly, proceeded to shoot himself" (*sovershenno dlia menia neozhidanno, no nesomnenno, Vronskii stal streliat'sia*; 1: 267). Tolstoy then leveled his anger at literary critics writing about *Anna Karenina*: "And if critics now already understand what I want to say [...] then I congratulate them and can confidently assure them *qu'ils en savent plus long que moi*" (1: 268). Twentieth-century literary critics tend to read this formula as a claim of art's superiority over other forms of expression, affirming its ability – and Tolstoy's – to produce inexhaustible meaning, perhaps to express the inexpressible. But at precisely the time Tolstoy coined this formula, he was considering retreating from literature and abandoning *Anna Karenina* for philosophical discourse. In the context of the Tolstoy–Strakhov correspondence, we may read Tolstoy's famous words differently: as an admission of art's inherent inability to deliver a clear and unambiguous message and a complaint about the author's lack of control over his text. Rather than struggle with the vicissitudes of artistic form, Tolstoy now wanted to find a form of expression that would indeed allow him to say, in words, what he wanted to, would allow him to say "I," and would convince instantly. It seemed to him that philosophical discourse, while it also required careful "linking," offered such a possibility.

Rather than agree to return to literature, Tolstoy tried to convince Strakhov, who himself wrote literary criticism (including critical articles on Tolstoy), to follow his example: "Give up literature altogether and write philosophical books. Who else is there? Who else will say what we think?" (1: 293; November 12, 1876). But Tolstoy must have known that the real problem was *how*: how to put one's thoughts into words.

Indeed, it was the problem of expression – artistic expression – that stood in the way of bringing *Anna Karenina* to completion. While Strakhov begged him not to leave thousands of readers in the dark, Tolstoy himself did not know "how it would all end." After the April 1876 issues, the publication came to a halt. At the end of July, still nothing appeared in press. Addressing Strakhov, Tolstoy grumbled: "I wish that you, instead of reading Anna Kar[enina], would finish it, and rescue me from this sword of Damocles" (1: 276; July 31, 1876).

Tolstoy finally completed the publication of the novel in July 1877, and entrusted Strakhov with the preparation of the revised separate edition (so in a way, Strakhov did finish the novel for Tolstoy).[8] Immediately after, in late July, the two men made their long-planned pilgrimage to the monastic community of Optina Pustyn', where they engaged the holy fathers and the elder Amvrosii in a conversation about religion and faith.

"TO EXPRESS, IN THE FORM OF CATECHISM, THAT WHICH I BELIEVE IN"

Not long after the completion of *Anna Karenina* Tolstoy again turned to his attempts to articulating his *profession de foi*. While his character, Levin, seemed to have found a response to the question "What am I?" in the faith that "filled his heart" as a "sensation," Tolstoy – the author who refrained from clearly articulating Levin's newly found faith in words – did not. Neither could he accept Levin's conclusion that there was "no need to speak," that this was "a mystery needed and valued by me alone and inexpressible in words." Tolstoy was still searching for the verbal means of speaking about his faith to others.

There were, after all, accepted forms. As Tolstoy wrote to Strakhov in November 1877, he had heard a priest teaching his children a lesson in Orthodox catechism, and, finding it odious and unconvincing, tried to write his own: "to express, in the form of catechism, what I believe" (1: 374). This attempt, too, showed Tolstoy how "hard" it was; he feared, even, that, for him, it might be "impossible." As often happened in these years, he felt overcome with despair (1: 374; November 6, 1877).

An unfinished fragment, "Christian catechism" (*Khristianskii katikhizis*), (*PSS* 17: 363–68), begins with a formula of his personal creed: "I believe in the one true holy church, living in the hearts of all men and on all the earth" (*PSS* 17: 363). But when he broke into the standard sequence of questions and answers, he found himself in difficulty. The first question ("What is necessary for the soul's salvation?"), found "A clear definition of that which we believe in." But the next question – "What is faith?" – led to a deadlock (*PSS* 17: 364).[9]

In a rough draft of yet another unfinished philosophical essay, "A definition of religion-faith" (*Opredelenie religii-very*), Tolstoy coined a new term, "religion-faith" – a fusion of religion and faith; and he focused on the word itself: "the word religion-faith is the word …"[10] "Clear and unquestionable" it might be for believers, but for those who did not believe (or "thought that they did not believe"), the word itself needed definition (*PSS* 17: 357). The untidy piece of paper (torn and crumpled as if discarded in despair) runs to less than half a page and ends in a half phrase (*PSS* 17: 781; undated).

After these failures, Tolstoy embarked on another project: extensive reading of the books that "define religion, faith." Strakhov – who held a post in the Imperial Public Library in St. Petersburg – served as his guide. In mid-December, Tolstoy reported that he had assembled a set of historical and philosophical studies of religion, including D. F. Strauss, Ernest Renan, Max Müller, Émile Burnouf, and Vladimir Soloviev (1: 385; December 17–18, 1877). On January 3, he acknowledged being somewhat "lost" in the thoughts of others (1: 389).

Still another attempt was a literary dialogue, entitled "Interlocutors" (*Sobesedniki*), which Tolstoy started on December 20, 1877. In its form, the extant draft resembles a Platonic dialogue. It is a conversation between seven participants who debate one topic: what is faith? Tolstoy defined the participants by their social roles and ideological positions, suggesting concrete prototypes: a "healthy idealist philosopher," aged 42 ("Fet – Strakhov – Schopenhauer – Kant"); a "natural scientist," who speaks for progress, aged 37 ("Virchow – Dubois Raimond – Tyndall – Mill"); a "positivist," aged 35 ("Bibikov"); a "clever priest," who denies reason, aged 56; a "dialectical thinker," aged 50, who justifies faith by sophisms ("Khomiakov – Urusov"); a "monk," aged 70 ("Father Pimen […] sleeps"), and, last, the "I," aged 49 and named "Ivan Ilych."[11] Here we gain a clue to what Tolstoy saw in his real-life correspondent, Strakhov: an idealist approximating Kant or Schopenhauer. But for the imaginary dialogue, Tolstoy expanded the team of interlocutors. The "priest" and the "monk" are clearly based on those Tolstoy had met during his recent pilgrimage with Strakhov to Optina Pustyn', where he was especially impressed with the sincerity and simplicity of Father Pimen, who had fallen asleep during a sophisticated conversation on faith.[12]

The participants in Tolstoy's dialogue discuss whether or not faith might be justified by different types of knowledge – science, pure reason (according to Kant), "dialectical reason," and experience (*opyt*). The "I" (Ivan Ilych), who initially demanded the definition of faith, first tries to circumvent the arguments of his interlocutors, momentarily insists on the "subjective ethical principle," but then, finally, "finds himself in a pitiful situation" (*PSS* 17: 371). Exactly a year later, December 20, 1878, Tolstoy returned to his unfinished dialogue, now reworking it as an interchange between two interlocutors (I. I., who is asked to define "faith-religion," but instead attempts to define *his own* faith, and K., who challenges I. I. from the point of view of reason). After several pages, Tolstoy stopped, and addressed himself: "I wanted to express the thought that had come to me directly in the form of a dialogue and I got into a muddle" (*PSS* 17: 373). He continued as a diary of sorts, with dated entries, asking, again and again, "Where is the source of faith?" "What am I?" This project, too, was abandoned.

To summarize: for more than three years now, Tolstoy had been trying to elucidate his religious views, or define his *profession de foi*, but all of his attempts (philosophical essays, a catechism, a literary dialogue) came to naught. Strakhov was implicated in most of these attempts, and, perhaps most importantly, he heard Tolstoy's confessional reflections on his struggle to define his faith, his frustration with *Anna Karenina*, his disillusionment with *littérature*, and his depression and despair.

I would suggest that Tolstoy's next attempt was to focus on the notion of "life." But first I will make a digression and introduce a groundbreaking attempt to define one's *profession de foi* that serves as an essential context for Tolstoy's endeavors.

ROUSSEAU AND HIS PROFESSION/CONFESSION

It was, of course, Jean-Jacques Rousseau who had famously confronted the problem of faith in the age of reason, and, placing himself between the two parties of his time – those who relied on reason and those who relied on the church – rejected both. Like Tolstoy after him, he embraced faith and could not stand the materialists.[13] But above all, he insisted that faith was to be found not in the official church, but in the hearts of all men. At a pivotal point in his life, Rousseau decided to abandon literature, and above all "the profession of writer," with all the social falsity it entails.[14] Holding pedagogy in higher esteem, he had embarked on a pedagogical novel, *Émile, ou de l'éducation*, devoting its core part, "Profession de foi du vicaire savoyard," to religion. (When "Profession de foi" appeared in 1762 as part of *Émile*'s volume 4, the whole work was banned.) In "Profession de foi," Rousseau, too, dismissed a lesson of catechism taught by a pedantic priest to children as a "heart-breaking stupidity," and decided to replace it with a confession of personal faith.[15] He, too, asked repeatedly: "What am I?" Rousseau took himself – a sense of his own being – as the fundamental truth and the starting point of reasoning about the world ("I exist").[16]

There is an intimate relationship between Tolstoy and Rousseau. As Tolstoy once said:

I read all of Rousseau, all twenty volumes [...] I more than admired him – I deified him. At age fifteen, I wore a medallion with his portrait around my neck in place of the cross. Many pages by him are so near to me, that it seems that I wrote them myself.[17]

In his *Confession*, Tolstoy mentions reading Rousseau as a formative experience of his early life. While the name of Rousseau does not appear in

Tolstoy's writings on faith from 1875 to 1879, it feels as if some phrases and paragraphs were written by Rousseau himself. Much has been said, and can still be said, on the topic Tolstoy and Rousseau.[18] Here, I will focus on one common concern that they shared: how to tell one's personal faith to others. The issue is not limited to establishing a direct link between Tolstoy and Rousseau. It hardly needs saying that Rousseau – in the "Profession de foi du vicaire savoyard" and in the *Confessions* – provided articles of faith and strategies of self-expression that could be used by generations of modern people, including those who felt a need to reconcile a strong sense of individual being and religious belief – such belief that would not be derived from established religion.

Scholars have long sought the secret of Rousseau's impact in his ingenious use of form, genre, and ways of communicating with the reader. In recent years, Dorothea von Mücke has shown how, in "Profession de foi du vicaire savoyard," Rousseau worked with two established religious genres, profession of faith and confession (merging them into one), with the dialogic form, and with the speaking "I." To summarize a complex argument in brief, she argues that Rousseau's "Profession de foi" achieves both the secularization of religious discourse, replacing it with a conversation about God between friends, and a sacralization of the intimate, confessional dialogue, endowing it with the promise of faith and salvation. This dialogic text invites the reader to enter into a similar dialogue with the author of the novel.[19]

Indeed, carefully situated within *Émile*, the inserted text of the "Profession de foi du vicaire savoyard" is set up as a dialogue: a "young man" is in a conversation with his mentor, the Vicar, who not only entrusts his friend with the profession of his personal faith but also "opens his soul," confessing intimate facts of his life, mainly his relationship to the church, religion, and faith. As the introductory narrative to the "Profession de foi" makes clear, before their decisive conversation the two friends routinely engaged in a reciprocal exchange of confessions. Finally, after the Savoyard Vicar makes his profession (on the side of a high hill), his young friend comes to share his non-canonical faith. A subtle play with the speaking "I" and its autobiographical potential underlies this exchange. The "young man" is the novel's first-person narrator, Émile's tutor, called "Jean-Jacques." The novel does not provide the reader with his confession, but shortly after the publication of the "Profession de foi du vicaire savoyard," in the *Confessions* (started in 1765), the author added a confessional story of his own life – the life of Jean-Jacques Rousseau. I would suggest treating them as twin texts that reinforce each other. It hardly comes as a surprise that many a reader took the "Profession de foi" as a profession of Rousseau's own faith and accepted Rousseau as their spiritual guide.[20]

As Mücke concludes, in the end, Rousseau performed a crucial part of the cultural work that prepared the displacement of religion in favor of an autonomous sphere of art and aesthetics. His "Profession de foi" "reframes the domain of belief in a secular manner," addressing "those questions that cannot be resolved by rational inquiry alone" – the questions of outlook onto the world – in a secular fashion.[21]

Rousseau, of course, had models to follow and to transform. Though in the *Confessions*, as a matter of principle, Rousseau does not acknowledge his predecessors, his title points to the *Confessions* of St. Augustine – a text that also fuses the confessional story of the author's past, sinful, life with the profession of his newly found faith, defining the finer points of early Christian doctrine.[22] An influential scholarly tradition relates Augustine's *Confessions* and Rousseau's *Confessions* to pose the trajectory of autobiography as a form of self-expression. After Augustine, the telling of one's life became linked to confession (in more than one sense – confessing sins and confessing belief) and to conversion. After Rousseau, the story of religious confession and conversion was transformed into a secular autobiographical narrative.[23] And yet, arguably, neither Rousseau's "Profession du foi," nor many of the secular biographical narratives that followed it, have cut all of their ties to the initial Christian pattern.

When, in the 1870s, Tolstoy invited his friend Strakhov to a confessional dialogue in which each was supposed to define his personal *profession de foi*, this whole tradition was at his disposal.[24] Moreover, whatever Tolstoy knew or did not know of this lineage, once his own conversion narrative appeared, soon assuming the title *A Confession*,[25] the link suggested itself: many readers have since mentioned Augustine, Rousseau, and Tolstoy in one phrase. With this in mind, I now return to Tolstoy.

TO WRITE ONE'S LIFE

In the letter of January 27 [?], 1878, Tolstoy sent Strakhov a brief report "On searching for faith" (*Ob iskanii very*). He returned to the initial Kantian questions Strakhov posed in November 1875, reiterated that all three could be easily expressed by one ("What am I?"), and reaffirmed his conviction that "reason did not, and could not, say anything in response." The answers, he said, lay in religion. But when one tried to formulate such answers, they inevitably became "meaningless": "Meaningless simply by virtue of the fact that they are expressed by the word [...] As expression, as form, they are meaningless, but as content, they alone are the truth" (1: 399; January 27 [?], 1878). How, then, to access that "truth" which lies apart from words? People, Tolstoy now claimed, give their answers "not through the word, the instrument of reason [...] but through their whole lives" (1: 399).

Strakhov responded that he could not share Tolstoy's trust in religion (he even found the Gospels unclear) (1: 402; February 3, 1878). Tolstoy sadly acknowledged the difference between them: "I see that my way is not your way" (1: 405; February 7, 1878). Two months later, Tolstoy expressed his disappointment in his friend and fellow traveler: in all this time, Strakhov had not covered much distance on his way to faith (1: 423; April 8, 1878).

Strakhov eagerly admitted his failures: Tolstoy expected something from him (he wrote), but "got nothing." He pictured himself as a man who was "vacillating," "negating," and who remained "incapable of firm belief": "Yes, such am I …" (1: 428; April 11, 1878). Still, he worked hard to search through various views on religion.

To this, Tolstoy responded that it was precisely this immersion in other people's views that was to blame (1: 429; April 17–18, 1878). He unveiled his new method and made another demand on Strakhov – to look for answers in the story of his own life: "You've lived through two thirds of your life. What has guided you, how have you known what is good and what is evil? This is what counts – tell your own self and tell us, without asking what other people say or how they speak" (1: 429). It could be that, like Rousseau in his *Confessions* he thought that "each individual only really knows himself," but, to achieve proper self-knowledge, one had to compare oneself to another.[26]

Strakhov did try to meet Tolstoy's new expectations; first, he rephrased Tolstoy's vague question: "You ask me: how have I lived up to this point?" His answer – which he called his "confession" – focused on his inability to engage actively in life:

Well this is how: I have never properly lived. In the period of greatest development of my powers (1857–67), I didn't so much live as submit to life, yield to temptations; but I was so tormented that then I renounced life [...] I did my service, worked, wrote, all so as just not to depend on others, so as not to be ashamed in front of friends and acquaintances [...] And so the whole time I did not live, but only *accepted* life [...] Here is my confession to you. (1: 432–33; April 25, 1878)

Thus, instead of a confessional story of his life, Strakhov offered a disclaimer: since he has never "lived," there is nothing to tell.

The failure of this exchange, I think, derived from uncertainty about the meaning each of the interlocutors attached to the idea of telling one's life.

In his evasive response, Tolstoy brought up the question of faith: "I hope that we shall be able to discuss the subject of our correspondence in person. In brief, what's strange to me is why you are not a believer. And this is just what I've been saying, though probably awkwardly and not so clearly" (1: 434; May 5–6, 1878). Thus, Tolstoy made clear that his veiled reproaches of the last months concerned Strakhov's failure to embrace religion. Perhaps what he now demanded from Strakhov, in place of his *profession de foi*, was a story of his life-long quest for faith. But Tolstoy was unable (or unwilling?) to put into clear words what it was that he expected. Strakhov realized that he had misunderstood, but decided that his mistake lay in his overly personal approach: "You don't want to continue the conversation […] I'm ashamed that I didn't understand, and turned the question to myself personally" (1: 436; May 14, 1878).

Tolstoy acknowledged: "A strange kind of misunderstanding has arisen between us" (1: 429; May 23–24, 1878). Then, he made another attempt to convey what he wanted: "I keep on at you about something that's tricky: give me a straight answer – how do you know what has guided and what guides you now in life?" (1: 439). Strakhov tried again, in much the same vein as in his first "confession":

You ask what I live by. But, first, I must say that I do not at all live. I've still got pride left, which moves me to serve, dress myself, look after my money […] Then I gain as much leisure as possible, read and keep thinking about that great mystery; you know that I am constantly preoccupied with the question of religion. (1: 441; late May 1878)

In his next philosophical letter, Tolstoy responded to Strakhov's new work, *On the fundamental concepts of psychology* (*Ob osnovnykh poniatiiakh psikhologii*), which was based on his voluminous reading:

Your merit lies in the fact that you have proved that philosophy – thought – cannot, in any manner, serve as the foundation for spiritual life, but your error lies in the fact that you do not admit that it is necessary that these foundations (if foundations are what they are) do exist […] [those foundations which we] cannot possibly gain by reason, or by our very nature, and which are therefore given to us. It is in this sense that I ask you: what do you live by – and you, about the most important thing, say in jest, mistakenly: I do not live. (1: 447; May 29, 1878)

From his insistent reiterations of these vague questions, it transpires that, for Tolstoy, what "one lives by" was faith; it followed that the way to tell one's faith was to tell one's life, and to tell one's life meant to tell a story of one's search for faith.

The next step in their dialogue took place in a face-to-face meeting in August 1878; we do not know what was said. Returning from his visit, Strakhov wrote to Tolstoy that, on his way back from Iasnaia Poliana, he had decided to take up Tolstoy's "challenge" to tell his life, but not as a "biography": "I will write *Instead of a Confession* and dedicate it to you" (1: 458; August 29, 1878).

Two weeks later, Strakhov confirmed his intention to write not-an-autobiography:

But what value, what meaning does my *life* have? [...] In what tone is it to be written? I could, I think, express a feeling of *disgust* most strongly of all:

> And I, repulsed, read the story of my life,
> I shudder and I curse
> I s otvrashcheniem chitaiu zhizn' svoiu
> Ia trepeshchu i proklinaiu

(1: 463; September 14, 1878)

(Strakhov borrows Pushkin's line, from the 1828 poem "Reminiscence" [*Vospominanie*], and therefore also quotes Levin in *Anna Karenina*.) He also affirmed his dependence on a dialogue with Tolstoy as an addressee of his alternative confession: "But I am prepared to write this for you, but for others – I wouldn't see the point" (1: 463). But Tolstoy was in such a troubled mental state – out of touch with his own self – that he could not properly respond to his friend's letter (1: 475; October 27, 1878).

A year later, the two friends were still discussing their shared plan to exchange self-revelations. Tolstoy now clearly defined the task as the writing of two parallel life stories. Echoing Strakhov, he accepted the idea that self-disgust was the most appropriate emotional key for one's life story told for the benefit of the others: "Write your life story; I still want to do the same thing. But we just need to set this up so as to arouse disgust for our lives in all our readers" (2: 540; November 1–2, 1879).

At this point, it would seem, Tolstoy had in mind not a *profession de foi*, but a confession of one's sins and faults. It should be noted that the Russian language encourages the ambiguity: the word *ispoved'* is equivalent to the French word *confession*; the phrase *ispovedanie very* – to the phrase *profession de foi*.

In response, Strakhov, once again, shared with Tolstoy his sense of uncertainty and lack of clear judgment:

It's very hard for me to judge my life, not just the most recent events, but also the most distant ones. Sometimes my life appears vulgar to me, sometimes heroic, sometimes moving, sometimes repulsive, sometimes unhappy to the point of despair, other times joyful […] These oscillations cause me great distress: I can't get any truth from myself! And it doesn't happen just in my reminiscences, but every day in all my affairs. I don't feel anything purely or directly, everything in me splits into two. (2: 541; November 17, 1879)

Tolstoy took Strakhov's ambivalence as an inability to discriminate between good and evil and, I think, ultimately, as a confession of unbelief. He reacted with a strong moral admonition:

You write as if to challenge me. And I know very well that you value my opinion, as I do yours, and so I'll tell you all I think […] The other is more visible than oneself. And I see you clearly. Your letter distressed me greatly. I have felt a lot and thought it over a lot. I think you are spiritually ill […] And it is impossible for you to write your life story. You don't know what is good and what is bad in it. And one needs to know.

But he realized that he might have gone too far: "I don't think I will send this. I am very busy with work for myself, which I will never publish. Forgive me" (2: 545–46; November 19–22, 1879). This letter, indeed, remained unsent. The one Tolstoy sent instead focused on his own ongoing work:

I wrote you a long letter, dear Nikolai Nikolaich, and I am not sending it. I am very busy, and very excited about my own work. Not artistic work and not work for publishing. And your letter saddened and troubled me greatly.

Your letter is not good and your spiritual condition is not good. And it's impossible for you to write your life story. You do not know what is good and what is bad. (2: 547; November 22–23, 1879)

Almost five years had passed since Tolstoy, as he said in his letter of May 5, 1875, had "penetrated" his friend's soul. In December 1879, he reevaluated his initial hopes that an interpenetration of two kindred souls would bring each to a higher state of self-awareness:

I was glad to look into your soul, since you opened it to me; but it has been distressing me that you are so unhappy, so troubled. I did not expect that […] You were not able to say what you have inside, and something incomprehensible came out. But you must not write your life story. You will not be able to. (2: 550; December 11–12, 1879)

So, in the end, Tolstoy's plan of reciprocal professions/confessions failed. Before, he had urged Strakhov to speak out; now, he tried to make him remain silent – on the strength of his conviction that others – himself, specifically – knew Strakhov better than he knew himself.

In the meantime, Tolstoy was intensely immersed in working on his own life story. When Strakhov visited him at Iasnaia Poliana in late December 1879, Tolstoy showed him a manuscript that (scholars believe) contained a preliminary variant of his *Confession*.[27] Whatever it was that Strakhov read, heard, and saw during his visit, when he returned home he affirmed his acceptance of Tolstoy's faith, describing the experience of religious conversion:

Something has as if suddenly dawned on me, and I feel more and more joy and view everything in this new light. I will tell you in all honesty why I was confused earlier, and why your present idea seems so new to me. Individual immortality in the form in which it is usually presented always seemed so incomprehensible and savage to me; in just the same way, the mystical rapture reached by the majority of religious people who talk in almost the same terms as you has always been abhorrent to me. But you have avoided both of these; acute as may be the movements of your soul, you do not seek salvation in self-oblivion or immobilization, but in clear and living consciousness. My God, how good this is! When I remember you, all your tastes, habits, pursuits, when I remember that unfailing, vehemently strong disgust of yours for forms of falsity in life, which resounds through all your writings and is reflected in all of your life, then I begin to understand how you have finally arrived at your present point of view. It could only be attained through strength of the soul, only through that long and arduous work which you have devoted yourself to. Please do not chastise me for praising you; I need to believe in you, this faith is my support. I've long called you the most complete and consistent writer; but above and beyond that, you are the most complete and consistent man. I am convinced of that by my reason and by my love for you; I will hold on to you and hope that I am saved. (2: 552; January 8, 1880)

Tolstoy's faith and – still more – Tolstoy's life, and Tolstoy the person, won Strakhov over: he addressed Tolstoy as his confessor and savior. Tolstoy – a layman – became a kind of holy *starets*, like those whom the two friends had visited in Optina Pustyn'.[28]

As to the work in which Tolstoy was involved at the time, at this point Strakhov alone was taken into Tolstoy's confidence, but (he wrote to Tolstoy) he found a way to tell others without betraying this trust: he would say that Tolstoy was writing a private – unpublishable – "history" of his "relationship to religion."

THE PARTING OF WAYS: TOLSTOY'S *CONFESSION* AND STRAKHOV'S EPISTOLARY CONFESSIONS

Contrary to Tolstoy's repeated claims that he would not publish his ongoing work, in 1882 he submitted for publication (after first reading it aloud to others) the text entitled *Introduction to an unpublished work*

(*Vstuplenie k nenapechatannomu sochineniiu*); within several years, it was circulating under the title *A Confession*. (Though promptly banned, this document did reach readers through illegal distribution.) Now, the general reader took the place that Strakhov had occupied in the "philosophical correspondence" of 1875–79, which had established the dialogic relationship of reciprocity and participation. (After 1879, Tolstoy's letters to Strakhov lost much of their confessional quality.) Tolstoy's *Confession* encouraged the reader to identify with the author (the speaking "I"), using his story – a typical story of a man of his generation and class – as a template for examining his own life and faith. But this is a topic for another study.

And what about Strakhov? In his letters, Strakhov continued to address his "confessions" to Tolstoy: "I will speak as if at confession" (2: 624; November 29, 1881); "I need to address God. And so, I want to confess before you" (2: 994; May 2, 1895). In one of the most elaborate of such confessions, on August 24, 1892, he speaks of his inability to carry his arguments to a conclusion. Strakhov points to a "celebrated precedent" that inspired him to embrace his hesitations. This was Plato: "his conversations do not have definitive conclusions" (2: 911; August 24, 1892). It appears that for Strakhov, a "concourse of thought" (his words), such as a Platonic dialogue, was an unfinished (Bakhtin would say unfinalized) message – "a boundless ocean," and not, as for Tolstoy, an interlinkage of notions into an integral, harmonious whole emblematized by a ball or globe.

Such letters indicate that, their differences notwithstanding, to the end of his days, Strakhov accepted Tolstoy as his confessor and "savior." And yet, in letters to another friend, Ivan Sergeevich Aksakov (one of Tolstoy's critics), Strakhov expressed his skepticism about Tolstoy's theological writings produced after 1880. But even when he wrote in a critical mode, Strakhov drew a distinction between Tolstoy's – poorly written – professions of faith and the man himself, as he knew him in direct and intimate contact:

Everything Tolstoy writes concerning his abstract interpretation of Christianity is *very poorly* written; but his *feelings*, which he is entirely unable to express but of which I have direct knowledge through his facial expression, his tone of voice, his conversations, are imbued with exceptional beauty. There is so much of everything in him; but I am struck, and forever will be struck by his *nature*, the Christian traits of his nature.[29]

Here, Strakhov put his finger on the essence of Tolstoy's struggle with his *profession de foi*: Tolstoy was entirely unable to put it into words. But his "life" – his whole being – carried the message of sin, despair, repentance, faith, and salvation.

CONCLUSIONS

I hope to have shown how Tolstoy's correspondence with Strakhov dramatizes the process of searching for faith and for an adequate definition of a personal faith, enacted in the conversation between the two intimate friends. Though they might have understood each other best in their face-to-face conversations, the correspondence, while retaining some of the immediacy, had the advantage of permanence.

How did Tolstoy (who obviously took the lead) organize and conduct their epistolary conversation and what did he hope to derive from the dialogic form? From the start, he set up an exchange of both philosophical reflections on faith and intimate self-revelations, that is, professions of faith and confessions. He expected Strakhov to validate his (Tolstoy's) ideas by retracing his train of thoughts. The dialogue proceeded slowly and hesitantly, over more than four years. Tolstoy started in the vaguely autobiographical mode (the fragment "I am forty-seven years old"), quickly moved to abstract philosophizing ("On the soul"), ran into a deadlock, and returned to the writing of "life." He would invite his interlocutor to object, then reject Strakhov's objections. Insisting on the truth of his convictions, he accepted the difficulty of expressing them in words. When Tolstoy returned to the autobiographical mode, he also sought help from his interlocutor by urging him to write *his* life. Trying two different modes – writing about "faith" and writing about "life" – Tolstoy might have hoped to come up with a synthetic form. In the end, he posed "faith" as something that both was derived from lived experience and propelled one's life forward. Consequently, to profess one's faith was to tell one's life – not as autobiography, but as a story of one's relations to religion. (Tolstoy did not go so far as to coin the neologism "life-faith," but he came close to posing such an entity.)

In fact, throughout the correspondence, Tolstoy was unclear and imprecise – and not only because he found it difficult to express himself, but also because he believed that religious experience, by its very essence, eluded verbal communication. To describe his situation, I will borrow from Tolstoy's correspondence with another with whom, throughout his life, he discussed questions of religion – his devout cousin Alexandra Andreevna Tolstaia. In February 1880, when his confessional–professional correspondence with Strakhov came to a halt, he wrote to Tolstaia: "to tell one's faith is impossible […] How to tell that which I live by. I'll tell you, all the same." (In the same breath he said: "You told your faith only because you said what the church says.")[30] I suggest that this same paradoxical position manifests itself in Tolstoy's philosophical correspondence with Strakhov in 1875–79.

Their correspondence unfolded at the time when Tolstoy, painfully unable to finish *Anna Karenina*, was eager to abandon *littérature* and the profession of the writer for another sphere, religion, and for another, as yet undefined, personal role. In the end, his interlocutor, Strakhov, helped put Tolstoy in the role of a religious sage, turning Iasnaia Poliana into a monastic habitat, on the model of Optina Pustyn'. The intimate conversation about faith between two friends took the place of religious rites administered by church (the sacrament of confession and the ritual presentation of one's profession of faith). In this sense, Tolstoy seemed to replay what happened in Rousseau's "Profession de foi du vicaire savoyard." But if Rousseau's "Profession de foi" and the *Confessions* had inaugurated (as scholars believe) the new autonomous sphere of art and aesthetics, Tolstoy, after more than a century, tried to do just the opposite. In the late 1870s, Tolstoy tried to return questions about the meaning of individual life – questions that could not be resolved by reason – from the sphere of literature in which the Enlightenment had placed them to that of (reformed) religion. By 1879, Tolstoy was working on a narrative (his future *Confession*) that would fuse the itinerary of personal conversion with the theological formulas of his new faith; in this sense, he turned from Rousseau to Augustine. As his correspondence with Strakhov shows, he was increasingly troubled by the uncertainty of the message delivered by a work of literature and by the freedom literature leaves the reader – to misunderstand or to understand only a part of the story, taking it for the whole. He longed for a form of expression that – while also based on a "system of linkages" – would "convince instantly," as a recital of a *profession de foi*. But in 1879, "faith" was not yet a creed (a formula) for Tolstoy: rather, it was a product of lived experience, presented to readers as a confessional story of his lifelong relations with religion and quest for faith. We know that, in the 1880s–90s, for many of Tolstoy's readers, the intimate intercourse between author and reader encouraged by his *Confession* (and by his subsequent religious writings) would result in conversion similar to that experienced by Strakhov in Iasnaia Poliana in December 1879. The relationship between the writer and the reader held a promise of salvation. This was not *littérature*.

NOTES

1. See *L. N. Tolstoi i N. N. Strakhov: Polnoe sobranie perepiski*, 2 vols. ed. and intro. Andrew Donskov, compiled by L. D. Gromova and T. G. Nikiforova (Ottawa and Moscow: Slavic Research Group at the University of Ottawa and the State L. N. Tolstoy Museum, 2003). The Tolstoy–Strakhov correspondence henceforth is cited in the text from this edition, by volume and page number.

Tolstoy's other texts are cited from *Polnoe sobranie sochinenii*, 90 vols. (Moscow: Khudozhestvennaia literatura, 1928–58); and henceforth cited in the text as *PSS* by volume and page. The author thanks Hugh McLean and Donna Orwin for valuable suggestions and Alyson Tapp for expert translations of the Russian texts.

2. See Donna Tussing Orwin, "Strakhov's *World as a Whole*: A Missing Link between Dostoevsky and Tolstoy," in Catherine O'Neil *et al.*, eds., *Poetics. Self. Place: Essays in Honor of Anna Lisa Crone* (Bloomington, IN: Slavica, 2007), 473–93.

3. For a thorough analysis of the Orthodox institution of *starchestvo*, Optina Pustyn', and Tolstoy, see Pål Kolstø, "Lev Tolstoi and the Orthodox *Starets* Tradition," *Kritika: Explorations in Russian and Eurasian History* 9, no. 3 (Summer 2008): 533–54.

4. From Donskov's comprehensive study, "Leo Tolstoy and Nikolaj Strakhov: a personal and literary dialogue" in the Tolstoy–Strakhov correspondence (1: xiv).

5. The most recent, and best, source on Tolstoy's religious views in the context of his time is Inessa Medzhibovskaya, *Tolstoy and the Religious Culture of His Time: A Biography of a Long Conversion, 1845–1887* (Lanham, MD: Lexington Books, 2008). The author treats Tolstoy's "conversion" as a lifelong engagement with religion.

6. Medzhibovskaya, *Tolstoy and the Religious Culture of His Time*, 162–63, analyzes this letter in detail.

7. The essay "O dushe …" (which is known to us only from a copy preserved in Tolstoy's archive; *PSS* 17: 340–52) and another unfinished fragment from this time, "O budushchei zhizni vne vremeni i prostranstva" (November 1875), have been analyzed by Medzhibovskaya, in *Tolstoy and the Religious Culture of His Time*, 166–67.

8. The complex story of the publication of the novel has been reconstructed by William Mills Todd, "The Responsibilities of (Co-)Authorship: Notes on Revising the Serialized Version of *Anna Karenina*," in Elizabeth Cheresh Allen and Gary Saul Morson, eds., *Freedom and Responsibility in Russian Literature: Essays in Honor of Robert Louis Jackson* (New Haven, CT: Yale University Press, 1995), 162–69.

9. Medzhibovskaya, *Tolstoy and the Religious Culture of His Time*, suggests that Tolstoy was aiming at Metropolitan Filaret's Catechism, which starts "I believe in one Holy, Universal, and Apostolic Church" (174–75 and 193–94 nn. 46 and 48).

10. Medzhibovskaya (*ibid.*) interprets Tolstoy's coinage "religiia-vera" differently (173).

11. For explication of the names, see *PSS* 17: 735–36.

12. The visit to Optina was discussed in the correspondence: see 1: 355 and 349. For a detailed description of this visit, see N. N. Gusev, *Lev Nikolaevich Tolstoi: materialy k biografii s 1870 po 1881 god* (Moscow: Izdatel'stvo Akademii nauk SSSR, 1963), 440–41.

13. I follow Jean-Guehenno, *Jean Jacques Rousseau*, trans. John and Doreen Weightman, 2 vols. (New York: Columbia University Press, 1966), vol. II, 27–28.

14. So Rousseau says in Book Ten of his *Confessions* (describing the year 1759). Guehenno, *Jean Jacques Rousseau*, vol. II, 13–15.

15. From "Profession de foi du vicaire savoyard," cited from *Émile* in Jean-Jacques Rousseau, *Œuvres complètes*, vol. IV (Paris: Pléiade, 1959), 554; hereafter cited as *OC*.

16. *OC* 570. The parallel, of course, is not complete: Tolstoy did not follow Rousseau in claiming his senses as the foundation of truth.

17. A reported conversation (1901); cited from the commentary to *PSS* 46: 317–18.

18. On the parallel between Rousseau's and Tolstoy's religious views, see Hugh McLean, "Rousseau's God and Tolstoy's God," in his *In Quest of Tolstoy* (Boston: Academic Studies Press, 2008), 143–58. Tolstoy's reading of "Profession de foi du vicaire savoyard" in 1852 has been described by Galina Galagan in her *L. N. Tolstoi: khudozhestvenno-eticheskie iskaniia* (Leningrad: Nauka, 1981), 55–58, and by Donna Tussing Orwin in her *Tolstoy's Art and Thought, 1847–1880* (Princeton, NJ: Princeton University Press, 1993), 39–49.

19. For the analysis of Rousseau's "Profession de foi du vicaire savoyard," I am much indebted to Dorothea von Mücke, "Profession/Confession," *New Literary History* 34, no. 2 (Spring 2003): 257–74. Here, I am paraphrasing von Mücke, "Profession/Confession," 266, 267, 270, 272.

20. In describing the set up of the "Profession de foi," I followed von Mücke. I bring in Rousseau's *Confessions* and add the notion of the twin texts.

21. Formulations from von Mücke, "Profession/Confession," 270–72.

22. Arguments connecting Rousseau and Augustine have been summarized by Guehenno, *Jean-Jacques Rousseau*, vol. II, 141.

23. For a prominent example of this scholarly tradition, see Karl Joachim Weintraub, *The Value of the Individual: Self and Circumstance in Autobiography* (Chicago: University of Chicago Press, 1978), 22, 300 and *passim*.

24. I deliberately leave aside the question of when exactly Tolstoy read Augustine. The most recent work on the topic is Alla Polosina, "L. N. Tolstoi i Avrelii Avgustin o pamiati, vremeni i pronstranstve," in Galina Alekseeva, ed., *Lev Tolstoi i mirovaia literatura* (Tula: Iasnaia Poliana, 2005), 65–76.

25. On his first attempt to publish it, in 1882, Tolstoy gave the work the title *Vstuplenie k nenapechatannomu sochineniiu*; it was in the 1884 edition, prepared without Tolstoy's participation, that the work first appeared under the title *Ispoved'*, and, after 1885 Tolstoy himself called it *Ispoved'*. Tolstoy's family and friends, including Strakhov, used the word *Ispoved'* much earlier; see *PSS* 23: 523–24.

26. Guehenno, *Jean-Jacques Rousseau*, vol. II, 298, commented on Rousseau's principle of confession by comparison.

27. Some scholars think that what Tolstoy showed to Strakhov in late December 1879 was a notebook of more than a hundred hand-written pages divided into five chapters: the first chapter uses the biographical "I" to relate the condition of his "soul" at the moment when he looked back at his life and started thinking about his faith; chs. 2 and 3 provide a critique of canonical theology.

In ch. 4, Tolstoy again relates the evolution of his religious thought. Finally, in ch. 5, which occupies three quarters of the notebook, Tolstoy retells – for clarity – all four Gospels. In conclusion, Tolstoy provides his profession of faith and critiques contemporary society from this point of view. It has been suggested that this work contains the core of Tolstoy's future four treatises: *Ispoved'* (*Vstuplenie k nenapechatannomu sochineniiu*) (1879–81; 1882), *Issledovanie dogmaticheskogo bogosloviia* (1879–80; 1884), *Soedinenie i perevod chetyrekh Evangelii* (1880–81), and *V chem moia vera?* (1883–84). To this day, this notebook has remained unpublished. T. G. Nikiforova published the first chapter and described the whole text in L. N. Tolstoy, "<Iskaniia istinnoi very>," in I. Borisova, ed., *Neizvestnyi Tolstoi v arkhivakh Rossii i SShA* (Moscow: AO-Tekhna-2, 1994), 122–30.

28. On Tolstoy's role as a "heterodox *starets*," see Kolstø, "Lev Tolstoi and the Orthodox *Starets* Tradition," 545–49.

29. Strakhov's letter to I. S. Aksakov, December 12, 1884 (archival document). The English translation from Donskov 1. xliv (translation adjusted). For the Russian, see 1: 51.

30. *Perepiska L. N. Tolstogo s gr. A. A. Tolstoi 1857–1903* (St. Petersburg: Tolstovskii muzei, 1911), 329.

CHAPTER 6

The worm of doubt: Prince Andrei's death and Russian spiritual awakening of the 1860s

Ilya Vinitsky

Where has he gone? There. Where? We don't know.
> G. R. Derzhavin. "On the Death of Prince Meshchersky"[1]

Hamlet. Not where he eats, but where he is eaten; a certain convocation of politic worms are e'en at him. Your worm is your only emperor for diet. We fat all creatures else to fat us, and we fat ourselves for maggots. Your fat king and your lean beggar is but variable service, two dishes, but to one table; that's the end.
> William Shakespeare, *Hamlet*

After death there might be chemical life, instead of the [kind of] physical life we have now. In my Father's house are many mansions.
> Leo Tolstoy[2]

In his seminal study *Tolstoy in the Sixties* Boris Eikhenbaum demonstrates how the philosophical and aesthetic doctrines of *War and Peace* are indebted to the ideological environment of its time, particularly the debate over historical forces and the laws of history. In this chapter I connect the psychological (or more precisely, spiritualist) aspects of the novel and concurrent debates of the 1860s concerning the essence of the soul and its existence in the afterlife. These psychological dimensions of the novel are, in turn, intimately related to the historical.

The soul is *the* central concept of Tolstoyan psychologism, in which it is alive and active, possessing a remarkable depth while retaining the capability to reflect the sky. Mercurial and dynamic (a force), both free and subjected to necessity, it is simultaneously autonomous and conditioned by the reality that surrounds it. It grows, flourishes, labors, thinks, seeks, hardens, softens, despairs, suffers, rejoices, and creates worlds (which then collapse only to rise again). The soul strives for happiness and receives God's love. It is located, it would seem, in the heart (as shown by the dying gesture of the old Prince Bolkonsky, who attempts to find a "place" for the soul in his chest). Importantly, it seems capable of endless development, which apparently exists in some unknown form before birth and continues in some unknown form even after the death of the individual.

The complexity of the subject matter and the sheer volume of material make exploring Tolstoyan psychologism within the ideological context of the 1860s a challenge to any scholar. In this chapter, I focus on the famous description of Prince Andrei's dying dream, which Konstantin Leontiev once called, "a crowning achievement in the field of psychic analysis."[3] Drawing on this scene, I will illustrate the ideological context of and the means by which *War and Peace* approaches the theme of the evolution of the human soul, or, as the spiritualists of the time would have put it, the ascent of the soul to the next step on the ladder of existence.

THE BATTLE FOR THE SOUL

In a programmatic article written in 1870, the philosopher Heinrich Struve (1840–1912) wrote: "The question of the independent origin of spiritual phenomena, or, as it is more often called, the existence of the soul, undoubtedly belongs among the most crucial questions of our time."[4] Indeed, in Russian intellectual history the "positivist" 1860s were a period of stormy debates on the soul, its essence, and relationships to the body and the external world; on the border between the material and spiritual worlds; and on the possibility of a scientific (physical, physiological, or psychological) understanding of spiritual phenomena. Other questions included the education (*Bildung*) of the soul, the innermost core of man's intellectual and moral nature, the stages and laws of spiritual/psychological development (or evolution), and the existence, in various aspects, of the soul beyond the grave.[5]

These debates were fueled by a radical materialist critique of Romantic idealism and a growing dissatisfaction with traditional religious worldviews on the part of some members of the intelligentsia. Recent discoveries in the fields of physiology, psychology, and the natural sciences, including Darwinian evolution, were well known in Russia and served as catalysts for them. Although the participants in these debates had different worldviews, one thing united them: the belief in the possibility of creating a "science of the soul" that could respond to questions posed by the new discoveries about the physical world, and simultaneously fulfill the moral demands of the contemporary individual.

The controversy over the status of the soul filled the pages of thick journals in the 1860s. The debate is perhaps best viewed within the context of what George Florovsky termed the "religio-philosophical awakening" of that period.[6] The awakening of the 1860s, with its various "optimistic" (progressive or evolutionary) doctrines about spiritual progress, ranging from post-Hegelian to post-Swedenborgian (Allan Kardec), was intimately related to a mixture of scientific thinking and moral idealism characteristic of the time. Thus, even Dmitry Pisarev, a pronounced opponent of the fantastical and metaphysical, noted that the reincarnational "hallucinations" of the socialist Pierre Leroux were founded on a passionate love for humanity and a belief in its unending perfectibility. Of course, according to Pisarev, all visionaries are insane. But in certain situations their insanity is akin to the ecstatic state of great poets and transformative leaders of humanity, who appear during key moments in human history.

TOLSTOY AND THE "DREADED QUESTION"

Literature and literary criticism played a central role in debates over the soul during this period. Artistic works served as a means for realist writers to declare their truths concerning the human soul in the world. In other words, psychologism (as seen in the works of Balzac, Dickens, George Sand, Hugo, Alexander Herzen, Ivan Turgenev, Ivan Goncharov, and Tolstoy) was understood by Russian critics not so much as a literary method, but as a means for objectively examining the human soul, placing it in its true (i.e., non-Romantic) relationship with social reality (which, naturally, each critic understood in his own fashion, as did the authors themselves). It was precisely in the 1860s that the Russian intelligentsia developed the cult of the writer as a psychologist "in the higher sense," of the writer as a kind of seer of spiritual depths.

In turn, the mystical doctrines of the soul that had become widespread in Russia in the second half of the nineteenth century found their echo in the work of authors who attempted to express the inner world of the individual in moments of a "crisis of faith." It is telling that one of the major themes of Russian Realism is the suffering of the human soul in the material world. The causes of this suffering were varied (social, economic, intellectual, moral), but its essence remains the same: the external world (a provincial town, a village, St. Petersburg, or all of Russia) becomes a ward in a madhouse or a Gothic dungeon, and the suffering protagonist attempts in vain to escape from it. It is no coincidence that the Realist constantly characterizes social reality using words such as "oppressive," "burdensome," "agonizing," "illusive," "miserable," and "dark," and deliverance from the "darkness" is symbolized in images such as "ray," "light," or "(re)awakening."

Tolstoy's psychologism is informed not only by the context of scientific and religious discourses during the "awakening" of the 1860s, but also to a significant degree by a struggle *against* theories that held the soul to be any kind of self-sufficient (or determined) entity and by juxtaposing these theories with literary renditions of the "inner world" of the individual. In one of the drafts to the second (historical) epilogue of *War and Peace*, Tolstoy writes:

Either the individual is free or he isn't; this is the dreaded question that humanity asks itself from the most varied positions and approaches. Physiology, psychology, statistics, even zoology take part in this struggle … some say there is no freedom, and the individual is subordinate to the laws of material … others say there is freedom in the soul, which comprises the free essence of the individual. (*PSS* 15: 231)[7]

According to Tolstoy, the solution to this "dreaded question" is possible if we can reject the conception of the soul as an immobile center:

As had been the case in astronomy [before Copernicus. *I.V.*], so too is it in the *literae humaniores* that all differences in approach are founded on either the acceptance or rejection of an absolute and static unit which serves as the measure for change in phenomena. In astronomy, this was the immobility of the earth, while in the humanities it is the immobility of the human personality (*lichnost'*), of the human soul. In both instances, there was a peaceful continuation of the scientific task of discovering the truth, and a struggle of fear and sorrow at the possible end of that as yet eternal building, that was to collapse upon the acceptance of that portentous truth. In astronomy, truth emerged the victor. In precisely the same way the truth of the fluidity (*podvizhnost'*) of personality will be victorious. (*PSS* 15: 233)[8]

In *War and Peace*, Tolstoy attempts to achieve a "Copernican" solution to the question of the human soul.

REALISTIC SPIRITUALISM

For contemporary critics, *War and Peace* was an apotheosis of the Tolstoyan method of psychological analysis. However, critics viewed the nature and goal of this analysis differently, in accordance with their own understandings of "the relationship of the physical world to the psychic one," as well as their own conceptions of human freedom. The philosopher and critic Nikolai Strakhov saw the novel as an example of "sound" psychological realism, the essence of which entailed "an unusually refined and true depiction of move-ments of the soul" of the novel's characters, an objective analysis of the "human soul," and an unveiling of the immutable laws of human nature. Strakhov juxtaposed this kind of realism with the "photographic" or "critical" realism then dominant in Russian literature. He understood Tolstoy's artistic task as depicting the human soul and life "in its real sense, not in the incorrect forms bequeathed to us by antiquity." Strakhov believed that Tolstoy strove to refute and vanquish all of the idols and phantoms of the past from the reader's consciousness: "Instead of the ideal, we must perceive the real." And the real "is the secret depths of life."[9] Strakhov's philosophical evaluation of Tolstoy's psychologism corresponds with his own understanding of man as the crowning achievement and central mystery of all of creation.[10]

The writer Nikolai Leskov, with characteristic polemical zeal, took issue with Strakhov's "scholastic" reading of Tolstoy in a series of remarks on the recently published fifth volume of *War and Peace*. In them, Leskov maintained that Tolstoy was hardly a realist obsessed with discovering the truth of earthly life, but rather a "spiritualist," capable of revealing to his reader the inner working of the human spirit which is not bound by its earthly existence. As evidence, Leskov drew upon the "truly beautiful and inimitable picture" of Andrei Bolkonsky's death scene.

In his argument, Leskov compares this with two famous scenes from English literature: the dream-vision of Shakespeare's Hamlet (act II, sc. I) and the supernatural "rapture" in Dickens' description of the death of Paul Dombey. Leskov claims that in *War and Peace* the death scene is free of ornamentation, and that all is majestically simple: no angel appears for the soul, nor is death any kind of "eternal sleep." Instead, it signifies a reawakening of the human soul from earthly life to a new one.[11] Leskov writes:

If it is absolutely necessary that we include Count Tolstoy into some category of "-*ists*" (*istov*), wouldn't it be more permissible not to count him among the ranks of the realists (which he has *never* been, not in a single line of his writing), but rather in a completely different category of thinkers, in a different pleiad of writers who understand earthly existence in a completely different fashion than it is understood by whatever coarse or sappy realists currently around?

Thus, for Leskov, the "spiritually inspired Prince Andrei" in facing death ascends "beyond the earthly individual," and, when *it* (death) enters, "the Prince's love for his beloved neither diminishes nor increases, it instead becomes a *different* kind of love, one that no realist could possibly understand."[12] Leskov sees the essence of Tolstoy's spiritualism in Andrei's discovery of the world as a united chain of existence, held fast together by divine love.[13] To elucidate his point further he introduces a citation from Alexei Tolstoy's *Don Juan* (1861), a mystical manifesto of idealist art in an era of sober realism. Prince Andrei, much like Alexei Tolstoy's protagonist, is:

> One link in the infinite chain,
> Which, connected with the entire universe,
> Eternally ascends higher towards the divine.[14]

The mystically inclined Leskov was a passionate individual, and an even more passionate critic. His polemical remarks on Tolstoy undoubtedly reflect his own beliefs and interests: the concept of transcendent love, the transfiguration of the individual upon death, and the "flight" of the spirit from the material prison of the body and the earthly world.[15] Despite Leskov's clear spiritualist bias, his reading of Prince Andrei's death nevertheless gives us an opportunity to consider the possibility of a *literary spiritualism* in Tolstoy, which is centered around the theme of the reawakening of the soul after death to a new kind of life, one that is higher on the ladder of existence than the human condition.

In his remarks written in the 1860s, Leskov noted how Tolstoy's "otherworldly currents" support spiritualist ideas.[16] Indeed, after the appearance of *War and Peace*, Tolstoy's work began to attract spiritualists of various orientations: disciples of Swedenborg and Kardec, "experimental" spiritualists, and, later on, followers of Madame Blavatsky, anthroposophists, and other mystics.[17] Tolstoy's own attitude toward such schools of thought was decidedly negative; he constantly attacked spiritualist beliefs in works such as *Anna Karenina, The Fruits of Enlightenment*, and *Resurrection*. At the same time, he was in constant contact with spiritualists, and showed an interest in their various doctrines concerning death, the reawakening of the spirit, and life beyond the grave. While Tolstoy radically disagreed with most of the tenets of mystical spiritualism, he nonetheless pursued similar goals.

DEATH AS REVELATION

Inessa Medzhibovskaya has correctly noted that "the dead body of Prince Andrei is the only body in the novel that does not induce horror."[18] It may be added that this is also the only moment in the novel where Tolstoy adopts the sentimental/pietistic tradition of depicting a "beautiful death" as opposed to the realist tradition of "La mort comme elle est"[19] or "dirty death."[20] In the former, people gather around the bed of the dying person, lovingly look into his or her eyes, and take in his or her dying words.[21] The death scene of Paul Dombey constitutes a part of this tradition, as Leskov pointed out. In Russian literature, this is a tradition which finds its roots in Karamzin and Zhukovsky, and would continue to be found in later works as well, such as in the death of Iliushechka in Dostoevsky's *Brothers Karamazov*. At the same time, Tolstoy defamiliarizes the traditional *topos* of the scene by including the consciousness of the dying Andrei into the narrative, which gradually builds to a revelation that is rather remote from the sentimental/Christian morals of Dickens or Zhukovsky.

Tolstoy was not the first to depict an inner world of a dying hero in Russian literature; in Romantic poetry the monologue of a dying character (including his vision of death) was commonplace. However, Tolstoy was one of the first who combined the realistic (objective, analytical) manner of depicting the experiences of the soul with poetic, idealistic ones. Andrei's death is shown by Tolstoy to be a revelatory one. Yet this portrayal of death attempts to "fulfill the demands of psychological realism" of the nineteenth century (all can be explained by the progression of disease, hallucinations, etc.).[22] However, as Leskov and many critics and readers of *War and Peace* have noticed, the *essence* of the description of Andrei's death strives to overcome the material realism of his contemporaries.

"The Tolstoian hero," Lydia Ginzburg writes, "exceeds the dimensions of his personality: that is, he functions not merely as a personality but also as someone in whom the laws and forms of life in general are manifest, and through whom they may be cognized. This is the source of those psychological features that transcend the merely personal and that seemed superfluous, that seemed to be mere luxuries of observations to those people who had been raised on the pre-Tolstoian novel."[23] In this sense, Tolstoy's method might best be defined as *transcendental realism* or *realistic spiritualism*.

Leskov juxtaposed Tolstoy's "death drama" with a scene from Dickens. However, the depiction of death as a mystical revelation which departs from church teachings could have French roots, namely, George Sand's *Consuelo* (1861), which Tolstoy knew quite well. In 1865, with work on *War and Peace* in full swing, Tolstoy reread this novel and was sharply critical of it in his diary (*PSS* 48: 63). Tolstoy's irritation (he never liked Sand) is understandable, but the similarities in the literary and spiritualist interests of these two very different writers are evident. Sand's novel relies upon the idea of reincarnation (metempsychosis) which Sand had adopted from the work of her friend, the socialist Leroux, who had written the famous tract *De l'humanité* (1840).[24] According to Leroux, death is a dream that results in a "reawakening" to an eternal life on earth. Past generations reawaken as today's living, and the total evolution of humanity will be the triumph of all those who lived before. Leroux's optimistic philosophy, as has already been mentioned, was well known in Russia (first and foremost through Sand's novels). Tolstoy was likewise familiar with Leroux; Eichenbaum discovered a citation from Leroux in one of Tolstoy's early diary writings.[25]

Consuelo concludes with the "beautiful death" of Count Albert (the mouthpiece for reincarnational ideas in the novel) in the arms of the heroine. This death does not terrify Consuelo, but rather fills her with faith and happiness.

The belief in the transmission of souls had received a strong foundation in her instinctive repugnance towards the idea of eternal punishment after death, and in her Christian faith in the immortality of the soul […] "No," thought she, "the divine spark still lingers, and hesitates to return to the hand which gave it, and who is about to resume his gift in order to send it forth under a renewed form into some loftier sphere. There is still, perhaps, a mysterious life existing in the yet warm bosom; and besides, wherever the soul of Albert is, it sees, understands, knows all that has taken place here. It seeks, perhaps, some aliment in my love – an impulsive power to aid it in some new and heavenly career."[26]

There are essential differences between this scene and Tolstoy's, both in depiction and in the authorial programs that underlie them. Tolstoy's centers on the consciousness of the dying individual (a man, in this case), not the witness of his death (in Sand's novel, a woman). Andrei's revelation remains opaque to his beloved (after the "departure" of the Prince, the shaken Natasha seems to think she has pierced the secret, but the news of Petya's death returns her to life, that is, to a state of non-knowledge).[27] Consuelo's exultation is juxtaposed with the mood of mystical resonance that Tolstoy borrowed from Schopenhauer during his last period of work on the novel.[28] At the same time, the very idea of death as a *happy* awakening into *this* life, as presented in Sand's novel, is close to Tolstoy. Ted Underwood, who has studied the role metempsychosis plays in nineteenth-century novels, correctly notes its importance for the philosophy of history present in *War and Peace*: "[B]y offering itself as an intimation of collective immortality, *War and Peace* gives clear and general expression to a tendency latent in many other mid-nineteenth century works," including those of Sand.[29]

Tolstoy would later elaborate on the idea of immortality as a kind of ascension to new forms of life in his teaching of death (*On Life*, 1886–87) and resurrection (see the eponymous novel of 1899). Most critics have pointed to Herder, Schopenhauer, or Buddhism as sources for Tolstoy's teachings on death as awakening. A. A. Kozlov, a gifted student of philosophy from the end of the nineteenth century, demonstrated the similarities between Tolstoy's teachings on immortality and those of the positivist philosopher Auguste Comte.[30] In particular, he focuses on Leroux's doctrine, which in Tolstoy is "developed and put into the context of a large body of philosophical and religious thought, making it incomparably more grounded."[31] Kozlov notes that readers who want to familiarize themselves with Leroux's theories need only to read Sand's *Consuelo*, who worked on this novel under the deep influence of her friend.

Kozlov's remarks were further developed by the foremost theorist of Russian spiritualism and an active participant in battles over psychology in the 1860s and 1870s, Alexander Aksakov. In his criticism on Tolstoy's last novel, polemically entitled "What Kind of Resurrection Is This? On Tolstoy's *Resurrection*," Aksakov claimed that Tolstoy's thoughts on human immortality were nothing new:

They [Tolstoy's thoughts] were espoused by French socialists with the light hand of Comte. In Pierre Leroux's, *"De l'humanité,"* which appeared more than a half century ago, they were developed particularly brilliantly and in great depth. They are based on the premise that the dualism of body and spirit, of heaven and earth, much like the idea of absolute goodness or absolute sin, is unconditionally false [...] Leroux claims that life is one, that it is both existential and earthly, and essentially eternal. He claims that the individual is immortal; given that he exists, thus he will continue to exist [...] We don't merely picture ourselves as the offspring of those who have already lived, but in essence and in actuality, we ourselves are the generations to come.[32]

Aksakov juxtaposes this philosophy of a false resurrection with his own spiritualist science, which proves with *experimental research* the existence of *psychic facts* of other individualized forms of existence after death: "In light of these facts an experimental metaphysics becomes possible, the likes of which Schopenhauer could have only dreamed about."[33]

WHY "THE HIGHEST"?

Leskov read Andrei's "awakening" from earthly life as an allusion to the religious doctrine on the *ascension* of the individual along the ladder of being: having refused the "Old Testament Adam," Tolstoy's hero nearly enters among the choirs of angels. This is the very same Herderian ladder of being recalled by Pierre Bezukhov in his conversation with Prince Andrei (*PSS* 10: 113; vol. 2, pt. 2, ch. 12).

Tolstoy's rough drafts bear witness to his interest in Herder's philosophy.[34] One of the later excluded scenes of the novel features a discussion between a Captain Tushin and a certain Belkin. While playing chess on the eve of the battle of Schöngrabern, Tushin and Belkin discuss Herder's article on metempsychosis, which first appeared in translation in *Herald of Europe* in 1804. In certain sketches of the scene Prince Andrei plays the role of either participant or observer in the discussion on the transmigration of souls.

We shall allow ourselves to cite a large portion of this discussion, which one might call a strikingly optimistic variation on the Shakespearean themes of the decay and sleep of death.[35]

"No, Herder writes well," said Tushin, "I still believe that my soul was once in a worm, then a frog, then a bird, then in everything else. Now it's in a human body and later it will be in an angel somewhere."

"Yes, but in what kind of angel? You don't know, and that's the nasty bit. Explain that to me."

"Well, he says that the organism …"

"What's an organism?"

"You know, any kind of living, whole thing: a worm, a Frenchman, Sergeant-major Marchenko. An organism is a whole, it can live by and for itself. In any case, every organism transforms into another kind of organism, and the highest kind of organism will go on forever, so that means people won't disappear either, they just become a higher kind of organism."

"All right, so this 'organist' (органист) (he smiled cleverly and pleasantly), this organist becomes something else, but why does it have to be higher? Explain that to me. We've just gotten rid of a bull over there, and you should see the yellow worms that have shown up. Those guys are your organists, they're not any kind of higher angels, but the filthiest organists around. And they're gonna take care of us in the same way. I'll get killed, and within a week those yella fellas will up and eat me?"

Tushin thought for a moment […]

"Yes, you're right […] but you know what, 'fine'. What do you think? You're right, why does it have to be a higher kind of organism? How are we better than dogs or these organists? We're the ones who call them filthy. Maybe it'll be better for us when we're made out of a million worms, or when we become grass. Maybe our lives will be brighter; maybe we'll be smarter. And I'll keep on living and enjoying life, whether I'm grass or a worm. If I become air, I'll rejoice and take flight like the air does. What do I know anyway, maybe it *is* better? Yes, it's got to be better." His eyes shone with tears. Listening to him made Belkin happy.

"You know what else?" continued Tushin, "Why do we all love everything: the grass, a bug, people, and occasionally even that colonel of yours?" (*PSS* 13: 367–8)

It is tempting to call the next part of this dialogue a Tolstoyan response to a moment in *Fathers and Children* where Bazarov, lying in a haystack, talks about the burdock that will grow out of him after his death (pt. 1, ch. 21):[36]

"You remember how back in the day," Tushin said, "when you'd lie in the grass and want to become the grass, or look at a cloud or some water, and it was as if you could become that grass or that cloud … you'd even want to become a worm. You know, be all nice and wiggly, that sort of thing. That's all because we've already been everything. I still think that we've been alive for millions of millions of years and have already actually been all of this."

"Yes, you know yesterday after we got here," said Belkin, "I drank some vodka to warm up and lied down there with the company, fell asleep on my back. Then suddenly it appeared to me that I was standing behind a door and there's something trying to get in from the other side, and that thing is … my death. And I already don't have anything left to hold it back with. It shoved the door open, I fell, and I see that I'm dead. I got so scared that I woke up. I woke up. I said to myself, 'See, you ain't dead'. I was overjoyed."

"Yes," Tushin added, eagerly taking it all in, "One bullet to your noodle, and you'll wake up and see that there's no Marchenko, no troops, nothing at all. You'll just wake up a bunch of young and healthy worms." "Ok, but how do you fall asleep and not wake up again?" (*PSS* 13: 369)

In the final version of the novel this passage finds its way into a number of motifs, uniting various characters in crucial moments: Natasha's peculiar version of metempsychosis,[37] Pierre's Masonic reflections on Herder, Prince Andrei's inner monologue at the moment the grenade explodes ("I love life – I love this grass, this earth, this air"), and his dream about the door. In addition, the words that describe the "flower of love" which begins to grow in Andrei's soul as he listens to Belkin and Tushin entered the new version of the novel in Andrei's dying revelation. Similarly, as we will see in the next section, Herder's idea of higher organisms "absorbing" lower ones is shifted to a scene that takes place after Pierre's capture.[38]

It is true that Tolstoy needed the "Herderian" episode for purposes of historical verisimilitude. But the idea of an ascending ladder of beings, as it is discussed by "people of the 1800s" was topical for the 1860s generation as well. The debates about biological and spiritual evolution were extremely important for Tolstoy himself. Origins of the Herderian strand of thought can be traced to Tolstoy's diary entries at the end of the 1850s. Of particular interest is an entry, dated April 11, 1858, which describes a dream:

I saw in a dream how the door to my dark room suddenly burst open. It gave me a fright. Then the door closed, silently. I was scared, and tried telling myself it was the wind. Someone said to me: "Come here, open up." I went to open the door, but something was holding me back. I wanted to run, but my legs wouldn't move, and I was overtaken by indescribable terror. I woke up, and was happy to have done so. Why was I happy? I regained consciousness, thus losing that which had been in the dream. Can't a man be just as happy in death as I was in waking up? He loses his self-consciousness, some say. But don't I lose that every night when I go to sleep, and go on living nonetheless? What do you lose? Your self? Your sense of individuality? Nothing dies, nothing is individual [...] We call people the highest creatures in existence. But what does higher or lower mean to God? Higher in activity (from our point of view), but lower in happiness, which is the essence of any kind of existence.

Man is not made of a tree, because a tree is happier than a man; rather both tree and grass are made of men.

Nothing dies, and I will never die. For eternity, I'll be happier and happier. Consciousness kills happiness and strength. (*PSS* 48: 75)

The reflections introduced above are most characteristic of Tolstoy's search for ideas from the late 1850s and early 1860s; they serve as a kind of philosophical commentary for the programmatic short story "Three Deaths" (1859) and an anticipation of the later *Strider* (1863, resumed and published 1885). But, as we have seen, the thoughts expressed in Tolstoy's diary in 1858 continued to occupy the writer during his work on *War and Peace* as well. Nor would they cease to occupy him even later. In one of his lengthy notes of 1870, while summarizing Schopenhauer (who also allowed for metempsychosis, or more precisely, palingenesis), Tolstoy demonstrates a skeptical relationship toward the idea of a ladder of being as indicative of an ascension from lower forms to the human individual: "Man is king over all creatures? How so? In the ranks of being there are no gradations. There is infinity, that is, obscurity" (*PSS* 48: 128). An even more radical summation can be found in an entry from November 17, 1873: "After death there might be chemical life, instead of the [kind of] physical life we have now. In my Father's house are many mansions" (*PSS* 48: 67).

"COPERNICAN REVOLT"

So what exactly does Prince Andrei awaken *to*? After his death, Natasha, looking through the door through which he has passed, unsuccessfully attempts to solve the enigma: "Where is he and *who* is he now?" (*PSS* 12: 173–74; vol. 4, pt. 4, ch. 1). Several years later, in his book *On Life*, Tolstoy formulates his philosophy of memory as evidence of the continuation of the lives of those who have died: memories of a dead friend, brother, or beloved create a new, more durable connection between two souls than could have existed if both were alive. Our dear ones continue to act upon us, raising us to their own condition, emanating from a centre that is beyond our earthly comprehension. The departed exists in the living one's consciousness and is represented as being encircled by some kind of invisible, incorporeal atmosphere (*PSS* 26: 411–15). Such a viewpoint can be seen as intending to give solace "to the self," that is, for the self that is still alive and mourning the loss of someone close to it. Characteristically, both Tolstoy's Natasha and Sand's Consuelo refer to their departed beloved as "who" not "what," and Tolstoy even goes so far as to italicize the pronoun. At the same time, there exists an idea of life after death in *War and Peace* (and elsewhere in Tolstoy's work) that takes such a radical form that neither Natasha nor Consuelo is capable of conceiving it: the awakening of "myself" not in any kind of "individual" angel, or in a new individual consciousness, or as a part of humanity at all, but rather as one of the countless phenomena of life in nature.

In the end, Tolstoy places into doubt any possible representation of the human individual as a kind of higher being on the ladder of existence. It was precisely this common image of humanity that had united materialists and spiritualists of the most varied convictions, starting from Plato and Aristotle.[39] In other words, Tolstoy's "Copernican revolt" rejects not only the idea of personal immortality, but also the concept of anthropocentric teleology (theodicy) as a whole.

The figure of Platon Karataev is most often treated as the clearest expression of Tolstoy's idea of a happy liberation from individuality. Likewise, the rejection of homocentrism in the novel can be most clearly seen in the bow-legged dog "of an uncertain colour" who chooses Platon as its master. Lacking name and pedigree, this dog is depicted by Tolstoy as perhaps the happiest being in existence during a time of terrible war and death: "Everything pleased it. Now it would roll on its back yelping with delight, now bask in the sun with a thoughtful air of importance, and now frolic about playing with a chip of wood or a straw" (*PSS* 12: 92; vol. 4, pt. 2, ch. 11). In one of the stranger scenes of the novel, on the eve of Platon's death, Pierre, along with a group of other prisoners, climbs a dirty, slippery mountain road in a rainstorm, while the lilac, bow-legged Grey (as Platon called him) runs merrily along the side of the road. Grey "was merrier and sleeker" than ever before, because "[a]ll around lay the flesh of different animals – from men to horses – in various stages of decomposition, and as the wolves were kept off by the passing men the dog could eat all it wanted" (*PSS* 12: 154; vol. 4, pt. 3, ch. 13).[40] This happy dog feeding on the corpses of animals, horse and human alike, is an echo of Tushin's reflections, which are themselves reworkings of Herder's theory of metempsychosis: "How are we better than dogs or these organists?" In all likelihood, Karataev's corpse would eventually become food for a similar happy mutt.[41]

CONCLUSION

In *War and Peace*, Tolstoy struggled with and eventually rejected various conceptions of the evolution of the soul that had been debated during the "awakened" 1860s. The result of this struggle with the "spirit of the age" was the creation of a kind of *negative pneumatology* equally juxtaposed to materialist[42] and spiritualist doctrines. Tolstoy's theodicy has no room for a Platonic representation of the transmigration of the soul that one would find in the *Timeus*, nor for a Hegelian phenomenology of the spirit, nor for the mystical dualism of Leskov, nor for any enlightened Orthodox spiritualism, such as was discerned by Konstantin Aksakov in Andrei's death scene.[43] There also was no room for Herder's or Kardec's visions of the progress of the soul, nor for the cult of human immortality as propagated by

Sand and Leroux. The materialist Bazarov's metaphysical *toska* (heart-ache), which recognizes one's own worthlessness in an infinite world, is also absent, as is the terror in the face of the metempsychosis of a Buddha or Schopenhauer. Not even that wise, resigned indifference, which Tolstoy attributed to the "truth" of the peasant attitude toward death as in the cases of Eroshka (*The Cossacks*), Platon Karataev, or Nabatov in *Resurrection*, is fully present. The thought that had occupied Tolstoy since the 1850s was that the human soul is merely a unit of the process of life like any other. The laws of this process are unknown, irrespective of whether one is closer or farther from God.[44] At the same time, Tolstoy, *in keeping* with the spirit of the 1860s, clearly attempted to give his philosophy an optimistic outlook.[45] As opposed to the tortured monologue of Shakespeare's Hamlet, whose "dread of something after death" Leskov juxtaposes with the triumphant death scene of Prince Andrei, Tolstoy's best characters are prepared to awaken to a new, unknown, state of existence, but one that is (probably) *happier* than earthly existence, in the form of a cloud, grass, air, or rain, or even in the form of young and healthy worms.

Translated from Russian by Timothy J. Portice.

NOTES

1. G. Derzhavin, *Stikhotvoreniia* (Leningrad: Sopovetskaia literatura, 1957), 55. All translations, unless otherwise noted, are by Timothy Portice.

2. A diary entry, November 7, 1873. *Lev Tolstoi. Polnoe sobranie sochinenii*, 90 vols. (Moscow: Gosudarstvennoe izdatel'stvo "Khudozhestvennaia literatura," 1928–58), 46: 67 (hereafter *PSS*). Henceforth references to Tolstoy's works are by volume and page number to this edition and are noted in the text.

3. K. Leont'ev, "O romanakh L. N. Tolstogo: analiz, stil', veianie: kriticheskii etiud," *Russkii vestnik* 6–8 (1890): 237.

4. *Russkii vestnik* 11 (1870): 435. Struve's article engendered much debate in the journals of the time.

5. On the 1860s polemics regarding the soul, see V. V. Zenkovskii, *Istoriia russkoi filosofii* (Leningrad: Ego, 1991 [reprint of 1948 YMCA Press edition]), vol. 1, pt. 2; Georgii Florovskii, *Puti russkogo bogosloviia* (Paris: YMCA, 1991), pt. 2, 7 ("Istoricheskaia shkola"); Fr. Seraphim Rose, *The Soul After Death: Contemporary "After-Death" Experiences in the Light of the Orthodox Teachings on the Afterlife* (Platina, CA: St. Herman of Alaska Brotherhood, 1994); E. A. Budilova, *Bor'ba materializma i idealizma v russkoi psikhologicheskoi nauke: vtoraia polovina XIX – nachalo XX veka* (Moscow: Izdatel'stvo Akademii nauk SSSR, 1960); M. G. Iaroshevskii, *Istoriia psikhologii* (Moscow: Mysl', 1985); David Joravsky, *Russian Psychology: A Critical History* (Oxford: Basil Blackwell, 1989).

6. Florovskii, *Puti russkogo bogosloviia*, 311.

7. In the final version of the epilogue Tolstoy focuses his critique on materialist (rationalistic) attempts to solve the problem of the soul, which he finds to be one-sided (*PSS* 12: 326).

8. In an earlier draft of the epilogue, Tolstoy writes that this "difficult, painstaking work" in search of a new truth is led by the fields of "zoology (Darwin), physiology (Sechenov), psychology (Wundt), philosophy ([*illegible*]) and history (Buckle)" (*PSS* 15: 233).

9. N. N. Strakhov, "Voina i mir. Sochinenie grafa L. N. Tolstogo. Tomy v i vi," in I. N. Sukhikh, ed., *Roman L. N. Tolstogo 'Voina i mir' v russkoi kritike* (Leningrad: LGU, 1980), 195, 205, 217, 197, 216.

10. As expressed in his book *Mir kak tseloe* (The World as a Whole), 1858–72. See Donna Tussing Orwin, "Strakhov's *World as a Whole*: A Missing Link between Dostoevsky and Tolstoy," in Catherine O'Neil *et al.*, *Poetics. Self. Place: Essays in Honor of Anna Lisa Crone* (Bloomington, IN: Slavica, 2007), 473–93; and also "'Mir kak tseloe' N. Strakhova: nedostaiushchee zveno mezhdu Tolstym i Dostoevskim," *Tolstoi. Novyi vek. Zhurnal razmyshlenii* 2 (2006): 197–221.

11. N. S. Leskov, *Polnoe sobranie sochinenii v 30 tomakh* (Moscow: Terra, 1996–2007), hereafter Leskov, *PSS* 6: 531.

12. Leskov, *PSS* 6: 576.

13. For Platonic idealism as a source of Tolstoy's conception of love, see Donna Tussing Orwin, *Consequences of Consciousness: Turgenev, Dostoevsky, and Tolstoy* (Palo Alto, CA: Stanford University Press, 2007), 63.

14. Leskov, *PSS* 6: 576–78.

15. In the second half of the 1860s Leskov participated in a circle of mystics seriously investigating "spiritism, magnetism, divine inspiration" as well as propagating "the denigration of nihilists." See A. I. Faresov, *Protiv techenii* (St. Petersburg: Tipografiia M. Merkusheva, 1904), 81–82. In his huge antinihilist novel, *At Daggers Drawn* (*Na nozhakh*, 1869–70), Leskov attempted to "overcome" materialism, which he associated with the social Darwinism of contemporary nihilists and the critical realism of left-wing writers. The novel's main protagonist, having been severely wounded in a duel, experiences visions extremely similar to those of Prince Andrei in *War and Peace*. The only significant departures from Tolstoy in Leskov's novel are the vision of the soul leaving the body (which Leskov borrowed from Kardec's *Book of Spirits*) and the fact that the struggle between life and death is resolved in favor of the former.

16. Leskov, *PSS* 8: 439.

17. Tolstoy maintained friendly relations with the ardent spiritualist Nikolai L'vov, who was presented in parodic form in *The Fruits of Enlightenment* (1890). In all likelihood, it was through L'vov's assistance that in 1884 the spiritualist journal *Rebus* was able to publish excerpts from Tolstoy's *Confession*, which had been forbidden by the censor. Proponents of spiritualism (Alexander Aksakov, Alexander Butlerov, Nikolai Vagner) often used examples from Tolstoy's writings in support of their own views. N. P. Vagner even went so far as to visit Tolstoy to attempt to convert him to spiritualist beliefs. Though claiming

to have been "sent by the call of the spirits," Vagner's mission failed. V. Shimkevich, "N. P. Vagner i N. N. Polezhaev. (Iz vospominanii zoologa)," *Zhurnal Ministerstva Narodnogo Prosveshcheniia* 16, no. 7 (1908): 10. In the 1880s and 1890s Madame Blavatsky and her followers considered Tolstoy to be an agent and secret follower of theosophy.

18. Inessa Medzhibovskaya, *Tolstoy and the Religious Culture of His Time: A Biography of a Long Conversion, 1845–1887* (Lanham, MD: Lexington Books, 2008), 94.

19. A chapter title from Balzac's *Le cousin Pons*, in which the protagonist's death is depicted.

20. Philippe Ariès, *The Hour of Our Death*, trans. Helen Weaver (New York: Barnes and Noble, 2000), 565–70. The most classic example of such a "dirty death" is Emma in Flaubert's *Madame Bovary*. In *War and Peace*, the death of the elder Count Bezukhov would also qualify.

21. The motif of looking deep into the eyes of the dying, as presented in the letters and works of Tolstoy, is typical of the Pietistic depiction of a "beautiful death." In one of his articles Leskov, in attempting to prove the verisimilitude of the Tolstoyan depiction of the last thoughts of a dying man, relies upon remarks from a Pietist brochure written by Pastor Rosenstrauch, *At the Bedside of the dying* (*Mittheilungen aus dem Nachlasse*; Russian translation of 1863), in which hundreds of deathbed scenes witnessed by the author are described. It should be remembered that for Tolstoy in the 1860s the Pietistic tradition was seen through the prism of Schopenhauer's thought, who explained the peaceful expression on the faces of the dead as proof that the process of dying was actually a process of awakening from the nightmare that is life.

22. Leont'ev, "O romanakh L. N. Tolstogo," 237.

23. Lydia Ginzburg, *On Psychological Prose*, trans. and ed. Judson Rosengrant (Princeton, NJ: Princeton University Press, 1991), 246–47.

24. The use of reincarnation as a hidden mechanism for driving a novelistic plot appears not only in Sand, but in Gautier (*Spirite*) and Eugene Sue (*Le Juif errant*); and in English literature – in George Eliot's *Daniel Deronda* and the work of Bulwer Lytton. See Lynn Sharp, *Secular Spirituality: Reincarnation and Spiritism in Nineteenth-Century France* (Lanham, MD: Lexington Books, 2006), 23, 56.

25. B. M. Eikhenbaum, "90-tomnoe sobranie sochinenii L. N. Tolstogo. (Kriticheskie zametki)," *Russkaia literatura* 4 (1956): 219.

26. George Sand, *Consuelo*, tome troisième, nouvelle édition (Paris: Michelle Lévy Frères, 1861), 393–94; George Sand, *Consuelo*, trans. Fayette Robinson (New York: Stringer and Townsend, 1851), 250.

27. In the sequel to *Consuelo*, *Comtesse Rudolstadt*, Albert actually does return, his death having been a rather elaborate hoax.

28. On the reflection of Schopenhauer's ideas in Prince Andrei's revelation, see Sigrid McLaughlin, "Some Aspects of Tolstoy's Intellectual Development: Tolstoy and Schopenhauer," *California Slavic Studies* 5 (1970): 198–200.

29. Ted Underwood, "Historical Difference as Immortality in the Mid-Nineteenth-Century Novel," *Modern Language Quarterly* 63, no. 4 (2002): 468.

30. On Kozlov's reading of *On Life* see James P. Scanlan, "Tolstoy among the Philosophers: His Book *On Life* and Its Critical Reception," *Tolstoy Studies Journal* 18 (2006): 61–4.

31. Cited in Boris Eikhenbaum, *Lev Tolstoi: semidesiatye gody* (Leningrad: Khudozhestvennaia literatura, 1974), 253.

32. A. Aksakov, *K chemu bylo voskresat'? Po povodu romana grafa Tolstogo "Voskresenie"* (St. Petersburg: Tipografiia V. Demakova, 1900), 14–15.

33. *Ibid.* 28.

34. On Tolstoy's reception of Herder see G. V. Krasnov, "Filosofiia Gerdera v tvorchestve Tolstogo," in G. K. Krasnov, ed., *L. N. Tolstoi. Stat'i i materialy* (Gorky, 1961), 157–74. In her new book, Lina Steiner discusses the resonance of Herder's ideas on the formation of the self and the spiritual composition of the nation in Tolstoy's epic (in manuscript).

35. For the significance of this scene in Tolstoy's search for the argument of the immortality of the soul, see Patricia Carden, "The Expressive Self in *War and Peace*," *Canadian-American Slavic Studies* 12 (1978): 526–28.

36. One can find the origin of Tolstoy's idea as early as in Eroshka's musings on death in *The Cossacks*.

37. "'If we have been angels, why have we fallen lower?' said Nicholas […] 'Not lower, who said we were lower? … How do I know what I was there?' Natasha rejoined with conviction" (vol. 2, pt. 4, ch. 10; *PSS* 10: 277). Also, see a draft version of this scene in *PSS* 13: 795–96, in which Sonya's soul, as the young people speculate, used to live in a cat before her birth and will reincarnate into a dog after her death. Here and below, translation of the novel by Louise and Aylmer Maude.

38. Carden believes that Tolstoy simply refrained from dealing with "the details about the consuming of one animal by another that had struck his sense of humor" and presented Herder's idea of the ladder of being "in an ennobled and elevated form." Carden, "The Expressive Self," 527.

39. The history of the idea of the ladder of being in the Western tradition from Plato to the Romantic philosophy is traced in Arthur Lovejoy's seminal *The Great Chain of Being: A Study of the History of an Idea* (Cambridge, MA: Harvard University Press, 1936).

40. It should be noted that only in the final version of the novel does the detailed description of the happy-go-lucky Grey exist. It is possible that while reworking this "character" Tolstoy was influenced by Schopenhauer's thoughts on dogs, which, as opposed to humanity, live directly (in the here and now), and do not fear death and individuality. Schopenhauer himself named all his poodles Atma, after the world-soul. See Arthur Schopenhauer, *The World as Will and Idea*, trans. R. B. Haldane and J. Kemp, vol. III (London: Trübner, 1886), 275. Grey's howling after his murdered master might also be connected with Schopenhauer, who believed that a dog is capable of remembering his master for a certain period of time. It is remarkable that soon after Karataev's death, Grey cheerfully goes up to another prisoner and wags his tail upon being petted (*PSS* 12: 159).

41. Rancour-Laferriere observes that "eventually [the dog] becomes a metonym for Karataev." Daniel Rancour-Laferriere, *Tolstoy's Pierre Bezukhov: A Psychoanalytic Study* (London: Bristol Classical Press, 1993), 196.

42. For Tolstoy's years-long struggle with Darwinism, see Hugh McLean's "Claws on the Behind: Tolstoy and Darwin," in *In Quest of Tolstoy* (Boston: Academic Studies Press, 2008), 159–80 (first published in *Tolstoy Studies Journal* 19 [2007]).

43. K. S. Aksakov and I. S. Aksakov, *Literaturnaia kritika* (Moscow: Sovremennik, 1981), 281.

44. Donna Orwin perceptively notes that Tolstoy's novel "contains a system of imagery drawn from nature that symbolizes the different parts of the soul and also joins the soul to nature": rivers, clouds, heavenly bodies. *Tolstoy's Art and Thought, 1847–1880* (Princeton, NJ: Princeton University Press, 1993), 138.

45. Zenkovsky once adroitly characterized Tolstoy's thought as a kind of "optimistically ornamented impersonalism." See *Istoriia russkoi filosofii*, 200. For a study of the polemical dimension of Tolstoy's teaching vis-à-vis Schopenhauer, see McLaughlin, "Some Aspects of Tolstoy's Intellectual Development," who locates the source of Tolstoy's optimism in Rousseau's "belief in the harmony and order of the world" (200).

CHAPTER 7

Tolstoy's spirituality

G. M. Hamburg

Perhaps no aspect of Tolstoy's vast oeuvre is more complicated or controversial than his spirituality. His large fictional narratives from *Childhood* through *Anna Karenina* derive much of their charm and a great deal of their intellectual intensity from his characters' agonized searches for the meaning of life. And from 1879 to his death in 1910 Tolstoy concentrated his attention almost exclusively on spiritual matters. His so-called "spiritual writings" – the "religious philosophical tracts" of the 1880s and 1890s, the compendia of 1903–10, and various fictional narratives, including the last great novel *Resurrection* – spelled out his views on such questions as the ethical content and truth of Christianity, the shortcomings of the Orthodox Church in Russia, the arbitrariness and violence of the Russian state, the hypocrisy and corruption of Russian society, the spiritual bankruptcy of modern ideologies, the meaning of life and death for ordinary Russians, and the common legacy of major world religions. Given the comprehensiveness of his spiritual vision, none of the "vexed questions" haunting Russian public life escaped his attention, yet his answers to these questions, expressed with his trademark erudition and clarity, engendered bitter disagreement. Secular readers like the novelist Ivan Sergeevich Turgenev condemned Tolstoy's spiritual writings for their "reliance on false premises" and their "dark negation of everything vital in human life."[1] On the other hand, the Holy Synod of the Orthodox Church excommunicated Tolstoy in February 1901 for denying eleven Christian dogmas, including the existence of the Trinity, the divinity of Christ, the virgin birth of Mary, and the efficacy of the sacraments.[2] Meanwhile, these same spiritual writings inspired hundreds of intellectuals and common people to adopt the Tolstoyan belief system as the basis for their lives and to persist in that belief well into the Stalinist period.[3]

   This chapter will explore Tolstoy's spirituality by focusing on the spiritual writings of the second half of his life. It will deal with three topics: Tolstoy's religious conversion; his effort to liberate "genuine Christians" from the bonds of social hypocrisy, of the state, and of false religious beliefs; and his idea of Christian self-discipline. The goal is to define Tolstoy's distinctiveness as a religious thinker against the Christian tradition from which he came.

Virtually all Tolstoy's writings from 1879 to 1910 touched on his conversion experience. Inessa Medzhibovskaya has recently argued that the conversion was the result of a long process of thought dating back at least a dozen years.[4] Tolstoy himself considered one of the triggers for the conversion crisis in the late 1870s to be the Russo-Turkish war, which for him posed the problem of whether any major religion could be considered "true."[5] Perhaps that war also reminded Tolstoy of the severe guilt he felt over his actions in the Caucasus as an observer and soldier in the early 1850s during Russia's attempt to put down Iman Shamil's mountain rebellion.[6]

The most famous of Tolstoy's conversion texts was *Confession* (*Ispoved'*) (written 1879–80, published 1882), which described his loss of religious faith by age 18, his embrace of a surrogate religion (belief in social progress), his fall into confusion and despair, and his rediscovery of faith as a guide to life. *Confession* was one of the conversion narratives analyzed by William James in *The Varieties of Religious Experience*.[7] It recounted a personal drama – Tolstoy was caught uncomfortably between old beliefs and new ones, between an old way of life and a new one – during which Tolstoy found himself mired in extreme anhedonia; he then experienced a cathartic transformation in his spiritual condition, as a result of which he accepted a new belief and new way of life, and thus effected an emotionally thrilling exit from existential despair. This conversion experience lacked the finality of many other conversions – for example, Augustine's conversion as presented in *Confession*. In 1879 Tolstoy had yet to define fully his new doctrinal outlook. Still, by that time he *had* decided that the rituals of Orthodox Church life were incomprehensible, and that he could not accept the Orthodox assertion that the non-Orthodox are victims either of falsehood or of heresy. Indeed, by then he already considered Orthodoxy's claim to be the one true Church nothing but a convenient fiction, "a means to enforce compliance with certain human duties" (pt. 15; *PSS* 23: 55). However, still finding much truth in the Church and in the faith of common Russian people, Tolstoy regarded Orthodox teaching as a mixture of truth and falsehood. He promised himself "to find the truth and the lie and to separate the one from the other" (pt. 16; *PSS* 23: 56–57).

What Do I Believe? (*V chem moia vera?*) (sometimes translated as *My Religion*) (written 1883–84, published 1884) returned to Tolstoy's conversion experience, now emphasizing his acceptance of Christian ethics as summarized by Jesus in the Sermon on the Mount. Here the key gospel text was Jesus' injunction, "Resist not evil," which Tolstoy interpreted as the essence of Christian teaching, as a requirement that every Christian unconditionally love others: "Resist not evil means not to resist evil ever – that is, never to commit violence, an act that always contradicts love" (pt. 2; *PSS* 23: 313). Jesus' other ethical demands were read in light of non-resistance. "Be not angry with others" meant to love others as oneself, to accept all human beings as equals. "Take no oaths" was a warning against swearing loyalty to institutions that might enjoin one to violate the command to love others. "Make no distinction between peoples and nations" required "love of everyone without reference to their ethnicity" (pt. 6; *PSS* 23: 365). "Keep to thine own wife" demanded adherence to a mutual vow of loving fidelity. *What Do I Believe?* clarified *Confession* by suggesting that the "truth" in Christianity to which Tolstoy had earlier alluded could be found in the ethics of non-resistance.

On Life (*O zhizni*) (written 1886–87, published 1888) offered a philosophical reflection on conversion from spiritual blindness to a life of faith. It abstracted from conversion the personal element: its focus was the nature of conversion in general rather than an individual believer's peculiar path to God. It cited Jesus' remark to the disciples that human beings "must be born again in spirit," but Tolstoy did not emphasize the need to accept Christian non-resistance so much as the demand that believers subordinate their "animal nature" to "reason." *On Life* depicted spiritual rebirth not as a dramatic event *à la Confession*, but as a slow-dawning awareness of the genuine life force within each human being" (ch. 17; *PSS* 26: 367–68), a process akin to "awakening" from a dream (ch. 15; *PSS* 26: 364), in which the source of life is "invisible" to the dreamer (ch. 9; *PSS* 26: 346). For Tolstoy, the "dream" from which rational people must awaken is the tyranny of fleshly desires; the "rational consciousness" or "reason" toward which the enlightened person must ascend is the ordered awareness invoked by the evangelist John in the word "Logos" and found in non-Christians' notions of self-control (chs. 10, 21; *PSS* 26: 347, 379–80). Ordered awareness leads human beings to control their "animal appetites" but also directs them to love others for their own sakes. According to Tolstoy, if one lives one's life rationally – that is, altruistically – then a kind of immortality may be achievable: after death, other people will remember one's "spiritual profile" (*dukhovnyi obraz*). In Tolstoy's opinion, Christ is "immortal" insofar as Christians have internalized his spiritual profile or "soul force," and, in principle, some form of immortality is available to all righteous men and women (ch. 31; *PSS* 26: 415). *On Life*, therefore, translated into philosophical terms the Christian ethical code discussed in *What Do I Believe?*, and it also refashioned Christian notions of personal immortality into a philosophical conception connecting altruism, memory of the good, and soul force.

Christian Teaching (*Khristianskoe uchenie*) (written 1894–96, published 1898) repeated the discussion of spiritual rebirth found in *On Life*, but juxtaposed the Christian idea of spirituality to ideas of spirituality obtaining in other faith traditions. Tolstoy remarked that a major obstacle confronting would-be Christians is the perplexity resulting from their confrontations with a multi-confessional world. This perplexity is a result of conflicting truth claims made by different faith communities, but it is also a result of deliberate and systematic deceptions designed to secure believers' blind submission to a particular confession. Thus, a person seeking faith has to confront Christian "polytheism" (i.e., the doctrine of the Trinity), Jewish "legalism," and the "perversions" of Buddhists, Daoists, and Zoroastrians who had departed from their spiritual masters' original insights. Tolstoy also underlined the "falsity" of Islam, a religion that, according to him, dignified the impossible notion of Muhammad's "flight to the seventh heaven" (pt. 35; *PSS* 39: 153–55).

In later writings, Tolstoy would maintain that all religions uphold the importance of love, and therefore all contribute something of value to the world. Yet he also argued that Christianity had lifted love to a metaphysical principle, "the basis of everything and practically the highest law of human life – that is, a law that allows no exceptions whatsoever." The fact that other faith traditions permit exceptions to the law of love undermines their utility, according to Tolstoy: "As soon as the law of love stopped being the highest, unalterable law of peoples' lives, the entire utility of the law was destroyed, and the teaching about love amounted to nothing but obligatory rhetorical instructions and words leaving the way of life of the nations the same as they had been before the law of love – that is, based on violence."[8]

From the texts cited above, it is possible to draw certain conclusions about Tolstoy's conversion. First, it was both an event and a process: the event (itself preceded by a process of thinking and existential angst) probably occurred as Tolstoy described it in *Confession*; but its full ethical, philosophical, and world-religious implications, as yet unknown to Tolstoy in 1878–79, required many years to ripen into consciousness. Second, Tolstoy regarded both the conversion event and the ensuing conversion process as crucial to his self-understanding. Conversion was not just an episode or even an epoch in his life, but the very essence of it after 1879. Third, Tolstoy thought of his conversion as a model for his followers.

They, too, might experience, by turns, a wrenching personal crisis, an awakening to the Christian law of love, a philosophical insight into the nature of rational consciousness and immortality, and a realization that, in spite of the spirit's oneness, Christianity is superior to all other faith traditions. Fourth, it follows from the first three points that Tolstoy's spirituality cannot be fathomed apart from his conversion. For him conversion was not only the trigger of spiritual thinking after 1879, but the actual unfolding of that thinking. That is why his references to conversion were so frequent, even obsessive: he lived in the wake of a cathartic event and in the midst of an ongoing spiritual awakening, wherein each day promised a new insight.

These conclusions may complicate the old debate among Tolstoy scholars about the existence of one or two Tolstoys – that is, whether Tolstoy's conversion constituted a "break" in his development as an artist and thinker. There are substantial reasons, of course, for rejecting a dichotomous view of Tolstoy: the main editor of the Jubilee Edition of Tolstoy's works, Nikolai Sergeevich Rodionov, passionately embraced the "one Tolstoy" theory,[9] and so has Richard Gustafson, the best American authority on Tolstoy's religion. Gustafson has written that there is no evidence "to suggest the radical shift in attitudes or theoretical understanding many have deduced from *Confession*."[10] Medzhibovskaya's idea that Tolstoy's spiritual transformation was the result of a "long conversion" has the virtue of underlining the continuity of Tolstoy's religious thought while still recognizing that the transformation was something "new" after all. My interpretation of this problem is that Tolstoy was all his life a spiritual seeker, but that *c.* 1878–79 he experienced a psychological "break" from his old convictions consistent with the typology of conversion described by James. For the rest of his life, Tolstoy worked out the implications of this break. In my view, it will not do to pretend that Tolstoy's conversion was nothing but literary artifice or that "nothing happened" to the writer of *Confession* to occasion that narrative.

In his major fiction before 1879, Tolstoy pitilessly exposed social pretension and hypocrisy. *War and Peace* showcased the unseemly struggle for the elder Bezukhov's fortune as the old count lay dying; the cold manipulation of short-sighted Pierre into his first marriage; the dishonesty attendant on adulterous affairs like the ones involving Pierre's first wife Hélène, the seductive but stupid Anatole Kuragin, and the mean-spirited ne'er-do-well Dolokhov; and the preposterous code of honor requiring old Count Ilya Rostov to cover young Nikolai Rostov's gambling debts. *Anna Karenina* dissected hypocrisy in high society from Russia's governing circles to nobles' drawing rooms and beyond. Throughout this early period, Tolstoy showed the profound influence of his intellectual hero, Jean-Jacques Rousseau, whose first discourse underscored the dangers of artifice and of upper-class hypocrisy. It therefore seems unsurprising that, after 1879, Tolstoy's spiritual writings continued in this vein of social criticism. However, the spiritual writings emphasized not so much the fact that wealthy Russians lived unexamined, cynical lives as the underlying pathology generating their social vices.

In *Confession* Tolstoy accused his peers of indifference to religion (pt. 1; *PSS* 23: 1–2), of selfishness and self-deception (pt. 10; *PSS* 23: 38), and of blindness to the virtues of common toilers, who, despite harboring a host of superstitions, managed to live more righteously and less unhappily than their social betters and to experience incomparably greater peace and joy. Tolstoy asserted: "All we rich, educated people are […] truly insane" (pt. 11; *PSS* 23: 42). The educated elites seemed to him not to comprehend that they were "not all of humanity" (pt. 8; *PSS* 23: 31). The elites lived unrighteously because they had asked themselves the wrong question – "Why should I live?" – instead of the right question – "How should I live?" Therefore, they had not built their lives on the rock of faith. According to Tolstoy, "faith is a life force. If a human being lives, then he or she must believe in something […] Without faith it is impossible to live" (pt. 9; *PSS* 23: 35). Thus, for the post-1879 Tolstoy, genuine life was inconceivable without God: "To know God and to live is one and the same thing. God is life" (pt. 12; *PSS* 23: 46).

In *What Do I Believe?* Tolstoy attacked the "false teaching of the world" as a cause of social hypocrisy. In pursuit of material gain, human beings had broken their bonds with nature to live in inhuman cities, given up healthy physical labor for unhealthy bureaucratic routines, disrupted their proper family lives for the sake of sexual flirtations, forsworn easy communication with the laboring classes in favor of the artifice of high society, and surrendered salutary alimentary regimes for addictions of every sort – all the while pretending that the new, irrational modern order represents progress. In reality, Tolstoy argued, the modern social arrangement requires its partisans to commit one "stupidity" after another, whereas following Christ entails precisely "avoiding stupidities" (pt. 10; *PSS* 23: 423). Paradoxically, the educated elites imagined that to leave modern amenities would cause them to suffer, whereas actually these amenities were a source of profound unhappiness, an onerous feature of a life akin to perpetual martyrdom (pt. 10; *PSS* 23: 416).

On Life classified modern societies as death cultures in which human beings operate "without rational explanations for their ways of living," deceive one another about the importance of their actions, and thus assign to these actions "a mysterious significance that they themselves cannot fathom" (ch. 5; *PSS* 26: 337). Modern societies are breeding grounds of conformity wherein individual behavior is susceptible to analysis by crowd psychology. According to Tolstoy, "this complex, seething activity of people, with their commerce, railroads, science and arts, is by and large only the pressure of a mad crowd pressing on the doors of life" (ch. 5; *PSS* 26: 338). On the other hand, the conformist public consists of solipsistic individuals, each crazily hoping that others "will not love themselves but him or her alone" (ch. 18; *PSS* 26: 369). The modern dream of individual bliss, Tolstoy declared, is an illusion, because it generates a competitive war of all against all for resources, because material satisfactions are by nature transient and often destructive, and because individual bliss is inevitably cancelled by the reality of death (ch. 18; *PSS* 26: 370–71).

The Kingdom of God Is within You (*Tsarstvo bozhie vnutri vas*) (written 1890–93, published 1893) argued that Tolstoy's contemporaries suffered from a "pervasive contradiction" between their declared moral values (humane treatment for all, universal brotherhood) and a "life centered on premises directly opposing all this" (pt. 5; *PSS* 28: 93). Thus, government officials think to themselves: "We are all brothers, but I receive a salary taken from poor workers' taxes, and I use this money to support a luxurious lifestyle for idlers and the rich" (pt. 5; *PSS* 28: 94). So, too, educated people experience a contradiction between their intellectual commitments (for example, to reason) and the sordid realities of politics, in which the state budget inevitably supports archaic institutions (such as the Russian imperial court) and immoral ones (the army). At root, Tolstoy's contemporaries were said to suffer from a contradiction between their declared love of humanity and their fealty to murderous institutions. From this contradiction came "a terrible inner tension that drives people of our time to numb themselves by wine, tobacco, opium, cards, the reading of newspapers, trips abroad, and by all types of diversions and spectacles" (pt. 5; *PSS* 28: 104). For Tolstoy in *The Kingdom of God Is within You*, hypocrisy was first a systemic phenomenon, and only second an individual vice.

According to Tolstoy, the state was deeply implicated in the modern culture of death. *What Do I Believe?* implied that the very existence of the state – with its oaths of allegiance, courts and penal system, injurious taxation schemes, armies, wars, and imperial ambitions – contradicted Jesus' command to love one's neighbour. Thus, to follow Christ's message of non-resistance would lead to a revolution more thoroughgoing than anything advocated by Russia's revolutionary parties.[11] In *The Kingdom of*

God Is within You Tolstoy maintained that the state, as an institution, was characteristic of a period in world history "dominated by social collectives," by entities larger than the individual but smaller than humanity. In this period social religions "had exalted the leaders of these collectives (tribal chiefs, ancestors, and political sovereigns) as the sole protectors of the collectives" (pt. 4; *PSS* 28: 69–70). Although the state was a by-product of the process of world historical development and was therefore "logical," it was also an inhumane and therefore irrational institution based on violence. In Tolstoy's view, "government is the application to human beings of the rope, of the chain that binds them or leads them, of the knout that beats them, or of the knife and axe that sever their limbs, nose, ears or head – the application of these instruments or the threat of them" (pt. 7; *PSS* 28: 131). Because they lived under the aegis of the state, modern people found themselves trapped "in a vicious cycle of violence, from which there is no possibility of escape" (pt. 8; *PSS* 28: 152). Tolstoy accused the state of cowing its subjects into submission, of paying officials exorbitant wages at the expense of the poor, of "hypnotizing the people" through the rituals of state religion and "the superstition of patriotism," and lastly of conscripting young men to be soldiers, thereby transforming these "hypnotized, physically strong young people supplied with instruments of murder [into] loyal supporters of the government ready to carry out its orders to commit violence" (pt. 8; *PSS* 28: 152–55). He called on genuine Christians to liberate themselves from this tyranny by refusing to collude with the state in violence. Non-resistance – what we might term "civil disobedience" – "would undermine the government's authority and inevitably lead to the liberation of everyone" (pt. 9; *PSS* 28: 176). Apparently, Tolstoy thought, non-resistance may have the effect of ending the "mass psychosis" induced by the state; it could awaken the people from the hypnotic trance induced by modern institutions.

Christian Teaching explored what Tolstoy called the five "false justifications" for sin, one of which he labeled the "temptation of the state." He observed that pseudo-Christians routinely justified violence by citing the government's authority, thereby shirking moral responsibility for their own deeds: "If I take other people's property, seize their families, execute them, if I kill members of another nation, ruin them, lob artillery shells at the women and children in their cities, I do so not on my own responsibility, but because I follow the will of a higher authority which I swore to uphold for the common good" (pt. 31; *PSS* 39: 149–50). Here Tolstoy interpreted the moral danger of the love of power as a temptation affecting not just high officials or the sovereign, but every person summoned to act in the sovereign's name. In his view, the "temptation of the state" was a modern phenomenon, for only in the modern age did this temptation begin to confront millions of people: "Almost all people living in a modern polity, as soon as they become conscious, find themselves entangled in political temptations" (pt. 49; *PSS* 39: 167). According to Tolstoy, the state was the "cruelest temptation" because it affected children by perverting their instincts from infancy, and because in its name "any measure can be justified, so long as a person supposes that even one life may be [legitimately] sacrificed for the good of the many." The temptation of the state could be overcome only if believers remembered that, "before belonging to any polity or nation, they belong to God as a member of the universal kingdom" (pt. 49; *PSS* 39: 168).

The most serious impediment to genuine spiritual life, according to Tolstoy, was the "pseudo-Christianity" preached by the Orthodox Church. Much of Tolstoy's spiritual writing was a polemic against this "false" faith. In *Critique of Dogmatic Theology* (*Issledovanie dogmaticheskogo bogosloviia*) (written 1880–84, published 1891) he attacked Orthodoxy's "mysterious discourse," in which "words do not have the same meaning they possess in ordinary language but some special meaning whose definition is nevertheless not provided" ("Introduction"; *PSS* 23: 62). He accused Metropolitan Makarii (Bulgakov) of writing nonsense in his catechism,[12] where Makarii attempted to reconcile the unity of God with the doctrine of the Trinity (ch. 5; *PSS* 23: 111). Tolstoy maintained that nothing in the Holy Scriptures even hints at the dogma of Christ's divinity. In his opinion, scriptural references to Jesus as the "son of God" apply not just to Jesus but to all people (ch. 11; *PSS* 23: 172–73). Tolstoy thought it outrageous of Makarii to describe the Church not as a "union of believers" but as a hierarchy with the authority to define doctrine and punish heretics. Tolstoy announced himself an opponent of the clerical hierarchy, of "corrupt, deceptive and ignorant men," to whom he attributed the ambition of controlling all of life ("Conclusion"; *PSS* 23: 296).

In *Harmony and Translation of the Four Gospels* (*Soedinenie i perevod chetyrekh evangelii*) (written 1880–84, published 1892) Tolstoy tried to identify the positive content of the Christian message. He stripped the Gospels of miracles and of Jesus' resurrection, these elements of the narrative being objectionable to him because Church authorities had used them as evidence for their picture of Jesus as the second person of the Trinity. Meanwhile, he sketched his own account of the Scriptures, interpreting God not as a person standing outside and above life, but instead as a presence found inside the natural order and thus within every human being. Jesus' wisdom consisted in a blissful awareness of this presence within himself and in complete self-identification with this presence or spirit. According to Tolstoy, Jesus' awareness of God gave him the inner resources to resist temptation and to master fleshly appetites. In principle, Tolstoy thought, other human beings can also lay claim to such inner resources. In his opinion, the universal accessibility to God's presence and the joy it affords are the "good news" propagated by the evangelists, but the spread of ecclesiastical religion has had nothing to do with this happy message. *Harmony and Translation of the Four Gospels* described the five injunctions of the Sermon on the Mount as the Gospels' core teaching (ch. 4; *PSS* 24: 197–284). However, in the book Tolstoy did not yet attempt to construct a fully elaborated ethical system based on them. He left that task for *What Do I Believe?*

In *What Do I Believe?* Tolstoy claimed that for 1,500 years the Church had interpreted Christ's ethical teaching in the Sermon on the Mount as "good" but "impracticable," as a "difficult" or utopian doctrine. According to Tolstoy, the Church had taught that "Christ's teaching is good for all people, yet unsatisfactory for them," and that earthly life is full of toil, suffering, and death, while the afterlife will bring prosperity, sinlessness, and immortal bliss. In Tolstoy's view, this dogma constituted a "fifteen-hundred-year-old pseudo-Christianity" (pt. 7; *PSS* 23: 377). It was an obstacle to the realization of the kingdom of God on earth; Tolstoy believed that the kingdom of God is within humans' grasp, if only we will love one another as Jesus had advised (pt. 9; *PSS* 23: 402). Tolstoy thought it no accident that the "pseudo-Christian" Church had opposed every measure of social progress from the end of slavery to the abolition of social Estates. He believed that false doctrine now stood in the way of the abolition of private property (pt. 11; *PSS* 23: 440).

In *The Kingdom of God Is within You* Tolstoy depicted the Church as an institution committed to power, an institution sustaining itself through its authority to label its critics as "heretics" and through its self-description as "infallible" (pt. 3; *PSS* 28: 47). He argued that "Churches, qua Churches, have always been and cannot fail to be institutions not only alien to Christ's teaching, but hostile to it" (pt. 3; PSS 28: 54). This was particularly so in Russia, with its despotic union of Church and state. There Orthodoxy "had held people in a condition of vulgar and primitive idol worship," and "had intensified and spread superstition and religious ignorance" (pt. 3; *PSS* 28: 62). Tolstoy addressed the nexus between pseudo-Christianity and the state in *Christian Teaching*, wherein he exposed what he called "the deceptions of faith." He claimed that false justifications for sin, such as the "temptation of the state" mentioned above, would have no authority over people were it not for the perversions of reason that occur in pseudo-religions. False believers teach their adherents "an understanding of life's meaning based not on reason, but on blind credulity" (pt. 33; *PSS* 39: 151). Whatever the confessional community, the deceptions operate in five ways: by deifying religious leaders and sanctifying religious institutions; by investing faith in "miracles"; by putting priestly intermediaries between believers and God; by manipulating the emotions of believers through rituals; and by inculcating false beliefs in children (pt. 33; *PSS* 39: 152–53). The best antidote to this system of deceptions, Tolstoy wrote, was "unperverted reason," that is, a believer's determination to trust his or her own logic rather than "sacred" books or deceptive preachers.

How should we position Tolstoy, a self-described "genuine Christian," within the Christian tradition he claimed to inhabit? As a matter of historical fact, as we noted above, in 1901 the Orthodox Church pronounced Tolstoy a heretic – that is, a deviant from Christian truth – and he accepted the logic of that classification. Already in *The Kingdom of God Is within You* he had observed that there could be no institutional Church without heresy against which to define itself. One should note parenthetically that Tolstoy's criticism of ecclesiastical dogmatism was a rejoinder to Aleksei Khomiakov's famous essay *The Church Is One*, and recognition of his own heterodoxy.[13] But if this consciously heterodox aspect of Tolstoy's relationship to Christianity is clear, other aspects are not.

Tolstoy explicitly associated himself with those teachers of the ancient Church who opposed the use of violence in politics:[14] with Tatian the Assyrian; with Clement of Alexandria, whose *Stromata* enjoined Christians to love their enemies; with Tertullian, whose *Apologeticus* rejected emperor worship and accepted martyrdom as preferable to armed resistance against the Roman state; with Cyprian of Carthage, who embraced martyrdom rather than resist Roman power by force; with Lactantius, whose *De mortibus persecutorum* celebrated the victims of Roman persecution; and with Origen, whose book *De principiis* underlined God's abhorrence at violence. Not every element of Tolstoy's self-drawn religious genealogy is persuasive, however. Although Tertullian, Clement, Cyprian, and Origen suffered persecution for their beliefs, all of them defended dogmatic positions that Tolstoy repudiated in his spiritual writings. And Tertullian was famous among Church Fathers for his vehement opposition to heresy. In the group of Church Fathers recommended by Tolstoy, perhaps Origen, with his somewhat heterodox understanding of the Trinity and his quirky views on the soul, was closest to Tolstoy's sensibility.

If we consider not Tolstoy's self-selected predecessors, but rather his own methods of analyzing Christian teachings – that is, his habit of appropriating portions of the Scriptures as "true" and of ignoring inconvenient passages – then his spiritual writings fit a different genealogy. In terms of method, Tolstoy's earliest predecessor may have been Marcion of Sinope, who rejected the Hebrew Scriptures and all but one Gospel – his own version of Luke. Marcion's near contemporary, Tatian the Assyrian, accepted all four canonic Gospels but "harmonized" them into his own consistent narrative, the *Diatessaron*, just as Tolstoy did 1,600 years later. Many Christian Gnostics rejected the canonicity of the Gospel of John but accepted the validity of the uncanonical Gospel of Thomas. In the sixteenth century Martin Luther rejected the Epistle of James as an uncanonical "straw epistle." In the early nineteenth century Thomas Jefferson composed his own version of the New Testament by discarding everything not said by Jesus, then collating and arranging Jesus' sayings in his own narrative.[15] In our own time, members of the "Jesus Seminar," organized by Robert Funk and John Dominic Crossan, have also disaggregated Jesus' sayings from the rest of the Gospel texts. Like Tolstoy before them, the leaders of the Jesus Seminar have treated certain of Jesus' reported sayings as probably inauthentic. Some members of the Jesus Seminar have seemed less interested in understanding Jesus as second person of the Trinity than in defining him as an ethical guide.

While bearing in mind these figures who took the liberty of discarding portions of the Gospels, amending its texts, or composing their own gospel narratives, one should also take note of the proclivity among certain Christian groups to focus on a single set of Christian teachings as the "true" basis of faith. Among them, the closest in spirit to Tolstoy were perhaps the Franciscan Spirituals of the late Middle Ages, members of the Moravian brotherhood, and certain Russian sectarians whose ethical outlooks derived from the Sermon on the Mount.

Finally, we should take note of Tolstoy's special interest in certain modern thinkers about Christianity. In *The Kingdom of God Is within You* Tolstoy declared his admiration for pacifists, starting with the Bohemian Peter Chelcicky and the English Quakers, the American Quaker William Lloyd Garrison, and the American Unitarian Adin Ballou.[16] In the compendia of 1903 and 1910, Tolstoy often cited Blaise Pascal's *Pensées* and the nonconformist Christian socialist John Ruskin's *Unto This Last*. Both books impressed him deeply. Although the spiritualist Tolstoy took some care to situate himself in the ancient Christian tradition, his connection with these modern thinkers was also real enough.

In general, then, Tolstoy's relationship to institutional Christianity was hostile, but his relationship to the broader tradition of Christian thinking had certain roots in the pacifists of the early and modern periods, in Pascal and Ruskin. Tolstoy's method of spiritual thinking hearkened back to Marcion, Tatian, and Luther, and perhaps to the Franciscan Spirituals. Yet if Tolstoy's thinking was neither entirely original nor idiosyncratic, it was well outside the mainstream of Christian thought on questions of dogma, ritual, and scriptural authority. Tolstoy was a liminal figure, definable as either inside or outside Christianity, depending on the aspect of his spirituality being scrutinized.

Tolstoy's critique of modern society, state, and Church pointed his followers toward the prospect of liberation from social and institutional constraints. In *The Kingdom of God Is within You* he asserted that, in his own lifetime, the final period of history had dawned, a period dominated by "God-centerdness" (*bozheskoe zhizneponimanie*), a way of viewing life which upheld neither the individual nor small collectives, but "the source of eternal, undying life – God" (pt. 4; *PSS* 28: 70). Eventually, he thought, the expansion of love would engulf all humanity, "everything living and existing" (pt. 4; *PSS* 28: 82–84). As this process reached completion, hypocritical modern society, the state, and the institutional Church would disappear. For genuine Christians, this prospect represented a final liberation from darkness, the end of history, the realization of the kingdom of God on earth. However, Tolstoy maintained, real Christians did not have to await the completion of this historical process to secure their individual freedom, for genuine Christianity affords the possibility of individual self-emancipation from the world's deceptions through the process of conversion or "awakening" that Tolstoy himself had undergone. In fact, the liberation of all humanity was to be the consequence of a series of auto-liberations. That was why, Tolstoy argued, "the higher understanding of life undercuts the state [...] Confessing genuine Christianity not only excludes the possibility of recognizing [the legitimacy of] the state, but undermines its foundations" (pt. 10; *PSS* 28: 186).

Tolstoy's Christian anarchism[17] appealed to his followers in at least three ways: it called on the higher angels of their natures to uphold universal love; it described their self-directed liberation from falsehood as an immediately attainable "awakening" from ignorance and a way to avoid the "martyrdom" of modern life; and it portrayed them as the instruments of God's will in history, able to bring down mighty institutions by non-violent means. This heady mixture of altruism and self-emancipation constituted one side of Tolstoyan spirituality. Another, too frequently neglected side of Tolstoy's spiritual vision lay in the iron self-discipline he demanded of himself and other genuine Christians.

Tolstoy's commitment to self-discipline was implicit in his ethics, and therefore was present *in nuce* in his discussion of Christ's five injunctions in *What Do I Believe?* and in his idea of inner awakening. In *The Kingdom of God Is within You* Tolstoy stressed that Christ's teaching "does not govern men by external rules but rather by an inner recognition of the possibility of divine perfection" (pt. 4; *PSS* 28: 78). Christian rules of conduct were not like legislative directives but were rather principles of "another, new, higher understanding of life" (pt. 8; *PSS* 28: 146).

However, the clearest indication of Tolstoy's thinking on Christian self-discipline may be found in his reflections on sin in *Christian Teaching*. Tolstoy asserted that there are three types of sin: "natural" or "innate" sin stemming from our "inherent inclinations" as human beings (Freud would have called these inclinations "drives"); "inherited" or "social" sin stemming from our inherited social status (such as nobiliary rank), from our legally ascribed privileges, or from customary social arrangements (such as the social superiority accorded men over women or the deference accorded to the wealthy by the poor or the myriad privileges afforded the well-educated over the unlettered); and "newly fabricated" (*pridumannye*) or "individual" sin stemming mostly from individuals' idiosyncratic efforts at self-aggrandizement (pt. 15; *PSS* 39: 131–32). The idea behind this typology of sin was to recognize that human beings are sinful. We are trapped in invidious social environments that vitiate our altruistic instincts, and we can also be inventively evil, if we are not restrained by the discipline of faith. Tolstoy's acknowledgment of human evil is significant, because just at the turn of the century he was attacked for his supposed naïveté on this point by Vladimir Solov'ev in *Three Dialogues*.[18]

Tolstoy expanded his discussion of sins in *Christian Teaching* by dividing them into six cardinal offenses against the law of love: drunkenness (*op'ianenie*), idleness or sloth (*prazdnost'*), immoderate desire or concupiscence (*pokhot'*), avarice or greed (*koryst'*), love of power (*vlastoliubie*), and fornication (*blud*). According to Tolstoy, an unrighteous person cannot rid himself or herself from a life of sin without attacking these sins in a particular sequence. First, one has to rid oneself of drunkenness, by which Tolstoy meant not only the stereotypical "Russian" vice of abusing alcohol but every form of self-intoxication, self-narcotization, or "dulling of the senses" (*odurenie*). Only after banishing intoxicants from our lives can we begin to overcome idleness. Having overcome idleness by accustoming ourselves to constant work, we may discover in ourselves a diminished desire to appropriate others' property, and we may then have less time to fantasize about fornication. After conquering idleness, he argued, we may also do battle against our immoderate desires, a category of vices in which Tolstoy included pleasure-seeking (*udovol'stvie*), the acquisition of goods beyond those necessary for satisfying material needs, and the pursuit of luxuries. He regarded immoderate desire as a sin stemming from inherent drives, from inherited or social sources, but also from the sinner's peculiar fancies (pt. 17; *PSS* 39: 133). After defeating immoderate desire, we may attack our inclination toward avarice. This sin Tolstoy described not as money-seeking per se, but as the pursuit of property: he was at this point in his life committed to the abolition of private property (pt. 19; *PSS* 39: 136).

After overcoming avarice, we may confront our love of power, a vice encompassing any form of competition designed to improve our social position at the expense of others, and thus to secure material or emotional advantages over them. Love of power may stem from personal inclinations or from the desire to maintain inherited privileges (pt. 20; *PSS* 39: 137). Tolstoy regarded love of power as potentially the deadliest of sins, because abuses of power by the individual or the state can so easily destroy human lives.

The final sin to overcome was fornication, a vice that Tolstoy viewed in some sense as the sum of the other offenses. It is a means of self-narcotization; it inclines the sinner to idleness; it is a form of immoderation, since it involves unnecessary sexual activity – that is, "sexual relations not for the purpose of procreation" (pt. 21; *PSS* 39: 138); it may entail avarice, since fornication's goal may sometimes be the acquisition of property, or the objectification and commodification of women (in prostitution); and for-nication often involves unequal power relationships, either between male and female, or amongst males (as when a serf owner claimed the right of *primae noctis*). Tolstoy assumed that our lustful desires cannot be eradi-cated, but he believed that the sin of fornication can be "reduced to a minimum" (*doveden do naimen'shei stepeni*) in most people and "virtually eliminated" (*doveden do polnogo tselomudriia*) in the wise minority of genuine Christians (pt. 58; *PSS* 39: 183).

The success of this program of controlling sin depends, according to Tolstoy, upon two prior steps: overcoming the five "false justifications" of sin (the temptations of procrastination, family, utility, partnership or "loy-alty," and the state); and exposing the deceptions of faith. Only after many individual Christians have banished temptations, have exposed the decep-tions of false religion, and have overcome the six sins haunting their lives, will society as a whole be able to dismantle the inherited structures of social privilege standing in the way of the kingdom of God.

Tolstoy's teaching on sin loosely resembled monastic treatises such as those found in the *Dobrotoliubie* (the Russian version of the *Philokalia*) or in the writings of Nil Sorskii, where the success of individual monks and of the entire community rests on self-disciplined avoidance of sin.[19] What is most interesting about Tolstoy's idea of Christian self-discipline, however, is the ways it simultaneously invoked and deviated from established Christian modes of analyzing sin.

Early Christian ideas of sin were elaborated by the Apostles, the Desert Fathers, and their successors. This legacy was systematized by Evagrius and Cassian, who posited the existence of eight capital sins: gluttony (Latin: *gastrimargia*, Russian: *chrevougodie*), lust or fornication (Latin: *fornicationus*, Russian: *blud*), avarice or greed (Latin: *avaritia*, Russian: *srebroliubie*), melancholia (Latin: *tristia*, Russian: *pechal'*), anger (Latin: *ira*, Russian: *gnev*), despair (Latin: *acedia*, Russian: *unynie*), vainglory (Latin: *inanis gloria*, Russian: *tshcheslavie*), and pride (Latin: *superbia*, Russian: *gordost'*).[20] The same eight sins were recorded by Nil of Sinai, Saint Efrem, and St. John Lestvichnik. All these sources were available to Tolstoy in the *Dobrotoliubie* – a handbook to which he often referred.[21] The notion of eight deadly sins became by the fifteenth century a standard trope of the Russian monastic tradition.[22]

Tolstoy's teaching on self-discipline dropped from the Orthodox list of eight cardinal sins melancholia, anger, despair, vainglory, and pride. Perhaps he regarded melancholia and despair as "monkish" vices unlikely to affect "genuine Christians" living outside the institutional Church. On the other hand, he might have expected these sins to be swept away by Christians' attack on idleness, the second in his list of sins. He probably thought of anger as a vice related to love of power, since anger involves putting oneself above others and may lead to attempts to dominate or kill them. By a similar logic, he may have regarded vainglory and pride as forms of love of power. Psychologically, the deletion of melancholia and despair from the list of deadly sins is telling in view of Tolstoy's own suicidal darkness *c.* 1878: by the mid-1890s, when he was writing *Christian Teaching*, he had apparently "overcome" his earlier inclination to suicidal depression. His decision to drop anger from the list of deadly sins is surprising, whatever its justification in his mind, given its prominence in the Sermon on the Mount. Tolstoy's demotion of pride, traditionally regarded by many Christian thinkers as the most serious of the capital sins or even as the root of evil, and his promotion of fornication to the place of ultimate sin were also curious deviations from the eastern Christian tradition. Perhaps as a Russian aristocrat with an imperious character, Tolstoy preferred not to confront his own pride. Although he insisted on wearing peasant clothes, performing manual labor, and learning from peasant wisdom, he retained to the end many traits of the willful lord. The importance he attached to avoiding fornication reflected his fascination with and perplexity over women, not to mention deep shame at his own sensuality.

Tolstoy's thinking about the hierarchy of sins may provide a fruitful perspective for analyzing two of his late fictional narratives – *The Kreutzer Sonata* and *Resurrection*. Both narratives highlighted the dangers of uncontrolled passions and revealed with special clarity the ways that different sinful impulses may cohabit in an undisciplined soul. Both narratives illustrated the connections between fornication (or the fear of it) and love of power. *Resurrection* was, among other things, a novel of spiritual "awakening" depicting an increasingly self-disciplined attack on temptations, spiritual deceptions, and sinfulness.

Before leaving the subject of Christian self-discipline, let us comment briefly on Western teachings about sin. In the West the hierarchy of seven deadly sins took shape between the sixth and twelfth centuries. The key figures here were Gregory the Great, who struck melancholia (*acedia*) from the list of capital sins, and replaced it with envy (*invidia*), and Hugues de Saint-Victor, who is often credited as the Western theologian first to speak of seven sins: lust (*luxuria*), gluttony (*gula*), greed (*avaritia*), melancholy (*tristia*), anger (*ira*), envy (*invidia*), and pride (*superbia*). Both Gregory and Hugues classified pride as the "root of all evil" – a position accepted by many, but not all Western spiritual writers thereafter. In the West, anger and pride, two sins left out of Tolstoy's list in *Christian Teaching*, drew the worried attention of religious commentators because these sins were understood to be closely related to violence and therefore to be dangerous to existing social arrangements.

The most powerful Western literary meditation on the hierarchy of sins was Dante's *Inferno*, a text that can be constructively compared to *Christian Teaching*.[23] In Dante's portrayal, his sojourners in hell encountered, in order of increasing seriousness, the ravages of lust, gluttony, avarice, sloth, heresy, violence, and fraud. Under fraud, this last and most serious category of sins, Dante included sorcery, false prophecy, corrupt politics, fraudulent advice, religious schism, and treachery – each a deliberate transgression against God but also a crime against the existing political order. What Dante, the politician, feared above all was rebellion against God, state, and Church. He was a lover of legitimate authority and thus, in a

Tolstoyan sense, a lover of power. Unlike Tolstoy, the great poet had no difficulty supporting the use of coercion by Church or state, so long as this coercion was exercised to advance salvation and righteous living. However, Dante shared with Tolstoy a hatred of deception, especially the fraudulence in which evil cloaks itself in order to resemble the good. Dante's hatred of imposture led him to abominate all varieties of fraud; the same hatred led Tolstoy to warn Christians against spiritual deceptions and the "illusion" of patriotism.

To some of Tolstoy's most religiously sensitive critics, his spirituality has seemed both primitive and negative in character. William James called him "one of those primitive oaks of men to whom the superfluities and insincerities, the cupidities, complications, and cruelties of our polite civilization are profoundly unsatisfying, and for whom eternal veracities lie with more natural and animal things. His crisis was the getting of his soul in order [...] the escape from falsehoods into what for him were the ways of truth."[24] Dmitrii Sergeevich Merezhkovskii saw Tolstoy's spirituality as a species of nihilism – a rejection of Orthodoxy without a corresponding affirmation.[25] Such criticisms issued from an appreciation of Tolstoy's critique of social conformism, state, and Church, and they are useful in reminding us just how forceful was Tolstoy's social criticism in the eyes of contemporaries. Yet, as we have seen in this chapter, Tolstoy's spirituality was built on the convert's hope of religious "awakening," on the law of brotherly love, on the energy generated by self-emancipation from the "deceptions" of the old pseudo-religion, but also on the fierce disciplining of inner resources needed to sustain a truly Christian life.

Tolstoy's spirituality was liminal with respect to the Christian tradition – simultaneously inside and outside it, depending on one's perspective and on the aspects of his teaching being examined at a given time. He depicted Jesus' ethical teachings as the "truth" of Christianity, reworked the Christian idea of the afterlife into an impersonal doctrine of immortality, and rethought Christian ideas of self-discipline. Meanwhile, he ruthlessly discarded "unnecessary," "irrational," and "mistaken" dogmas as well as the Church's teaching authority. Tolstoy's admission – half-elated, half-rueful – in *What Do I Believe?* that he alone, after 1,800 years, "had discovered the law of Christ as something new"[26] testified to his awareness of his outsider's perspective on received Christian wisdom. His outlook bespoke extraordinary independence of mind, but also a fierce pride that certain defenders of Russian Orthodoxy did not hestitate to label Satanic.

Given Tolstoy's complex attitude toward Christianity, his attitudes toward sectarianism and non-Christian religions should surprise no one.

In his lifetime, he eloquently defended Russian sectarians, especially pacifist groups, against state persecution. He decried government persecution of the Jews. He praised all major religious traditions, Occidental and Oriental, to the degree that they promoted universal love. Yet he was the first to attack superstitions, empty rituals, and religious deceptions by sectarians and non-Christians. To these groups, marginal and often imperiled in Russia, he was a powerful friend but not a comrade in faith.

"Tolstoy," according to his admirer Vasilii Vasil'evich Rozanov, "even granting his terrible and criminal blunders, errors and impudent words, is an *enormous* religious phenomenon, perhaps the greatest phenomenon of Russian religious history in the nineteenth century, however perverse. But a crooked oak is an oak nonetheless, and it cannot be judged by a mechanical institution fashioned by human hands."[27] Rozanov's remark was, of course, a protest against the Holy Synod's decision to excommunicate Tolstoy from the Orthodox Church, but it was also tacit recognition of the difficulty of classifying a strange, complicated, willful figure whose idiosyncratic religious vision, twisting toward the vaulted heavens like the branches of a mighty oak, even today, astonishes.

NOTES

1. See Turgenev's letter to Dmitrii Vasil'evich Grigorovich on October 31 / November 12, 1882, in *Perepiska I. S. Turgeneva v dvukh tomakh*, vol. 1 ed. Konstantin Ivanovich Tiunkin (Moscow: Khudozhestvennaia literatura, 1986), 57.

2. "Opredelenie Sviateishego Sinoda ot 20–22 fevralia 1901 goda. No. 557. S poslaniem vernym chadam Pravoslavnoi Greko-Rossiiskoi tserkvi o Grafe L've Tolstom," in E. F. Fomina, ed., *Za chto Lev Tolstoi byl otluchen ot tserkvi* (Moscow: Izdatel'stvo Dar, 2006), 10–11.

3. See Mark Aleksandrovich Popovskii, *Russkie muzhiki rasskazyvaiut: posledovateli L. N. Tolstogo v Sovetskom Soiuze, 1918–1977* (London: Overseas Publications Exchange, 1983); William Edgerton, ed., *Memoirs of Peasant Tolstoyans in Soviet Russia* (Bloomington, IN: Indiana University Press, 1993); Elena Dmitrievna Meleshko, "Tolstovskie zemledel'cheskie kommuny," in Ruben Grantovich Apresian, ed., *Opyt nenasiliia v XX stoletii: sotsial'no-eticheskie ocherki* (Moscow: Aslan, 1996), 157–66; Meleshko, *Khristianskie etiki L. N. Tolstogo* (Moscow: Nauka, 2006), 251–93.

4. Inessa Medzhibovskaya, *Tolstoy and the Religious Culture of His Time: A Biography of a Long Conversion, 1845–1887* (Lanham, MD: Lexington Books, 2008).

5. See his poignant remark in *Christian Teaching* in Tolstoi, *Khristianskoe uchenie*; *PSS* 39: 118: "The main thing that prevented me from believing [Christian] teaching was that I knew that alongside this Orthodox Christian teaching, which claimed it was alone in truth, there were the Christian Catholic teaching,

the Lutheran and Reformed teaching, and all the other various Christian teachings, each of which asserted it was alone in truth; and I knew that, alongside these Christian teachings exist the non-Christian religious teachings – of Buddhism, Brahminism, Islam, Confucianism and so on, each regarding itself as true and other teachings as mistaken. And I could neither return to the faith I had learned since childhood nor believe in any of those confessed by other peoples, because they all had one and the same contradictions, illogic, miracles, rejection of the faiths of others, and – the main thing, deception, the demand of blind adherence to their teaching." All translations in this chapter, unless otherwise noted, are my own.

6. This is my argument in the commentary essay, "War of Worlds," in Thomas Sanders, Ernest Tucker, and Gary Hamburg, eds., *Russian-Muslim Confrontation in the Caucasus, 1829–1859* (London and New York: Routledge and Curzon, 2004), 171–238, especially 221–23.

7. William James, *The Varieties of Religious Experience: A Study in Human Nature: Being the Gifford Lectures on Natural Religion Delivered at Edinburgh in 1901–1902*, ed. Martin Marty ([1902] New York and London: Penguin, 1982).

8. Tolstoi, "Zakon nasiliia i zakon liubvi," *PSS* 37: 166, 169.

9. See Lev Abramovich Osterman, *Srazhenie za Tolstogo* (Moscow: Grant, 2002), 109, citation from the diary of Nikolai Sergeevich Rodionov: "Two Tolstoys or one? One Tolstoy! And there is no contradiction!"

10. Richard F. Gustafson, *Leo Tolstoy: Resident and Stranger* (Princeton, NJ: Princeton University Press, 1986), xvi.

11. Tolstoi, *V chem moia vera? PSS* 23: 368–70.

12. Makarii (Bulgakov), *Pravoslavno-dogmaticheskoe bogoslovie*, 3rd edn, 2 vols. (St. Petersburg: Tipografiia "A. Treia," 1868).

13. Khomiakov's essay asserted: "the Church's unity follows inevitably from God's unity […] Its unity is true and unconditional." Khomiakov upheld the truth of "Greco-Russian Orthodoxy" against all "false teachings." See "Tserkov' odna," in A. S. Khomiakov, *Sochineniia v dvukh tomakh, Tom 2, Raboty po bogosloviiu* (Moskovskii filosofskii fond. Moscow: Izdatel'stvo Medium. Zhurnal "Voprosy filosofii," 1994) 5, 23.

14. Tolstoi, "Zakon nasiliia i zakon liubvi," *PSS* 37: 165.

15. Thomas Jefferson, *The Jefferson Bible: The Life and Morals of Jesus of Nazareth* (New York: Holt, 1995).

16. Tolstoi, *Tsarstvo bozhie vnutri vas*, pt. 1, *PSS* 28: 2–18.

17. For a short comment on Tolstoy's "Christian anarchism," see Andrzej Walicki, *A History of Russian Thought from the Enlightenment to Marxism* (Stanford, CA: Stanford University Press, 1979), 347–48.

18. Vladimir Sergeevich Solov'ev, *Tri razgovora. 1899–1900*, in *Sobranie sochinenii V. Solov'eva: fototipicheskoe izdanie* (Brussels: Foyer Oriental Chrétien, 1966), vol. x, 81–221. Tolstoy is the model for "The Prince," a character who is pilloried by Solov'ev's spokesman "Mr. Z" in the first two dialogues.

19. On Sorskii's monastic charter, see George A. Maloney, S. J., ed., *Nil Sorskii: The Complete Writings* (New York and Mahnah, NJ: Paulist Press, 2003), 50–120.

20. See Avva Evagriia, "Ob os'mi pomyslakh k Antonii," in *Dobrotoliubie* (Paris: YMCA Press, 1988), vol. 1, 603–5; Sviatoi Ioann Kassian Rimlianin, "Obozrenie dukhovnoi brani," in *Dobrotoliubie* (Paris: YMCA Press, 1988), vol. 2, 21–84. To be more precise, Evagrius actually wrote not about eight cardinal "sins," but about eight "temptations," "illusions," or "veils," which phenomena were classified as "sins" by subsequent Christian writers.

21. Prepobodnyi Nil' Sinaiskii, "Ob os'mi dukhakh zla," in *Dobrotoliubie*, vol. 2, 229–70; "Podvizhnicheskiia nastavleniia Sv. Efrema," in *Dobrotoliubie*, vol. 2, 377–429; "Podvizhnicheskie uroki Sv. Ioanna Lestvichnika," in *Dobrotoliubie*, vol. 2, 515 et seq.

22. Maloney, ed., *Nil Sorskii*, 71–85. On the problem of the eight deadly sins in Orthodox theology, see Aimé Solignac, "Péchés capitaux," *Dictionnaire de spiritualité* (Paris: Beauchesne, 1984), vol. XII, pt. 1, 853–62; and I. Hausherr, "L'origine de la théorie orientale des huit péchés capitaux," *Orientalia Christiana* 30 (1933): 164–75.

23. In *Purgatorio*, Dante offered a different hierarchy of sin. As the poet and his guide Virgil ascend the Mountain of Purgatory, they enter seven terraces, on each of which a certain sin is punished. In ascending order (and in decreasing order of spiritual seriousness), those sins are: pride, envy, anger, sloth, avarice (and its "opposite" prodigality), gluttony, and lust.

24. William James, *The Varieties of Religious Experience*, ed. Marty, 186.

25. D. S. Merezhkovskii, *L. Tolstoi i Dostoevskii*, ed. E. A. Andrushchenko (Moscow: Nauka, 2000), 196–97.

26. Tolstoi, *V chem moia vera? PSS* 23: 477.

27. V. V. Rozanov, "Ob otluchenii gr. L. Tolstogo ot tserkvi," in *Okolo tserkovnykh sten. Sobranie sochinenii*, ed. A. N. Nikoliukin (Moscow: Respublika, 1995), 478; also quoted, without attribution to the primary source, in Aleksei Zverev and Vladimir Tunimanov, *Lev Tolstoi* (Moscow: Molodaia gvardiia, 2006), 573.

CHAPTER 8

Tracking the English novel in Anna Karenina: *who wrote the English novel that Anna reads?*

Edwina Cruise

England merits the title of most *novelistic* country … Nowhere does the novel thrive so readily as in England. Dozens of new novels come out every month.

Fatherland Notes, 1866[1]

Anna […] asked Annushka to bring out a little lamp, attached it to the armrest of her seat, and took a paper-knife and an English novel from her handbag. At first she was unable to read […] and [then] Anna began to read and to understand what she was reading […] Anna Arkadyevna read and understood, but it was unpleasant for her to read, that is, to follow the reflection of other people's lives. She wanted too much to live herself. When she would read about the heroine of the novel taking care of a sick man, she wanted to walk with inaudible steps round the sick man's room; when she would read about a Member of Parliament giving a speech, she wanted to give that speech; when she would read about how Lady Mary rode to hounds, taunting her sister-in-law and amazing everyone with her courage, she wanted to do it herself. But there was nothing to do, and so, fingering the smooth knife with her small hands, she forced herself to read.

The hero of the novel was already beginning to achieve his English happiness, a baronetcy and an estate, and Anna wished to go with him to this estate, when suddenly she felt that he must be ashamed and that she was ashamed of the same thing.

(*Anna Karenina*, pt. 1, ch. 29: 99–100; *PSS* 18: 106–7)[2]

Anna's stormy night train journey is one of the most celebrated passages in Russian literature. It is in this scene that she tries to make sense of her deeply conflicted responses to an encounter the previous evening with Vronsky, her future lover. In his brilliant analysis of Anna's emotional state Robert Jackson writes of "a powerful passion [that] crashes through a barrier of will and conscience."[3] As soon as Vronsky enters Anna's English novel, she puts the book down. Warmed by her own shame, she mentally wrestles Vronsky's image into an insignificant "boy-officer." The text continues: "She smiled scornfully and again picked up the book, but now was decidedly unable to understand what she was reading" (pt. 1, ch. 29: 100–1; *PSS* 18: 107). Anna has read her novel for the last time.

The English novel that Anna reads on the train has not yet been identified by critics, if by that is meant a single novel that includes all four scenes: the heroine walking silently around the bedside of an ailing man; a Member of Parliament giving a speech; Lady Mary boldly riding to hounds, taunting her sister-in-law; and, in the last scene that Anna vicariously inhabits, the hero about to achieve his "English happiness," a baronetcy and an estate, and she – that is, Anna – wishing to join him. To the contrary, these scenes identify tropes that are the ubiquitous baggage of Victorian novels. Take a baronetcy, for example. The destination of hordes of heroes and heroines, played out on the final pages of innumerable English novels, it signals marriage, prosperity, and lifelong happiness. Or the "horsey heroine," often straddling the grey area between respectable and "fast" behavior.[4] In other words – with profound apologies to those who have yearned for the scholar's Eureka – there seems to be no such thing as any "long-lost English novel" waiting to be rediscovered.

The would-be detective like myself who spends years reading obscure, excessively long, and now mostly out-of-print English novels in hopes of tracking down the one specific title that Anna reads will be obliged to concede (as I have) that Anna's novel is Tolstoy's carefully calculated invention, a composite of prototypically English scenes and images, liberally reflected in the English novels that were in fashion in Russia by the 1860s. The pervasive English theme in Tolstoy's novel has been superbly documented by Barbara Lönnqvist.[5] Tolstoy has indeed infused his novel with the compelling aura of contemporaneous English language and culture. Thanks to reading English novels, both Dolly and Anna comfortably use the English word "skeletons" to allude to the guilt that the latter is feeling after the ball (pt. 1, ch. 28: 98; *PSS* 18: 104). Dolly is able to recognize the mirror of fashionable English culture in the furnishings at Vronsky's estate (pt. 6, ch. 29: 616; *PSS* 19: 191). And thanks to that kind of novel reading, first readers of *Anna Karenina* must have had an especially keen appreciation for Tolstoy's interaction with the English novel. These same readers might have noted that the pre-Vronsky Anna has her dresses refashioned, invoking the famous thrift so prized in the Victorian wife (pt. 1, ch. 33: 110; *PSS* 19: 117). And they probably would have rushed to a few English-novel-driven conclusions as soon as they read that Anna calls the crushed railroad worker's death "a bad omen" (pt. 1, ch. 18: 65; *PSS* 18: 70), or, later in the novel, that she has repeated nightmares.[6]

Such impressionistic evidence is not persuasive, of course. The text quoted above, however, contains the most convincing proof that Anna reads more than one novel, and on more than one occasion. The thrice-repeated, iterative verb phrase "when she would read" / "if she read" (*chitala li ona*) marks a habitual pattern of reading, with well-established roots in Anna's psyche.[7] As I see it, and will argue below, whether viewed as a single novel or several novels, a single and exceptional "read" or a pattern of reading, Anna's novel is the reader's "Open, Sesame" to the generic and culture-defining traits of the English novel in Tolstoy's *Anna Karenina*.

With apologies to Henry James, what exactly is this baggy monster of elephantine proportions that we have been calling "the English novel in *Anna Karenina*"? Boris Eikhenbaum defines *Anna Karenina* by reference to the English and French novel: "Initially the novel seems made according to the European model: something on the order of the traditions of the English family novel and the French 'adultery' novel."[8] That sweeping cultural distinction between English and French novels is true in a sense, but not when applied to the English novels that Tolstoy read, i.e., to the novels that most influenced *Anna Karenina*. By the mid-1860s, whether lifted from the French novel or from Dickens, borrowed from stage melodrama or "ripped from today's headlines," English novels reflected the reading public's voyeuristic interest in scandal, crime, and other deviant behavior. These novels, featuring adultery, bigamy, homicide, arson, and sleuthing detectives in the bushes, sold exceptionally well at home and abroad, conspicuously including Russia. It is not possible to imagine Tolstoy's perception of the English novel in the 1860s and early 1870s without including the sensation novel.[9] In an 1864 literary review in *Fatherland Notes* (*Otechestvennye zapiski*) an unnamed critic wrote: "English *belle lettres*, at least some of its representatives, is turning away from its ancient heritage of simplicity and realism, and striving for sensation [...] We have no doubts that the success of sensation novels is a result of the temporary corruption of public taste."[10] The critic dismisses Braddon's latest novel, *John Marchmount's Legacy* (1864), as no better than her earlier novels. S/he much prefers Trollope's latest novel, *Rachel Ray* (1864).[11] Although lower on the artistic totem pole than Eliot's *Adam Bede* (1859) and *Romola* (1863), which the critic describes as "greater than anything that has ever come from the pen of a woman," or William Thackeray, whose best works "are imbued with the most simple and practical every-day philosophy," Trollope nonetheless elicits the critic's praise: "His novels, though they inhabit a more modest terrain, represent common sense and everyday life; they not only engage the reader, they also provide nourishment for the mind."[12] To translate: Trollope eschewed unmotivated and unnatural sensation; he would rather have the scary part be when the heroine gets a chill, or the hero is thrown from his horse. The novels of early Trollope could be left in public rooms in the best of homes.

The number and types of English novels that Tolstoy knew and may have read is enormous. So, in the interests of space and focus, let us discard two heavyweights, Charles Dickens and William Thackeray – not because they didn't write splendid novels in the 1860s, but because their influence on Tolstoy and in Russia came at an earlier period. Let us also lop off novels that Tolstoy might have read before he wrote his provocatively titled *Family Happiness* (1859), a first-person account of a young woman's emotional and moral growth into dedicated and entirely domesticated motherhood. Another good reason for starting with 1859: it marks the approximate time when Tolstoy began making a conscious effort to read English novels in English.[13] And we shall end our inquiry with novels published after December 1872, just three months before Tolstoy began *Anna Karenina*.

And now, the only limitation of real consequence: let's confine the "suspects of interest" to four novelists whom Tolstoy held in high regard; they are – in the order I will discuss them – Anthony Trollope, George Eliot, Mary Elizabeth Braddon, and Mrs. Henry Wood. Trollope was well known in Russia before 1860, whereas Eliot, Wood, and Braddon burst onto the English literary scene in 1859, 1861, and 1862, respectively. Taken as a composite of the English novel, including its sensational aspects, this mismatched quartet profoundly influenced Tolstoy's conception of the English theme in *Anna Karenina*. Their novels are among the primary contributors to the English novel that Anna reads (see Appendix 1).

First readers of *Anna Karenina* had easy access to the contemporaneous English novel that I have circumscribed above. Three different translations of Eliot's maiden novel, *Adam Bede*, for example, were serialized in 1859 in three different Russian journals, within a year of its London publication. In a more typical example, the journal *Fatherland Notes* began serializing Braddon's *Lady Audley's Secret* only three months after its book publication in late November 1862. As one Russian critic half-jestingly complained, "As soon as a critic feels like grabbing his pen to talk about a new novel, just blink, and it's already out in four translations, written by forty hands, published in journals, and sometimes distorted beyond comprehension."[14] Whatever the ideological bias of the leading Russian journals, the editors recognized the commercial advantages of translating "free" (no copyright fees) novels from abroad; it was cheaper to pay for translation than to pay Russian authors for original works. And there were many popular new novels to be had! Between 1859 and 1872 Trollope and Wood each produced over twenty-two novels. Braddon, even with two large broods of children to care for, managed to extrude fourteen major novels during that time. Eliot comes in a distant fourth with a comparatively meager seven titles. With the exception of Wood, who bypassed serial publication in Russia, each of these novelists was well represented in the major journals; all four novelists were translated into Russian for book publication.

As I have mentioned above, Tolstoy preferred to read English novels in English. His extensive library at Iasnaia Poliana contains very few English novels in French or Russian translation. The overwhelming majority of his fiction in English is from the "Collection of British Authors" (COBA) series, created by the Leipzig publisher Christian Bernhard Tauchnitz.[15] Remembered as a brilliant publisher and a devoted Anglophile, Tauchnitz was in his time the single most important purveyor–ambassador of British literary culture around the world. Tauchnitz acquired a loyal following because he paid authors for publication rights outside of the British Empire – an unprecedented gesture in the days before international copyright laws. By 1860 Tauchnitz had achieved a virtual monopoly in the publication and distribution of British literary culture. More to the point for Anna's novel, the Tauchnitz COBA series was widely distributed throughout western Europe, as well as in the capital cities of Russia. Tolstoy shopped in Moscow at J. Deubner Buchhandlung.[16]

The descriptive bibliography of foreign books in the library at Iasnaia Poliana (published in 1999) is essential reading for any sleuth tracking Anna's novel.[17] Even more revealing are the actual English novels that Tolstoy and his family read; once the shock and awe of touching them passes, the Tauchnitz titles on Tolstoy's library shelves have a rich story to tell. The novels of Braddon and Wood show signs of numerous readers; the covers are well-worn, many rebound in her distinctive way by S. A. Tolstaia. Often missing are pages within a volume, or a whole volume from a multi-volume novel. Tolstoy's well-known markings are there – thumb-nail imprints and double folds on page corners – but so are underlinings (not typical for Tolstoy), a child's crayon scribbles, a portrait in pencil, signs of a food stain or two here and there, drops of candle wax, and vocabulary notes in a few languages, especially in the Braddon novels.

This treasure trove of Tauchnitz volumes comes with a few caveats, however. The library is not always a good guide to what Tolstoy read or when he read it. Several novels that we know he read are no longer (or never were) on the shelves.[18] Most conspicuously, the best of Trollope is missing, perhaps a result of Tolstoy's habit of sharing favorite books with family and friends. I suspect that several novels went missing after Tolstoy sent them to his brother Sergei, who lived nearby.[19] It is often difficult to date Tauchnitz volumes: the original date of publication on the title page was never changed for subsequent editions. Lastly, in a few volumes – I did not catch this at first – there are faint signs that double-folded corners, Tolstoy's most common reading signature, have been unfolded and flattened, probably in the process of rebinding.

Having collected the physical evidence from the English novels in Tolstoy's library, I turn to the substantive areas of our investigation: the quartet of novelists themselves, and their contemporaneous reception in Russia and by Tolstoy. Anthony Trollope (1815–82) is the logical place to start. His work as a whole best conforms to Eikhenbaum's definition of the English family novel quoted above, and he was the most popular English novelist in Russia in the early 1870s. He was a frequent topic of conversation, especially in the *European Herald* (*Vestnik Evropy*).[20] Typical of literary criticism at the time, there was often a great deal of retelling and extensive quotation from the novels under discussion; even a reader who only read reviews of Trollope's novels and not the novels themselves would have been familiar with Trollope's trademark traits. As L. Polonsky, foreign-literature critic for the *European Herald* in 1870 wrote in an essay entitled "Sketches of English Society in the Novels of A. Trollope":

There is no truer representative of English society [...] than Anthony Trollope. An artful storyteller, who has described all the layers of high- and middle-class society, a true realist, alien to any sort of unbridled fantasy, a fine observer, not lacking in mellow humor [...] the most popular man of letters, author of a slew of novels, some of which have been translated into Russian.[21]

Trollope's novels served up an affable and confident narrative presence, benign satire, vivid characterizations, and entertaining confirmation of the power of love. He appealed equally to male and female readers. Recognized in Russia especially for his independent and feisty women characters who have a sense of their own self-worth, he was at his best when he worked within the conventional themes of the English novel: social and financial barriers to marriage, a dramatic change in circumstances, leading more likely than not to a marriage or two (or maybe a baby's cry) on the last page, and the expectation of stability and happiness within the domestic sphere. Far from breaking with English-novel conventions, Trollope perfected them. In short, Trollope produced the perfect model of a proper English novel. (By contrast, the final moments of *Anna Karenina*, when Levin realizes that he cannot share his interior life with his wife, threaten the idyll of family happiness.)

Tolstoy's diaries for late September–early October 1865 show an intense period of novel reading, including Trollope's *The Bertrams* (1859), which he did not seem able to put down. There is an often-quoted diary entry by S. A. Tolstaia about her husband dated 1878 (after the book publication of *Anna Karenina*) and the English novel: "I know that when Levochka turns to reading English novels he is near to writing."[22] That is very likely. He also read English novels when he had writer's block. Consider these diary extracts, written at a time when he was feeling out of sorts, and having trouble finishing volume 1, part 2 of *War and Peace* (the first military conflicts):

Sept. 24:	I read *Consuelo* [by George Sand]. What dithering twaddle […]
Sept. 27:	I read that stupid Julia Kavanah. [*sic*][23]
Sept. 28:	Stupid J[ulia] K[avanagh] […]
Sept. 29:	I read Trollope. – If it weren't for the diffuseness. Good.
Sept. 30:	I read Trollope. Good.
Oct. 1:	I'm reading *Bertrams* – Splendid!
Oct. 2:	Trollope slays me with his mastery. I console myself that he has his talent, and I have mine. To know what's my own – or, rather, what's *not mine* – that's the main art.
Oct. 3:	Finished Trollope. Too much convention.

(*PSS* 48: 63–64)[24]

Tolstoy's comment on convention (*uslovnogo*) is puzzling. I interpret Tolstoy's "too much convention" here – at least in part – as a childish swipe at a writer whom he did not want to admire so much. Tolstoy's criticism of *Adam Bede* (see below) seems tainted by the same insecure envy. In fact, *The Bertrams* is not a conventional novel, at least not a conventional Trollope novel. The tasteless Egyptian whirling Dervishes scene in the travelogue part of Trollope's story surely does not register as conventional. While Tolstoy is correct in general – a lot of the same plot complications and literally many of the same characters appear from one Trollope novel to the next – he is wrong in the particulars. *The Bertrams* is an atypical novel, somber, psychological, and focused on suppressed feelings. Trollope's themes – avarice, marriage for money and station rather than love, and the ongoing debates on women's rights – are not so unusual, but the novel's outcome is. On the last page, barriers to marriage finally surmounted, the formerly engaged Caroline and George wed. "But," writes the apologetic storyteller,

Sweet ladies, sweetest, fairest maidens, there were no soft, honeyed words of love then spoken; no happy, eager vows, which a novelist may repeat, hoping to move the soft sympathy of your bosoms. It was a cold, sad, dreary matter, that offer of his; her melancholy, silent acquiescence, and that marriage in Hadley church, at which none were present but Adela, and Arthur, and Miss Baker [...] They now live together, very quietly, very soberly, but yet happily [...] No baby lies in Caroline's arms, no noisy boy climbs on the arm of George Bertram's chair. Their house is childless, and very, very quiet; but they are not unhappy.[25]

The story of Caroline and George, with its denial of a "happily ever after," runs counter to the Trollope pattern. The final image of his paralyzed characters, silent and motionless in a house that is not a home, is disquieting. Nonetheless, overall, Trollope's genius as a storyteller was not preoccupied with innovation; to that extent, Tolstoy is right. What Trollope did do, and that exceptionally well, was to give vivid form to the manners and mores that define what Gertrude Himmelfarb describes as the "Victorian virtues."[26] More to the point, Trollope's corpus provided rich source material for Anna's novel. Trollope wrote the kind of popular, family-oriented fiction that Anna would read, but it is not what Tolstoy himself most enjoyed.

In contrast to Trollope, George Eliot (1819–80) regarded literary convention as a threatening plague. In her 1856 essay "Silly Novels by Lady Novelists," published in the intellectually prestigious *Westminster Review*, Eliot skewered the perfect heroines favored by the burgeoning numbers of lady novelists.

The heroine is usually an heiress [...] with perhaps a vicious baronet [...] in the foreground [...] Her eyes and wit are both dazzling; her nose and her morals are alike free from any tendency to irregularity; she has a superb *contralto* and a superb intellect, she is perfectly well dressed and perfectly religious; she dances like a sylph, and reads the Bible in the original tongues [...] [Men] see her at a ball, and are dazzled; at a flower show, and they are fascinated; on a riding excursion, and they are witched by her noble horsemanship; at church and they are awed by the sweet solemnity of her demeanor. She is the ideal woman in feelings, faculties, and flounces.[27]

Soon after Eliot wrote this piece (she attributed its uncharacteristic bile to a toothache), she began her first fiction, initially serialized, and then published under the title *Scenes of Clerical Life* (1859).

These are three somber sketches, with death a common denominator, in which the narrator is alternately witty, wise, sympathetic, but not sentimental. When Tolstoy read *Scenes* he immediately recognized Eliot's talent. To a favorite relative, A. A. Tolstaia, Tolstoy wrote: "Were you in Russia now, I would send you Elliot [*sic*] *Scenes of clerical life*, but I can only ask you now to read it, particularly 'Janet's Repentance'."[28] Tolstoy continues: "Happy are the people who, like the English, imbibe their Christian training with mother's milk, and in such a high and pure form as evangelical

Protestantism. – Here is a moral and religious book, but I really liked it and it made a strong impression" (*PSS* 60: 300). Tolstoy saw more Christian significance in these sketches than Eliot intended, but what stands out in his assessment is the "I really liked it and it made a strong impression." When and how Tolstoy read *Scenes* is revealing. They appeared anonymously – even the publisher did not know the author's identity – in several installments of *Blackwood's Edinburgh Magazine*, concluding with the November 1857 issue; and then they came out in book form in London in January 1858. Tauchnitz, usually much faster out of the gate, did not negotiate republication rights until late November 1858; *Scenes* came out in the COBA series in February 1859. Nonetheless, since the first Russian translations did not appear until 1860, Tolstoy must have read *Scenes* in English, most likely in the Tauchnitz edition. There is no record that *Scenes* was ever in his library.

Most Russian readers first encountered the yet-unidentified George Eliot by way of *Adam Bede* in 1859, in Russian translation. Tolstoy's often-quoted reaction to *Adam Bede* (below, in italics) in his diary, October 11, 1859, is cryptic, but perhaps less so when read in the context of the whole day's entry:

With each passing day, my moral state gets worse and worse, and already I've almost gotten into my summer rut. I will try to resist. *I've been reading* Adam Bede. *Powerfully tragic, although it doesn't ring true (neverno) and it's full of one thought. There's none of that in me.* The horses are worse and worse. I got angry at Lukyan. (*PSS* 48: 22)

Tolstoy's grouchy mood – his perceived moral failings and anger that his horses were not thriving – is sandwiched around his sketchy take on *Adam Bede*. I suspect that Tolstoy, still on the uncertain threshold of a brilliant career as a writer, may have been in equal measure attracted to and threatened by Eliot's capacious talent. Whatever Tolstoy had in mind by his remarks, W. Gareth Jones has made a good argument that "*Adam Bede* must […] have profoundly influenced Tolstoy's conception of […] *Anna Karenina*."[29]

Not in any doubt is the extraordinary adulation that Russian critics poured on George Eliot after the publication of *The Mill on the Floss* (1860): "The English novel stands first, of course [among foreign novels] […] The triumvirate of Dickens, Thackeray, and Eliot has no rivals."[30] Eliot's major work belonged to the future: *Romola* (1863), *Middlemarch* (1872), and *Daniel Deronda* (1876); nonetheless, her generous, reflective, and probing narrative voice had already captured the Russian propensity for soulful and intellectually charged novels.[31] E. J. Blumberg has made a good case for the influence of *Middlemarch* on *Anna Karenina*, but, as a rule, the study of a single English novel relative to *Anna Karenina* tends to obscure the more consequential connections that several English novels may have to *Anna Karenina*.[32] Quite probably, as S. Knapp has noted, Tolstoy – and Russian readers as well, I would add – were more strongly engaged by the early, less polished, Eliot.[33] Eliot's early, philanthropic focus on the humbly born (somewhat reminiscent of the physiological sketch, a generic corner-stone of early Russian Realism in the 1840s) appealed to the Russian imagination. Whether the early or late Eliot, and Tolstoy's tastes changed over time, she engaged his mind throughout his life in a way that Trollope did not.

The prodigious artistic invention and seriousness of purpose that put Eliot's novels into the category of high culture find no counterpart in the novels of Mary Elizabeth Braddon (Maxwell) (1837–1915), "Queen of the Sensation Novel." She earned that reputation on the basis of *Lady Audley's Secret* (1862) and *Aurora Floyd* (1863), two bigamy novels that *Fatherland Notes* hailed as "the major event of this year's English literary season [...] The success was enormous; there hasn't been one like it since the time of Walter Scott."[34] The following year, however, the same journal had cooled its enthusiasm; while acknowledging that Wilkie Collins[35] and Mistress Braddon were masters of sensation, the critic's condescending tone implied that sensationalism itself was under attack.[36] In 1866, continuing the epigraph that begins this chapter, *Fatherland Notes* wrote its most icy rebuke: "The sensational tone in the novel that is so popular these days has had a significant impact on the decline of taste and common sense."[37]

Mary Elizabeth Braddon was a favorite "read" for the recently wedded Tolstoys. Memoirs attest that Tolstoy, who loved to read aloud, would often read English novels with his wife and family: picture a fun, cozy, family evening, entertainment served up by the happy husband and proud father of the house – and a comic actor of first rank in family theatricals. T. A. Kuzminskaia, who often visited Iasnaia Poliana, recalls of that time: "Sometimes he [her brother-in-law, Tolstoy] would read to us aloud. I remember how he read in translation an English novel by Mistress Braddon – *Aurora Floyd*. He liked this novel and interrupted his reading with exclamations: 'What masterful writers these English are! All these small details portray life!'"[38] Kuzminskaia goes on to record that Tolstoy "half in jest, half-seriously" remarked on her resemblance to the eponymous heroine, Aurora, who enjoys fast riding, elopes with her groom, conceals her bigamy by throwing her blackmailing first husband down a well on her second husband's estate, and considers poisoning her second husband, all this just for starters. Kuzminskaia (proud of her presence in the character of Natasha in *War and Peace*) was amused, but recoiled that Tolstoy would think that she, like Braddon's heroine, would stoop to marry a groom. "Lev Nikolaevich [Tolstoy] had a good laugh and continued to read."[39] Braddon, in short, was a source of merriment and predictable, light-hearted humor in the Tolstoy household. Through the bizarre lens of an English novelist whose early novels portray powerful and calculating women who bring criminal and mental depravity to the mid-Victorian hearth, we are privy to an intimate family gathering in the Tolstoy home. In the mid-1860s, Iasnaia Poliana was an English-novel idyll in the making.

Memoirs are always suspect,[40] but there is confirming evidence of Braddon's role in family gatherings by Tolstoy himself. In an often-quoted letter to his wife, dated December 1864, he wrote: "Yesterday morning I read an English novel by the author of *Aurora Floyd*. I bought ten parts of these English novels not read yet, and I dream of reading them with you" (*PSS* 83: 85). At the time, Tolstoy was in Moscow, recovering from surgery to correct a badly set broken arm; a week earlier his doctors had cautioned him against "even the smallest movement" (*PSS* 43: 383; 83: 61). Imagine, then, Tolstoy hustling around town with his right arm in a cast – furthermore in slippery winter weather – to buy up Braddon's novels as if they were a scarce and highly prized item. He surely would not have done that for Trollope or Eliot, and maybe not even for Mrs. Henry Wood.

What are missing from these snapshots of Braddon at Iasnaia Poliana are the novels that he read *after* her first two wildly popular sensation novels. In the decade before Tolstoy began writing *Anna Karenina*, Tauchnitz published fourteen Braddon novels in the COBA series, six of which are in the Tolstoy library. A turned corner in vol. 2, p. 354, is the only evidence that Tolstoy read *John Marchmont's Legacy*, the novel that he may have purchased in Moscow in December 1864 (mentioned above). Braddon took more time writing this novel than was her custom; responding to the frequent critique that sensation novels placed a higher priority on the action than on the actors, she made a special effort to strengthen characterization. Her most successful character, Olivia Arundel, is a rigidly proper and unsympathetic woman, unrequited in love, yet twice married. At the end of the novel, her jealousy, bitterness, and frustration have morphed into madness. Robert Lee Wolff, a distinguished authority on Braddon, writes about *Legacy*: "The reader encounters no identical twins, no forged wills, few stock properties, and only an incidental corpse. Though the villainy is black indeed, behind it there lies convincing human motivation."[41] The critics were not as generous in their assessments.

Or perhaps Tolstoy bought on that December day Braddon's ambi-tiously serious – i.e., no sensation – adaptation of Gustave Flaubert's *Madame Bovary*, *The Doctor's Wife*, also published by Tauchnitz in 1864. Alas, that title is not on Tolstoy's library shelves – not proof, of course, that he did not read it. Braddon's unhappily married Isabel reads too many romantic novels and falls in love with a local womanizer. Isabel, like Flaubert's Emma, is one of those heroines who uses characters in novels to imagine a life different from and better than her own reality. But Braddon's heroine does not read her way down Pauline's perilous slope to an adulterous liaison; neither does she take her own life. Such a bold infringement of English mores, unlike the faked bigamies of Braddon's first two novels, would have transgressed the impassable Victorian Rubicon of respectability. Wolff writes of this social and ethical line that Braddon could not cross: "Victorian English convention made it impossible for Isabel to follow Emma's example, to run off with Lansdell, or to have an affair with him."[42] One of several novels in which Braddon's heroines rebel against the stultifying life that married women are expected to endure, *The Doctor's Wife* ends with an affirmation of Isabel's spiritual development. She has cast off the novel-induced views of romantic love, and "the chastening influence of sorrow [both her husband and her platonic lover have died] has trans-formed a sentimental girl into a good and noble woman."[43]

And then, of course, there is also *Only a Clod* (1865), *The Lady's Mile* (1866), and *Fenton's Quest* (1871), all in Tolstoy's library. The most interest-ing of these, *The Lady's Mile*, takes its title from the narrow and often crowded bridle path for recreational driving and horse-back riding in London's famously upper-class Hyde Park, a potent symbol for the rigid social code that so constricted the public and private lives of women. In 1864, before the publication of *Mile*, the literary critic for *Fatherland Notes* played an ideological riff on the new English phrase "pretty horsebreakers," characterizing it as a euphemism for high-society playgirls whom "strictly moralistic, puritanical England" used to pretend did not exist.[44]

Evidence that Tolstoy read the more mature Braddon, after 1863, is scanty. What we do know, however, is that he took Braddon seriously as a writer. The September 30, 1865 diary entry quoted above, "I read Trollope. Good." continues:

The novelist has his poetry: (1) in his attention to the way that events are combined – Braddon, my *Cossacks*, my future work; (2) in the picture of mores, based on historical events – the *Odyssey*, the *Iliad*, my *1805* [the first title of *War and Peace*]; (3) in the beauty and cheerfulness of situations [...]; (4) and in the characters of people. (*PSS* 48: 64)

Tolstoy admired the way Braddon meticulously structured her narrative. Her pursuit of innovation – Braddon's reader craved mystery, danger, and surprise – may have resonated with Tolstoy's own search for form in *War and Peace*.[45] On the other hand, I do not think he took Braddon's characters too seriously; otherwise he would not have been able to enjoy her novels so much. What did Tolstoy make of Braddon's strong and independent woman characters, not always heroines, who memorably break out of the tightly corseted and cosseted lives that society has prescribed for them? Perhaps Tolstoy had Braddon's delightfully deviant heroines in mind when he wrote his anti-feminist remarks in part 1 of the epilogue of *War and Peace*:

Then as now much time was spent arguing about the rights of women, husband-and-wife relationships, and freedom and rights within marriage (though these things were not called "serious issues," as they are now), but Natasha had no interest in any such questions and had no knowledge of them. (*PSS* 12: 267–68)[46]

And now on to the *pièce de résistance*. The least-studied source for Anna's novel is Mrs. Henry (Ellen née Price) Wood (1814–87), sometimes mis-identified as Mrs. Humphrey Ward, now best remembered by her most atypical novel, *East Lynne* (1861), and yet to be adequately recognized for her influence on Tolstoy.[47] Wood, like Braddon, burst onto the literary scene in the same sensationalist bubble. Each of them knew how to write an engaging and entertaining story quickly, and to cater to popular tastes. Each of them became publisher and editor of her own low-middle-brow, family-oriented magazine. And each of them, especially Wood, borrowed extensively from other writers and themselves.

It is no accident that Braddon wrote under her own name, or that Mary Ann Evans, more circumspect, wrote under the pseudonym of George Eliot, while Ellen Price Wood chose to write under her husband's name, even after his death. "Mrs. Henry Wood" conveys the image of a devoted wife and protector of the hearth. Her typical reader – let us take, for example, Anna or Dolly – was a married woman and mother who defined herself by reference to the family. Wood incorporated into her novels not only the characteristic elements of the English family novel – love, duty, desire, marriage, and family – but also a few corpses, suspected adulterers, detectives, trials, bad omens, Gothic ruins, etc. After *East Lynne* Wood consciously struck out on a path that would separate her from more overtly sensationalist rivals. Her next two novels, *The Channings* (1862) and *Mrs. Halliburton's Troubles* (1862), oppose an ideal, "pattern" family, with a devoted mother at the helm, to a barely house-broken motley crew;

excepting a small scandal (just one quick murder), these novels elaborately characterize the right and proper upbringing for children and mothers. Wood did not eliminate sensation from her subsequent repertoire, but her narrator could be counted on to mentor the (woman) reader's moral development, especially on issues of family. Her novels, like those of Braddon, tend to end on a predictable, happy note: the villains are punished, true love triumphs, and moral order is restored. Braddon's "Trollopized" endings, however, sometimes seem like a belated bow to propriety, whereas Wood's pious messages are more categorically integrated into her stories.

Tolstoy perceived Braddon and Wood quite differently. To appreciate the enormous distinction he made between them, let us take one last detour, to Tolstoy's well-known habit of making lists, in this case lists of English novelists. In the draft of an 1887 letter from the so-called "Tiflis Young Ladies" correspondence, Tolstoy recommends translation of "good classical novels by Dickens, George Eliot, ~~Hugo, Wood, Braddon~~ and even good novels by ~~Wood, Walter Scott~~ Bulwer, Wood and Braddon, and others" (*PSS* 64: 30). Such a curious list![48] Wood is crossed off the list twice, and Braddon once, before they make the final roster. It is a testimonial to both writers, but especially to Braddon, who is so little known in Tolstoy studies.

In a much more famous letter, from 1891, Tolstoy includes Wood – but not Braddon – among the writers who most influenced him. From the age of 35 to 50 – in other words, from 1863, the year in which he began *War and Peace*, to 1878, the year after he finished *Anna Karenina* – Tolstoy lists:

The Odyssey and *The Iliad* (in Greek)	v. great [influence]
Byliny	v. great
Xenophon *Anabasis*	v. great
Victor Hugo. <u>*Misérables*</u>	enormous
<u>Mrs. Wood. Novels</u>	great
<u>George Elliot [*sic*]. Novels</u>	great
Trollope – novels[49]	great

                                                                    (*PSS* 66: 68)

That Braddon does not make the cut should come as no surprise; the images of Braddon in the Tolstoy home suggest that her novels were entertaining ephemera: tasty while consumed, but not memorable. Short-lived popularity has generally been Wood's legacy as well; with the exception of *East Lynne*, her novels are no longer in print. Wood's presence on Tolstoy's 1891 list has confounded at least one modern critic.[50] Indeed, why is she there at all, and why is she first among the English novelists – even before Eliot? Tolstoy perfectly well recognized that, compared to Eliot, Wood was a vastly inferior writer and mediocre thinker. Nonetheless, relative to Eliot, I think it is safe to say that Wood exerted a more *obvious* influence on Tolstoy.

The best scholarship on Wood and Tolstoy, Amy Mandelker's *Framing Anna Karenina*, locates in Wood's sensational *East Lynne* (1861) a "source of seduction in the Victorian domestic ethos rather than in the illicit passion of the continental romance."[51] I am obliged to her discussion that Tolstoy "borrows Victorian social and textual conventions in order to expose them."[52] My own research, however, persuades me that the greater part of Tolstoy's indebtedness to Wood comes from the novels that she wrote after *East Lynne*.[53]

Tolstoy first expressed his pleasure in reading Wood only in 1872. In a note to his brother Sergei, Tolstoy wrote: "I am really busy with astronomy and physics and reading Wood, a marvelous novel" (*PSS*: 61: 276). Tolstoy did not need to explain who Wood was: Sergei obviously already knew. But what unidentified Wood novel so pleasured Tolstoy that he called it "marvelous"?[54] If we accept that Anna's novel is a composite, then one English novel more or less should not matter. Especially in the case of Wood, who was sometimes guilty of sleep-inducing prolixity, superfluous repetition, and redundancy, etc., etc. She so often repeats her favorite ideas, images, motifs, and character types that it is sometimes hard to disentangle one novel from another. And no wonder: from 1861 to the end of 1872 Wood produced the equivalent of eight novels the size of *War and Peace*! As early as 1863 a Russian critic cited Wood for writing four novels at the same time: "This fact alone best proves the decline, in an artistic sense, of refined English literature."[55] Her often derivative graphomania weighs the odds against locating textual evidence that might identify the particular Wood novel Tolstoy was reading in March 1872. I nonetheless cannot resist sharing my suspicion that at that time Tolstoy might have been reading the "three-decker" (in three volumes) *The Shadow of Ashlydyat* (1863), apparently Wood's favorite among all her books. I will collapse my evidence to one suggestive connection between Lady Mary, riding to hounds in Anna's novel, and an earlier incarnation of the horsey female, Charlotte Pain, the daring and captivating "baddie" of Wood's *Shadow*. Anna's Lady Mary is endowed with the same boisterous equestrian energy as Charlotte Pain, who makes a dramatic entrance in the first scene of *Shadow*. Before her appearance, the narrator gossips disparagingly about the image of the Amazon.

Ladies were mostly in carriages; a few were mounted, who would ride quietly home again when the hounds had thrown off; a very few – they might be counted by units – would follow the field. [The neighborhood] was supplied in a very limited degree with what they were pleased to call masculine women: for the term "fast" had not yet then come in.[56]

After this, on to the hunting field astride a fine hunter rides Charlotte Pain, an alluring woman, provocatively attired, and a fearless rider. She occupies the hero, also astride, in idle chatter. It is apparent that Charlotte takes pleasure in her power over men and animals. A moment later, the hero's mother and his future bride drive up in a barouche; between themselves they express disapproval of the flashy and gaudy Amazon. (Curiously, at the end of the novel, with the exception of the reformed hero's belated contempt, the indiscreet and independent Charlotte Pain manages to evade society's censure.) The possible connection between Charlotte Pain and Lady Mary is intriguing. But even if Tolstoy had read *Shadow* a year before he started *Anna Karenina*, it is not plausible that the portrait of Charlotte Pain is the only, or even the major, source for Lady Mary; this literary and cultural trope – the provocative equestrienne – has many sources. Such freighted linkages – in this instance not a literal linkage, but Tolstoy's one-way connection to the English novel – give Anna's novel its symbolic power.

Anna's novel aside, Wood's influence on *Anna Karenina* is more strongly evident elsewhere in part 1 of the novel. Wood's brand of "domesticated sensationalism," for all its corpses, and secret garden mazes where miscreants skulk, is firmly rooted in English respectability and the idea of the family as the center of the universe.[57] Earlier, Anna conducts her mission of mercy to reconcile Dolly to Stiva with great skill, gently prevailing over her sister-in-law's initial reservations. Anticipating Anna's arrival, Dolly recalls the Karenin home and her intuition that "there was something false in the whole make-up of their family life" (pt. 1, ch. 19: 66; *PSS* 18: 71). There is an odd disconnect between Dolly's naïveté about Stiva's womanizing and the precision with which she imagines what Anna will say: "All these consolations and exhortations and Christian forgiveness" (pt. 1, ch. 19: 66; *PSS* 18: 71). Where does that righteous piety come from, if not from the English novels that Dolly reads? And how is it that Anna plays so well the role of ministering angel for preservation of the family? We know very little about Anna at this moment in the novel, but short of the implausible assumption of adultery in the Karenin marriage, and, therefore, that she is speaking from personal knowledge, we may attribute Anna's trained intuition to the English novels that she reads:

I know how people like Stiva look at it [adultery and the family]. You say he talked with *her* about you. That never happened. These people may be unfaithful, but their hearth and wife are sacred to them. Somehow for them these women remain despised and don't interfere with the family. Between them and the family they draw some kind of line that can't be crossed. (pt. 1, ch. 19: 70; *PSS* 18: 75)

The "woman-to-woman" conversations in Wood's novels cover much of the same adulterous terrain, but ultimately, as the lines below from *Within the Maze* make explicit, there is only one practical message for women who suspect their husbands of infidelity.

Men and women are different. A separated man – say a divorced man, if you like – can go abroad, here, there and everywhere; and enjoy life without hindrance, and take his pleasure at will: but a woman, if she be a right-minded woman, must stay in her home-shell, and eat her heart away […] My dear little friend, at all costs, *stay with your husband.*[58]

In part 6 of *Anna Karenina*, during her second heart-to-heart with Anna, Dolly independently arrives at that same conclusion, but by a different logic. By putting her children's needs before her own desires, she will, by default, stay with her errant husband. Wood would have heartily approved of Dolly's behavior. Surely part of Tolstoy's fondness for Wood must have been their similar views on the essential role in the family of dedicated and nurturing mothers.

The greater part of Wood's influence on Tolstoy concerns, I suspect, their shared obsession with death – and that theme takes us beyond *Anna Karenina*. Here we could detour into the images of death in the Victorian novel at the time that Wood wrote, but that digression would only confirm that she surpasses every other English novelist of her time in her fixation on death. As Malcolm Elwin so acerbically puts it: "There are always three or four tragic deaths in one of her books, every one of which contains some death-bed scene comparable in oppressive anguish and sentimental melo-drama with those of little Nell or Paul Dombey."[59] Imitator of Dickens she was – who was not at that time? – but Wood added her own twist on death. Her virtuous heroes, old and young, tend to die slow and conscious deaths, ideal conditions for tranquil and soulful conversation. They die in their bedrooms, at home, surrounded by devoted family and caretakers. Wood's death narratives focus on faith in an after-life; her dying heroes speak confidently and joyfully about their future lives in paradise. Often in their last words they look heavenward and seem to see and speak to someone who has gone on before. Wood, strong in her Anglican faith, often wrote about model deportment in death. Compressed into a few lines, her advice would go something like this: children should be taught about death and heaven at an early age; adults should reconcile themselves with death before they die;

and during the prolonged dying process, the one going to heaven and those remaining behind should console themselves with thoughts of their next and certain meeting. This is programmatic Wood at her evangelical best. By contrast, rarely do Tolstoy's characters embrace death without conflict. The servant Gerasim in Tolstoy's *The Death of Ivan Ilych*, so wise, accommodating, respectful, and non-judgmental, is able to deal righteously with the dying Ivan Ilych because he is sanguine about his own death. This is fine for servants, or peasants like Platon Karataev (*War and Peace*) and the title character in "Alyosha Gorshok," but Tolstoy could not write about protagonists from his own, privileged class with any of Wood's secure faith in life after death. Nonetheless, given the frequency with which Wood wrote about death, and the esteem in which he held her, Tolstoy must have found inspiration in her portraits of death and dying. I would like to think that in March 1872, Tolstoy was marveling at Wood's comforting vision of the transitory nature of death, and death as a bridge to a certain life in heaven.

So, let us return to the topic, and address the question posed in the subtitle to this chapter. "Who wrote the English novel that Anna reads?" Now, however, we can rephrase the question into something more concrete, albeit far less tidy. "What English novelists whom Tolstoy read most contributed to Anna's novel?" With all the tracking and detouring we have done, the answers should come easily. We can immediately eliminate Braddon. Braddonesque sensationalism would not have been proper for Anna to read, and certainly not in public. The saccharinely pious hypocrite, Lydia Ivanovna, public standard-bearer for the commandments of her faith, but not the generous spirit of Christianity, would surely not have approved. Neither does Anna read Eliot. *Romola* and *Middlemarch* were too highbrow for her. If she had read Eliot, perhaps Anna would have a more reasoned, less melodramatic, view of herself. Anna's reading choices come from current English novels in which the story-line, however bold or even sensational, espouses the virtues of a family-centered life. She read Trollope, of course. His name comes readily to mind, because he is still published and read in the twenty-first century. And, no less certainly, Anna read Wood. The only reason that the Wood–Tolstoy connection is not well known is that – and here I repeat myself – Wood is still an unknown figure. Thus, Anna is reading a composite novel in which Trollope (the most *popular* English novelist in Russia before *Anna Karenina*) and Wood (the most *representative* English novelist for that same period) play prominent roles. To this list, we could probably add a few more lady novelists whose ghosts still lurk in Tolstoy's library, waiting to be recognized for their possible connections to *Anna Karenina*.[60]

Just one last question, before I take my leave. If, as I have argued, Anna does not seem to derive pleasure from English novels, then why has she been reading them? Unlike her cohort group of fictional readers, Anna does not fall prey to the seductive lures of her stories for the obvious reason that there are very few such lures in them. Any novelistic lapses in propriety are overwhelmed by the demands of virtue. The trope of the "reading woman" does not in work in Anna's case. Anna is reading not only, and not primarily, to relieve her boredom by imagining herself in other people's lives. Her novels clarify virtue; they send subtle (Trollope) or explicitly mentoring (Wood) messages reinforcing appropriate behavior and worthy values in a model English family.

Let's see how that works out in *Anna Karenina*. We left Anna in part 1, chapter 29, on the train with her English novel. Before the completion of her journey back home, even before she meets Vronsky again, on the snow-swept station platform, she closes it for good because she can no longer read about the idealized family. Her own life as a woman, a wife, and a mother has been so bewilderingly unsatisfactory, unlike the contented, virtuous lives she finds in English novels. Her immediate back story is embedded in them: virtue and duty have reigned in her married life. Anna has always enjoyed and merited an irreproachable reputation in the highest circles of St. Petersburg. Vronsky, however, has broken through that barrier of integrity. And when he pops up again in her English novel, what Anna has moments before called her "good and usual life" cannot go on as before.

On her first evening back in St. Petersburg, "Anna sat by the fire place with her English novel and waited for her husband" (pt. 1, ch. 33: 110; *PSS* 18: 117). She holds the book one last time, but does not open it. Without its dogmatic prescriptions to guide her, she has begun to see the world differently, with less charity toward her husband and Lydia Ivanovna. She finds temporary sanctuary – "moral peace," she calls it – in the company of her son, but she still cannot rid her thoughts of Vronsky's fascination (pt. 1, ch. 32: 107; *PSS* 1: 114). After her sojourn in Moscow, Anna is never at home, both in the literal sense and in the "make yourself at home" family sense. The remainder of her life is spent in temporary lodgings. Anna never reaches a satisfied and stable state of being. Vronsky's estate is no more than a vacation resort, where she reads voraciously, but indiscriminately, like a vacuum cleaner, sucking up "novels and the books that were in vogue. She ordered all the books that were mentioned with praise in the foreign newspapers and magazines she received […] and all the subjects that interested Vronsky […] agronomy, architecture and, occasionally, even horse-breeding and sports" (pt. 6, ch. 25, p. 643; *PSS* 19: 219).

But the English novel is no longer a presence in Anna's life; she has cast off the restraining influence imposed by that kind of book-reading. From its perspective, Anna is doomed from the moment she stops reading stories that reify the values and conventions of mid-Victorian England. Forsaking the English novel is a marker of the onset of Anna's demise.

APPENDIX I

Titles in the library at Iasnaia Poliana from the Collection of British Authors series, published by C. B. Tauchnitz, Leipzig.

Braddon, [Maxwell], Mary Elizabeth.

    58 titles published by Tauchnitz 1862–1908

    14 titles published 1862–71

    8 Tauchnitz titles at Iasnaia Poliana

        6 titles, or 44%, of total works dating 1862–72

            Lady Audley's Secret, 1862

            Aurora Floyd, 1863

            John Marchmont's Legacy, 1864

            Only a Clod, 1865

            The Lady's Mile, 1866

            Fenton's Quest, 1871

Eliot, George.

    11 titles published by Tauchnitz 1859–85

    7 titles published 1859–72

    5 titles (4 Tauchnitz and 1 Asher) at Iasnaia Poliana

        5 titles, or 71% of total works dating 1859–72

            Adam Bede, 1859

            The Mill on the Floss, 1860

            Romola, 1863

            Felix Holt, 1867

            Middlemarch, 1872 (Asher)

Trollope, Anthony.

    45 titles published by Tauchnitz 1859–84

    22 titles published 1859–71

    12 titles at Iasnaia Poliana

        4 titles, or 18% of total works dating 1859–71

            The Warden, 1859

            The West Indies and the Spanish Main, 1860

            The Last Chronicle of Barset, 1867

            Sir Harry Hotspur, 1871

Wood, Mrs. Henry.
> 36 titles published by Tauchnitz 1861–85
> 22 titles published 1861–72
> > 6 titles at Iasnaia Poliana
> > > 5 titles, or 22% of total works dating 1861–72
> > > > *East Lynne*, 1861
> > > > *Lord Oakburn's Daughters*, 1865*
> > > > *The Red Court Farm*, 1868
> > > > *Oswald Cray*, 1865
> > > > *George Canterbury's Will*, 1870*
> > > *Included in V. F. Bulgakov's manuscript bibliographic list

NOTES

1. (Unsigned), "Interesy nauki i literatury na Zapade," *Otechestvennye zapiski* 167, nos. 7–8 (1866): 25.
2. *Anna Karenina* is quoted from the R. Pevear and L. Volokhonsky translation (New York: Viking, 2001). I have made a small number of changes for greater accuracy. References to this edition of *Anna Karenina* are cited in the text by part, chapter, and page; references to the Russian Jubilee edition (*PSS*) are cited by volume and page.
3. R. L. Jackson, "The Night Journey, Anna Karenina's Return to Saint Petersburg," in L. Knapp and A. Mandelker, eds., *Approaches to Teaching Tolstoy's* Anna Karenina (New York: Modern Language Association of America, 2003), 150.
4. See Gina M. Dorré, *Victorian Fiction and the Cult of the Horse* (Aldershot, UK and Burlington, VT: Ashgate Publishing Company, 2006).
5. B. Lönnqvist, "The English Theme in *Anna Karenina*," *Essays in Poetics: The Journal of the British Neo-Formalist Circle* 24 (Autumn 1999): 58–90.
6. Mrs. Henry Wood was especially well known for ratcheting up the tension in her novels with omens, and anxious, prescient dreams. Creating suspense by way of portentous foreboding was a common trait of the sensation novel.
7. For a reading of this phrase that disagrees with mine, see D. Sloane, "Anna Reading and Women Reading in *Anna Karenina*," in Knapp and Mandelker, eds., *Approaches to Teaching Tolstoy's* Anna Karenina, 124–30.
8. B. Eikhenbaum, *Tolstoi in the Seventies*, trans. Albert Kaspin (Ann Arbor, MI: Ardis, 1982), 111.
9. For a superb article on the sensation novel, see P. Brantlinger, "What Is Sensational about the Sensation Novel?" in Lyn Pykett, ed., *Wilkie Collins* (New York: St. Martin's Press, 1998), 30–57.
10. (Unsigned), "Inostrannaia literaturnaia letopis'," *Otechestvennye zapiski* 152, 1–2 (1864): 265–66.
11. All dates of English novels refer to their English-language publication in Leipzig by C. B. Tauchnitz in his "Collection of British Authors" series. See note 15.

12. (Unsigned), "Inostrannaia literaturnaia letopis'," 266.

13. For a good short account of Tolstoy and the English language, see W. G. Jones, "Introduction," in Jones, ed., *Tolstoi and Britain* (Oxford: Berg Publishers, 1995), 1–30.

14. (Unsigned), "Obzor inostrannoi literatury III," *Otechestvennye zapiski* 134, nos. 1–2 (1861): 56.

15. See W. B. Todd and A. Bowden, *Tauchnitz International Editions in English 1841–1955: A Bibliographical History* (New York: Bibliographical Society of America, 1988).

16. The book store's imprint is on the soft cover of volume 2 of the Tauchnitz edition of Braddon's *John Marchmont's Legacy* in Tolstoy's library.

17. See *Biblioteka L'va Nikolaevicha Tolstogo v Iasnoi Poliane: bibliograficheskoe opisanie*, pt. III, *Knigi na inostrannykh iazykakh*, 2 vols. (Tula: Izd. Iasnaia Poliana, 1999).

18. Two titles by Wood, *Lord Oakburn's Daughters* (1865) and *George Canterbury's Will* (1870), are listed in V. F. Bulgakov's manuscript bibliography, but not listed in the published 1999 bibliography. See D. Goubert, "Did Tolstoy Read *East Lynne?" Slavonic and East European Review* 58, no. 1 (1980): 24.

19. Tolstoy sent the second part of an unidentified Braddon novel to his brother Sergei on May 6, 1868 (*PSS* 61: 201). Missing from the library are vol. 2 of *Aurora Floyd* and of *Only a Clod*. In a letter of August 9, 1891, Tolstoy recommended to L. P. Nikiforov a Braddon reading which he would send, if he could get it back from Sergei (*PSS* 66: 30–31). That title, identified as *In Great Waters, and Other Tales* (1877), is not in the Tolstoy library.

20. L. Polonskii, "Ocherki angliiskogo obshchestva v romanakh A. Trollopa," *Vestnik Evropy* 8 (1870): 613–75; 10 (1870): 667–716; N. A Tal', "Angliiskie semeinye khroniki," *Vestnik Evropy* 3 (1871): 306–30; L. Polonskii, "Zhenskie tipy v romanakh A. Trollopa," *Vestnik Evropy* 8 (1871): 513–68.

21. Polonskii, "Ocherki angliiskogo obshchestva," 623.

22. S. A. Tolstaia, *Dnevniki* (Moscow: Khudozhestvennaia literatura, 1978), vol. 1, 100. Quoted in C. J. G. Turner, *A Karenina Companion* (Waterloo, Ontario: Wilfrid Laurier University Press, 1993), 109.

23. Julia Kavanagh (1824–77), a third-rate writer, now entirely forgotten, of stories and novels. Tauchnitz published eighteen Kavanagh titles in the COBA series, nine for the period 1859–72. John Sutherland describes her work as "aimed at younger women readers and [...] fashionably domestic in style while remaining wholly 'ladylike' in tone." See J. Sutherland, *The Stanford Guide to Victorian Fiction* (Stanford, CA: Stanford University Press, 1999), 343. Kavanagh is not represented in Tolstoy's library, which is noteworthy because Tolstoy twice records that he read her. I suspect that some of the grumpiness in Tolstoy's critique, "too conventional," about *The Bertrams*, may have come from his strong reaction against Kavanagh.

24. Tolstoy wrote the underlined words in English.

25. Anthony Trollope, *The Bertrams* (New York: Harper and Brothers, 1859), 528.

26. See Gertrude Himmelfarb, *The De-moralization of Society: From Victorian Virtues to Modern Values* (New York: Alfred A. Knopf, 1995), 3–52.

27. George Eliot, *Selected Essays, Poems and Other Writings* (London: Penguin, 1990), 140–41.

28. The underlined words are in English in the original text.

29. G. W. Jones, "George Eliot's *Adam Bede* and Tolstoy's Conception of *Anna Karenina*," in Jones, ed., *Tolstoi and Britain*, 79.

30. (Unsigned), "Obzor inostrannoi literatury," 57.

31. See K. E. Harper and B. A. Booth, "Russian Translations of Nineteenth-Century English Fiction," *Nineteenth-Century Fiction* 8, no. 3 (1953): 192.

32. E. J. Blumberg, "Tolstoy and the English Novel: A Note on *Middlemarch* and *Anna Karenina*," in Jones, ed., *Tolstoi and Britain*, 93–103.

33. S. Knapp, "Tolstoj's Readings of George Eliot: Visions and Revisions," *Slavic and East European Journal* 27, no. 3 (1983): 318–19.

34. (Unsigned), "Inostrannaia literatura," *Otechestvennye zapiski* 147, nos. 3–4 (1863): 101.

35. Wilkie Collins (1824–89), "the King of the Sensation Novel," wrote action-packed detective stories that were regularly translated for serial publication in the journal *Russian Herald* (*Russkii vestnik*). A protégé and colleague of Charles Dickens, he is represented in the COBA series by nine novels between 1859 and 1872. More the wonder, then, that Tolstoy seems not to have read Collins, nor is there any record of a Collins novel in his library. Perhaps Tolstoy drew the line at the unadulterated sensationalism that Collins proffered. Or, perhaps, excepting Trollope – with his gallery of richly portrayed women – Tolstoy seemed to prefer English novels by *women* novelists at this time.

36. (Unsigned), "Inostrannaia literaturnaia letopis'," 266.

37. (Unsigned), "Interesy nauki i literatury na Zapade," 26.

38. T. A. Kuzminskaia, *Moia zhizn' doma i v Iasnoi Poliane, Vospominanie*, 3rd edn (Tula: Tul'skoe Knizhnoe Izdatel'stvo, 1958), 258.

39. *Ibid.*

40. Tolstoy's eldest child, S. L. Tolstoy, born in 1863, could not have had some of the memories that he claimed. He has led more than one scholar astray with his recollections of English novelists whom his father read: "From English literature he read Dickens, Thackeray and family novels: Trollope, Humphrey Ward, George Eliot, Broughton (?), Braddon, etc." (S. L. Tolstoi, *Ocherki bylogo* [Moscow: Gosudarstvennoe izdatel'stvo "Khudozhestvennaia literatura," 1956], 79). He confuses Mrs. Henry Wood with Mrs. Humphrey Ward (1851–1920), whose first novel published by Tauchnitz dates from 1888. That error has crept into R. F. Christian's fine study, *Tolstoy: A Critical Introduction*, where he writes of "Trollope, George Eliot, and Mrs. Ward" ([Cambridge: Cambridge University Press, 1969], 165). S. L. Tolstoy also does not seem clear on the difference between Braddon and Rhoda Broughton (1840–1920), most of whose novels were written after 1872. Broughton is represented in the Tolstoy library by the COBA edition of *Tales for Christmas Eve* (1872), but the book is in its original binding, suggesting that it was not often read.

41. R. L. Wolff, *Sensational Victorian: The Life and Fiction of Mary Elizabeth Braddon* (New York and London: Garland Publishing, 1979), 160.

42. *Ibid.* 162–63.

43. M. E. Braddon, *The Doctor's Wife*, ed. Lyn Pykett (Oxford and New York: Oxford University Press, 1998), 402–3.

44. (Unsigned), "Inostrannaia literaturnaia letopis'," 276. The underlined words are in English in the Russian text.

45. In *War and Peace*, however, Tolstoy seems to restrict his interaction to the shopworn clichés of an earlier English novel, most conspicuously in the creaky, melodramatic plot devices that enable Pierre's instant transformation from an ursine bastard into a high-born, wealthy, and therefore eminently eligible, bachelor – all in one quick death and a brief contest over a "found" will.

46. Leo Tolstoy, *War and Peace*, trans. Anthony Briggs (New York: Viking, 2006), 1290.

47. See note 40.

48. Walter Scott (1771–1832), central to any comprehensive discussion of the English novel and Russian literary culture, pops out of nowhere to make a brief walk-on, only to be blue-penciled.

49. Tolstoy wrote the underlined words in English or French within the Russian text. It is curious that Tolstoy wrote "Trollope" in Russian, but "Mrs. Wood" and "Eliot" in English. I speculate that he read more novels of Trollope in Russian translation than in English, thus the choice of Cyrillic for his name.

50. Goubert, "Did Tolstoy Read *East Lynne*?" 22–39.

51. A. Mandelker, *Framing Anna Karenina: Tolstoy, the Woman Question, and the Victorian Novel* (Columbus, OH: Ohio State University Press, 1993), 60.

52. *Ibid.* 66.

53. For support of that view, see Stella Nuralova, "Missis Genri Vud i Lev Tolstoi (Zaiavka temy)," *Studia Litteraria Polono-Slavica* 5 (2000): 187–90.

54. The Jubilee edition misidentifies the novel as *Within the Maze* (1872; *PSS* 61: 276). It is likely that Tolstoy read *Within the Maze*, but not in March 1872; the Tauchnitz COBA edition was not published until nine months later, in December.

55. (Unsigned), "Inostrannaia literatura," *Otechestvennye zapiski* 147, nos. 3–4 (1863): 101.

56. *The Shadow of Ashlydyat*, in three volumes, vol. 1 (London: Richard Bentley, 1863), 7.

57. I have borrowed the term "domesticated sensationalism" from Jennifer Phegley, "Domesticating the Sensation Novelist: Ellen Price Wood as Author and Editor of the *Argosy* Magazine," *Victorian Periodicals Review* 38, no. 2 (2005): 180–98.

58. *Within the Maze* (London: Macmillan and Co.: 1904), 226.

59. M. Elwin, *Victorian Wallflowers* (London: Jonathan Cape, 1937), 250.

60. For example, Dinah Craik (1826–87), represented by three titles in the Tolstoy library, two from the period 1859–72; Florence Lean (1837–99), five titles in the library, two in our time period; and Charlotte Mary Yonge (1823–1901), with five titles on Tolstoy's shelves, but only one, a French (!) translation of *The Book of Gold* (1866), from the relevant years.

CHAPTER 9

Violence and the role of drama in the late Tolstoy: The Realm of Darkness

Justin Weir

> NIKITA […] My dear Pa, you also forgive me, a sinner! Yuh told me at the beginnin' when I started this whorin' nasty life, yuh told me: "If a claw gets stuck, the bird is lost." I didn't listen t'yer words, no good dog that I am, an' it turned out like yuh said. Forgive me, for God's sake. (90; *PSS* 26: 242)[1]
>
> *The Realm of Darkness: If a Claw Gets Stuck, the Bird is Lost*

Tolstoy's plays have gone relatively unstudied by scholars.[2] Unlike his fiction, his plays do not so thoroughly engage in psychological analysis and introspection. In cases of sinful, violent behavior, however, sometimes reason and rationalization cannot explain why a character acts the way he or she does, and thus the stage is an ideal forum for conveying an aesthetic and moral idea. The preeminent example, and one of Tolstoy's most successful plays, is *The Realm of Darkness: If a Claw Gets Stuck, the Bird is Lost* (1886). The purpose of this chapter is to illuminate the aesthetic context for Tolstoy's depiction of violence in *The Realm of Darkness*, a work that exemplifies many of the artistic goals Tolstoy had for his fiction in the latter part of his career.

Three critical points of view may be assumed for viewing the less significant work of a major author, in this case the plays of Tolstoy. To start, there are of course shared themes and formal strategies, though a common theme is often transformed by the constrictions and potentials of a different genre and medium. Tolstoy's fascination with revealing the interior psychology of a character and use of free-indirect discourse, for example, does not translate into drama very well. Second, philosophical ideas transcend genre and medium in Tolstoy's oeuvre. It would be surprising if Tolstoy's plays were to address issues fundamentally different from the ones that occupied him in other genres. His commitment in the latter half of his career to nonviolence, for example, can be found in his dramatic works as well as in his fiction and essays. Finally, facts from the author's biography may emphasize or minimize his decision to write drama. Why did Tolstoy feel compelled to write plays at all? How did he envision his role as a playwright and how did that role fit into his larger vision of himself as an author and Christian thinker? Tolstoy wrote plays early and late in his career, sometimes just for home entertainment at his estate, Iasnaia Poliana; the post-conversion plays, however, occupy a more significant place among his late fiction.

From all three critical points of view, *The Realm of Darkness* makes an especially compelling interpretive case. Thematically it treats sexual transgression, violence, and repentance – key motifs from Tolstoy's earliest works and crucial to his late fiction. Moreover, in its graphic treatment of infanticide, the play participates in Tolstoy's evolving philosophy of non-violence and his ongoing investigation of the nature of sin. At every juncture the play also bespeaks not just the later Tolstoy's reexamination of Christianity but also his enduring interest in the peasants with whom he spent so much time. Their beliefs, ways of life, and especially their speech, are brilliantly depicted in the play by Tolstoy.[3] Although individual idealized portraits of peasants may be found in Tolstoy's fiction, such as Platon Karataev in *War and Peace*, he strived to understand but not romanticize them. *The Realm of Darkness* starkly demonstrates that infidelity, violence, and moral despair are not restricted to the upper classes. It is a singular work with universal aims. As Andrew Wachtel writes: "With its constant use of peasant dialect and its shocking violence, *The Realm of Darkness* stands practically alone in the Russian dramatic tradition."[4] And yet it is essential for understanding Tolstoy's view of drama.

The plot of *The Realm of Darkness* is as follows. Anisya is the young second wife of a rich old peasant, Pyotr, and she is having an affair with the hired hand, Nikita. (Nikita has previously had an affair with Marinka, an unmarried peasant girl, and abandoned her.) Anisya and Nikita, with the active encouragement of Nikita's mother Matryona, conspire to kill Pyotr in order to obtain his money and to marry. Once Anisya has poisoned Pyotr, and Nikita has secured the old man's money, he marries Anisya; but carries on an affair with Akulina, Pyotr's daughter from his first marriage. Anisya can say or do nothing to protest, since Akulina knows from Nikita that she, Anisya, killed Pyotr. The situation cannot continue indefinitely, and after several months Nikita agrees to marry off Akulina. But she is pregnant with Nikita's child. With encouragement from Anisya and again from his own mother (the play takes an especially harsh view of women), Nikita aims to conceal his sin. He crushes the newborn infant to death and buries it in the cellar. Now distraught, he nearly hangs himself from guilt, before reconsidering. As the play concludes, he appears before the people gathered for the wedding, confesses, and turns himself in, taking full blame upon himself and accepting his sins before God. The arc of the plot suggests that sin leads to violence and, fortunately in this instance, repentance – but it is the harrowing violence that sticks with many readers and viewers of the play.

The events of *The Realm of Darkness* were based on a real murder confessed to by Efrem Koloskov at his stepdaughter's wedding.[5] Tolstoy heard about the case from his friend, local prosecutor N. V. Davydov. (Tolstoy was always interested in local court cases, even taking on the unsuccessful role of defense attorney in 1866 for a soldier accused of striking his senior officer.)[6] Besides changing the names, Tolstoy made only a few significant alterations. He added the first murder, the poisoning of Pyotr, and chose not to depict an additional attempted murder by Koloskov of his 16-year-old daughter.[7] The addition of the poisoning of Pyotr is in accord with the sentiment underscored by the play's subtitle (and original working title) "if a claw gets stuck, the bird is lost"; that is, even a single sin (illicit sex) can lead perilously to a life of sin (first one murder then another). Tolstoy designed the play to be realistic, but he worried about the reaction of the censor to the naturalistic violence of the fourth act, when the infant is crushed to death. He wrote a less explicit variant of the fourth act in an unsuccessful attempt to get the play staged in 1887.[8] Perhaps to highlight further the play's realism, Davydov subsequently wrote that Tolstoy had actually met twice with Koloskov; Tolstoy's scrupulous diary and other writings of that time record no such meetings, however.[9] The timing of his first drafts indicate that Tolstoy was probably prompted to begin writing the play by a request for material from M. V. Lentovsky, the director of the Moscow people's theater Skomorokh.[10]

Tolstoy attempted to stage *The Realm of Darkness*. Tsar Alexander III liked the play when it was read to him, but he rescinded his approval at the request of Procurator of the Holy Synod Konstantin Pobedonostsev. The play was not performed in Russia until 1895, though it was staged to acclaim in Paris by the Théâtre-Libre in 1888 with the encouragement of Émile Zola.[11] In 1890 the play also opened successfully in Berlin; by the time the Maly Theater in Moscow staged *The Realm of Darkness* in 1895, it had already been influential in Europe.[12] But it was nevertheless published in 1887 in Russia and widely read.[13] It thus had an effect on the reading public in Russia well before it was realized on the stage.

An overriding interpretive rationale for untying the thematic, philosophical, and biographical knots of *The Realm of Darkness* is that the play serves as an important touchstone of Tolstoy's evolving aesthetics. W. Gareth Jones goes so far as to call it "the one play that bears the mark of Tolstoy's genius."[14] By reflecting on past literary motifs and new philosophical priorities in the play, Tolstoy displays how traditional literary forms, such as drama, may still serve well to transmit his new ideas to the Russian audience and reading public. In general, the late 1880s and 1890s mark a tentative return by Tolstoy to fiction aimed at the educated reading public: *The Death of Ivan Ilych* (1886), *The Kreutzer Sonata* (1889), *Master and Man* (1895), *Resurrection* (1899), as well as work on *Father Sergius*, all date from this period. *The Realm of Darkness*, like the aforementioned, transcends its moral or pedagogical purpose and meditates on the possibility of art to convey meaning. But it was not Tolstoy's first attempt at drama.

Before *The Realm of Darkness*, Tolstoy had written a number of plays and dramatic fragments, including *An Infected Family* (1864), a complete play that Tolstoy attempted to have staged, and *The Nihilist* (1866), a fragment that was written to be performed at home. *An Infected Family* and *The Nihilist* were primarily topical, responding to themes of political radicalism in the new generation of the sixties that appeared in such novels as Turgenev's *Fathers and Sons* (1862) and Chernyshevsky's *What Is To Be Done?* (1863). One of Tolstoy's earlier dramatic fragments, *Free Love* (1856), responded to the question of women's rights a few years in advance of a broader cultural discussion of the "woman question" in Russia.[15] Regardless of the relative success of any of these early dramatic works, one could not argue that Tolstoy intended them to take a place within the aesthetic vanguard of his other fiction. They did not consume his attention in the same way as his novels did, nor did he pursue staging them with any dedication. They are primarily curiosities for both the Tolstoy scholar and for scholars of Russian drama.

By contrast, Tolstoy took *The Realm of Darkness* seriously, though he remained ambivalent about whether plays in general could achieve the aesthetic goals he had for his other fiction. The relatively impoverished ability of drama (when compared to novels) to engage in psychological introspection was acknowledged by Tolstoy as a key limitation of the form:

> Here [on the stage] it is impossible to prepare for the moments lived through by the hero, impossible to make him think and call up memories, or to throw light on the characters by referring back to the past. It all comes out dull, forced and unnatural. A ready-formed state of mind, ready-formed resolutions, must be presented to the public. But monologues and modulations of colours and scenes only disgust the spectator. It is true, I myself could not resist it and put a few monologues into *Vlast' t'my*, but while doing so I felt it was not the right thing.[16]

Tolstoy makes two points here on thought and memory that are worth emphasizing. First, showing how the character thinks is an aesthetic challenge for the dramatist.[17] In *The Realm of Darkness*, Tolstoy on the contrary accentuates how sin begets sin almost in spite of one's ability to reflect on one's behavior. It thus follows that Nikita's preliminary sins – having affairs with Marinka and Anisya – are within the scope of normally acceptable behavior. Nikita is just sowing wild oats, with his mother's approval. One cannot help recall how Tolstoy was told by his beloved Aunt Tatiana Ergol'skaia that nothing completes a young man like an affair with a married woman.[18]

The second point, on memory, is perhaps more important. For much of Tolstoy's career he would have considered not just thought but memory in particular as essential for the creation of art. He referred to the effect of music on memory, for example, in *Childhood* (1852). As his mother plays the piano, the hero Nikolenka remarks: "I well remember the feelings [those pieces] aroused in me. They resembled memories – but memories of what? It almost seemed as if I were remembering something that had never been" (*PSS* 1: 31).[19] As Natasha Sankovitch, Patricia Carden, and others have noted, Tolstoy frequently uses "imagination" for "memory."[20] In a late diary entry (January 20, 1905) on music and memory Tolstoy writes:

Music is the stenography of feelings [...] Music without speech takes those expressions of feelings and their nuances and unites them, and we receive the play of feelings without that which called them forth. (*PSS* 55: 116–117)

And Pozdnyshev, the protagonist of *The Kreutzer Sonata*, complains that:

[music] merely irritates me. How can I put it? Music makes me forget myself, my true condition, it carries me off into another state of being, one that isn't my own: under the influence of music I have the illusion of feeling things I don't really feel, of understanding things I don't understand, being able to do things I'm not able to do. (*PSS* 27: 61)[21]

Tolstoy, himself often keen to control his reader's experience, is disturbed by the uncontrollability of music, its unpredictable effect on the listener, and its shaky ontology. There is no overt music playing in *The Realm of Darkness*, though women singing in both the opening and closing scenes frame the play. But when Nikita repeatedly thinks he hears the murdered baby whimpering at the end of the fourth act, Tolstoy alludes to the unpredictable and multivalent nature of aural perception. The cries of the baby are imagined, not real, and thus characterize Nikita's despair and pain, which is real. The first thing said about Nikita in the play is in the opening scene when Pyotr calls out to him, asking if he's "gone deaf" (*Oglokh!*). Until his crisis, Nikita loses the ability to hear the voice of conscience. Like the cries of the dying baby in *The Realm of Darkness*, screams of pain merge with a droning inhuman music in the late story "After the Ball" (1903), where the narrator witnesses soldiers beating a Tatar forced to run the gauntlet. The music in "After the Ball" and the whimpering cries heard by Nikita in *The Realm of Darkness* do not suggest meaning in memory, but rather a lack of meaning and a loss of memory, an existential crisis that has culminated in violence. As Pozdnyshev says, there is an illusion of understanding in music but no real understanding. Since Tolstoy sees drama as somewhat limited in its ability to depict thought and memory, one is not surprised to find violence and sin represented in drama as counter-rational: they are the result of a world rendered senseless by the loss of faith. If sin destroys thought and memory, two essential aspects of human being, then drama is an ideal medium to depict it. One wonders whether it was primarily the difficulty in getting *The Realm of Darkness* staged that dissuaded Tolstoy from authoring even more plays after it than he did.[22]

Whereas in early works Tolstoy's consideration of violence turns on psychological analysis and tests the rational or irrational basis for acting violently, his later non-introspective representations of violence are more often connected to actual violent behavior. I purposely leave aside here dueling and the extensive body of Tolstoy's war fiction, which have their own complex set of moral and aesthetic issues, and which in some cases may contradict my general argument, in order to focus on violence that is unsanctioned by political and social institutions, violence for which one can rarely share blame. Consider one of Tolstoy's most famous violent images from *Anna Karenina* in the post-coital scene between Vronsky and Anna:

He felt what a murderer must feel when looking at the body he has deprived of life. The body he had deprived of life was their love, the first period of their love [...] But in spite of the murderer's horror of the body of his victim, that body must be cut in pieces and hidden away, and he must make use of what he has obtained by the murder. Then, as the murderer desperately throws himself on the body, as though with passion, and drags it and hacks it, so Vronsky covered her face and shoulders with kisses. (*PSS* 18: 156)[23]

But Vronsky, unlike Nikita in *The Realm of Darkness* or Pozdnyshev in *The Kreutzer Sonata*, does not actually kill anyone. The violence is a metaphor through which one glimpses Vronsky's moral horror, which he himself could scarcely characterize in words. It is not just the dramatic form of the later plays that causes Tolstoy to shift his analysis of violence, then, but also his shifting ideas. Sexual transgression leads not to violence of thought, but to violent action in the later Tolstoy. For in *Anna Karenina* the link between adultery and Anna's suicide is not at all as direct and incontrovertible.

Especially in the latter half of his career, Tolstoy was of course an unparalleled advocate of non-violence, and he wrote about it at length in his nonfictional work *The Kingdom of God Is within You* (1893). But violence was a touchstone for Tolstoy's fictional aesthetics throughout his career. *The Realm of Darkness* is a transitional point between early and late belletristic representations. There are two murders that bookend the play: Anisya's poisoning of her husband Pyotr at the beginning and Nikita's crushing of the baby at the end. In between, however, Tolstoy implies that through his sin Nikita has damaged himself: he has perpetrated violence upon his soul that nearly erupts into the physical world as he contemplates committing suicide at the end of the play. As Donskov writes, "[f]rom the external events, so to say, the conflict becomes internal, as Nikita utters 'I stopped bein' a man!' The fact that he recognizes this – and recognition, as the word itself indicates, is a change from ignorance to knowledge – affects a change, a change toward his rebirth."[24] What is left unsaid and forms a mystery throughout the play is the inner workings of the mind of Nikita, which, as time goes by, is dulled more and more by drinking.

A crucial and early example of the narrative use of introspection to understand violent behavior is made most strikingly in Tolstoy's *Boyhood* (1854), where violence is the subject of intense introspection after Tolstoy's autobiographical hero, Nikolai Irtenev, sees his brother kiss Sonya.[25] In a passage that needs to be quoted at length, he reflects on the predilection for violence of boys who are no longer children yet not adolescents:

I can quite appreciate the possibility of the most frightful crime being committed without object or intent to injure but just because – out of curiosity, or to satisfy an unconscious craving for action. There are moments when the future looks so black that one is afraid to let one's thoughts dwell on it, refuses to let one's mind function and tries to convince oneself that the future will not be, and the past has not been. At such moments, when the will is not governed or modified by reflection and the only incentives that remain in life are our physical instincts, I can understand how a child, being particularly prone owing to lack of experience to fall into such a state, may without the least hesitation or fear, with a smile of curiosity deliberately set fire to his own house – and then fan the flames where his brothers, his father and his mother, all of whom he loves dearly, are sleeping. Under the influence of a similar absence of thought – absentmindedness almost – a peasant lad of seventeen, examining the blade of a newly-sharpened axe lying near the bench on which his old father lies face downward asleep, suddenly swings the axe and with vacant curiosity watches the blood oozing under the bench from the severed neck. It is under the same influence – the same absence of thought, the same instinct of curiosity – that a man finds a certain pleasure in standing on the very brink of a precipice and thinking, "What if I throw myself down?" Or raising a loaded pistol to his forehead says to himself: "Suppose I pull the trigger?" (*PSS* 2: 40–41)[26]

It is not violence toward others or violence toward the self, nor the theory or morality of violence, but violence per se that especially interests Tolstoy in this passage. As in *The Realm of Darkness* violence toward others can quickly turn against oneself. Here he explicitly correlates violence with a favorite existential topic, a curiosity about one's own death. It is an important paradox that Tolstoy ties violence to absentmindedness within a passage of sustained introspective narrative. Like Nikolai, who elsewhere in *Boyhood* turns round quickly to see if the world is still there, Tolstoy sometimes seems to be thinking his way back to non-thought, reconstructing how an idea is born from nothing.[27]

For the later Tolstoy, by contrast, one's internal moral compass is often profoundly disrupted as one passes out of childhood. In *The Death of Ivan Ilych* (1886), a work contemporaneous with *The Realm of Darkness*, puberty and social ambition push Ivan off course. He leads an immoral, though not violent, life. For violent behavior, in particular, the voice of conscience must usually be further quelled. In an important essay from 1890, *Why Do Men Stupefy Themselves?*, Tolstoy blames the use of drugs, alcohol, and even smoking for allowing one's conscience to be muted, if only for a moment, as one contemplates violent actions of one sort or another. He associates such lapses of conscience with all sorts of crime and degradation, from murder to prostitution to bad writing (during which tobacco silences the writer's internal editor). As in the case of violence in *Boyhood*, Tolstoy focuses on an act of violence without apparent motive. Why do people use stupefying substances and how is it connected to the perpetration of crime? He writes: "Ask a smoker why he began smoking tobacco and smokes now, and he will answer the same: 'just because, out of boredom, everyone smokes.' The users of opium, hashish, morphine, hallucinogenic mushrooms would in all likelihood answer just the same" (*PSS* 27: 269). What is the reason one begins smoking? No reason. Simply out of boredom, or for recreation. It's common. That is the story the perpetrators tell when asked to report on their motives.

There is a correlation in these violent retellings with Tolstoy's notion of the authentic life of childhood, ruined by sex and society. "When do boys begin smoking? – Almost always at the same time they lose their childhood innocence" (*PSS* 27: 270). In *Boyhood*, there was no cause for violence. Now Tolstoy suggests that the use of conscience-repressing substances has a purpose, in order to forget sexual transgression. This boundary between the innocence of childhood and the onset of sexual awareness, and with it, inauthenticity, is suggested in *The Death of Ivan Ilych* when Pyotr, a colleague of Ivan Ilych present at the funeral, recognizes in the tired eyes of the dead man's son an unspoken cause, his sexual maturation. In *The Realm of Darkness*, we are meant to blame Nikita's mother, Matryona, who early in the play encourages him not to marry but to enjoy his sexual freedom: "Why not have some fun? That's what young's for" (8; *PSS* 26: 130). Using stupefying substances, and Nikita drinks heavily as the play goes on, gives conscience an alibi: "The reason for the universal circulation of hashish, opium, wine, tobacco is not for taste, or pleasure, or diversion, or for fun, but only for its use in concealing the instruction of conscience" (*PSS* 27: 273). Hiding from one's conscience is not a motive for crime in the traditional sense. It is a behavior that accompanies illicit actions, and functions as an alibi. Violence, no matter how unthinkable and absent-minded, was once just a stage of life (as in *Boyhood*), but is now a sign of an authentic childhood that has been spoiled, and of the repression of conscience.

Drowning out the voice of one's conscience substitutes for a missing motive, but it also makes a good, engaging, and exciting narrative. Tolstoy is repeatedly drawn to sensational examples, not just in the infanticide of *The Realm of Darkness* or the chopping off of a finger in *Father Sergius* (where Sergius is clearly intoxicated by lust), but also in his nonfiction. In another memorable passage from *Why Do Men Stupefy Themselves?*, he recalls how a cigarette provided a murderer with the strength to finish the job.

That cook who killed his barin's wife told of when, entering the bedroom, he cut her throat with a knife and she fell, croaking, and the blood gushed out, he lost his nerve. "I couldn't finish her off," he said, "and I walked out of the bedroom into the living room, sat there and smoked a cigarette." Only after having stupefied himself with tobacco did he feel himself strong enough to return to the bedroom to finish off the old woman and look into what property she had. (*PSS* 27: 275–76)

Is it redundant to point out that Tolstoy did not need to describe how the murderer cut her, she fell, croaking, and the blood gushed out? Or that we do not need Nikita to describe the sound of the crushing of the infant's bones? Tolstoy wishes us to remain so attentive to consciousness that we will have perfect clarity if and when a big moral question arrives. Conscience must assume control over consciousness at just the right moment. Tolstoy writes unsympathetically: "They drink and smoke not just because, or out of boredom, or for fun, not because it is pleasant, but in order to drown out one's conscience. And if that is so, how horrible the consequences must very well be!" (*PSS* 27: 282). It is a pitiless condemnation from a man who for much of his life controlled poorly his own impulses – to gamble, smoke, womanize, and so forth. Knowing the reflexivity of Tolstoy's philosophy, however, and that he puts himself first among transgressors, one may regard such statements not just as the harsh condemnations they appear to be, but also as a radical self-censure we know them to be.

In a well-known example from his essay "Art as Device," Viktor Shklovsky examines a diary entry from 1897 in which Tolstoy writes that he cannot remember whether he has dusted the sofa or not, and he is horrified that habit has consumed so much of his conscious life: "if the whole complex life of many people passes by unconsciously, then it is as if that life had never been."[28] Shklovsky continues, memorably: "So life disappears, turning into nothing. Automatization consumes things, clothes, furniture, one's wife and the fear of war."[29] Tolstoy vows not to lose life to a habitualized loss of consciousness. Shklovsky in turn defines art as a process of revitalizing perception of things that are known to us, of "defamiliariz-ing" the world, of "making the stone stony" again. Crucial to Shklovsky's understanding of art in this regard, and made explicit elsewhere, is his attention to the role of the past, the literary tradition. Defamiliarization as a purposeful reworking of literary formulas takes old and familiar ways of describing life in art and destroys them in order to renew their perceptibility and significance for the reader or observer. For Tolstoy, the total attentive-ness required for monitoring one's present moral behavior pays conscience the price of the past – past art, past habit are, theoretically, subject to destruction in order that we remain aware, vigilant, in our conscious tracking of our behavior. Tolstoy is willing to give up his refined art of introspective psychological analysis, at least in *The Realm of Darkness*, if that is what a moral aesthetics requires.

The first verse of the biblical epigraph of *The Realm of Darkness* (taken from Christ's Sermon on the Mount, Matthew 5:28, 29) reminds us of the link between attentive consciousness and one's conscience: "But I say unto you, That whosoever looketh on a woman to lust after her hath committed adultery with her already in his heart" (1; *PSS* 26: 123). The epigraph is unusual for the play. Not only is an epigraph unspoken in a work of drama, but the meaning of the verse, that lust means sinning in one's heart if not in one's deeds, is itself undramatic. The play actually contradicts the sense of the epigraph, since it opens with infidelity already ongoing and not just contemplated. Anisya and Nikita have long since moved from desire to deed. The second verse of the epigraph speaks with violent and complicated imagery: "And if thy right eye offend thee, pluck it out, and cast it from thee: for it is profitable for thee that one of thy members should perish, and not that thy whole body should be cast into hell" (1; *PSS* 26: 123). Like other late stories, such as *The Kreutzer Sonata* and *Father Sergius*, *The Realm of Darkness* makes a clear and substantial link between sexual transgression and violence. The same epigraph here in *The Realm of Darkness* is used again by Tolstoy just a few years later in *The Devil* (1889), a posthumously published story that has alternative endings: one in which the protagonist kills the peasant woman who tempts him, and the other in which he kills himself. Along with the subtitle of the play, "if a claw gets stuck, the bird is lost," the epigraph forces us (readers in the case of the subtitle and epigraph) to meditate on questions of mind/body connections as well as bodily integrity per se. Does an evil thought equal an evil deed? Can one really sever sexual desire from one's whole self? A younger Tolstoy would probably have equivocated: did Pierre's lust for Hélène in *War and Peace* make him wholly bad? No. And Stiva's criticism of Levin in *Anna Karenina* that he is too much of a piece ("ty ochen' tsel'nyi chelovek") is a just one in the context of the novel (pt. 1, ch. 11; *PSS* 18: 46). In the later period we witness more frequent attempts by Tolstoy to integrate human being entirely through conscience; that is, to see contradictory and self-defeating behavior as an index of one's moral failing rather than as a sign of the breadth and fragility of human character.

Here the logic is all consuming. To take one step down the road of sinfulness is to cross over into an irresistibly sinful life. His willingness to sin once makes Nikita much more likely to sin again. It is a slippery slope for Nikita, as one sin leads easily to another without an easily identifiable cause to blame. Of lying, he remarks: "What a break that somethin' told me t'swear before the icon. Right away I put an end t'the whole mess. They say it's scary t'swear t'a lie. That's all alotta bunk. Nothin' but talk. Plain an' simple" (18; *PSS* 26: 143). The words "somethin' told me" (literally "like someone nudged me" [*i kak eto menia kak tolkonul kto*]) are essential – an unnamed, unanalyzed, non-introspective cause compelled him to act. Tolstoy transforms the inability to provide introspective analysis in a play into the dangerous infinite negativity of sinful life.

A cause is missing in Nikita's motivation to perpetrate ever greater crimes, because he has lost in the deepest sense his memory, the ability to recollect oneself, one's actions, and God.[30] The play asks viewers to make a very dramatic jump from his dalliance with Marinka to his crushing an infant to death in order to hide his affair with his stepdaughter Akulina. Must sex lead ineluctably to murder? For Tolstoy the equation is never quite that simple, though it may seem so for characters like Pozdnyshev in *The Kreutzer Sonata*. The crucial fact is that Nikita has forgotten his soul. Memory, that cornerstone of creativity in the fiction of the early Tolstoy, is now tied essentially to the maintenance of the spiritual self. In the important essay *On Life* (1887), which Tolstoy wrote along with *The Realm of Darkness* while convalescing from an injury to his leg, he distinguishes between the animal and spiritual sides of human being.[31] Through his sexual transgressions and other sins, Nikita extinguishes his spiritual side and gives into the animal side of his being. He kills part of himself, Tolstoy would argue, before killing anyone else. Nikita's father Akim, who approximates a *raissoneur* in the play, phrases it in terms of having "forgotten" God. He says: "It seems, d'ya, the end's at hand […] Oh, God's been forgotten. Forgotten, I mean. We've forgotten, forgotten God, God" (46; *PSS* 26: 183). It is as though the action of the play realizes Nikolai's nightmarish thought from *Boyhood* that "the future will not be, and the past has not been."

Partly because it is in a different genre than his previous belletristic work, one that resists mnemonic narrative devices, *The Realm of Darkness* reflects Tolstoy's changing aesthetics, that memory is not just creative but essentially spiritual. Thus the following key exchange between Akim and Nikita forebodes the play's frightful climax:

AKIM.   I told yuh, d'ya, 'bout the orphan girl, that yuh wronged the orphan girl, Marina, I mean, wronged.
NIKITA.   Look what he remembered! Let sleepin' dogs lie. That's over'n done with.
AKIM (ANGRILY).   Over? No, pal, 'tain't over. Sin, I mean, latches onto sin an' pulls yuh along, an' yuh're stuck in sin, Mikishka. Yuh're stuck in sin, I see. Yuh're stuck, yuh've sunk in it, I mean. (55; *PSS* 26: 196) …
AKIM (OPENS THE DOOR).   Come t'yer senses, Mikita. Yuh need a soul. (56; *PSS* 26: 197)

Nikita does violence to himself by forgetting his soul. Half a man, he is destined to treat others inhumanly. Akim suggests he cannot live without a soul, and indeed Nikita is nearly driven to suicide before he ultimately confesses his crimes.

Throughout the play, then, Nikita's lack of reflection bespeaks two authorial strategies. In terms of the play's broader themes, Nikita has forgotten God in his sinful behavior. In terms of the play's aesthetics, his lack of reflection, and thus introspection, accords with the demands of the dramatic genre. The overarching suggestion that modern life dulls consciousness and makes one deaf to conscience is writ large across the works of the last quarter century of Tolstoy's life. The ensuing threat of violence reaches from dark corners of the peasant village in *The Realm of Darkness* to continents across which nations move in war. Acknowledging the 60,000 suicides in Europe, Tolstoy remarks in *The Kingdom of God Is within You* that he is surprised there are not more:

Every man of the present day, if we go deep enough into the contradiction between his conscience and his life, is in a state of despair. Not to speak of all the other contradictions between modern life and the conscience, the permanently armed condition of Europe together with its profession of Christianity is alone enough to drive any man to despair, to doubt of the sanity of mankind, and to terminate an existence in this senseless and brutal world. This contradiction, which is the quintessence of all the other contradictions, is so terrible that to live and to take part in it is only possible if one does not think of it – if one is able to forget it. (*PSS* 28: 104)[32]

Nikita is deaf to conscience, forgets God, and engages in savage brutality. But Tolstoy is sympathetic.

NOTES

1. Unless otherwise noted, all English quotes are taken from the excellent and explicitly colloquial translation by Marvin Kantor: Leo Tolstoy, *Plays: Volume Two, 1886–1889*, trans. Marvin Kantor with Tanya Tulchinsky, intro. Andrew Baruch Wachtel (Evanston, IL: Northwestern University Press, 1996). *Vlast' t'my* is often translated as *The Power of Darkness*. Kantor and Tulchinsky choose "realm" for "vlast'." Wachtel notes: "The word 'power,' however, tends to connote some kind of outside force, whereas what Tolstoy seems to have had in mind was that evil can be inherent in human nature. Thus, his focus is on the entire closed world in which the crimes described in this play were committed rather than on any external power. That is why we have opted for 'realm' here" (xi).
2. Andrew Donskov provides an excellent bibliography in his *Essays on L. N. Tolstoj's Dramatic Art* (Wiesbaden: Harrassowitz, 1988).
3. Donskov (*Essays*, 69) argues that Tolstoy used dialect not just for comic but also for serious effect.
4. Wachtel, Introduction, *Plays*, xiii.
5. L. N. Tolstoi. *Polnoe sobranie sochinenii* [*PSS*]. 90 vols. Moscow: Gosudarstvennoe izdatel'stvo "Khudozhestvennaia literatura," 1928–58; 26: 706. Hereafter cited as *PSS*, and in the text. N. Gudzii, "'Vlast' t'my'. Istoriia pisaniia, pechataniia i postanovki na stsene 'Vlasti t'my'," *PSS* 26: 705–36. Among literary influences, Wachtel discusses Pisemsky's drama *A Bitter Fate* (1859) and Dostoevsky's *Crime and Punishment* (Wachtel, Introduction, *Plays*, viii, x). George Steiner sees a reflection of Raskolnikov's confession in the scene where Nikita admits his sins before the wedding crowd (*Tolstoy or Dostoevsky: An Essay in the Old Criticism* [New York: Knopf, 1959], 128). Tolstoy clearly has Raskolnikov's crime in mind

during these years. He discusses the question of why Raskolnikov kills the old pawnbroker and her sister in an essay from a few years later, *Why Do Men Stupefy Themselves?* (1890), which I discuss below.

6. He wrote his biographer Pavel Biriukov in 1908 that the event of the trial and execution "had a much greater influence on my entire life than all other seemingly more important events of life: the loss or restoration of a fortune, successes or failures in literature, even the loss of those people closest to [me]" (*PSS* 37: 67). See also Walter Kerr, *The Shabunin Affair: An Episode in the Life of Leo Tolstoy* (Ithaca, NY: Cornell University Press, 1982).

7. Gudzii, "'Vlast' t'my'," 706.

8. *Ibid.* 713.

9. *Ibid.* 706–7.

10. *Ibid.* 708.

11. Neil Carruthers, "The Paris Première of Tolstoy's *Vlast' t'my* (*The Power of Darkness*)," *New Zealand Slavonic Journal* (1987): 83.

12. See W. Gareth Jones, "Tolstoy Staged in Paris, Berlin, and London," in Donna Tussing Orwin, ed., *The Cambridge Companion to Tolstoy* (Cambridge: Cambridge University Press, 2002), 142–60.

13. *Ibid.* 143.

14. *Ibid.* 142.

15. Wachtel writes: "Tolstoy was already writing an anti-woman's liberation work before any pro-woman's liberation works had appeared in Russian literature" (Introduction, *Plays*, x).

16. Quoted by Donskov (*Essays* 19). The quote is originally from a published interview in the weekly *Teatr i iskusstvo* 34 (1908): 580–81.

17. Donskov, following R. Christian, is right to reject oversimplification: "Reference has been made to Tolstoj's statement that one must not 'make him [the character] think [on the stage] and call up memories … A ready-formed state of mind, ready-formed resolutions, must be presented to the public.' This assertion that characters must be already formed, and that there is no room for them to think anew or to develop into something different is, according to Christian, an absurdly constricting one. But in practice, it was not so simple since Tolstoj's heroes do digress into the past and they certainly do develop" (*Essays*, 22). Donskov references R. F. Christian, *Tolstoy: A Critical Introduction* (Cambridge: Cambridge University Press, 1969), 257–58.

18. An often repeated anecdote, but see, for example: A. N. Wilson, *Tolstoy: A Biography* (New York: W. W. Norton, 1988), 61.

19. Translation from Leo Tolstoy, *Childhood, Boyhood, Youth*, trans. Rosemary Edmonds (New York: Penguin, 1964), 40.

20. Natasha Sankovitch writes: "In his fiction Tolstoy rarely uses the word *pamiat'* ("memory") to refer to that part of the mind where memories or reminiscences (*vospominaniia*) are, metaphorically speaking, awakened; instead, he uses the word *voobrazhenie* ("imagination")" (*Creating and Recovering Experience: Repetition in Tolstoy* [Stanford, CA: Stanford University Press, 1998], 113.). In subsequent pages, Sankovitch addresses music and memory extensively

(*Ibid.* 215–24). Patricia Carden writes that Tolstoy affirmed the notion that "the capacity for remembering is a sign of the expressive capacity of the self" ("The Recuperative Powers of Memory: Tolstoy's *War and Peace*," in John Garrard, ed., *The Russian Novel from Pushkin to Pasternak* (New Haven, CT: Yale University Press, 1983), 89.

21. Translation from Leo Tolstoy, *Tolstoy's Short Fiction*, trans. and ed. Michael R. Katz (New York: Norton, 1991), 218.

22. Tolstoy did write several more plays, notably *The Fruits of Enlightenment* (1889) and *The Living Corpse* (1900).

23. Translation by Louise and Aylmer Maude taken from Leo Tolstoy, *Anna Karenina* (New York: W. W. Norton 1970), 135–36.

24. Donskov, *Essays*, 25.

25. Donna Orwin discusses this passage and several others from Tolstoy's war stories, *The Kreutzer Sonata* and *Resurrection* in the context of his understanding of how rational consciousness (*razumnoe soznanie*) plays the role of suppressing evil and violent impulses. See *Consequences of Consciousness: Turgenev, Dostoevsky, and Tolstoy* (Palo Alto, CA: Stanford University Press, 2007), 158–79. Of the passage I quote from *Boyhood* below, she writes: "So two conditions are necessary for the adolescent to contemplate such terrible crimes: there must be great energy, and the loving milieu and moral 'thought' by which it is normally controlled must be absent" (*ibid.* 160).

26. Translation from Tolstoy, *Childhood*, 143.

27. In a key chapter of *Boyhood*, entitled "Boyhood," he discusses his fascination with solipsistic skepticism: "But not one of these philosophical theories held me so much as skepticism, which at one time brought me to the verge of insanity. I fancied that besides myself nobody and nothing existed in the universe, that objects were not real at all but images which appeared when I directed my attention at them, and that so soon as I stopped thinking of them these images immediately vanished. In short, I came to the same conclusion as Schelling, that objects do not exist but only my relation to them exists. There were moments when I became so deranged by this *idée fixe* that I would glance sharply round in some opposite direction, hoping to catch unawares the void (the *neant*) where I was not" (Tolstoy, *Childhood*, 159). Irina Paperno describes Tolstoy's encounter in his diaries with his "inaccessible self" as similar to an experience of death: "[T]he search for the true self turned into an impossible mission of defining the non-self of the true being, which lay outside language. His last hope was death: it was in death that the author hoped to finally experience the truth of a selfless being. It would seem that, against reason, he hoped to leave a record of this experience" ("'Who, What Is I?': Tolstoy in his Diaries," *Tolstoy Studies Journal* 11 [1999]: 32–54, 32).

28. V. Shklovsky, "Art as Technique," Lee T. Lemon and Marions J. Reis, eds., in *Russian Formalist Criticism: Four Essays* (Lincoln, NE: University of Nebraska Press, 1965), 12. The quote of Tolstoy is from his diary of March 1, 1897 (*PSS* 53: 142).

29. "Art as Technique," 13.

30. Richard Gustafson's work provides the key insight here with his analysis of prayer in Tolstoy as a form of "recollective consciousness," an assessment of human vocation in the context of the divine. See *Leo Tolstoy: Resident and Stranger: A Study in Fiction and Theology* (Princeton, NJ: Princeton University Press, 1986), 331.

31. Simmons remarks that as Tolstoy's attention turned from trying to stage *The Power of Darkness*, he became consumed with completing *On Life*. See Ernest J. Simmons, *Leo Tolstoy*, 2 vols. (New York: Vintage Books, 1960), vol. II, 420.

32. The translation is taken from Leo Tolstoy, *The Kingdom of God Is within You: Christianity not as a Mystic Religion but as a New Theory of Life*, trans. Constance Garnett (Lincoln, NE: University of Nebraska Press, 1984), 131–32.

CHAPTER 10

What men quote by: Tolstoy, wise sayings, and moral tales

Gary Saul Morson

THE SHORTEST LITERARY WORKS

The author of *War and Peace* also mastered short forms, including moral tales and the shortest of all literary forms, the quotation.

Tolstoy loved quotations. By "quotations" I mean not any set of cited words, but the sort of memorable short saying that we find in *Bartlett's Familiar Quotations* and similar volumes. Although it is often assumed that Bartlett invented the anthology of quotations, it derives from a tradition extending back to the Renaissance (Erasmus' *Adagia*), medieval florilegia, ancient classics including Diogenes Laertius, and the biblical Book of Proverbs, which is itself a collection of collections of Middle Eastern proverbs.

To be a *quotation* in this sense, a set of words must be able to stand on its own as a complete, if brief, literary work. It must be *quotable*. We may therefore distinguish what I shall call a quotation – a short literary work – from an extract, in the sense of any set of cited words. Extracts, such as the sort of citations footnoted in scholarly articles, are neither offered nor taken as complete works capable of standing on their own.

Clearly, not all extracts are quotations. But neither are all quotations extracts. For one thing, although a quotation may have an extract as a source, it may and often does differ from its source if for no other reason than to stand on its own. Becoming a quotation is a change in status that often involves a change in text. In Matthew, Jesus says: "whoever shall smite thee on one cheek, turn to him the other also" but we nevertheless have the quotation "turn the other cheek" for the obvious reason that the extract "turn to him the other" makes no sense.[1] Although inaccurate as an extract, "turn the other cheek" is indeed accurate as the quotation; for the quotation is precisely the form that is most commonly quoted.

It is as if the extract acquires a sort of second speaker when it becomes a quotation. As we distinguish between a quotation and an extract, so a

199

misquotation differs from what we might call a misextraction. "Turn the other cheek" is a misextraction but an accurate quotation; "turn to him the other" is an accurate extract but would be a misquotation.

Not all quotations are extracts for another reason. Some are not extracted from anything at all. Rather, like the maxims of La Rochefoucauld, they were composed *as* complete works from the outset. Tolstoy collected such works by La Rochefoucauld and others. The sayings of Heraclitus represent a more complex case, because although we presume they at one time must have been fragments of a lost whole, they have survived on their own since antiquity and have long been treated as complete. The thoughts in Pascal's *Pensées* were assembled into a volume by others, and so, although presumably written as notes for some projected work, now function as complete.

Sometimes, authors doubly design works so that individual lines can be read either as parts of a larger whole or as wholes in themselves. Alexander Pope explicitly states as much in his preface to *An Essay on Man*, which has indeed survived as both a rhymed essay and a sort of anthology of famous couplets on the human condition.

TOLSTOY AND QUOTATIONS

Both the quotation and the anthology of quotations fascinated Tolstoy. As early as 1847, when he was attending Kazan University, he wrote in his diary: "I read Catherine [the Great]'s *Instructions* and since I made the general rule for myself to think over and write down the remarkable thoughts of any serious work I am reading, I here write my opinion of the first six chapters of this remarkable work."[2] By March 15, 1885, he had conceived the idea of publishing "for everyone" an anthology of great quotations. His diary enthusiastically mentions the project: "I must put together for myself a Circle of Reading: Epictetus, Marcus Aurelius, Lao Tzu, Buddha, Pascal, the Gospel. This is also necessary for everyone." In 1903, he published *Thoughts of Wise People for Every Day*, which collects quotations from forty-one authors. His much larger *Circle of Reading* (1906), which contains 250 authors, is also arranged according to the calendar.[3] Among the authors is Tolstoy himself, who quoted from his own works and wrote new quotations for the occasion.

Tolstoy produced other anthologies, such as *For Every Day* (1910), *The Path of Life* (1910), and his *Calendar of Proverbs* (1886). He also compiled "Selections" devoted to single authors. If one looks at the table of contents of volume 40 in his complete works, one finds some eighteen short collections of quotations – the longer *Circle of Reading* occupies volumes

41 and 42 – including "Selected Thoughts of La Bruyère," "Selected Aphorisms and Maxims of La Rochefoucauld," "Selected Thoughts of Montesquieu," "Sayings of Mohammed, Not Included in the Koran," and two collections of quotations from Lao Tzu.

Most important, in his great novels, author, narrator, and characters write or speak quotable phrases of their own, obviously indebted to the masters of the form. The famous first sentence of *Anna Karenina* – "All happy families resemble each other; each unhappy family is unhappy in its own way" – reworks earlier versions of this line, including a French saying, "Les peoples heureux n'ont pas d'histoire," which appears in *War and Peace*, and a remark of Montesquieu, "Happy the people whose annals are blank in history books!" Montesquieu's comment became well known, and by the time Tolstoy wrote *Anna* had already inspired George Eliot's observation in *The Mill on the Floss* (1860): "The happiest women, like the happiest nations, have no history." For that matter, as early as 1740 we find in *Poor Richard's Almanack* (Tolstoy loved Franklin): "Happy the Nation, – fortunate that age, whose history is not diverting."[4]

Numerous quotable lines appear in Tolstoy's works, some indebted to other thinkers, others Tolstoy's own but reflecting an intimate knowledge of various genres of quotation. In his salon scenes, characters formulate quotable witticisms and in *War and Peace* several widely circulated witticisms of the time appear. Platon Karataev speaks in proverbs, and in *Anna Karenina* a peasant's proverb-like saying inspires Levin's discovery of life's meaning, which itself takes the form of numerous quotable lines. *War and Peace* traces how famous statements by Napoleon and Tsar Alexander came to be uttered. It shows them to be not inspiring pronouncements made under fire but, as calculated imitations of earlier pronouncements, pretentious bombast reflecting sheer vanity. Many of Tolstoy's works use epigraphs, and *Resurrection* ends on biblical quotations. Like other works we will examine, *The Kingdom of God Is within You* makes a quotation its title.

Quotations, in short, play a key role in Tolstoy's thought and poetics. It is therefore surprising that even critics who discuss Tolstoy's short works and consider their relation to the long novels typically focus on his short tales or essays but do not even consider the shortest works, the quotations. Boris Eikhenbaum's classic study *The Young Tolstoi* insists, oddly enough, that the novel and long forms in general were alien to the author of *War and Peace*, but in discussing the short forms that were natural to Tolstoy he omits the quotation. In fact, Eikhenbaum and other Formalists misunderstood the relation of short to long forms, in Tolstoy as elsewhere, because they thought of short genres as collections of devices linked together and long genres as collections of short genres. The Formalists took great delight in showing that even such a didactic author as Tolstoy, so concerned with problems of moral and meaning, was really only playing with literary forms as he invented new ones to replace worn-out older ones. But if one thinks of genres as ways to express a given sense of experience, then we can more easily see the relation of Tolstoy's short works to his long ones, beginning with quotations at one extreme and extending to the great novels at the other.

In the present chapter, I must limit myself to quotations and the ways in which they shaped Tolstoy's moral tales, with some hints at how quotations also contributed to his longer works. I hope that this approach will allow readers to see not just the moral tales and short stories but also the novellas and the novels in a new way.

GENRES OF QUOTATION

Quotations come in genres. In speaking of genres, I have in mind Bakhtin's idea of "form-shaping ideology."[5] Each genre embodies and is defined by a sense of experience. Forms express that sense. They do not define the genre but result from the "ideology" that does.

Tolstoy was fascinated with several genres of quotation. He loved, and in his novels used, the sardonic maxim, by which I mean the ironic and disillusioned commentaries on human nature exemplified by La Rochefoucauld: "Each of us has the fortitude to bear the misfortunes of others." An old man's form, such sayings *unmask* the way in which self-love (*amour-propre*) deceives us in unexpected ways.

Several Tolstoy characters, usually his shallower ones, love another genre, the witticism. Witticisms demonstrate the power of mind over contingent circumstances. In an instant, the wit masters all the complexities of a situation and utters a perfectly appropriate remark. Speed therefore matters, and so witticisms, which we often know through anecdotes, are typically preceded by a phrase like "promptly replied" or "immediately quipped." Stiva, in *Anna Karenina*, and Speransky, in *War and Peace*, appreciate witticisms. We know that Andrei has grown wiser when Speransky's conversation seems to him like the recitation of a joke book. In his final dream, Andrei astonishes others with shallow witticisms before he achieves the real insight that "death is an awakening."

"Death is an awakening" represents a third genre of quotation, the aphorism. Aphorisms in this sense evoke the ultimate unknowability of the world, as in Lao Tzu ("The way that can be spoken of is not the true way"), Heraclitus, or Pascal. Prince Andrei begins believing in intellect, but grows to recognize unfathomable, aphoristic mystery: "All is vanity, all is delusion, except those infinite heavens. There is nothing but that. And even that does not exist."[6]

This chapter focuses on a fourth genre, one that Tolstoy favored especially when older, the wise saying. Wise sayings particularly suited Tolstoy's attempt to found his own religion and to reform human life. Wise sayings underlie, and sometimes provide the title for, several of Tolstoy's moral tales.

Stories, plays, and novels may embody the sensibility of quotations, as *The Importance of Being Earnest* expands the witticism, Byron's *Don Juan* the sardonic maxim, and *Rasselas* the aphorism. In this sense, *War and Peace* is the longest aphorism in the world. Long works may also enter into dialogue with a quotational genre's sensibility. Tolstoy's moral tales use wise sayings both ways. They exhibit more complexity than meets the eye.

I first explore wise sayings as a genre and then discuss some of Tolstoy's tales that depend on that genre.

WISE SAYINGS

Whether oral or written, wise sayings, which are probably the oldest literary form, collect the wisdom of ancestors. In the Bible, their sensibility shapes both Proverbs and Psalms and is questioned in Job and Ecclesiastes. They also appear as proverbs and as the sayings of Confucius, Mozi, and Mencius; of the Seven Sages of ancient Greece; of rabbis and the Talmud; and of sages around the world.

As "the wisdom of ages," wise sayings typically either lack an author, as proverbs do, or are ascribed to a semi-legendary avatar of wisdom, like Solomon or Confucius. Many are "Anonymous," an attribution quite different from "author unknown."

If proverbs or wise sayings do have a particular author, they contrive to lose that anchor over time. They "anonymize" themselves. Sometimes scholars can identify a particular author for a saying typically used as if it belonged to no one. How many people know that the common sayings "one swallow does not make a summer" and "the whole is more than the sum of its parts" occur first in Aristotle, or "Pandora's box" as a mistranslation in Erasmus?

The Bible testifies that Solomon "excelled [...] all the wisdom of Egypt. For he was wiser than all men [...] And he spake three thousand proverbs; and his songs were a thousand and five" (1 Kings 4:30–32). Therefore most of Proverbs and Psalms is traditionally ascribed to him. By the Greek classical period, Aesop, too, was a semi-legendary figure, whose fables continued to accumulate. Their morals are spoken sometimes by a character in the fable (an endomythium) and sometimes by the author, either before or after the fable (a promythium or epimythium). In the same way, daily entries in the *Circle of Reading* include quotations from Tolstoy as well as his advance and concluding summaries. In his moral tales, Tolstoy used all three types of morals.

Proverbs are still being coined, but we treat many new ones as old because proverbial status itself confers a sense of antiquity. That sense is not a fact about the saying but a constituent part of it.

To use a saying as a proverb is not to say but to cite it. A speaker uses a proverb because it is not only what he wants to say but also what is generally said. That is why Aristotle recommends their use in the *Rhetoric*.

Wise sayings typically imply a dialogic situation. Often addressed to those who will not hear, they *demand* our attention. In the Bible, a personified Wisdom "standeth in the top of high places, by the way in the places of the paths. She crieth at the gates [...] at the coming in at the doors: Unto you, O men, I call; and my voice is to the sons of man" (Proverbs 8:1–4). Tolstoy also seemed to cry at the gates.

Sometimes the situation presumed by wise sayings is pedagogic. The old teach the young. Tolstoy's cultivation of his image as a wise old man speaking almost from the other world also suggests this situation. He was nothing if not a pedagogue.

In Proverbs, wise sayings are addressed to "my son," and in ancient Egypt they occur in "instructions" (*The Instructions of Amem-em-ope*). Wise sayings may also imply a Master answering his followers or anyone seeking wisdom, as with Confucius, Mozi, and Mencius. When a ruler asks Confucius what should come first, the Master answers "the rectification of names," for without that "affairs will not be successfully carried out."[7]

As this example illustrates, in traditional wise sayings, advice is above all *practical*: it exists so that "affairs are successfully carried out." According to Proverbs, if one acts wisely, that is, both prudently and justly, one is bound to succeed. Some proverbs stress prudence, others righteousness, and some both.

Proverbs advise: work hard, restrain your impulses, overcome pride, do not employ unjust means, and you will eventually come out ahead. Exercise self-control: "He that is slow to anger is better than the mighty; and he that ruleth his spirit than he that taketh a city" (Proverbs 16:32); "Pride goeth before destruction, and a haughty spirit before a fall" (Proverbs 16:18).

The idea that prudence and righteousness are rewarded, and that folly and evil are punished, easily leads to a sense of a providential world order: "Be not deceived, God is not mocked: for whatever a man soweth, that also shall he reap" (Galatians 6:7); "The righteous is delivered out of trouble, and the wicked cometh in his stead" (Proverbs 11:8). Such Providence may come from God, as in the Bible, or from "Heaven," as with the Chinese sages.

Such statements often anticipate a second kind of listener, a "scorner," who mocks Providence as a fool's belief. Answering them in advance, Proverbs "scorns the scorners": "How long [...] will [...] the scorners delight in their scorning, and the fools hate knowledge?" (Proverbs 1:22). Not forever, for God Himself "scorneth the scorners" (Proverbs 3:34).

Wisdom herself constantly answers this mocking voice. Wise sayings therefore insist that virtue triumphs *in spite of appearances*. "Wisdom crieth without [...] How long, ye simple ones, will ye love simplicity? and the scorners delight in their scorning, and the fools hate knowledge? [...] the prosperity of fools shall destroy them. But whoso hearkeneth unto me shall dwell safely" (Proverbs 1:20–33). Wisdom and the teacher caution against the scorner precisely because he is so persuasive. They tell him: existing facts notwithstanding, the time will come when "thou mourn at the last, when thy flesh and body are consumed" (Proverbs 5:11). The fact that this punishment will happen only "at the last" suggests why it appears that Providence fails.

We can be sure Wisdom will triumph because she suffuses the very nature of things. She explains: "The Lord possessed me in the beginning of his way, before his works of old. I was set up from everlasting, from the beginning, or ever the earth was [...] all they that hate me loveth death" (Proverbs 8:22–36).

The Book of Psalms addresses the same doubts, answers the same scoffing voices, and refutes the same contrary evidence. The psalmist affirms what Robert Alter calls "the traditional moral calculus."[8] He hears the scorner's boast: "He hath said in his heart, God hath forgotten: he hideth his face; he will never see it" (Psalms 10:11). In response, the psalmist demands God provide justice and expresses assurance that He will.

One important clarification is in order. I do not mean to say that all short sayings enunciate the sort of providential worldview conveyed by Psalms and Proverbs. Lao Tzu clearly is up to something different, and Machiavelli the very opposite. For that matter, so is Ecclesiastes, and the insights of Montaigne and La Rochefoucauld do not resemble those of Confucius or Franklin. Rather, there exists an identifiable group of quotations that do endorse a providential view, and it is these and these alone I refer to as wise sayings. Tolstoy knew many genres of quotations, and as he grew into his role as sage and master, he interacted more and more intensely with the providential ones that I am calling wise sayings.

THE SERMON ON THE MOUNT AS PROVERBS

Tolstoy's moral tales typically vindicate Providence, but in a surprising way and with unexpected significance. Several take proverbial phrases as their titles: "A Spark Neglected Burns the House," "Evil Allures, But God Endures," and "Where Love Is, God Is." Others begin or conclude with a biblical saying.

It is easy to misread these stories as simpler than they are. For one thing, their style is not straightforwardly simple, but polemically so. We never forget that these are *Tolstoy's* "simple" stories. In *What Is Art?*, he describes hearing an astronomer's complex lecture. Reminding him that many in his audience did not even know why day follows night, Tolstoy suggested that basic topic. The wise astronomer answered, "Yes it would be a good thing, but it is very difficult. To lecture on the spectrum analysis of the Milky Way is far easier." Tolstoy adds:

And so it is in art. To write a rhymed poem dealing with the times of Cleopatra, or paint a picture of Nero burning Rome, or compose a symphony in the manner of Brahms or Richard Strauss, or an opera like Wagner's, is far easier than to tell a simple story without any unnecessary details, yet so that it should transmit the feelings of the narrator.[9]

Some stories do work relatively simply. They illustrate a proverb or answer a question. "A Spark Neglected Burns the House" (*Ustupish' ogon' – ne potushish'*) confirms its title both literally and figuratively. The old man cautions his son to forget offenses, and prosperity returns only when he listens. The old man's wisdom is both Christian and practical:

malice blinds you. Others' sins are before your eyes, but your own are behind your back […] Is strife among men ever bred by one alone? […] No, lad! Christ, when He walked the earth, taught us fools something very different […] If you get a slap, turn the other cheek […] And his own conscience will rebuke him.[10]

He recommends Christ's teachings as *practical*. They convey essentially the same wisdom as Proverbs: "A soft answer turneth away wrath" (Proverbs 15:1). Needless to say, that is hardly the only way to read the Sermon on the Mount, which has seemed to many to be quite the opposite, a recommendation of all that is impractical.

Interestingly enough, *Resurrection* follows a similar logic as "A Spark Neglected." It is essentially a moral tale expanded to novel length, and, like those tales, ends with biblical quotations and Christian lessons. In the last chapter, Nekhliudov recognizes the Sermon on the Mount precisely as *practical* wisdom. Here again, Christ's apparently impossible commands turn out to be the most hard-headed and effective method for success in *this* world. "'But surely it cannot be so simple,' thought Nekhliudov; and yet he saw with certainty, strange as it had seemed at first, that it was not only a theoretical but also a practical (*prakticheskoe*) solution of the question."[11] Nekhliudov anticipates "the usual objection" – how can one let evil-doers go unpunished? – but he knows that it is forgiveness, not punishment, that truly works. Jesus' commands are not "exaggerated and impossible demands, but simple, clear, practical laws, which, if carried out in fact (and this was quite possible) would establish [...] the greatest blessing attainable by men – the Kingdom of Heaven on earth" (*Resurrection*, 517; *PSS* 32: 443).

HOW THE TITLE "GOD SEES THE TRUTH" MISLEADS

Not all Tolstoy's moral tales work so directly. At first glance, the title "God Sees the Truth, but Waits To Tell" refutes scorners who deny God's justice or claim He hides His face. Given this title, we look for some compensation, however tardy, for Aksyonov's sufferings, although we can hardly imagine what would be sufficient – and for some adequate punishment for the murderer and scorner, Makar Semyonovich.

Readers demand *justice*. But God proves wiser than that. It turns out that the entire sequence of events – unjust condemnation, years of prison, and the eventual meeting of the innocent with the guilty – happens to give Aksyonov something much more valuable than justice: the opportunity to forgive. Aksyonov knows that turning Makar Semyonovich in would be not only revenge but also justice, all the sweeter, and all the more just, because the victim gets to be its agent.

And yet, to grasp the story one must recognize not, as the title initially seems to suggest, that justice eventually triumphs, but that the desire for justice is to be overcome. To read "God Sees the Truth" as a story about the triumph of justice is to miss its point.

Meeting the real murderer, Aksyonov craves such justice. He remembers his flogging, his years in prison, and his premature old age. These thoughts drive him almost to suicide, and he can only think with anger that the villain Makar Semyonovich is responsible for it all.

Like the psalmist, the victim demands justice, and if that were the moral, the opportunity to inflict it would complete its pattern.

And yet, at the moment of truth, Aksyonov forgoes justice and protects Makar. He does not know why. When Makar Semyonovich comes to see him, Aksyonov remains angry, all the more so for his "weakness," and threatens to summon the guard.

Makar Semyonovich begs forgiveness, but Aksyonov refuses: it's all very well for you to talk, but I have still suffered all these years and lost my family. Makar Semyonovich can only say that it would be easier to bear flogging than to see Aksyonov at that very moment. And it is then that the real reason for Aksyonov's suffering becomes apparent. He suddenly begins to weep, says God will forgive you, and declares sincerely that perhaps he is a hundred times worse. Immediately, Aksyonov's heart grows light. He loses all desire to leave prison and hopes only for his last hour.

God *has* rewarded him, but not with justice. No, God has given something higher than justice, the joy that can come only from forgiveness. The greatness of the injury makes the forgiveness all the sweeter. Aksyonov suddenly realizes he has indeed lived a meaningful life in a way he never expected. Nothing could be more valuable than that.

The story looks at first as if its key event were the false arrest, and so Aksyonov has regarded his life. But this dramatic, outwardly visible event does not define it; the inward, prosaic one does. Aksyonov gets to change his life story. Unexpectedly, the answer to unjust imprisonment becomes not release, but the end of the desire for it.

The story could end here, but it contains one more twist: Makar Semyonovich does confess, but when the order for Aksyonov's release comes, Aksyonov is already dead. If we read this story as a tale about how God insures justice at last, this ending should seem profoundly unsettling. For here the triumph of justice is entirely pointless, since it does the victim no good. Quite the contrary: vindication precisely when it no longer can compensate for anything seems more like mockery. It is almost as if not God, but a scorner, arranged events.

But that is just the point: *Providence is not justice*, and *meaning is not compensation*. The story's ending questions not Providence but the identification of it with what Job and the psalmist demand, and what Proverbs promises, the proportionate reward of good and punishment of evil. We should look for meaning not in compensation but in forgiveness and love.

By this measure, the story has two providential endings. Makar Semyonovich achieves meaning as well when he sincerely confesses.

Indeed, one reason God "does not soon tell" (English: waits to tell) is to give Makar Semyonovich the chance to confess and repent, which he can only do after he has seen Aksyonov's sufferings. Aksyonov's suffering, then, has saved two people.

The story's title proves a decoy. It names where the reader begins. But the reader must, like Aksyonov, arrive at a wholly different understanding of life.

TWO MORE MISLEADING TITLES

"God Sees the Truth" is not Tolstoy's only misleading title. *The Death of Ivan Ilych* is not about the death of Ivan Ilych at all. It is about his dying. The story tries to teach us the radical difference between the two.

One's death is an event in the life of others, as Ivan Ilych's death provokes conversation in chapter 1. The dead Ivan Ilych continues to fulfill a social role.

Death is for Caius, the generalized man. But one's dying is for oneself alone. It is an experience that cannot be shared and must be unique. Each person's dying differs radically not only from his death but also from the dying of each other person. We are all alike in our uniqueness. Pascal famously wrote that "we shall die alone" (*on mourra seul*)[12] and Tolstoy's story may be read as a narrativization of this famous aphorism.

Like Aksyonov, Ivan Ilych learns that the story of his life is not what he imagined. Its key moment is none of the usual, noticeable ones, but the private chance he gets at the very end to make it meaningful. Like Aksyonov, he does.

Master and Man also narrates a life story that changes at its very end. This title misleads because the story proves to be not about a master (*khoziain*) and his man (*rabotnik*), but about the disappearance of that distinction, and of everything else separating people, when we understand life as love.

Proverbs and the sages remind us that in death we are all equal. But here it is not death but dying that reveals our essential equality. "We shall die alone" means that we die beyond social roles.

Indeed, the master Brekhunov not only becomes equal to his servant Nikita but also becomes Nikita:

He remembered that Nikita was lying under him [...] and it seemed to him that he was Nikita, and Nikita was he [...] "Nikita is alive, so I too am alive!" he said to himself triumphantly.[13]

As with Aksyonov, everything unexpectedly turns out to have been preparation for that key final choice. In one story, the hero forgives his enemy, in the other he loves another *as himself.*

Brekhunov's sense of his life changes so thoroughly that he talks of himself in the third person:

And he remembered his money, his shop, and his house [...] and it was hard for him to understand why that man, called Vasili Brekhunov, had troubled himself with all those things with which he had been troubled.

"Well, it was because he did not know what the real thing was," he thought concerning that Vasili Brekhunov. "He did not know, but now I know and know for sure. Now I know!" [...] and his whole being was filled with joyful emotion.

Brekhunov's story also resembles Aksyonov's because its key moment occurs without preparation, as if from nowhere. Brekhunov chooses to save Nikita "suddenly, with the same resolution with which he used to strike hands when making a good purchase" (*M and M*, 287–88; *PSS* 29: 42). Brekhunov's gestures, like his life, reverse their meaning *suddenly* – suddenly, because love derives from nothing and is an independent impulse. As Tolstoy would say in his tracts, it represents not our human but our divine nature. So surprising is Brekhunov's choice that he does not at first recognize it:

But to his great surprise he could say no more, for tears came to his eyes and his lower jaw began to quiver rapidly [...] "Seems I was badly frightened and have grown quite weak," he thought. But this weakness [...] gave him a peculiar joy such as he had never felt before. (*M and M*, 288; *PSS* 29: 42)

He experiences love "to his great surprise" because the feeling is entirely new and therefore unanticipated.

Brekhunov tries to tell Nikita, but fails: "His eyes began to fill with tears, and he could say no more. 'Well, never mind,' he thought. 'I know about myself what I know'" (*ibid.*). Aksyonov and Ivan Ilych also cannot express what they have discovered. And so it must be, because Christian love is not a doctrine to be taught but an experience one must undergo. For Tolstoy's greatest follower, Ludwig Wittgenstein, that is why "those who have found after a long period of doubt that the sense of life became clear to them have been unable to say what constituted that sense [...] There are, indeed, things that cannot be put into words. *They make themselves manifest.*"[14]

Ivan Ilych's change is invisible to outsiders who see two final hours of agony while he experiences "a single instant" whose meaning does not change. As readers, we too are outsiders. The story seeks not to argue us into love but to induce a rethinking of our lives.

TAKE NO NEED FOR THE MORROW

Several stories vindicate providence while questioning Proverbs (and proverbs). Far from counseling prudence, they implicitly allude to Jesus' command – which Tolstoy often endorsed – to live only in the present and not worry about the future.

Behold the fowls of the air: for they sow not, neither do they reap, nor gather in barns; yet your heavenly Father feedeth them [...] Therefore take no thought, saying, What shall we eat? What shall we drink? or Wherewithal shall we be clothed? [...] But seek ye first the kingdom of God [...] Take therefore no thought for the morrow: for the morrow shall take thought for the things of itself. (Matthew 6:26–34)[15]

In "Ilyas," the couple achieves happiness only when, having lost their wealth and become servants, they need no longer worry about the future. "'Don't laugh [...] God has disclosed the truth to us now, and we have told it to you, not for your amusement, but for your own good.' [...] And the guests stopped laughing and started thinking" (*Tales*, 249–50; *PSS* 25: 34). And so must we.

In "Two Old Men," the one who cites proverbs and practical wisdom misses his opportunity for a successful pilgrimage, but the one who lives in the present seizes it. "Walk in the Light while There Is Light" – one title that does not mislead – tells us to ignore all consequences. Practical wisdom is placed in the mouth of the "wise physician," who repeatedly dissuades the hero from joining the Christians. The crucial thing to recognize is that, if one's standard is prudential wisdom, the physician's arguments are correct. One must educate one's children and not leave one's responsibilities to others; and even the Christians depend on others to protect them from foreign invaders and violent men. The hero must learn not, as Nekhliudov does, that Christianity is indeed practical, but to forget about practical consequences altogether and take no heed for the morrow.

"WHAT DO PEOPLE LIVE BY?" AS A DOUBLE TITLE

Tolstoy's greatest moral tale, "What Do People Live By?," also considers wise sayings and uses a title that, though not exactly misleading, turns out to require not one but two readings.[16] We usually read it as "What Do People *Live* By?," but it is also "What Do *People* Live By?"

Understood the first way, the title alludes to the devil's temptation to turn stones into bread. Jesus answers: "Man shall not live by bread alone, but by every word that proceedeth out of the mouth of God" (Matthew 4:4). It is not bread alone that people live by, but the word of God, which in this story means love.

With the emphasis on "live," the title also recalls two others, *Who Is To Blame? (Kto vinovat?)* and *What Is To Be Done? (Chto delat'?)*. It seems to say: those are the wrong questions. One must not blame at all, and we can understand what is to be done only when we understand what people live by. And people live not by "utility," as Chernyshevsky has it, but by love.

Read the other way, with the emphasis on "people," the title asks what makes us humans as opposed to angels. After all, the plot centers on an angel whom God compels to learn the nature of *human* life. As the angel learns, so do we.

Tolstoy defamiliarizes human life as we look at it from a non-human perspective. Each incident is told first from Semyon's and then from the angel's point of view.

NEEDS AND LOVE

Three characteristics differentiate human from angelic life. The first is that it costs something to give. To love in a human way involves sacrifice. For angels, who have no material body, who live without suffering, and who do not die, that is not the case. It is precisely to teach the angel the difference that God makes him human.

Turned into man as he fundamentally is, the angel finds himself naked, freezing, and helpless. With a material body, he now feels pain and want: "I had never known human needs [...] till I became a man. I was famished, frozen, and did not know what to do [...] For the first time since I became a man, I saw the mortal face of a man, and his face seemed terrible to me" (*Tales*, 141–42; *PSS* 25: 23). "Human needs" changes the angel's view of humans. Semyon's face is at first terrible because humans must provide for their own needs. Therefore giving is not costless and automatic. That is why the angel hears Semyon talking to himself about how to feed and clothe his family. The angel thinks: "I am perishing of cold and hunger, and here is a man thinking only of how to clothe himself and his wife, and how to get bread for themselves. He cannot help me" (*Tales*, 142; *PSS* 25: 23). And indeed, if Semyon considers only his pressing needs, there is no reason to help.

When the angel recognizes why Semyon cannot help, he feels desperate. That new feeling teaches him another consequence of human needs: despair that they cannot be satisfied. The angel then witnesses something else new to him, the man's inner struggle and subsequent change. Should he pass by or help? Again, needs insure that such conflicts always exist, because love requires that we care for others before ourselves.

Semyon wonders whether he would be walking into a trap or, if not, how he could care for the man when he has so little. After all, Semyon has just failed to buy warm clothing, and knows there is no bread for tomorrow. But his conscience strikes him – all of a sudden – and he returns to help.

At first, the angel hardly recognizes him. Apparently, wholly distinct forces conflict within us. As love wins out over needs, life overcomes death. The angel has seen death in Semyon's face, but now he "was suddenly wholly alive, and in his face I recognized God" (*Tales*, 142; *PSS* 25: 23).

Just before her husband arrives, Semyon's wife Matryona is patching a shirt and planning how to make the bread last a little longer. She takes heed for the morrow, working to satisfy the basic human needs, food and clothing. She is understandably angry when Semyon arrives smelling of drink and with a naked man. She says, quite correctly, that they cannot clothe all the naked. But that is just the point: it is because one cannot do everything, because giving always costs, that care for others has its peculiar human value.

When Semyon reminds his wife that we will all die some day, "she glanced at the stranger and suddenly the word entered her heart" (*Tales*, 129; *PSS* 25: 13). Again the change is sudden, because it comes from a part of us distinct from needs. Matryona, too, experiences two forces that conflict: "When she remembered that he had eaten their last piece of bread [...] she felt grieved; but when she remembered how he [the stranger] had smiled, her heart leapt" (*Tales*, 130; *PSS* 25: 14). Late at night, still conflicted, she tells Semyon they have no more bread. He replies: "If we live, we will eat" (*Tales*, 130; *PSS* 25: 14). Consider the birds.

From the angelic perspective, her first reaction literally carries the stench of death. Paradoxically enough, death results from considering what we need to live. "He that loveth not abideth in death," as the story's first epigraph reminds us. The angel knows that if she does not relent she will die. But she suddenly loves, and death disappears.

Now the angel learns his first lesson, *in man dwells love*. He learns that love is a distinct force within us, that it runs contrary to our needs and so costs us something; and yet it is a force for life.

UNCERTAINTY AND DOUBT

The angel's next lesson concerns another defining feature of human life, radical uncertainty.

The angel knows God exists, for God speaks directly to him. But people live in a world of doubt, which conditions everything important.

Unlike the angel, people never see God. Two of the story's biblical epigraphs mention this important fact: "No man hath seen God at any time" (1 John 4:12) and "for he that loveth not his brother whom he has seen, how can he love God, whom he hath not seen?" (1 John 4:20). What is more, the angel knows just what God's will is, even if he once chooses to disobey it. But people must follow His will without being sure what it is, or even that God exists.

Semyon's plan to buy a sheepskin goes awry, as human plans do. When he meets the freezing man, doubt assails him. By contrast, the angel both knows and knows that he knows. Each time he understands God's lesson, he recognizes that he does (*PSS* 25: 24). He is literally as well as figuratively illumined, until, when he knows all three answers, he is "clothed in light so that the eye could not look on him, and his voice grew louder, as though it came not from him but from heaven above" (*Tales*, 143: *PSS* 25: 24). No human has such testimony.[17]

To comprehend human life, the angel must learn what it is to doubt. He first experiences it when, naked and helpless, he "did not know what to do" (*Tales*, 141; *PSS* 25: 23).

The story of the wealthy man who orders shoes to last a year illustrates this constituent fact of human life. "As if cast in iron" (*Tales*, 132; *PSS* 25: 16), this man seems, as Matryona comments, to be beyond the power of death. His sudden demise therefore comes as a complete surprise.

But the angel, we learn later, has detected the angel of death over the man's shoulder. Seeing what people cannot, he knows for sure that the man will die that day. Consequently, he makes not the ordered boots but slippers for the man's corpse. No human would ever be sure enough of the future to do that. Human expectations can never be more than hopes or fears.

The angel therefore learns that, because people cannot know the future, it is not given to them to know their own needs. The angel thinks: the rich man is making preparations for a year though he will not last the day.

Uncertainty conditions everything we do. We easily aim for the wrong thing. We must choose to obey God's uncertain will and, unlike the angel, will never know if we have.

MORTAL LOVE

The angel's third lesson concerns the most crucial difference between angels and people, mortality. Mortality changes the very nature of love.

Unlike angels, we love in the face of death, and love all the more what we must leave ere long. Mortal ourselves, we see our own mortality in others. We pity and love them for undergoing the suffering that only mortals fear and feel.

Semyon appeals to his wife's generosity by reminding her that we all die. Taken logically, the answer makes little sense, because the threat of death would by itself lead us to conserve resources, not give them to strangers. Nor does Semyon mean that she faces heaven or hell after death. Consequences, whether in this world or the next, are entirely beside the point. The fact that we will all die does not point to some reason to love; it is itself the reason. When people love, the sense of mortality is never absent.

That is the love that *people* live by. It is also the love that people *live* by, because without it, they could not live at all.

It is not our efforts that sustain us, because they must always be as insufficient as the struggles of a naked, helpless man. The angel has not understood this, and has therefore responded to the mother's plea to live to help her newborns. He has thought, quite reasonably, in terms of consequences.

The angel thinks, again correctly, that it would be unjust for her to die. By sheer accident, her husband has been killed by a falling tree. Now the woman herself is dying and so her infants seem punished for what could not be their fault. True enough, but in God's providential order justice is not the most important thing.

What is most important is the love that binds us together as fellow mortals. Though it leaves her children orphans, the mother's death enables love in others. That love involves risk in a world of death. The woman who adopts the girls does so in spite of fearing she will have insufficient milk for her own child. First she plans not to feed the crippled girl, who will probably not survive in any case, but then, for that very reason, she pities her. Her own child indeed dies. That event, which cannot be understood in terms of justice, makes her love the girls even more.

The angel disobeys God in response to the proverb the dying mother quotes, that one cannot live without mother and father. By the story's end, the angel has understood matters more deeply:

Having heard the story, I thought, "Their mother besought me for the children's sake, and I believed her when she said that children cannot live without father or mother; but a stranger has nursed them and brought them up." And when the woman showed her love for the children that were not her own […] I saw in her the living God, and understood what people live by […] I have learned that all people live not by care of themselves, but by love. (*Tales*, 143–44: *PSS* 25: 34)

Such love is entirely gratuitous. It promises no reward and repays no debt. Performed for their own sake, the woman's loving actions derive from a part of our nature that lies beyond justice and consequences. Mortal ourselves, we love mortal others.

We do not love this way for any purpose, and yet, as God has made the world, it does serve a purpose. Without it we could not survive. The angel recognizes that in each incident this is the love he has seen.

"I remained alive when I was a man not by care of myself, but because love was present in a passerby […] The orphans remained alive, not because of their mother's care, but because there was love in the heart of a woman, a stranger to them, who pitied and loved them. And all people live not by the thought they spend on their own welfare but because love exists in people." (*Tales*, 144; *PSS* 25: 25)

We all resemble newborns or naked men in the cold. Like them, we cannot survive by our own efforts. And yet we live, because of purely gratuitous acts of love.

In each case, the one who loved was a stranger, that is a person with no ties to, and no interest in, the one helped. Such help cannot be foreseen and its results cannot be known. That is why mortal love demands a world of uncertainty.

Strangely enough, God has deliberately misled us. "I have now understood," the angel explains, "that though it seems to people that they live by care for themselves, in truth it is love alone by which they live" (*Tales*, 144; *PSS* 25: 25). Why should God have found it necessary we should be so mistaken?

The answer is that it is precisely because we think that we live by our own efforts that we regard such love as senseless and gratuitous. Done for mutual advantage, it would be an economic bargain and so not love at all.[18]

The angel learns: God does not want us to live apart, but bound by our gratuitous love for each other. So he gives us love that must be senseless to exist at all.

As one of the story's epigraphs tells us, "God abideth in him" who loves. Therefore the dying woman's proverb, that children cannot live without mother and father, is answered by a different one:

And Matryona sighed, and said; "The proverb is true that says, 'One may live without father and mother, but one cannot live without God.'" (*Tales*, 139; *PSS* 25: 21)

One proverb reminds us of our needs. It expresses the conventional, and reasonable, proverbial wisdom. The other tells us of the senseless love that truly sustains us and gives meaning to life. The story moves from one to the other. The distance between them marks the difference between the wisdom Tolstoy found insufficient and the wisdom he recommended. The story voices a wise saying but goes beyond it to a truth still wiser. God's world is providential not because it rewards prudence and justice, as in traditional wise sayings, but because it allows for gratuitous, mortal human love.

Tolstoy adapts the wise saying to his own wisdom.

NOTES

1. Matthew 5:39. Unless otherwise indicated, all citations from the Bible are from the King James Version (1611).
2. As cited from Tolstoy's diaries in Boris Eikhenbaum, *The Young Tolstoi*, trans. Gary Kern (Ann Arbor, MI: Ardis, 1972), 10.
3. On these anthologies, see S. M. Vreitberg's foreword to volumes 39 to 42 of the Academy "Jubilee" Tolstoy, *L. N. Tolstoi. Polnoe sobranie sochinenii*, 90 vols. (Moscow: Gosudarstvennoe izdatel'stvo "Khudozhestvennaia literatura," 1928–58), 39: v–xxxviii.
4. I give a more detailed account of Tolstoy's line and its sources in Morson, *"Anna Karenina" in Our Time: Seeing More Wisely* (New Haven, CT: Yale University Press, 2007), 35, 235–36.
5. On Bakhtin's genre theories, see Gary Saul Morson and Caryl Emerson, *Mikhail Bakhtin: Creation of a Prosaics* (Stanford, CA: Stanford University Press, 1990), 271–305.
6. Leo Tolstoy, *War and Peace*, trans. Ann Dunnigan (Harmondsworth: Signet, 1968), 344; *PSS* 9: 344.
7. Theodore de Bary and Irene Bloom, eds., *Sources of Chinese Tradition*, 2nd edn, vol. 1 (New York: Columbia University Press, 1999), 56.
8. *The Book of Psalms: A Translation with Commentary*, trans. Robert Alter (New York: Norton, 2007), 3.
9. Leo N. Tolstoy, *What Is Art?*, trans. Aylmer Maude (New York: Bobbs-Merrill, 1960), 179; *PSS* 30: 184.
10. Leo Tolstoy, *Walk in the Light and Twenty-Three Tales* [henceforth *Tales*], trans. Louise and Aylmer Maude (Maryknoll, NY: Orbis, 2003), 152–53; *PSS* 25: 51–52. Translations modified for accuracy.
11. Leo Tolstoy, *Resurrection*, trans. Louise Maude (New York: Dodd, Mead, 1901), 517; *PSS* 32: 442.
12. Blaise Pascal, *Pensées*, trans. A. J. Krailsheimer (Harmondsworth: Penguin, 1966), 80.
13. All citations from *Master and Man* are from Leo Tolstoy, *"The Death of Ivan Ilych" and Other Stories* [henceforth *M and M*], ed. David Magarshack (New York: Signet, 1960), 288–91; *PSS* 29: 41.
14. Ludwig Wittgenstein, *Tractatus Logico-Philosophicus*, trans. D. F. Pears and B. F. McGuiness (London: Routledge, 1961), 73 (6.521–6.522).

15. Cited, for instance, in *The Kingdom of God Is within You*, *PSS* 28: 73–74.
16. The Table of Contents for *PSS* 25 gives the title as "*Chem liudi zhivy?*" but in the text of the story the title lacks the question mark. The commentary (*PSS* 25: 666–67) insists that Tolstoy settled on the title with the question mark.
17. It is as if Tolstoy meant to endorse the description of human life offered in Dostoevsky's Grand Inquisitor legend. God has placed us in a world in which the essential condition of action is uncertainty. We must do right without ever being sure what it is or whether we have succeeded.
18. Again the story seems to echo the Grand Inquisitor legend: if one acts like a Christian because Christ can perform miracles, God can save, and heaven can reward, then one is not a Christian at all. Such calculations are economic. A true Christian would follow Christ even if He had no supernatural power at all.

CHAPTER 11

The *"proletarian lord": Leo Tolstoy's image during the Russian revolutionary period*

Michael A. Denner

> Too, those who are caught by Tolstoy's eyes, in the various portraits, room after room after room, are not unaffected by the experience. It is like, people say, committing a small crime and being discovered at it by your father, who stands in four doorways, looking at you.
> Barthelme, "At the Tolstoy Museum"[1]

Leo Tolstoy figured large in the deeply partisan and impassioned debates during the Russian revolutionary period (1917–24). In the uncharted social and political chaos of disappearing and emerging institutions, competing centers of authority vied for validation and credibility by reciting and creating stories about Tolstoy: how he foretold the Revolution, warned against it, or caused it; why he would have rejected or embraced it; what he would have said or done had he lived to see it. Regardless of political position, these commentators saw Tolstoy as the code that, when correctly interpreted, offered a truer understanding of the Revolution's cipher, because both Tolstoy and the Revolution were equally products of a uniquely Russian experience.

An examination of the stories people told about Tolstoy in primary historical documents from the Russian and international press provides a fuller and more nuanced historical understanding of debates about the authenticity, inevitability, and justness of the Russian Revolution. While the storytellers intended only to influence the perception of the Revolution by invoking Tolstoy, making what was new and unfamiliar into something comprehensible by referencing something known, these stories nonetheless altered Tolstoy's image as well. The new images generated by texts about Tolstoy and the Revolution entered into a reciprocal relationship with existing social-historical texts of every kind about him. Although they were incidental, potent and new images of Tolstoy arose in response to the Revolution.

The historical examination of Tolstoy and revolution is therefore simultaneously literary criticism stimulated by a desire to uncover the full trajectory of Tolstoy's image. The author is more than the biological source of texts. It is rather a complex and constantly unfolding social process that operates on, inter alia, literary interpretations and their validity, authorial biographies, textological assumptions and priorities, and publishing practices. Discursive interests (e.g., those competing centers of authority) become part of the story we tell about Tolstoy, and this story influences our interpretive assumptions about his texts. A fuller understanding of our received image of Tolstoy therefore enhances and desimplifies our interpretations of his literary works. While we can never develop a totally *authentic* image of Tolstoy, we can be more and less naïve in our handling of his representation. This chapter dwells on Tolstoy both as a "great singular figure" and as a generalizable phenomenon. By studying how Tolstoy's images have been generated, we learn about collective representation as an act of social behavior, one determined and constrained by social conditions.

TOLSTOY AND REVOLUTIONS

Tolstoy had his own political views, of course. In a note dated January 22, 1905, to his English biographer, Aylmer Maude, Tolstoy's second daughter Mar'ia L'vovna wrote:

I have lately returned from Yasnaya [Tolstoy's estate] where I spent two months. My father was well but he is tormented by demands made on him to take part in current events. The Liberals want to draw him into their camp, the Conservatives into theirs, and the Revolutionists into theirs; and he does not belong to any one of them and only asks to be left in peace. People do not understand and do not admit his point of view and think that in consequence of what is happening in Russia he must come down from his Christian standpoint and say something new and something they want him to say.[2]

The letter was published in Maude's 1910 biography, as Mar'ia L'vovna knew it would be. It was a public statement about Tolstoy's reluctance to make public statements. Like all of Tolstoy's familiars, Mar'ia L'vovna took an active part in the social construction of Tolstoy, and her letter elaborates some essential and stable features of Tolstoy's relationship with public debates on politics. In the chaos of worldly concerns, the unruly masses torment Tolstoy with demands. He must come down to their level, he must say something new, and he must say something they want him to say.

Tolstoy's carefully crafted image partakes of what Leo Braudy calls "the best fame: [I]ts aloneness, its separation from the crowd, even though the famous, more clearly than ever, had emerged from the crowd to assert their personal distinctiveness and thereby demonstrate its potentiality in every member of their audience."[3] A star must successfully navigate the opposed poles of ordinary and extraordinary, of access and detachment. Tolstoy executed this maneuver brilliantly as the genius count cum ploughman prophet. His recent English biographer, A. N. Wilson, observed acutely Tolstoy's convoluted interactions with his own fame and nobility: "He was not 'Sir' or 'Count': just plain Lev Nikolaevich, and woe betide the servant who forgot this."[4]

Of course Tolstoy came down to say something to the masses; celebrities and prophets can remain so only if they sometimes leave their compounds and deserts. Responding to the events of 1905, Tolstoy wrote several articles and booklets on the meaning of revolution, which were printed in vast quantities in Russia and translated in the press abroad. But he said nothing new, and certainly not what people wanted to hear. The gist of his response was predictable for anyone even rudimentarily familiar with Tolstoy's social and political beliefs:

These complex and difficult circumstances among which we now live in Russia demand from us not articles sent to newspapers, nor speeches at meetings, nor going into the street with revolvers, nor dishonest and irresponsible inciting of the peasantry. What's needed now is a strict attitude toward oneself, toward one's own life, which alone is in our power and the improvement of which alone can improve the general condition of people.[5]

Tolstoy's rejection of revolution was unequivocal and consistent. All societal progress depended upon personal moral improvement consisting primarily of the self-abnegation of an individual "subjecting his animal personality to reason and making manifest the power of love" (*On Life*, ch. 14). Such was the "Christian standpoint" from which Tolstoy refused to come down during the 1905 Revolution, and one he held at least from the 1870s until his death in 1910.

Though he rejected with equal vehemence both the tsarist regime and any revolutionary movement that appealed to force, it is important to realize that Tolstoy was in no sense a Liberal. Tolstoy once remarked to Dushan Makovitsky that to ask him about democratic representation "is like asking the Pope – no, not the Pope, but a monk – about how to organize prostitution."[6] Yet, despite Tolstoy's resolutely anti-Liberal stance and his rejection of revolution, to be a progressive *intelligent* during the decade before the Revolution meant embracing, at some level of commitment, ideas associated among the broad public directly with Tolstoyism.

These included, on the one hand, a rejection of official Christianity, militant imperialism, nationalism, materialistic culture, and, above all, a bourgeois lifestyle; and on the other hand, an embrace of "Tolstoyan virtues" like physical labor, rural life, pacifism, asceticism, voluntary poverty, spiritual enlightenment based loosely on Eastern metaphysics, a concern for the downtrodden, and, of course, vegetarianism. (Tolstoy may have invented the hippie life.) The Bolsheviks were well aware of this affinity because so many of them (Bonch-Bruevich, Armand, Krupskaia, Lunacharsky) had toyed with Tolstoyism. Lenin himself acknowledged it in 1908 during Tolstoy's eightieth birthday celebrations:

The whole of this press is steeped to nausea in hypocrisy, hypocrisy of a double kind: official and liberal. The former is the crude hypocrisy of the venal hack [...] Much more refined and, therefore, much more pernicious and dangerous is liberal hypocrisy [...] Their calculated declamations and pompous phrases about the "great seeker after God" are false from beginning to end, for no Russian liberal believes in Tolstoy's God, or sympathizes with Tolstoy's criticism of the existing social order. He associates himself with a popular name in order to increase his political capital, in order to pose as a leader of the nation-wide opposition.[7]

Lenin did not exaggerate the Tolstoy cachet and, despite what he says, plenty of people believed, at least a bit, in Tolstoy's God, or at least in Tolstoy. He represented Russian popular discontent with the status quo. In 1909, the journal *Herald of Knowledge* (*Vestnik znania*) polled "working intelligentsia" for the writer most widely read. Tolstoy was placed first, with 295 votes. Darwin was second at 152 votes, with Karl Marx a distant sixteenth at 52 votes.[8]

An international *impersonal* political cult, disconnected from Tolstoy's own ideas, grew up around the *idea* of Tolstoy, his image as a prophet and rebel. As William Nickell has argued, after his death Tolstoy was transformed into a "cultural endowment" where every mention of his name was "an investment" upon a potential for Tolstoy to "encompass, signify and engender what it was to be Russian in 1910."[9] This potential existed long before 1910, but it intensified after his death. Such is the fate of many prophets.

THE REVOLUTIONS OF 1917

Lenin described the 1905 Revolution as "the great dress rehearsal" for the Bolshevik Revolution of 1917.[10] Tolstoy, whom Lenin acknowledged as having played a major role in the "failure" of the 1905 Revolution, obviously missed opening night in 1917. His no-show notwithstanding, after the revolutions of 1917 widespread demands once again emerged for Tolstoy to "take part in current events." Once again, from all sides, politicians, émigrés, intellectuals, and revolutionaries used the media of the age to *make* Tolstoy "say something new and something they want him to say." Perhaps because Tolstoy no longer could exercise ultimate, "authorial" control over his own image, Tolstoy's myth during the 1917 revolutions became the object of far more bitter and partisan wrangling than during the 1905 Revolution.

Tolstoy's *influence* on the revolutionary period and the use of Tolstoy's *image* during that period are very different, albeit related, phenomena. Though it is difficult to validate, no doubt Tolstoy, like many others, indirectly *influenced* to some degree the course of events in 1917 and later. He might have done this through texts he wrote, the "moral authority" derived from his outspoken opposition to the tsarist regime, the international acclaim associated with his name, or his direct and indirect personal influence on political actors. The study of the use of Tolstoy's *image* involves an analysis of the various expressions of devotion to, or rejection of, Tolstoy's diverse representations in various media. A further, even finer distinction needs to be made between Tolstoy's actual influence and the influence that contemporaries *attributed* to him. One manifesto or article or speech invoking Tolstoy's image – be it either to condone or to condemn something – gave rise to a reaction, often an outraged one, from opponents who invoked Tolstoy's name in making their own counterargument. His assumed influence increased enormously as a result of these debates. Tolstoy was credited with, or condemned for, exerting influence that seems incommensurate with the cause.

There was no "Tolstoy bloc" with an independent existence or rationale of its own. Instead there existed a collective and impersonal narrative that derived from a sense of Tolstoy's representativeness, an expression of the influence that contemporaries assumed Tolstoy had on this period.

The scores of media references to Tolstoy and the 1917 revolutions reveal a complex trajectory. Initially, in 1917, the newly erupted revolutions needed to be absorbed into the preexisting myth of Tolstoy. Was it a Tolstoyan revolution, one caused for better or for worse by the societal trends associated with his teaching and influence? To what degree was the cult of Tolstoy responsible? Primary documents show that to a significant extent, in Russia and abroad, the breakdown of tsarist social institutions and the creation of new revolutionary ones were popularly perceived as Tolstoyan in character and origination.

As the revolutionary period took shape and its violent features became known during the civil war period, Tolstoy's image became something against which one tested the validity and authenticity of what had recently happened. In particular, the November 1920 commemoration of the tenth anniversary of Tolstoy's death in Russia and abroad set off a debate. Writers repeatedly asked the same questions, often verbatim: "For whom would Tolstoy have been? On which side of the barricades would Tolstoy have stood?"

By the end of the civil war, as the Bolsheviks consolidated control and set to work building the state, the debate changed fundamentally. No longer was the Revolution to be measured against Tolstoy; rather Tolstoy's myth had to be assessed against the stories told about the Bolshevik Revolution, its aims and achievements. Contemporaries argued whether there would be a place for Tolstoy's bust in the new pantheon of the Revolution.

The primary documents upon which I have based this research are rich and diverse, and largely overlooked since they are too historical for literary scholars and too literary for historians. This chapter offers examples from the most representative or overlooked pieces.

TOLSTOY AND THE FEBRUARY REVOLUTION

The ubiquity of Tolstoy's image in the revolutionary-era media has been numerically documented in the "Miscellany of the Commission" (*Sbornik komissii*) charged with marking one hundred years from Tolstoy's birth in 1928. This project demonstrates both the contemporary importance of Tolstoy's image and the fanatical embrace of bean-counting gripping the planned economy of Stalin's Soviet Union in 1928. The authors claim to have surveyed all newspapers and books published in Russia between March 1, 1917 and August 24, 1924, seeking to substantiate "a picture of exceptional interest for L. N. Tolstoy" among the "wide masses of the Russian population" during the revolutionary years.[11] They consulted "academic criticism" about Tolstoy as a writer, biographies, "a few articles" about Tolstoy as a thinker and moralist,[12] and finally "the most difficult of all categories for which to provide statistics," the thousands of references to Tolstoy in the popular press. In addition to all the books and academic journals, these include about four dozen periodicals and "many minor provincial newspapers" as well. Over 2,710 days, the total number of mentions of Tolstoy in these various categories during the period comes to 4,681, or about one allusion "every half day."[13]

Tolstoy's image sometimes quite literally appeared as an idol or icon. On March 17, 1917, the newspaper *Russian Bulletin* (*Russkie vedomosti*) printed an account by Count A. N. Tolstoy (a distant relative of Leo Tolstoy) of peaceful demonstrations on March 12 by "a battalion of workers, soldiers, female workers, Kirghiz in bright vests, and orchestras." Count A. N. reported seeing banners with "Long Live the Russian People," "Long Live the Brotherhood of All People," and, above it all, a "touching" portrait of Tolstoy.[14] The "Miscellany of the Commission" reports the frequent "mass expressions" of revolutionary zeal recorded in the press after the Revolution. These consisted of "proclamations never to forget Tolstoy at numerous rallies in Moscow, St. Petersburg, and the provinces, the bearing of his portraits during every possible demonstration, and the placing of busts of Tolstoy where the tsarist memorials had been dismantled."[15]

The foreign press likewise initially tended to identify the revolutionary period with Tolstoy's image. In its reporting on the February Revolution in Russia, on the same page as a detailed description of Tsar Nicholas' arrest ("Ex-Czar, Guarded, Has Fits of Crying: Son Well, Empress Better"), the *New York Times* printed the following tableau of class harmony under the title "Great Crowd of Soldiers and Workers Greet His Widow at Her Home."

A great crowd of peasants, soldiers, and workmen, says a Reuter dispatch from Petrograd, went singing and cheering to the house of the late Count Tolstoy at Yasnaya Poliana and sent a deputation to greet the widowed Countess in behalf of the Russian people. The Countess was asked to come out with the portrait of Count Tolstoy, and she complied. Thereupon all knelt and chanted.[16]

Such accounts were widespread. In her introduction to Tolstoy's much-anticipated diaries, published in the United States during the inter-revolutionary period, Rose Strunsky repeats the story of the impromptu ceremony at Iasnaia Poliana, and makes explicit the connection between Tolstoy and the Revolution:

The ultimate meaning of the Russian Revolution which took place in March, 1917, can best be understood through the pages of the Journal of Leo Tolstoi which is here printed. The spiritual qualities which make up the mind and personality of Tolstoi are the spiritual qualities which make up the new era [...] [N]o land but Russia could have produced a Tolstoi, and in no land but Russia could Tolstoi have been so embraced and so absorbed. The first act of the March Revolution was to redecorate the grave of Tolstoi in the forest of Zakaz, to make the sacred pilgrimage to his resting place and tell the father of the good news – the will of God is being established, reason is awakened in man.[17]

For those who had no sympathy for the Revolution, Tolstoy was likewise the clue to what was happening. Since he was virtually synonymous with opposition to war and refusal to comply with military conscription, he was often blamed in the Russian press for Russian desertions on the fronts of World War I. In June 1917, amid widespread reports of Russian desertion, the Swiss newspaper *Gazette de Lausanne* reported that the Germans were newly optimistic about their chances in the war and laid the blame "principally on the influence of Tolstoy's theories." A month later, the *New York Times* editorial board attributed the collapse of the Russian front in northern Galicia in July 1917 to the "senile vaporings" of Tolstoy.[18]

Within Russia, Tolstoy was also used to make sense of the new institutions arising out of the collapsed tsarist order. In addition to conscientious objection to military service, his name was closely associated with land reform, "the land question." His position on it was derived mostly from the American political economist Henry George, who recommended that the state abolish private property and nationalize all agricultural land. M. Gauzner, in a pamphlet published in 1917 and entitled "L. N. Tolstoy on Land," argued that the Constituent Assembly operated with Tolstoy's authority in its planned land reform.[19] Gauzner's explanation for Tolstoy's importance in deciding the just allocation of property was somewhat paradoxical. Only a nobleman and owner of vast tracts of land, who had witnessed first hand the consequences of the unjust system, could understand the importance of land to the Russian people. Tolstoy was the chief spokesman on the question of how land was to be divided in Russia, and he foresaw that private ownership of land would disappear.

Gauzner's account of Tolstoy's influence on the present moment begins with the latter's article "The Great Sin," written in the wake of the 1905 Revolution. In it, according to Gauzner, Tolstoy correctly identified land as the "only thing of importance and interest" for the entire people. Now that the old system had been destroyed, the Constituent Assembly, once convened, would finally realize Tolstoy's vision and "private ownership of land will disappear." However Gauzner warns that it will be "far from easy to divide the land" so "before the decision of the Constituent Assembly, before the decision of the entire people, it will be useful to recall the opinion of the great writer of the Russian land, Lev Nikolaevich Tolstoy."[20]

Much of the rest of the pamphlet is devoted to recounting Tolstoy's and Gauzner's views on the "land question." George recommended a system in which land was essentially nationalized and rented out to the peasants.[21] Having detailed the system, Gauzner poses the question of why Tolstoy, given his generally progressive views, would have defended George's "relatively measured, incomplete and bourgeois idea." The answer, proposes Gauzner, resides in Tolstoy's own complicity – he was himself a landholder, and for him George's system "offered the least effect on landowners while simultaneously promising a successful solution to the problem." Tolstoy understood that it was "impossible to begrudge the people the land" because they were its "rightful owners" but he was "too dreamy, too kind a man, and his heart could not come to terms with the violent expropriation of land." Therefore, Gauzner claims, it is "our duty to hearken to the voice of L. N. Tolstoy, and not to become violators arbitrarily taking land, for that is not our personal affair, but the affair of all the people and all the people, [and] the entire 'commune' (*mir*) should do it in the Constituent Assembly."[22] The February Revolution and the Constituent Assembly were completing the Tolstoyan project of demolishing private ownership of land. The pamphlet ends with Gauzner's claim that "people have recognized their great sin, and will no longer commit it. Tolstoy's enormous achievement consists of his having helped people to acknowledge this sin, the sin of landownership."[23]

For Gauzner, Tolstoy – a landowner who preached the necessary destruction of his own class – offered a potential model for peaceable progress. As a unifying image before whom the people owed "a debt," Tolstoy was a sign of continuity and a connection.

THE OCTOBER REVOLUTION

After the Bolshevik's ouster of the Provisional Government, the ensuing civil war, and the violent breakdown of social institutions in the new Soviet Union, the Revolution was no longer perceived as Tolstoyan. It no longer could be claimed to represent the "mutual harmony" and "democracy" that Strunsky associated with Tolstoy's image. Vladimir Chertkov, Tolstoy's literary executor and most prominent representative, noted that the revolutionaries in early 1918 "love to refer to themselves as 'not-Tolstoyans'." "As for influencing those who are presently committing these atrocities: [the revolutionaries] know very well how Tolstoy felt about activities such as theirs."[24]

Despite the avowedly "not-Tolstoyan" orientation of the revolutionary leaders, Tolstoy's image remained a powerful influence. He was often re-imagined in the popular press as an observer and judge of the events of the era. The polemics shifted, and one question was repeatedly asked: "Who would Tolstoy have backed?" (*Za kogo by byl Tolstoy?*) Given Tolstoy's rejection of violence and political activity, many participants made the reasonable argument that he would have rejected the Revolution and its *modi operandi*. However, surprisingly robust and creative arguments on all sides of the debate, for the Revolution, against it, and undecided, still insisted that the Revolution bore Tolstoy's mark.

THE TOLSTOYANS

Leading Tolstoyans in Russia and abroad initially embraced the Bolsheviks as the party of peace, and cautiously hoped the new Soviet government might evolve into something better than its tsarist predecessor. The Bolsheviks carried the Russian masses, and with them the Tolstoyans, largely on their appeal to end all Russian participation in the European war. The Bolsheviks furthermore promised to divide the land fairly, educate the peasants, and disestablish the Orthodox Church – policies any Tolstoyan might support. Although their views of the Bolsheviks' motives and goals soured by the early 1920s, this did not prevent Tolstoyans from working closely with the Soviet government throughout the 1920s and 1930s.

Despite initial misgivings, Chertkov made an argument in favor of the Revolution in a pamphlet he published in London during the fall of 1919, at the height of Western intervention in the Russian Civil War. In "Save Russia," he beseeched British readers to withhold judgment against the Bolsheviks.[25] Given the violence and class hatred that existed in Russia, Chertkov warned outside observers against a summary judgment against the Revolution and urged them to consider its several beneficial results. The "automatic demobilization" of Russian soldiers during the chaotic year of 1917 represented "one of those historical achievements the significance of which for the whole future of mankind is so far-reaching that it can scarcely be adequately appreciated by the current generation." Readers would have immediately understood that this "demobilization" was motivated in part by Tolstoy's pacifistic writings. According to Chertkov, having shaken off the "corrupting influence of Church and State" – another clear reference to Tolstoy's influence – the Russian soldiers in turn inspired the German soldiers to discontinue fighting. "And undoubtedly this example offered by the Russian people has greatly contributed to the cessation of the European war." The Bolshevik Revolution furthermore brought an end to the ecclesiastical censorship that had endured even after the 1905 Revolution and this had the unintended result of making Tolstoy's religious writings available.

Thus the writings of Tolstoy, which have now for the first time become accessible to the masses in Russia, afford pre-eminent satisfaction to our working classes. In

Tolstoy the people find a clear and powerful expression of their own most sacred beliefs and highest aspirations [...] No wonder therefore that amidst the Russian people there is at present so enormous a demand for the writings of Tolstoy that we, Tolstoy's publishers, can only regret the impossibility of satisfying it in a sufficient degree.[26]

These unintended and even anti-revolutionary consequences of the Bolshevik Revolution led Chertkov to hope that "this odious civil war would automatically exhaust itself for want of combatants, as was the case with Russia when her troops withdrew from the international war." An end to the internecine war was impeded by one thing, "that some of the conflicting armies are receiving support from foreign powers." Chertkov therefore implores his British readers to compel their governments to "desist from affording the slightest material support to any of the parties involved in our civil war." He ends his letter by repeating his claim that the Bolshevik Revolution was "a great spiritual upheaval" and beseeching British working-class readers to "endeavor to prevent the dark forces of governments" from obstructing "our advance towards the realization of the universal brotherhood on earth" foreseen by Tolstoy.[27]

Appended to Chertkov's letter is a second appeal, described on the frontispiece as "reprinted from *Foreign Affair* by Paul Birukoff [Pavel Biriukov], well-known to the world as the biographer of Tolstoy, whose close personal friend he was." Biriukov follows roughly the same argument as Chertkov, underscoring what he hoped was the temporary nature of the Bolsheviks' regime, and describing "Russia's vivid new life," which he links explicitly with Tolstoy. Like Chertkov, Biriukov calls on the common working British citizen to exercise pressure to cause the government to cease its blockade and meddling in Russian affairs. He ends his plea to "save Russia" by reanimating Tolstoy:

I was the intimate friend of the great master, Leo Tolstoy, whom the world long recognized as the embodiment of the conscience of humanity. I know that were he alive to-day, his powerful voice would thunder through the world and bring the powerful to their knees ... In the name of my great dead master, I appeal to you, brothers, workers, save Russia![28]

A year later, on the tenth anniversary of Tolstoy's death, another notable Tolstoyan, I. M. Tregubov, published an article entitled "Tolstoy the Communist" on the front page of *Izvestia*. Tregubov had worked closely with Tolstoy on resettling the Dukhobors in Canada in the 1890s. To ground his argument that Tolstoy would have sided with the Bolsheviks had he lived to see the Revolution, Tregubov quotes from correspondence with the Dukhobors in which Tolstoy recommends that they forbid private property and work for the common good. This letter and other writings against private property prove that Tolstoy was a "fervent supporter of Communism" and believed that the "capitalist system should be destroyed and replaced with a communist system." The article is followed by a curious rejoinder from the editorial board: "Though it does not agree with all the opinions of the author [Tregubov], the editors have given space on this tenth anniversary of Tolstoy's death to an article belonging to the pen of one of his most notable followers." The same issue of *Izvestia* carries a short announcement, from the National Commissariat for Education, that a "Tolstoy museum," the future State Tolstoy Museum described by Barthelme in the epigraph, had been opened on Prichistenka Street.

THE WHITES

Russians in exile often blamed the October Revolution on Tolstoy. The popular American digest *Current Opinion* ran an article entitled "Tolstoy as the Great Patriarch of the Bolsheviki Family." It quotes I. I. Bunakov, a member of the Socialist Revolutionary Party and the Union for the Renaissance of Russia (*Soiuz Vozrozhdenia Rossii*), that "the fault and the responsibility of Lenin are insignificant in comparison with that of the giant Tolstoy, that pure representative of Russian culture." Tolstoy deserved the blame because he was the main spokesman for "the ideal of cosmopolitanism, of pan-humanism, of universality" which had long gripped Russia. The Revolution was a (paradoxical) sign of the profoundly national character of the Russians, because it has revealed itself "as so opposed to the ideas of Nation, *Patrie* and State."[29]

Symbolist novelist and literary critic Dmitry Sergeevich Merezhkovsky, and Duma representative Vasily Alekseevich Maklakov, both living in Europe in exile after the Revolution, saw Tolstoy's role in sharply partisan terms, but in ways significantly more nuanced than Bunakov's. In 1921 Merezhkovsky, whose best-known work of criticism was *Tolstoy and Dostoevsky*, published an essay entitled "Tolstoy and Bolshevism."[30] He argues that Tolstoy's ideas had led directly to the Revolution, and that the Revolution itself indicated a dire turn in European history: "Bolshevism is the suicide of Europe. Tolstoy inspired the act; Lenin completed it." However, on the question of which side Tolstoy would have favored, Merezhkovsky's analysis is more nuanced.

Which party does Tolstoy favor? Both sides, the White and the Red, quote him in their favor, and both seem to be right. But the question is not an easy one. Let us be more honest than our enemies and frankly admit that if we measure Tolstoy with the usual yardsticks – his ethics, his art canons, his politics, and his metaphysics – Tolstoy is not with us. At the best, he is midway between – or else above us and our opponents.[31]

Merezhkovsky admits that Tolstoy would have rejected the Bolsheviks for their use of force, but acknowledges that the forces opposed to the Bolsheviks – Merezhkovsky's own political party – do not abjure the use of violence, and therefore would likewise have been rejected by Tolstoy. Socially and politically, Merezhkovsky argues, Tolstoy was a part of Old Russia and therefore anathema to the Bolsheviks; however, like the Bolsheviks, Tolstoy sought the destruction of that world with a "blind rage." Whether Tolstoy would have joined the Bolsheviks in casting the "withered branch" of Russia into the "fire of world revolution" is ultimately uncertain, Merezhkovsky proposes. One area, though, in which Tolstoy would clearly have taken the Bolsheviks' side is aesthetics and metaphysics.

But at heart [Tolstoy] did feel as [the Bolsheviks] feel. He responded to that popular impulse which has exalted and sustained Bolshevism. What is Bolshevism? A denial of all culture as morbid and unnatural complication, a will to simplify, in its final analysis a metaphysical urge backward towards the condition of primitive man. But Tolstoy's genius is inspired by the same will.[32]

In Merezhkovsky's analysis, Tolstoy offers the most salient example of the "Scythian mind" that has dominated Russian thought with its plan to "convert Russia into a vacant level plain" and, having finished that task, to "leave the globe a perfect plain."

Merezhkovsky revisits his original question: "Are the Bolsheviki right then? Is Tolstoy one of them, and not one of us?" The question, he claims, cannot be fully answered on shared aesthetic and metaphysical grounds because "these are not the yardsticks by which you can measure Tolstoy […] His measure is religion." As soon as Tolstoy is recognized as a religious thinker, "we find Tolstoy with us."[33] While both Lenin and Tolstoy may share a desire for the destruction of present civilization, "a return to wildness," Tolstoy's metaphysics aims at the creation of a new culture, with religion as its foundation. Like "every revolution in the past," Lenin's will end "in an abyss of terror because there was no religion behind it." It is therefore "religious blasphemy to identify Tolstoy with Lenin."

Merezhkovsky ends the essay with a prediction made by Tolstoy's aunt and guardian, Countess Alexandra Il'inichna Osten-Sakin,[34] that one day "people would address her nephew with these words: 'Holy Leo, pray God for us'."

Is [Tolstoy] therefore a saint? No, in spite of his greatness, he is a sinner like ourselves […] Russian Bolshevism is Tolstoy's fire of Purgatory. All Russia is now burning in the first of its sins. But it will not be consumed […] Only its sins will be burned away in the purifying fire, and then will the Holy Russia of Leo arise. "Holy Leo, pray God for us!" – until we say that, we shall not save Russia.[35]

Strikingly similar to Chertkov and Biriukov, Merezhkovsky sees Tolstoy, or at least a Tolstoyan force, as the cause of a revolution which, despite a period of "burning" and purification, will eventually resolve into a new Tolstoyan phase.

In January of the same year (1921), in Paris, V. A. Maklakov[36] published a pamphlet with the same title as Merezhkovsky's article, and like Merezhkovsky he asks whether Tolstoy would have sided with the Bolsheviks. The pamphlet is based on a speech during a commemoratory event for Tolstoy, presumably the tenth anniversary of his death. Maklakov begins by wondering whether it was right to celebrate Tolstoy while Bolshevism was "in full swing," given the widespread perception that "the moral responsibility for [Bolshevism] lies with Tolstoy."[37] This perception derives its validity not merely from the argument that Tolstoyism and Bolshevism were equally products of the Russian national character.[38] Instead it was becoming increasingly clear that the Bolsheviks and Tolstoy shared an "internal affinity" demonstrated by "the honour with which the Bolsheviks surround Tolstoy's memory." As examples Maklakov cites the celebrations of the tenth anniversary of the author's death, the naming of streets, and plans to create a museum at Iasnaia Poliana. Furthermore, the Tolstoyans were collaborating with the Bolsheviks. They continued to publish their works in Soviet Russia, and even those who were living abroad "in full freedom" spoke out on behalf of the Bolsheviks.[39]

Maklakov does not mention, but surely has in mind, Chertkov's pamphlet "Save Russia" with its addendum by Biriukov, as well as the several journals and publishing houses – Unity (*Edinenie*), The Voice of Tolstoy (*Golos Tolstogo*), True Freedom (*Istinnaia Svoboda*) and Brotherhood (*Bratstvo*) – affiliated with V. F. Bulgakov, Chertkov, N. N. Gusev, and other visible Tolstoyans working in Russia, that continued to work more or less independently until 1922. And though Chertkov made official his plans to work with the Soviet government on a new, Jubilee edition of Tolstoy's works only in March 1921 (thus after Maklakov's speech), the plan had been openly advertised almost from the moment of the Revolution.[40]

Were he alive to see the events of 1917, claims Maklakov, Tolstoy would not have had the same views on Bolshevism as "one of us," i.e., as a member of the émigré community. He would have instead pointed out that

Bolshevism was the "logical result of the teachings and beliefs we ourselves hold" as "people of the world." Maklakov reminds the reader that Tolstoy was an idealist and an anarchist who categorically rejected all use of force and government. Thus, in Communism there was "nothing that would entice him" any more than other systems since there were "basically no differences" among governments.[41] In fact, inasmuch as a Communist government would try to practice fairness and equality, it would appear to Tolstoy to be "the most dangerous of teachings" because it would provide a "justification for evil, a justification for the idea of government, an apology for violence and coercion."[42] Therefore, Maklakov surmises, "Tolstoy and all of us would stand on different sides of the barricades, but we would not stand on the same side as Tolstoy, but rather on the same side as the Bolsheviks."[43]

Maklakov asks whether Tolstoy might nonetheless be "attracted by something in the Communist ideal in such a way that he would forgive the Bolsheviks in their striving after that ideal?"[44] He answers unequivocally in the negative: Tolstoy would have condemned the Bolsheviks because, in their attempts to advance the war between haves and have-nots, they had committed what, for Tolstoy and Christ, was the only unforgivable sin: the corruption of innocent souls by sowing hatred among the classes.[45] Returning to the question of why Tolstoyans accept the Bolsheviks, Maklakov says that the adherents of Tolstoy might very well *understand* what he preached, but they do not *accept* it. Tolstoy came to his beliefs through a crisis in which he "conceived a hatred for worldly life and the teachings of the world,"[46] and to accept his views requires one to "undergo, and not fleetingly, a similar frame of mind."[47] Tolstoyans might agree with Tolstoy's "denunciations and attacks on the rich and famous, with his criticisms, and therefore think that they agree with his teaching," finding common ground with the Bolsheviks. However they do not *accept* those teachings in the same way that Tolstoy did. Maklakov compares the Tolstoyans "who seriously claim that Tolstoy would have forgiven the Bolsheviks for their brutality" to the Inquisitors, followers of Christ's teachings, who "imagined that they too understood Him, as they lit the bonfires."[48]

As for why the Bolsheviks would "bow their heads before their own enemy and castigator," Maklakov is dissatisfied with the explanation that they do so as "merely an advertisement." They have Marx and Engels, so why do they need Tolstoy? To answer that question fully requires an understanding of Tolstoy's importance to Russia. While he was alive, Tolstoy was Russia's "consolation," and Russia calmed itself during troubled times with the idea that "it had Tolstoy, that he was not a myth or a legend, that he was a living reality, that there really existed this elder, upon whom the whole world gazed, and that he would never leave Russia, that he wouldn't trade her for anything."[49] Given Tolstoy's importance to Russia, Maklakov is led to wonder what the Bolsheviks might have done had Tolstoy lived to see the Revolution:

Would they have touched him? No doubt, no. They would have surrounded him with superficial honour, they would have honoured him as a "respected member of the proletariat," would have given him special bread cards, they would have sought to demonstrate through him their tolerance, their high level of culture, and their love for the people. But they would have had no more success bribing him with their honours and flattery than if they threatened him with death. They couldn't have fooled and flattered him, as they have flattered his nearsighted friends.

In the Bolshevik cult of Tolstoy, Maklakov concludes, "there is a measure of sincerity, like enemies who lay a laurel wreath on the tomb of a fallen warlord-enemy. In the depths of their souls they can sincerely honour his memory; they are glad that death has rid them of such an opponent."[50]

RED TOLSTOY

The Bolsheviks during this revolutionary period remained fundamentally ambivalent toward the political cult of Tolstoy. On the one hand, they believed that his popularity revealed both the exceptionality and the universality of the Russian people: the promises of selflessness, social cooperation, and rejection of bourgeois European culture that were implicit in the "cloud" of ideas and associations that swirled about Tolstoy's image. On the other hand, as a direct competitor with Socialist and Marxist thought – a third way, an alternative to western European constitutional government – his cult represented a discursive competitor from the intellectual and liberal bourgeois realm. Tolstoyan magazines published in the period often mention the competition between the Bolsheviks and their camp for the Russian ear. After reprinting a public lecture by the Tolstoyan N. N. Gusev, for instance, the editors of *Unity* (*Edinenie*) offered the following anecdote:

On the twenty-sixth of May [1918], this lecture ["Tolstoy and the Russian Revolution"] was repeated at the request of the workers at the Mikhel'son factory. This lecture had a paid entry with the profits going to support the [Tolstoyan] Society of True Freedom. For some reason, a *free* Bolshevik lecture on the separation of church and state was organized at the very same time and in the very same place as this lecture by N. N. Gusev. And yet Gusev's lecture attracted far more listeners.[51]

The Bolsheviks also had to worry about their own international image being overshadowed by Tolstoy's legacy. Many foreign commentators simply assumed either that the Bolsheviks were nothing more than Tolstoyans or that their revolution was merely a waypoint on the pathway to a Tolstoyan society. Since leading Bolsheviks dismissed Tolstoy as a superannuated relic of Russia's agrarian past, such conflations surely would have frustrated them. In one example, a 1919 *New York Times* article dismissed the Bolsheviks as "little Tolstoys."[52] In a 1920 article "Light from Tolstoy on Russia," Durant Drake (a leading American sociologist), criticizing the United States' press coverage of the Soviet government, rejected the idea that the Russians "longed to be delivered from their Bolshevik masters."[53] The outside world should know that the Bolshevik Revolution is not something imposed from above, but instead expresses an authentic Russian desire enshrining the tenets of Tolstoyism: economic equality, peace, and a rejection of bourgeois privilege.[54] Drake concludes by remarking that whatever might be said "in the press discussions of Western nations," "[t]his much, at least, is clear to the student of Tolstoy. The ideal of the Bolsheviki is a genuine ideal, not a mere mask for cupidity and love of power. To the degree in which it follows the ideal of Tolstoy, it undoubtedly has a deep hold upon the Russian soul."[55]

Today there is a strong (and well-founded) tendency to identify all Soviet criticism of Tolstoy's political ideas as little more than Lenin's doctrinal dismissals *réchauffés*.[56] At least before the end of the 1920s, however, there was debate among Bolsheviks themselves concerning the relevance of Tolstoy's political cult for the Soviet Union. The desire for approval from Tolstoy caused many to imagine that he might have changed his views had he lived another decade to see the revolutions. At least at this point in time, then, Tolstoy's image was not exactly a tool of propaganda, and no attempt was made to bias or oversimplify the representation. Instead, when Tolstoy's views were made to buttress one side or another of a debate, his views were represented as *more* nuanced, *more* ambiguous than they actually were.

On the tenth anniversary of Tolstoy's death, *The Whistle* (*Gudok*) – the "official newspaper for railway workers" – published a front-page editorial by M. Volokhov entitled "The All-Russian Tolstoy." Tolstoy deserves to be called "All-Russian" because his works are "the property of working class in Russia" and he wrote "exclusively for the Russian oppressed, the Russian poor, the Russian dark and ignorant countryside." Calling Tolstoy "the proletarian lord," Volokhov concludes that one "need not be a prophet" to know that, "were he alive today, [Tolstoy] would likely be among the ranks of the active builders of a new Russia, along with Gorky and Timiryazev. On this day, ten years after his death, proletarian Russia bares her head before his grave and believes passionately that he belongs to her."[57]

Echoing *The Whistle*'s panegyric, *Communist Labour* (*Kommunisticheskii trud*) ran a similar piece the same day, "Leo Tolstoy. Tenth Anniversary, 1910–1920," concluding that "the truth of our teachings and actions could not have escaped the penetrating gaze of the brilliant moralist, and precisely for this reason, he would have been on our side!"[58]

Ivan Knizhnik articulated a more careful attempt to reconcile Tolstoy with the Bolshevik program in a long, front-page article in *Petrograd Pravda* (*Petrogradskaia Pravda*). Knizhnik, a member of the Petrograd soviet during the October Revolution, begins by noting that, during the celebrations held all over Russia on the tenth anniversary of Tolstoy's death, there were sure to be many speeches on "what makes Tolstoy great and why he is dear to mankind." However, since most of those who know Tolstoy's works "belong to the bourgeois camp," speakers in all likelihood would "use the memory of Tolstoy to demonstrate that he would have not approved of our revolution, founded on violence, as it contradicts his moral teaching, etc." But Knizhnik warns his readers against accepting how the "bourgeois and false-socialist counterrevolutionaries" depict Tolstoy and claims instead that "the vast majority of his ideas could be used to demonstrate the rightness of our revolution."

The most important of Tolstoy's ideas – "the rejection of private ownership of land and the means of labor, the rejection of government and of all bourgeois culture" – were contained in books that had been forbidden by the censor "right up to the February Revolution." These forbidden works reveal that Tolstoy's positions were, in fact, "just like those of scientific socialism." "The military, police, and court exist in the modern state for the protection of the property of the few, the capitalists and the owning class against the vaster number of dispossessed, and [...] science, religion and art in the conditions of the bourgeois system not only do not serve to enlighten the people but, just the opposite, they serve the cause of its pollution."

Knizhnik explains that for Tolstoy there were only two solutions to "ridding the people of bourgeois supremacy": the first, a call to "go to the people" and work the land ("a vestige of Populism"); and the other, for "all conscious people to refuse to fulfill the duties that the bourgeois government calls them to do." Tolstoy gave up on direct revolution through violence, explains Knizhnik, because after the defeat of the People's Will revolutionaries in the 1870s he decided that revolution through violence was impossible "when the Tsar had millions of soldiers." However, "had Tolstoy lived until our days and had he seen how our soldiers during the October Revolution had turned from blind servants of the bourgeois government into its gravediggers, who knows, maybe Tolstoy would have changed his views on violence," especially inasmuch as the Revolution had been "almost bloodless."

Knizhnik then turns to the question of how Tolstoy would have reacted to the new Soviet way of life. Tolstoy was great precisely because "he absorbed into himself, granted from a peculiar perspective, all the greatest hopes of the people including the proletariat." In this sense of Tolstoy as peculiarly representative of Russia, "Tolstoy was a forerunner of our Revolution and many of the significant characteristics of our proletarian revolution were approved of by him in advance." To prove the point, Knizhnik elaborates the many points of similarity between Tolstoy's teachings and the policies recently instituted by the Soviet government. He mentions separation of church and state, the Bolsheviks' policies on art and education, the abolishment of capital punishment and the attempts to reform criminals "through public service," and the "comprehensive development of every individual." He concludes that Tolstoy would "undoubtedly have welcomed the decision of the Soviet power to teach every cook how to run a government and be a conscious member of it. He would have welcomed our system of public education [...] and the rejection of all coercion, just as Tolstoy taught in the 1860s." He ends the article by telling the "bourgeoisie and false-socialists: Hands off of Tolstoy! He's more likely with us than with you!"[59]

TOLSTOY, OUR COMPETITOR

By the end of the Civil War (the summer of 1923), the political cult of Tolstoy was being subjected to increasing criticism from within the Soviet Union. The above-mentioned Tolstoyan periodicals and publishers had ceased to exist by late 1921. A cursory glance through the bibliographic data from Pokrovskaia's extensive bibliography[60] or the card catalogue at the National Library of Russia indicates a dramatic shift in the tenor and number of Tolstoy publications. While dozens of publishers and newspapers published literally hundreds of Tolstoy's writings – belletristic and publicistic – and writings about Tolstoy during the 1917–21 period, the flow of such works dropped sharply toward the end of the Civil War. By 1923,

virtually the only publisher of Tolstoy's works was the new State Tolstoy
Museum. This decline is all the more striking as it occurred during the
relatively open time of the New Economic Policy (NEP), when private
printing presses were allowed to operate with relatively little interference
from the Soviet authority.

One plausible explanation for this clear shift in Tolstoy's social presence
in the Soviet Union can be found in a lengthy 1924 public lecture (published
in two separate, fairly large runs of 5,000 the same year) by one of the leaders
of the Bolshevik party, A. V. Lunacharsky, chairman of the Commission for
the People's Commissariat of Education from 1917 to 1929. In "Tolstoy and
Marx," Lunacharsky, who had written more than thirty articles and lectures
on Tolstoy,[61] begins by observing that, in Russia and other countries,
Marxism and Tolstoyism are two of the main ideologies, though certainly
not all the enemies of Marxism belong to the "Tolstoy camp."[62] Though the
bourgeoisie has no ideology of its own, it uses Menshevism as a "fig leaf to
hide its shame" before the masses. (For Lunacharsky, Menshivism means a
"perverted Marxism" that preaches against revolution and for "patience"
and "fatalism.") This pact between the bourgeoisie and Menshevism represents the "most dreadful enemy" to the Soviet Union. But, according to
Lunacharsky, "Tolstoyism is the worldview that should stand in the second
place in the ranks of our enemies" because, though it "does not exert an
influence on the proletariat," it is nonetheless "the strongest influence on
the intelligentsia" and more importantly it acts as "our competitor in
exercising influence on the best part of the peasants not only in Europe
but in the depths of Asia as well."[63] Next, Lunacharsky presents professions
of faith in Tolstoyism by two of the most notable intellectuals and political
actors of the day – the French intellectual and Nobel Laureate
Romain Rolland, and the leader of anti-imperialism in "Indostan,"
Mahatma Gandhi – to support his claim that Tolstoyism was the "leading
opponent" of Marxism. Their very public adherence to Tolstoyism indicates how, "whenever our task has to do with the most important allied
forces for the proletariat, that's when we have to deal with Tolstoyism."

Having established Tolstoy's influence on progressive leaders outside of
Russia, Lunacharsky then launches into a long-winded discussion of the
"relations between Marxism and Tolstoyism." Tolstoyism is "nothing new:
whenever there appears a new social formation – concentration of capital,
significant wealth, growth of trade and manufacturing – whenever these
things arise in whatever country, there appears a movement analogous to
Tolstoyism."[64] He delineates the similarities between Tolstoyism and, inter
alia, the Old Testament prophets, Rousseau, Jesus Christ, and Carlyle,

concluding that Tolstoyism is a social teaching which "raises the flag of revolution against capitalism [...] in the name of the past that, transfigured, is projected forward as the future."[65] This criticism is followed by not unexpected paeans to Marxism as a movement that "accepts civilization completely, accepts completely science and art and even wealth, the accumulation of wealth, capitalism. Marxism is the progeny of the city, and not the countryside; it looks forward and not back."[66]

Lunacharsky's closing statement on the competition between Marxism and Tolstoyism indicates that leading Bolsheviks had, by the early 1920s, begun to consider Tolstoyism a competitor and discursive threat to their attempts to win over the Russian intelligentsia and to expand their revolution beyond Russia. Lunacharsky observes that in contemporary Germany, the intelligentsia, in "great internal vacillation" in its search for "non-bourgeois" governance, has "divided into two tendencies." One group has embraced Communism, the "rational organization of human life"; and the other, mysticism, "in which a central role is played by Tolstoy, precisely because he appeals to credulity, because he says things that seem rational."[67] Predicting an eventual victory for the more pragmatic and worldly Communism, Lunacharsky nonetheless worries that Tolstoy's political cult might distract and delay the world intelligentsia from aiding the proletariat.

> We hope that this still-strong position, which has its moral arguments, its artistic authority in the great Tolstoy, and in various places is putting out new offshoots, we hope that it does not delay the intelligentsia in their path to unity with the proletariat, who needs it, who needs the intelligentsia at this early stage so much that without it the proletariat simply cannot set to work on building the new communist regime. We will wage a battle with this attractive and corrupting Tolstoyan superstition which saps the conscience and energy.[68]

And a battle was certainly waged against Tolstoy's social presence, or at least the political cult connected to him. In very short order – certainly by the centenary celebration of Tolstoy's birth in 1928 – even an *acknowledgment* of Tolstoy's political influence in Russia, much less a claim that Tolstoyism represented an important discursive competitor, would become simply impossible in the Soviet Union.[69] Probably no other artist has ever been the object of such pervasive, governmentally funded, and successful mediation and construction as Tolstoy underwent during the twentieth century in Soviet Russia. The powerful but contradictory image of Tolstoy generated by mass culture, his impersonal political cult, was dismantled in Stalin's Russia. (It eventually ceased to exist even outside of the Soviet Union.) A new, purely literary cult was crafted to replace it. Tolstoy's image was

1. *K stoletiiu L. N. Tolstogo: Sbornik komissii po oznamenovaniiu stoletiia so dnia rozhdeniia L. N. Tolstogo.* This amateurishly retouched photograph, published in the *Miscellany of the Commission* to mark the 1928 centenary of Tolstoy's birth, depicts the entryway to the Iasnaia Poliana school near Tula, Russia. Banners of Lenin and Stalin, the latter at least probably added, flank a statue of Tolstoy.

honed to produce a model appropriate for Socialist Realism: the consummate artist who never sank to aestheticism, a "critical realist" who raged against the economic, social, and religious conditions of his time, and an internationalist who remained thoroughly Russian. Here is not the place to discuss how Soviet educational, redactorial, and printing practices have refigured Tolstoy; I have instead chosen to concentrate on how Tolstoy was represented *before* the formation of what Nickell calls "the Leninist center" of Tolstoyan criticism.[70] Suffice to say that the Soviet image of Tolstoy is not at all historically continuous and is only contingently related to the discourse about him during the Revolution.

NOTES

1. D. Barthelme, "At the Tolstoy Museum," in Ann Charters, ed., *The Story and Its Writer* (Boston: Bedford/St. Martin's, 1999), 135.

2. A. Maude, *Life of Tolstoy, Later Years* (New York: Dodd, Mead and Co., 1911), 622.

3. L. Braudy, *The Frenzy of Renown: Fame and Its History* (Oxford: Oxford University Press, 1986), 403.

4. A. N. Wilson, *Tolstoy: A Biography* (New York: W. W. Norton, 1988), 346.

5. All translations, unless otherwise indicated, are mine. L. N. Tolstoi, "Obrashchenie k russkim liud'iam. K pravitel'stvu, revoliutsioneram i narodu," in *Polnoe sobraniie sochinenii v 90-i tomakh, akademicheskoe iubileinoe izdanie* (Moscow: Gosudarstvennoe izdatel'stvo khud. lit., 1928–1958), 36: 314.

6. D. P. Makovitskii, "U Tolstogo: 'Iasnopolianskie zapiski' D. P. Makovitskogo," in Shcherbina *et al.*, eds., *Literaturnoe nasledstvo*, vol. 90, book 1 [1904–5] (Moscow: Nauka, 1979), entry 36 for November 1905.

7. V. I. Lenin, "Leo Tolstoy as the Mirror of the Russian Revolution," in M. Solomon, ed., *Marxism and Art: Essays Classic and Contemporary* (New York: Wayne State University Press, 1979), 169–74.

8. Cited in V. Kantor, "Lev Tolstoi: iskushenie neistorii: Samyi, Samyi, Samyi, ili Tolstoi contra Gete," *Voprosy literatury* 4 (2000): 120–81.

9. W. Nickell, *Tolstoy in the Public Domain: His Death as a National Narrative*, PhD dissertation, UCLA at Berkeley, 1998 (Ann Arbor: UMI, 1998), xx.

10. V. I. Lenin, *"Left Wing" Communism: An Infantile Disorder* (Detroit, MI: The Marxian Educational Society 1921), 21.

11. N. Apostolov, "L. N. Tolstoi v gody russkoi revoliutsii," in *K stoletiiu L. N. Tolstogo: sbornik* (Moscow: Komissiia po oznamenovaniiu stoletiia so dnia rozhdeniia L. N. Tolstogo, 1928), 21.

12. *Ibid.* 22. The author suggests that such articles were "no doubt caused by the demands and moods of the time."

13. *Ibid.* 23.

14. A. Tolstoi, "Dvenadtsatogo marta," *Russkiie vedomosti* 61 (March 17).

15. Apostolov, "L. N. Tolstoi," 21.

16. "Kneel to Tolstoy's Portrait: Great Crowd of Soldiers and Workers Greet His Widow at Her Home," *New York Times* (March 27, 1917): 4.

17. R. Strunsky in her foreword to *The Journal of Leo Tolstoi: First Volume – 1895–1899* (New York: Alfred A. Knopf, 1917), xii.

18. "The Russian Danger," *New York Times* (July 27, 1917): 8.

19. Though democratically elected in November 1917, the Assembly never had a chance to deliberate the land question since it was dissolved by the Bolshevik decree in December. Gauzner was evidently a member of the Socialist Revolutionary Party, which had drafted a "Law on the Land" proposal for deliberation by the Assembly. See Michael Melancon, "The Left Socialist Revolutionaries, 1917–1918," in Edward Acton, Vladimir I. Cherniaev, William G. Rosenberg, eds., *Critical Companion to the Russian Revolution, 1914–1921* (London: Hodder Arnold, 1997), 296.

20. M. Gauzner, *Lev Nikolaevich Tolstoi o zemle* (Petrograd: Kn-vo M. A. Iasnogo b. Popova), 6.

21. *Ibid.* 12.

22. *Ibid.* 13–14.

23. *Ibid.* 15.

24. V. Chertkov, "Pomoshch' Tolstogo," *Golos Tolstogo i Edinenie* 2, no. 8 (1918), 9.

25. As a direct result of his association with Tolstoy, Chertkov had spent nearly a decade (1897–1906) in exile in England. He was well known to the British as a public intellectual and founder of the New Age Press.

26. V. Tchertkoff (Chertkov) and Paul Birukoff (Pavel Biriukov), *Save Russia: A Remarkable Appeal to England by Tolstoy's Literary Executor in a Letter to His English Friends* (London: C. W. Daniel, 1919), 5. Chertkov oversimplifies the status of Tolstoy's works. Although the publication of many of Tolstoy's religious works had remained officially banned by the Holy Synod on ecclesiastical grounds, these works were printed in Russian by presses abroad, including Chertkov's own publisher in London, and widely distributed in Russia before 1917.

27. *Ibid.* 12–13.

28. *Ibid.* 17–18.

29. Cited in "Tolstoy as the Great Patriarch of the Bolsheviki Family," *Current Opinion* (January 1919): 49.

30. D. Merezhkovskii, "Tolstoy and Bolshevism," *The Living Age* (May 7, 1921): 331–37. (First published in German in *Deutsche Allgemeine Zeitung* March 15–16, 1921, later collected [in Russian] in *Tsarstvo antikhrista* [Munich 1921].) It was widely republished in the Western press.

31. *Ibid.* 333.

32. *Ibid.* 334.

33. *Ibid.* 335–36.

34. Merezhkovsky incorrectly refers to her as Alexandra Andreevna.

35. *Ibid.* 337.

36. Maklakov, a lawyer and high-ranking Duma deputy from the Kadet party, was a personal friend of Tolstoy who also represented him in several personal legal matters. Tolstoy also made use of his judicial expertise while writing *Resurrection*.

37. B. A. Maklakov, *Tolstoi i bol'shevizm. Rech'* (Paris: Knigaizdatel'stvo Russkaia zemlia, 1921), 5.

38. This argument was put forth most famously in Nikolai Berdiaev's 1918 academic essay, "Spirits of the Russian Revolution" "Dukhi russkoi revoliutsii," in S. A. Askol'dov *et al.*, eds., *Iz glubiny: Sbornik statei o russkoi revol'utsii* (Moscow and Petrograd: Russkaia mysl', 1918), 37–74.

39. Maklakov, *Tolstoi i bol'shevizm*, 7.

40. For an excellent history of the publication of the Jubilee Edition of Tolstoy's *Complete Collected Works*, which details Chertkov's and Gusev's complex relations with the Bolsheviks during this period, see L. Osterman, *Srazhenie za Tolstogo* (Moscow: Grant, 2002).

41. Maklakov, *Tolstoi i bol'shevizm*, 12.

42. *Ibid.* 13.

43. *Ibid.* 14.

44. *Ibid.* 15.

45. *Ibid.* 23.
46. *Ibid.* 40.
47. *Ibid.* 45.
48. *Ibid.* 48.
49. *Ibid.* 50.
50. *Ibid.* 53.
51. N. N. Gusev, "Tolstoi i russkaia revoliutsiia. Lektsiia," *Golos Tolstogo i Edinenie* 2, no. 8 (1918): 16.
52. "New Forces of Disintegration in Russia: Syndicalism, More Violent than Bolshevism, Threatens To Thrust Unhappy Nation into New Chaos of Lawlessness, Says Manuel Komroff, Just Back from Russia," *New York Times* (January 19, 1919): 66.
53. D. Drake, "Light from Tolstoy on Russia," *International Journal of Ethics* 30, no. 2 (1920): 190–95.
54. *Ibid.* 192.
55. *Ibid.* 195.
56. See, for instance, G. Struve, "Tolstoy in Soviet Criticism," *Russian Review* 19, no. 2 (1960): 171–86. He quotes L. Opul'skaia, a leading Soviet Tolstoy critic of the twentieth century, as writing in 1958: "It is not just this brevity which makes Lenin's judgments about Tolstoy […] a *program* for further study … It is necessary to investigate in detail the way in which the fundamental contradiction between Tolstoy's art and world outlook, revealed by Lenin's analysis, comes to light whenever he touches, as an artist or thinker, upon any new sphere" (173).
57. M. Volokhov, "Vserossiisskii Tolstoi. (K 10-letiiu so dnia ego smerti)," *Gudok* (November 20, 1920): 1.
58. A. Kavkazskii, "Desiataia godovshchina. (1910–1920)," *Kommunisticheskii trud* (November 20, 1920): 1.
59. All quotes are from the same page of Ivan Knizhnik, "Lev Tolstoi i proletarskaia revoliutsiia. (K desiatiletiiu so dnia ego smerti)," *Leningradskaia Pravda* (November 20, 1920): 1.
60. N. D. Pokrovskaia (Khaimovich), *L. N. Tolstoi: Bibliografiia proizvedenii L. Tolstogo i literatury o nem., 1917–1927*, ed. N. K. Piksanova (Moscow: Izdanie Tolstovskogo Muzeia, 1928), 97–157. Pokrovskaia's bibliography appears to be remarkably complete, considering the year it was published (1928). (It contains, for example, mentions of works by Trotsky and books published abroad by émigrés.) I have cross-checked her bibliography against the card catalogue at the St. Petersburg National Library of Russia, which contains a complete record of books published in Russia during these years (or, in the least, the most complete record available).
61. K. N. Lomunov, "Predislovie" (to "A. V. Lunacharskii o Tolstom. Neopublikovannaia lektsiia 1928 g."), in *Lev Tolstoi v 2-kh knigakh* (Moscow: Izd-vo AN SSSR, 1961), 403.
62. A. V. Lunacharskii, *Tolstoi i Marks* (Leningrad: Academia, 1924), 5.
63. *Ibid.* 7–9.

64. *Ibid.* 12.
65. *Ibid.* 21.
66. *Ibid.* 37.
67. *Ibid.* 46.
68. *Ibid.* 48.
69. For an excellent discussion of the strident and dangerous debates surrounding Tolstoy's legacy during 1928, see William Nickell, "Tolstoi in 1928: In the Mirror of the Revolution," in Kevin M. F. Platt and Davis Brandenberger, eds., *Epic Revisionism: Russian History and Literature as Stalinist Propaganda* (Madison, WI: University of Wisconsin Press, 2006).
70. *Ibid.* 31.

Bibliography

This list does not include the English translations of Tolstoy used by various authors, and cited by them in their notes.

Afanaseva, M. L., G. V. Alekseeva, *et al.*, eds. *Biblioteka L'va Nikolaevicha Tolstogo v Iasnoi Poliane: bibliograficheskoe opisanie*, part III: *Knigi na inostrannykh iazykakh*. 2 vols. Tula: Izdatel'skii dom, "Iasnaia Poliana," 1999.

Aksakov, A. *K chemu bylo voskresat'? Po povodu romana grafa Tolstogo "Voskresenie."* St. Petersburg: Tipografiia V. Demakova, 1900.

Aksakov, K. S., and I. S. Aksakov. *Literaturnaia kritika*. Moscow: Sovremennik, 1981.

Apostolov, N. *Lev Tolstoi nad strannitsami istorii: istoriko-literaturnye nabliudeniia*. Moscow: Komissiia po oznamenovaniiu stoletiia so dnia rozhdeniia L. N. Tolstogo, 1928.

    "L. N. Tolstoi v gody russkoi revoliutsii." In *K stoletiiu L. N. Tolstogo: sbornik*. Moscow: Komissiia po oznamenovaniiu stoletiia so dnia rozhdeniia L. N. Tolstogo, 1928. 20–23.

Apresian, Ruben Grantovich, ed. *Opyt nenasiliia v XX stoletii: sotsial'no-eticheskie ocherki*. Moscow: Aslan, 1996.

Ariès, P. *The Hour of Death*. Trans. H. Weaver. New York: Oxford University Press, 1991.

Ariès, Philippe. *The Hour of Our Death*. Trans. Helen Weaver. New York: Barnes and Noble, 2000.

Barthelme, Donald. "At the Tolstoy Museum." In Ann Charters, ed., *The Story and Its Writer*. Boston: Bedford/St. Martin's, 1999. 129–38.

Bary, Theodore de, and Irene Bloom, eds. *Sources of Chinese Tradition*. 2nd edn. Vol. 1. New York: Columbia University Press, 1999.

Berdiaev, N. A. "Dukhi russkoi revoliutsii. In S. A. Askol'dov *et al.*, eds., *Iz glubiny: sbornik statei o russkoi revol'utsii*. Moscow and Petrograd: Russkaia mysl', 1918. 37–74.

Biriukov, P. *L. N. Tolstoi: Biografiia*. 3 vols. Berlin: Izd. I. P. Ladyzhnikova, 1921.

Bloom H. "Introduction." In H. Bloom, ed., *Poets of Sensibility and the Sublime*. New York: Chelsea House Publishers, 1986. 1–9.

Blumberg, E. J. "Tolstoy and the English Novel: A Note on *Middlemarch* and *Anna Karenina*." In W. G. Jones, ed., *Tolstoi and Britain*. Oxford: Berg, 1995. 93–104.

The Book of Psalms: A Translation with Commentary. Trans. Robert Alter. New York: Norton, 2007.

Braddon, M. E. *The Doctor's Wife*. Ed. Lyn Pykett. Oxford and New York: Oxford University Press, 1998.

Brantlinger, P. "What Is Sensational about the Sensation Novel?" In Lyn Pykett, ed., *Wilkie Collins*. New York, St. Martin's Press, 1989. 30–57.

Braudy, Leo. *The Frenzy of Renown: Fame and Its History*. Oxford: Oxford University Press, 1986.

Budilova, E. A. *Bor'ba materializma i idealizma v russkoi psikhologicheskoi nauke: vtoraia polovina XIX – nachalo XX veka*. Moscow: Izdatel'stvo Akademii nauk SSSR, 1960.

Bulgakov, V. *L. N. Tolstoi v poslednii god ego zhizni*. Moscow: Pravda, 1989.

Etimologicheskii slovar' russkogo iazyka. Ed. A. F. Zhuravlev and N. M. Shanskii. Vol. 10. Moscow: Izdatel'stvo Moskovskogo universiteta, 2007.

Bulgarin, Faddei. *Vospominaniia*. Moscow: Zakharov, 2001.

Burke E. *A Philosophical Enquiry into the Origin of Our Ideas of the Sublime and Beautiful*. Oxford: Oxford University Press, 1990.

Carden, Patricia. "The Expressive Self in *War and Peace*." *Canadian-American Slavic Studies* 12 (1978): 519–34.

"The Recuperative Powers of Memory: Tolstoy's *War and Peace*." In John Garrard, ed., *The Russian Novel from Pushkin to Pasternak*. New Haven, CT: Yale University Press, 1983. 81–102.

Carruthers, Neil. "The Paris Première of Tolstoy's *Vlast' t'my* (*The Power of Darkness*)." *New Zealand Slavonic Journal* (1987): 81–92.

Chernyshev, V., ed. *Slovar' sovremennogo russkogo literaturnogo iazyka*. 17 vols. Moscow and Leningrad: Akademiia Nauk, 1950–65.

Chertkov, V. "Pomoshch' Tolstogo." *Golos Tolstogo i Edinenie* 2, no. 8 (1918): 9.

Chertkov, V. G., and Pavel Birukov. *Save Russia: A Remarkable Appeal to England by Tolstoy's Literary Executor in a Letter to his English Friends*. London: C. W. Daniel, 1919.

Christian, R. F. *Tolstoy: A Critical Introduction*. Cambridge: Cambridge University Press, 1969.

Chubakov, S. *Lev Tolstoi o voine i militarizme*. Minsk: Izdatel'stvo BFU, 1973.

Coetzee, J. M. *The Lives of Animals*. Ed. and intro. Amy Gutman. Princeton, NJ: Princeton University Press, 1999.

Crowther, P. *The Kantian Sublime: From Morality to Art*. Oxford: Clarendon Press, 1989.

Curtiss, John Shelton. *Russia's Crimean War*. Durham, NC: Duke University Press, 1979.

Davydov, Denis. *Voennye zapiski partizana Denisa Davydova*. Moscow: Gosudarstvennoe izdatel'stvo "Khudozhestvennaia literatura," 1940.

Denner, Michael A. "Accidental Art: Tolstoy's Poetics of Unintentionality." *Philosophy and Literature* 27 (2003): 284–303.

Derzhavin, G. *Stikhotvoreniia*. Leningrad: Supovetskaia literatura, 1957.

Dobrotoliubie. 5 vols. Paris: YMCA Press, 1988.

Donskov, A. A. *Essays on L. N. Tolstoj's Dramatic Art.* Wiesbaden: Harrassowitz, 1988.

    L. N. Tolstoy i N. N. Strakhov: Epistolianyi dialog o zhizni i literature. Ottawa and Moscow: Slavic Research Group at the University of Ottawa and the State L. N. Tolstoy Museum, 2006.

Doroshenko, S. *Lev Tolstoi – voin i patriot: voennaia sud'ba i voennaia deiatel'nost'.* Moscow: Sovetskii pisatel', 1966.

Dorré, G. M. *Victorian Fiction and the Cult of the Horse.* Aldershot, UK and Burlington, VT: Ashgate, 2006.

Dostoevskii, F. M. *Polnoe sobranie sochinenii v tridstati tomakh.* Ed. G. M. Fridlender *et al.* Leningrad: Nauka, 1972–90.

Drake, Durant. "Light from Tolstoy on Russia." *International Journal of Ethics* 30, no. 2 (1920): 190–95.

Edgerton, William, ed. *Memoirs of Peasant Tolstoyans in Soviet Russia.* Bloomington, IN: Indiana University Press, 1993.

Eiges, Iosif. "Vozzrenie Tolstogo na muzyku." In P. N. Sakulin, ed., *Estetika L'va Tolstogo: sbornik statei.* Moscow: Gosudarstvennaia Akademiia Khudozhestvennykh Nauk, 1929. 241–308.

Eikhenbaum, B. M. "90-tomnoe sobranie sochinenii L. N. Tolstogo. (Kriticheskie zametki)." *Russkaia literatura* 4 (1956): 216–23.

    Lev Tolstoi: semidesiatye gody. Leningrad: Khudozhestvennaia literatura, 1974.

    The Young Tolstoi. Trans. Gary Kern. Ann Arbor, MI: Ardis, 1972.

    Tolstoi in the Seventies. Trans. Albert Kaspin. Ann Arbor, MI: Ardis, 1982.

    Tolstoy in the Sixties. Trans. Duffield White. Ann Arbor, MI: Ardis, 1982.

Eliot, G. "Silly Novels by Lady Novelists." In *Selected Essays, Poems, and Other Writings.* Ed. A. S. Byatt and Nicholas Warren. London: Penguin, 1990. 140–63.

Elwin, M. *Victorian Wallflowers.* London: Jonathan Cape, 1937.

Fanger, Donald, ed., trans., intro. *Gorky's Tolstoy and Other Reminiscences: Key Writings by and about Maxim Gorky.* New Haven, CT: Yale University Press, 2008.

    "Nazarov's Mother: Notes toward an Interpretation of *Hadji Murat.*" *Iberomania* (1974): 99–104.

Faresov, A. I. *Protiv techenii.* St. Petersburg: Tipografiia M. Merkusheva, 1904.

Ferguson F. *Solitude and the Sublime: Romanticism and the Aesthetics of Individuation.* New York and London: Routledge, 1992.

Flerovskii, N. "Iziashchnyi romanist i ego iziashchnye kritiki." *Delo* 6 (1868): Sovremennoe obozrenie, 1–28.

Florovskii, Georgii [Florovsky]. *Puti russkogo bogosloviia.* Paris: YMCA Press, 1991.

Fomina, E. F., ed. *Za chto Lev Tolstoi byl otluchen ot tserkvi.* Moscow: Izdatel'stvo Dar, 2006.

Franklin, Julian H. *Animal Rights and Moral Philosophy.* New York: Columbia University Press, 2005.

Galagan, Galina. *L. N. Tolstoi: khudozhestvenno-eticheskie iskaniia.* Leningrad: Nauka, 1981.

Gauzner, M. *Lev Nikolaevich Tolstoi o zemle*. Petrograd: Kn-vo M. A. Iasnogo b. Popova, 1917.

Ginzburg, Lydia [Lidiia]. *On Psychological Prose*. Trans. and ed. Judson Rosengrant. Foreword by Edward J. Brown. Princeton, NJ: Princeton University Press, 1991.

"O romane Tolstogo 'Voina i mir'." *Zvezda* 1 (1944): 125–38.

Glebov, P. "Zapiski Porfiriia Nikolaevicha Glebova." *Russkaia starina* 3 (1905): 528–29.

Gol'denveizer, A. B. *Talks with Tolstoy*. Trans. S. S. Koteliansky and Virginia Woolf. London: The Hogarth Press, 1923.

Vblizi Tolstogo. Moscow: Goslitizdat, 1959.

Goubert, D. "Did Tolstoy Read *East Lynne*?" *Slavonic and East European Review* 58, no. 1 (1980): 22–39.

Grossman, Leonid. "Stendal' i Tolstoi." *Russkaia mysl'* (June 1916): 32–51.

Gudzii, N. K. "'Vlast' t'my'. Istoriia pisaniia, pechataniia i postanovki na stsene 'Vlasti t'my'." In *L. N. Tolstoi: Polnoe sobranie sochinenii*. Vol. 26 (Moscow: Gos. izd-vo, 1936). 705–36.

Guehenno, Jean. *Jean-Jacques Rousseau*. Trans. John and Doreen Weightman. 2 vols. London: Routledge and Kegan Paul; New York: Columbia University Press, 1966.

Gulak, A. T. "'Raspuskaiushchiisia': stilistiko-rechevye kraski obraza iunogo voina v rasskazakh L. Tolstogo 50-kh gg." *Russkii iazyk v shkole* 5 (September 2000): 70–74.

Gusev, N. N. *Letopis' zhizni i tvorchestva L. N. Tolstogo*. Moscow: Academia, 1936.

Lev Nikolaevich Tolstoi: materialy k biografii s 1870 po 1881 god. Moscow: Izdatel'stvo Akademii nauk SSSR, 1963.

"Tolstoi i russkaia revoliutsiia. Lektsiia." *Golos Tolstogo i Edinenie* 2, no. 8 (1918): 16.

Gustafson, Richard F. *Leo Tolstoy. Resident and Stranger: A Study in Fiction and Theology*. Princeton, NJ: Princeton University Press, 1986.

Harper, K. E., and B. A. Booth. "Russian Translations of Nineteenth-Century English Fiction." *Nineteenth-Century Fiction* 8, no. 3 (1953): 188–97.

Hausherr, I. "L'origine de la théorie orientale des huit péchés capitaux." *Orientalia Christiana* 30 (1933): 164–75.

Hertz, N. *The End of the Line*. New York: Columbia University Press, 1985.

Himmelfarb, Gertrude. *The De-moralization of Society: From Victorian Virtues to Modern Values*. New York: Alfred A. Knopf, 1995.

Iankovskii, I. *Chelovek i voina v tvorchestve L. N. Tolstogo*. Kiev: Vishcha shkola, 1978.

Iaroshevskii, M. G. *Istoriia psikhologii*. Moscow: Mysl', 1985.

Iunge, E. F. "Iz besed Tolstogo s Polem Deruledom: Neizvestnye zapisi E. F. Iunge." In I. I. Anisimov et al., eds., *Literaturnoe nasledstvo: Tolstoi i zarubezhnyi mir. Kniga Pervaia*. vol. 75, no.1 (Moscow: Nauka, 1965): 535–41.

Jackson, R. L. "The Ethics of Vision II: The Tolstoyan Synthesis." In *Dialogues with Dostoevsky; The Overwhelming Questions*. Stanford, CA: Stanford University Press, 1993. 55–74.

"The Night Journey, Anna Karenina's Return to Saint Petersburg." In Liza Knapp and Amy Mandelker, eds., *Approaches to Teaching Tolstoy's* Anna Karenina. New York: Modern Language Association of America, 2003. 150–60.

Jahn, G. R. "Tolstoi and Kant." In G. J. Gutsche, and L. G. Leighton, eds., *New Perspectives on Nineteenth-Century Prose*. Columbus, OH: Slavica, 1982. 60–70.

James, William. *The Varieties of Religious Experience: A Study in Human Nature: Being the Gifford Lectures on Natural Religion Delivered at Edinburgh in 1901– 1902* [1902] Ed. Martin Marty. Harmondsworth and New York: Penguin, 1982.

Jauss H. R. *Ästhetische Erfahrung und literarische Hermeneutik*. Munich: Fink, 1977.

Jefferson, Thomas. *The Jefferson Bible: The Life and Morals of Jesus of Nazareth*. New York: Holt, 1995.

Jones, W. Gareth. "George Eliot's *Adam Bede* and Tolstoy's Conception of *Anna Karenina*." In W. G. Jones, ed., *Tolstoi and Britain*. Oxford: Berg, 1995. 79–92. ed. *Tolstoi and Britain*. Oxford: Berg, 1995.

"Tolstoy Staged in Paris, Berlin, and London." In Donna Tussing Orwin, ed., *The Cambridge Companion to Tolstoy*. Cambridge University Press, 2002. 142–60.

Joravsky, David. *Russian Psychology: A Critical History*. Oxford: Basil Blackwell, 1989.

Kalinin, I. A. "Istoriia kak iskusstvo chlenorazdel'nosti (istoricheskii opyt i metal-iteraturnaia praktika russkikh formalistov)." *Novoe literaturnoe obozrenie* 71, no. 1 (2005): 103–31.

"Vernut': veshchi, plat'e, mebel', zhenu i strakh voiny. Viktor Shklovskii mezhdu revoliutsionnym bytom i teoriei ostraneniia." *Wiener Slawistischer Almanach* 62 (2005): 351–86.

Kant, I. *Critique of Judgment*. Trans. W. S. Pluhar. Indianapolis, IN: Hackett Publishing Company, 1987.

Kantor, V. "Lev Tolstoi: iskushenie neistorei: samyi, samyi, samyi, ili Tolstoi contra Gete." *Voprosy literatury* 4 (2000): 120–81.

Kavkazskii, A. "Desiataia godovshchina. (1910–1920)." *Kommunisticheskii trud* 20 (1920): 1.

Keep, John L. N. *Soldiers of the Tsar: Army and Society in Russia, 1462–1874*. Oxford: Clarendon Press, 1985.

Kerr, Walter. *The Shabunin Affair: An Episode in the Life of Leo Tolstoy*. Ithaca: Cornell University Press, 1982.

Khomiakov, A. S. *Sochineniia v dvukh tomakh*. Tom 2. *Raboty po bogosloviiu*. Moskovskii filosofskii fond. Moscow: Izdatel'stvo Medium. Zhurnal "Voprosi filosofi," 1994, 5, 23.

Kleman, M. K., and N. P. Piksanov, eds. *I. S. Turgenev v vospominaniiakh revoliutsionerov-semidesiatnikov*. Moscow: Academia, 1930.

Knapp, L. "'Tue-la, Tue-la!': Death Sentences, Words, and Inner Monologues in Tolstoy's *Anna Karenina* and Three More Deaths." *Tolstoy Studies Journal* 11 (1999): 1–19.

Knapp, L., and Mandelker, A., eds. *Approaches to Teaching Tolstoy's* Anna Karenina. New York: The Modern Language Association of America, 2003.

Knapp, S. "Tolstoj's Readings of George Eliot: Visions and Revisions." *Slavic and East European Journal* 27, no. 3 (1983): 318–26.

Knizhnik, Ivan. "Lev Tolstoi i proletarskaia revoliutsiia. (K desiatiletiiu so dnia ego smerti)." *Petrogradskaia Pravda* (November 20, 1920): 1.

Kodjak, Andrej. "Tolstoy's Personal Myth of Immortality." In Andrej Kodjak, Krystyna Pomorska and Stephen Rudy, eds., *Myth in Literature*. Columbus, OH: Slavica, 1985. 188–207.

Kolstø, Pål. "Lev Tolstoi and the Orthodox *Starets* Tradition." *Kritika: Explorations in Russian and Eurasian History* 9, no. 3 (Summer 2008): 533–54.

Krasnov, G. K. "Filosofiia Gerdera v tvorchestve Tolstogo." In G. K. Krasnov, ed., *L. N. Tolstoi: Stat'i i materialy. IV. Uchenye Zapiski Gor'kovskogo gosudarstvennogo universiteta im. N. I. Lobachevskogo*. Gorky: Gor'kovskii gosudarstvennyi universitet imeni N. I. Lobachevskogo, 1961. 56: 157–74.

Kuzminskaia, T. A. *Moia zhizn' doma i v Iasnoi Poliane, Vospominaniia*. 3rd edn. Tula: Tul'skoe knizhnoe izdatel'stvo, 1958.

Layton, Susan. *Russian Literature and Empire: The Conquest of the Caucasus from Pushkin to Tolstoy*. Cambridge: Cambridge University Press, 1994.

Leighton, Laurence. "Denis Davydov's Hussar Style." *Slavic and East European Journal* 7 (1963): 349–60.

Lenin, V. I. *"Left Wing" Communism: An Infantile Disorder*. Detroit, MI: The Marxian Educational Society, 1921.

  "Leo Tolstoy as the Mirror of the Russian Revolution." In M. Solomon, ed., *Marxism and Art: Essays Classic and Contemporary*. New York: Wayne State University Press, 1979. 169–74.

Leont'ev [Leontiev], K. "O romanakh L. N. Tolstogo: analiz, stil', veianie: kriticheskii etiud." *Russkii vestnik* 6–8 (1890): 245–77, 234–69, 205–44.

Leskov, N. S. *Polnoe sobranie sochinenii v 30 tomakh*. Moscow: Terra, 1996–.

Lomunov K. N. "Predislovie" (to "A. V. Lunacharskii o Tolstom. Neopublikovannaia lektsiia 1928 g."). In *Lev Tolstoi v 2-kh knigakh*. Ed. K. N. Lomunov. Moscow: Izd-vo AN SSSR, 1961. 403–5.

Lönnqvist, B. "The English Theme in *Anna Karenina*." *Essays in Poetics: The Journal of the British Neo-Formalist Circle* 24 (Autumn 1999): 58–90.

Lovejoy, Arthur O. *The Great Chain of Being: A Study of the History of an Idea*. Cambridge, MA: Harvard University Press, 1936.

Lunacharskii, A. V. *Tolstoi i Marks*. Leningrad: Akademia, 1924.

Lyotard, J.-F. "Answering the Question: What Is Postmodernism?" In T. Docherty, ed., *Postmodernism: A Reader*. New York: Columbia University Press, 1993. 38–46.

  Lessons on the Analytic of the Sublime. Palo Alto, CA: Stanford University Press, 1994.

Makarii (Bulgakov). *Pravoslavno-dogmaticheskoe bogoslovie*. 3rd edn. 2 vols. St. Petersburg: Tipografiia "A. Treia," 1868.

Maklakov, B. A. *Tolstoi i bol'shevizm: Rech'*. Paris: Knigaizdatel'stvo Russkaia zemlia, 1921.

Makovitskii, D. P. "U Tolstogo: 'Iasnopolianskie zapiski' D. P. Makovitskogo." In V. R. Shcherbina *et al*., eds., *Literaturnoe nasledstvo* 90, no. 1 [1904–5]. Moscow: Nauka, 1979.

Maloney, George A., ed. *Nil Sorskii: The Complete Writings*. New York and Mahnah, NJ: Paulist Press, 2003.

Mandelker, Amy. *Framing Anna Karenina: Tolstoy, the Woman Question, and the Victorian Novel*. Columbus, OH: Ohio State University Press, 1993.

"Tolstoy's Eucharistic Aesthetics." In Andrew Donskov and John Woodsworth, eds., *Lev Tolstoy and the Concept of Brotherhood*. New York and Ottawa: Legas, 1996. 116–27.

Maude, Aylmer. *Life of Tolstoy, Later Years*. New York: Dodd, Mead and Co., 1911.

McLaughlin S., "Some Aspects of Tolstoy's Intellectual Development: Tolstoy and Schopenhauer." *California Slavic Studies* 5 (1970): 187–248.

McLean, Hugh. "Claws on the Behind: Tolstoy and Darwin." In *In Quest of Tolstoy*. Boston: Academic Studies Press, 2008. 159–80. First publ. *Tolstoy Studies Journal* 19 (2007): 15–32.

"Rousseau's God and Tolstoy's God." In *In Quest of Tolstoy*. Boston: Academic Studies Press, 2008. 143–58.

Medzhibovskaya, Inessa. *Tolstoy and the Religious Culture of His Time: A Biography of a Long Conversion, 1845–1887*. Lanham, MD and Boulder, CO: Lexington Books, 2008.

Melancon, Michael. "The Left Socialist Revolutionaries, 1917–1918." In Edward Acton, Vladimir I. Cherniaev and William G. Rosenberg, eds., *Critical Companion to the Russian Revolution, 1914–1921*. London: Hodder Arnold, 1997. 281–91.

Meleshko, Elena Dmitrievna. *Khristianskie etiki L. N. Tolstogo*. Moscow: Nauka, 2006.

Merezhkovskii [Merezhkovski, Merezhkovsky], Dmitrii Sergeevich. *L. Tolstoi i Dostoevskii*. Ed. E. A. Andrushchenko. Moscow: Nauka, 2000.

"Tolstoy and Bolshevism." *The Living Age* (May 7, 1921): 331–37.

Meyer, Leonard B. *Emotion and Meaning in Music*. Chicago: University of Chicago Press, 1956.

Monk, S. *The Sublime: A Study of Critical Theories in Eighteenth-Century England*. 1935. Ann Arbor, MI: University of Michigan Press, 1960.

Morrison, Simon. *The People's Artist: Prokofiev's Soviet Years*. Oxford: Oxford University Press, 2008.

Morson, Gary. *"Anna Karenina" in Our Time: Seeing More Wisely*. New Haven, CT: Yale University Press, 2007.

Hidden in Plain View: Narrative, and Creative Potentials in War and Peace. Stanford, CA: Stanford University Press, 1987.

Morson, Gary Saul, and Caryl Emerson. *Mikhail Bakhtin: Creation of a Prosaics*. Stanford, CA: Stanford University Press, 1990.

The Musorgsky Reader: A Life of Modeste Petrovich Musorgsky in Letters and Documents. Ed. and trans. Jay Leyda and Sergei Bertensson. New York: Norton, 1947.

The New York Times. "Kneel to Tolstoy's Portrait: Great Crowd of Soldiers and Workers Greet His Widow at Her Home." *The New York Times* (March 27, 1917): 4. (Retrieved July 18, 2008, ProQuest Historical Newspapers, *The New York Times* [1851–2004] database, Stetson University. www.proquest.com/.)

"New Forces of Disintegration in Russia: Syndicalism, More Violent than Bolshevism, Threatens To Thrust Unhappy Nation into New Chaos of Lawlessness, Says Manuel Komroff, Just Back from Russia." *The New York Times* (January 19, 1919): 66–67. (Retrieved July 16, 2008, ProQuest Historical Newspapers, *The New York Times* [1851–2004] database, Stetson University. www.proquest.com/.)

"The Russian Danger." *The New York Times* (July 27, 1917): 8. (Retrieved October 3, 2008, ProQuest Historical Newspapers, *The New York Times* [1851–2005] database, Stetson University. www.proquest.com/.)

Nickell, William Scott. "Tolstoi in 1928: In the Mirror of the Revolution." In Kevin M. F. Platt and Davis Brandenberger, eds., *Epic Revisionism: Russian History and Literature as Stalinist Propaganda*. Madison, WI: University of Wisconsin Press, 2006. 17–38.

"Tolstoy in the Public Domain: His Death as a National Narrative." PhD dissertation, UCLA at Berkeley, 1998. Ann Arbor: UMI, 1998. 9902182. Dissertation Abstracts International, Section A: The Humanities and Social Sciences, vol. 59, no. 8, 3017–18, February 1999.

Nussbaum, Martha. "Beyond 'Compassion and Humanity': Justice for Nonhuman Animals." In Cass R. Sunstein and Martha Nussbaum, eds., *Animal Rights: Current Debates and New Directions*. Oxford and New York: Oxford University Press, 2004. 299–320.

Nuralova, S. "Missis Genri Vud i Lev Tolstoi (Zaiavka temy)." *Studia Litteraria Polono-Slavica* 5 (2000): 187–90.

Orwin, Donna Tussing. *Consequences of Consciousness: Turgenev, Dostoevsky, and Tolstoy*. Palo Alto, CA: Stanford University Press, 2007.

"'Mir kak tseloe' N. Strakhova: nedostaiushchee zveno mezhdu Tolstym i Dostoevskim." *Tolstoi. Novyi vek. Zhurnal razmyshlenii* 2 (2006): 197–221.

"Strakhov's *World as a Whole*: A Missing Link between Dostoevsky and Tolstoy." In Catherine O'Neil, *et al*, eds., *Poetics. Self. Place: Essays in Honor of Anna Lisa Crone*. Bloomington, IN: Slavica, 2007. 473–93.

ed. *The Cambridge Companion to Tolstoy*. Cambridge: Cambridge University Press, 2002.

"Tolstoy and Courage." In Donna Tussing Orwin, ed., *The Cambridge Companion to Tolstoy*. Cambridge: Cambridge University Press, 2002. 222–36.

Tolstoy's Art and Thought, 1847–1880. Princeton, NJ: Princeton University Press, 1993.

Osterman, Lev Abramovich. *Srazhenie za Tolstogo*. Moscow: Grant, 2002.

Paliukh, Z. G., and A. V. Prokhorova, eds. *Lev Tolstoi i muzyka: khronika, notografiia, bibliografiia*. Moscow: Sovetskii kompozitor, 1977.

Paperno, Irina. "'Who, What Is I?': Tolstoy in His Diaries." *Tolstoy Studies Journal* 11 (1999): 32–54.

Parthé, K., "Death Masks in Tolstoi." *Slavic Review* 41, no. 2 (1982): 297–305.

Pascal, Blaise. *Pensées*. Trans. A. J. Krailsheimer. Harmondsworth: Penguin, 1966.

Phegley, J. "Domesticating the Sensation Novelist: Ellen Price Wood as Author and Editor of the *Argosy* Magazine." *Victorian Periodicals Review* 38, no. 2 (2005): 180–98.

N. D. Pokrovskaia (Khaimovich). *L. N. Tolstoi: Bibliografiia proizvedenii L. Tolstogo i literatury o nem. 1917–1927*. Ed. N. K. Piksanov. In N. N. Gusev and V. G. Chertkov, eds., *Tolstoi i o Tolstom. Novye materialy. Sbornik 4*. Moscow: Izdanie Tolstovskogo Muzeia, 1928. 19–199.

Polonskii, L. "Ocherki angliiskogo obshchestva v romanakh A. Trollopa." *Vestnik Evropy* 8 (1870): 613–75; 10 (1870): 667–716.

"Zhenskie tipy v romanakh A. Trollopa." *Vestnik Evropy* 8 (1871): 513–68.

Polosina, Alla. "L. N. Tolstoi i Avrelii Avgustin o pamiati, vremeni i pronstranstve." In Galina Alekseeva, ed., *Lev Tolstoi i mirovaia literatura*. Tula: Iasnaia Poliana, 2005. 65–76.

Popovskii, Mark Aleksandrovich. *Russkie muzhiki rasskazyvaiut: posledovateli L. N. Tolstogo v Sovetskom Soiuze, 1918–1977*. London: Overseas Publications Exchange, 1983.

Powelstock, David. *Becoming Mikhail Lermontov: The Ironies of Romantic Individualism in Nicholas I's Russia*. Evanston, IL: Northwestern University Press, 2005.

Rancour-Laferriere, Daniel. *Tolstoy's Pierre Bezukhov: A Psychoanalytic Study*. London: Bristol Classical Press, 1993.

Reyfman, I. *Ritualized Violence Russian Style: The Duel in Russian Culture and Literature*. Stanford, CA.: Stanford University Press, 1999.

"Turgenev's 'Death' and Tolstoy's 'Three Deaths'." In Lazar Fleishman, Gabriella Safran and Michael Wachtel, eds., *Word, Music, History: A Festschrift for Caryl Emerson. Stanford Slavic Studies* 29/30 (2005), pt. 1: 312–26.

Ritter J. "Landschaft: Zur Funktion des Ästhetischen in der modernen Gesellschaft." In Ritter, *Subjektivität*. Frankfurt a. M.: Suhrkamp, 1974. 141–63.

Rose, Seraphim. *The Soul after Death: Contemporary "After-Death" Experiences in the Light of the Orthodox Teachings on the Afterlife*. Platina, CA: S. Herman of Alaska Brotherhood, 1994.

Rosen, Margo. "Natasha Rostova at Meyerbeer's *Robert le Diable*." *Tolstoy Studies Journal* 17 (2005): 71–90.

Rousseau, Jean-Jacques. *Émile. Œuvres complètes*. Vol. 4. Paris: Pléiade, 1959.

Rozanov, Vasilii Vasil'evich. *Okolo tserkovnykh sten: Sobranie sochinenii*. Ed. A. N. Nikoliukin. Moscow: Respublika, 1995.

Saburov, A. A. "Obraz russkogo voina v 'Voine i mire'." In D. D. Blagoi, ed., *L. N. Tolstoi: sbornik stat'ei i materialov*. Moscow: Izdatel'stvo Akademii nauk SSSR, 1951. 390–424.

Sacks, Oliver. *Musicophilia: Tales of Music and the Brain*. New York: Knopf, 2007.

Sand, George. *Consuelo*. Tome troisième, nouvelle édition. Paris: Michelle Lévy Frères, 1857.

  Consuelo. Trans. Fayette Robinson. New York: Stringer and Townsend, 1851.

Sanders, Thomas, Ernest Tucker and Gary Hamburg, eds. *Russian–Muslim Confrontation in the Caucasus, 1829–1859*. London and New York: Routledge and Curzon, 2004.

Sankovitch, Natasha. *Creating and Recovering Experience: Repetition in Tolstoy*. Stanford, CA: Stanford University Press, 1998.

Scanlan, James P. "Tolstoy among the Philosophers: His Book *On Life* and Its Critical Reception." *Tolstoy Studies Journal* 18 (2006): 52–69.

Schönle A. "Modernity as a 'Destroyed Anthill': Tolstoi on History and the Aesthetics of Ruins." In J. Hell and A. Schönle, eds., *Ruins of Modernity*. Durham, NC: Duke University Press. In press.

Schopenhauer, A. *The World as Will and Idea*. Trans. R. B. Haldane, and J. Kemp. Vol. 3. London: Trübner, 1886.

  The World as Will and Representation. Trans. E. F. J. Payne. 2 vols. New York: Dover Publications, 1969.

Sergeenko, P. A. *Kak zhivet i rabotaet L. N. Tolstoi*. Moscow, 1908.

  "Tantseval'naia muzyka." In *L. N. Tolstoi v vospominaniakh sovremennikov*. Vol. 2. Moscow: GoslzdKhudLit, 1960. 219–21.

Slovar' sovremennogo russkogo literaturnogo iazyka. Ed. V. Chernyshev. Vol. 6. Moscow and Leningrad, 1957.

Shanskii, N. M., and A. F. Zhuravlev, eds. *Etimologicheskii slovar' russkogo iazyka*. Multi volume. Moscow: Izdatel'stvo Moskovskogo universiteta, 1963–.

Sharp, Lynn. *Secular Spirituality: Reincarnation and Spiritism in Nineteenth-Century France*. Lanham, MD: Lexington Books, 2006.

Shestov, L. *Dostoevskii i Nitshe, Sochineniia v dvukh tomakh*. Vol. 1. Tomsk: Vodolei, 1996.

  "Dostoevskii i Nitshe." In *Filosofiia tragedii*. Moscow: Folio, 2001. 135–316.

Shimkevich, V. "N. P. Vagner i N. N. Polezhaev. (Iz vospominanii zoologa)." *Zhurnal Ministerstva Narodnogo Prosveshcheniia* 16, no. 7 (1908): 1–18.

Shklovsky, Viktor. *Lev Tolstoy*. Trans. Olga Shartze. Moscow: Progress Publishers, 1978.

  "Art as Technique." In Lee T. Lemon and Marion J. Reis, eds., *Russian Formalist Criticism: Four Essays*. Lincoln: University of Nebraska Press, 1965. 12.

  "O staroi russkoi voennoi i o sovetskoi oboronnoi proze." *Znamia* 1 (1936): 218–27.

Simmons, Ernest J. *Leo Tolstoy*. 2 vols. New York: Vintage Books, 1960.

  Leo Tolstoy. Special limited edition. Boston: Little, Brown and Company, 1946.

Singer, Peter. *Animal Liberation*. New York: HarperCollins, 2002.

Sloane, David. "Anna Reading and Women Reading." In Liza Knapp and Amy Mandelker, eds., *Approaches to Teaching Tolstoy's* Anna Karenina. New York: Modern Language Association of America, 2003. 124–30.

Solignac, Aimé. "Péchés capitaux." In *Dictionnaire de spiritualité*. Vol. XII, pt. 1. Paris: Beauchesne, 1984. 853–62.

Solov'ev, Vladimir Sergeevich. *Sobranie sochinenii V. Solov'eva: fototipicheskoe izdanie.* Brussels: Foyer Oriental Chrétien, 1966.

Stadt, Janneke van de. "L. N. Tolstoi i muzyka (iz arkhiva N. N. Guseva)." In *Iasnopolianskii sbornik.* Tula: Priokskoe knizhnoe izdatel'stvo, 1986. 167–76.

    "Narrative, Music, and Performance: Tolstoy's *Kreutzer Sonata* and the Example of Beethoven." *Tolstoy Studies Journal* 12 (2000): 57–70.

Steiner, George. *Tolstoy or Dostoevsky: An Essay in the Old Criticism.* New York: Knopf, 1959.

Strakhov, N. N. "Voina i mir. Sochinenie grafa L. N. Tolstogo. Tomy v i vi." In I. N. Sukhikh, ed., *Roman L. N. Tolstogo 'Voina i mir' v russkoi kritike.* Leningrad: LGU, 1980. 257–84.

See also Tolstoi, L. N.

Strunsky, Rose, ed. *The Journal of Leo Tolstoi: First Volume – 1895–1899.* New York: Alfred A. Knopf, 1917.

Struve, Gleb. "Tolstoy in Soviet Criticism." *Russian Review* 19, no. 2 (1960): 171–86

Sutherland, John. *The Stanford Companion to Victorian Fiction.* Stanford, CA: Stanford University Press, 1999.

Swift, Johathan. *Gulliver's Travels.* New York: New American Library, 1960.

Tal', N. A. "Angliiskie semeinye khroniki." *Vestnik Evropy* 3 (1871): 306–30.

Tiunkin, Konstantin Ivanovich, ed. *Perepiska I. S. Turgeneva v dvukh tomakh.* Vol. 1. Moscow: Khudozhestvennaia literatura, 1986.

Tkachev, P. N. "Tkachov Attacks Tolstoy's Aristocratism: 1875." In A. V. Knowles, ed. and trans., *Tolstoy: The Critical Heritage.* London: Routledge and Kegan Paul, 1978. 250–61.

Todd, W. B., and A. Bowden. *Tauchnitz International Editions in English 1841–1955: A Bibliographical History.* New York: Bibliographical Society of America, 1988.

Todd, William Mills III. "The Responsibilities of (Co-)Authorship: Notes on Revising the Serialized Version of *Anna Karenina.*" In Elizabeth Cheresh Allen and Gary Saul Morson, eds., *Freedom and Responsibility in Russian Literature: Essays in Honor of Robert Louis Jackson.* Evanston, IL: Northwestern University Press; New Haven, CT: Yale Center for International and Area Studies, 1995. 159–69.

Tolstaia, S. A. *Dnevniki.* Moscow: Khudozhestvennaia literatura, 1978.

Tolstoi, A., gr[af]. "Dvenadtsatogo marta." *Russkiie vedomosti* 61 (March 17, 1917): [un-numbered].

Tolstoi [Tolstoy], L. N. *Tolstoy's Diaries.* Ed. and trans. R. F. Christian. 2 vols. London: Athlone, 1985. 473.

    "'Iskaniia istinnoi very'." Ed. T. G. Nikiforova. In I. Borisova, ed., *Neizvestnyi Tolstoi v arkhivakh Rossii i SShA.* Moscow: AO-Tekhna-2, 1994. 122–30.

    L. N. Tolstoi i N. N. Strakhov: Polnoe sobranie perepiski. 2 vols. Ed. and intro. Andrew Donskov; comp. L. D. Gromova and T. G. Nikiforova. Ottawa and Moscow: Slavic Research Group at the University of Ottawa and the State L. N. Tolstoy Museum, 2003.

Perepiska L. N. Tolstogo s gr. A. A. Tolstoi 1857–1903. St. Petersburg: Tolstovskii muzei, 1911.

Perepiska L. N. Tolstogo s sestrami i brat'iami. Moscow: Khudozhestvennaia literatura, 1990.

Polnoe sobranie sochinenii [PSS]. 90 vols. Moscow: Gosudarstvennoe izdatel'stvo "Khudozhestvennaia literatura," 1928–58.

Polnoe sobranie sochinenii v sta tomakh. Moscow: Nauka, 2000–.

Tolstoi, S. L. *Ocherki bylogo.* Moscow: Gosudarstvennoe izdatel'stvo "Khudozhestvennaia literatura," 1956.

Townsend, Charles E. *Russian Word-Formation.* New York: McGraw-Hill, 1968.

Tregubov, Ivan 1920. "Tolstoi-kommunist." *Izvestiia VTsIK* (November 24, 1920): 1.

Trollope, A. *The Bertrams.* New York: Harper and Brothers, 1859.

Tsiavlovskii, M. "Lev Tolstoi na voine." *Literaturnaia gazeta* (November 17, 1940).

Tumanov, Alexander. *The Life and Artistry of Maria Olenina-d'Alheim.* Trans. Christopher Barnes. Edmonton: University of Alberta Press, 2000.

Turner, C. J. G. *A Karenina Companion.* Waterloo, Ontario: Wilfrid Laurier University Press, 1993.

Underwood, Ted. "Historical Difference as Immortality in the Mid-Nineteenth-Century Novel." *Modern Language Quarterly* 63, no. 4 (2002): 441–69.

Unsigned. "Interesy nauki i literatury na Zapade." *Otechestvennye zapiski* 167, nos. 7–8 (1866): 25–29.

"Inostrannaia literatura." *Otechestvennye zapiski* 147, nos. 3–4 (1863): 99–105.

"Inostrannaia literaturnaia letopis'." *Otechestvennye zapiski* 152, nos. 1–2 (1864): 245–79.

"Obzor inostrannoi literatury III." *Otechestvennye zapiski* 134, nos. 1–2 (1861): 56–61.

"Tolstoy as the Great Patriarch of the Bolsheviki Family." *Current Opinion* (January 1919): 49–50.

Ushakov, D., ed. *Tolkovyi slovar' russkogo iazyka*, ed. D. Ushakov. 4 vols. Moscow: Gosudarstvennoe izdatel'stvo inostrannykh i natsional'nykh slovarei, 1938.

Volokhov, Mark "Vserossiiskii Tolstoi. (K 10-letiiu so dnia ego smerti)." *Gudok* (November 20, 1920): 1.

von Mücke, Dorothea. "Profession/Confession." *New Literary History* 34, no. 2 (Spring 2003): 257–74.

Walicki, Andrzej. *A History of Russian Thought from the Enlightenment to Marxism.* Stanford, CA: Stanford University Press, 1979.

Ward, Charles. "How to Sing Tolstoy/Tolstoy Transformed." *Houston Chronicle* (Sunday, April 18, 1999), 1, 9.

Weintraub, Karl Joachim. *The Value of the Individual: Self and Circumstance in Autobiography.* Chicago: University of Chicago Press, 1978.

Weiskel, T. *The Romantic Sublime: Studies in the Structure and Psychology of Transcendence.* Baltimore, MD: Johns Hopkins University Press, 1976.

Wilson, A. N. *Tolstoy: A Biography.* New York: W. W. Norton, 1988.

Wittgenstein, Ludwig. *Tractatus Logico-Philosophicus*. Trans. D. F. Pears and B. F. McGuiness. London: Routledge, 1961.

Wolff, R. L. *Sensational Victorian: The Life and Fiction of Mary Elizabeth Braddon*. New York and London: Garland Publishing, 1979.

Wood, Mrs. H. *The Shadow of Ashlydyat*. London: Richard Bentley, 1863.

Within the Maze. London: Macmillan and Co., 1904.

Zenkovskii, V. V. *Istoriia russkoi filosofii. 1948*. Leningrad: Ego, 1991.

Zhiliakova, E. M. "Denis Davydov i povest' L. N. Tolstogo *Dva gusara*." In A. S. Ianushkevich, ed., *Russkaia povest' kak forma vremeni*. Tomsk: Izd. Tomskogo un-ta, 2002. 216–26.

Zimmer, Carl. "From Ants to People, An Instinct to Swarm." *New York Times* (November 13, 2007): D1.

Zverev, Aleksei, and Vladimir Tunimanov. *Lev Tolstoi*. Moscow: Molodaia gvardiia, 2006.

Index

Achilles, 91
Addams, Jane, 1
adultery, 161, 189
Aesop, 204
aesthetics, 35, 108, 116, 185, 189, 192, 194, 231;
    aestheticism, 240; consciousness, aesthetic, 35;
    European, 23; experience, aesthetic, 35; goals,
    aesthetic, 186; Schopenhauer's, 36; Tolstoy's,
    2–3, 4, 17, 26, 34, 57, 59. *See also* death;
    Schopenhauer
Aksakov, A. N., 128, 134
Aksakov, I. S., 114, 119
Aksakov, K. S., 132
Alexander I, Tsar, 89, 94, 201
Alexander III, Tsar, 185
Alter, Robert, 205
amour-propre. See under vanity
Amvrosii. *See under* Optina Pustyn'
analysis, psychological, 72, 123, 183, 188, 192;
    Tolstoy's psychologism, 120, 122, 124
anarchism, "Christian," Tolstoy's, 2, 5, 150, 157,
    233; Tolstoy's rejection of the existing social
    order and culture, 145–6, 150, 222, 226–7,
    230, 233, 234, 236. *See also* Bolshevism;
    Christianity; patriotism; religion; revolution;
    war; women
Andrei, Prince. *See* Bolkonsky.
anger, 41, 44, 53; as a pleasure, 88; fury, 85, 88; joy
    of, 3; justifiable, 86; in overcoming fear, 86; in
    War and Peace, 86; rage, 10, 86–8, 91; *zloba*,
    85–6, 87. *See also* revenge; sin.
animal, 3, 6, 61, 73, 74, 136, 174; "capabilities
    approach," 53; French army as an, 57, 65, 74;
    Houyhnhnms, 68; human being as, 3, 8, 64, 68,
    70, 86, 87, 194, 221; in Tolstoy's fiction, 52, 54,
    55, 56, 57, 62–6, 68, 69, 71–3; in various Russian
    writers, 72; kingdom, 52, 58, 70, 71;
    liberationists, 54; Platon Karataev's dog, 132,
    136, 137; reason in, 54; respect for, 53; rights of,
    52, 53, 73; suffering of, 56; violence toward, 55,
    56. *See also* Swift; Tolstoy (works): "Strider"

"Ant Brotherhood" (*Muraveinye braty*). *See under*
    Tolstoy, N. N.
aphorism, 202, 203, 209. *See also* proverb;
    quotation; saying; wisdom
Apostolov, N. 93
Ariès, Philippe, *The Hour of Our*
    Death, 33
Aristotle, 203
Armand, I. F., 222
army, 16, 77, 87; French, 26, 74; Russian, 65;
    Tsarist, 92
art, 5, 17, 52, 60–1, 103, 108, 186, 187, 192, 206, 239;
    as an "infection," 2, 9, 14, 16–18, 19, 20, 23, 28,
    62, 74; authentic, 17; Bolsheviks' policies on,
    237; for art's sake, 59; musical, 8, 13, 18, 24;
    Tolstoy on, 2, 9, 10, 12, 14, 59, 231; Tolstoy's,
    3–4, 62, 142, 201, 239, 243. *See also* aesthetics;
    Bolsheviks; music
Asia, 238
Assembly, Constituent (*Uchreditel'noe Sobranie*),
    the, 226, 227, 241
Astapovo, 1
Augustine, 108, 116, 118, 139

Bakhtin, M. M., 114, 202, 217
Balakirev, M. A., "King Lear on the Heath"
    (*Korol' Lir v Stepi*), 20
Ballou, Adin, 149
Balzac, H. de, 122, 135
Barthelme, D., 219, 230
Bartlett's Familiar Quotations, 199
battle, 55, 63, 78, 81, 85, 86; Austerlitz, 16;
    Borodino, 13, 83, 84, 85, 86, 87; chance and loss
    of control in, 83–4; Inkerman, 94; Jena 84;
    killing in, 86; merriment in, 87; soldier in, 87;
    Schöngraben, 128; Rostov in, 63; Tolstoy's first,
    92; Waterloo, 82. *See also* Bolkonsky; courage;
    death; soldier; war
Bayreuth, 21
Beethoven, Ludwig van, 11–13, 16–19,
    23, 59